DEFIANT ACTS / ACTOS DESAFIANTES

Defiant Acts
Four Plays by Diana Raznovich

Actos Desafiantes
Cuatro Obras de Diana Raznovich

Edited by
Diana Taylor and Victoria Martinez

Drawings by
Diana Raznovich

Lewisburg

Bucknell University Press

London: Associated University Presses

Authorization to photocopy items for internal or personal use, or the internal or personal use of specific clients, is granted by the copyright owner, provided that a base fee of $10.00, plus eight cents per page, per copy is paid directly to the Copyright Clearance Center, 222 Rosewood Drive, Danvers, Massachusetts 01923. [0-8387-5479-1/02 $10.00 + 8 pp, pc.] Diana Raznovich maintains all rights to the production of any of these plays either in English or in Spanish. Contact information can be obtained through Argentores: J. A. Pacheco de Melo, 1820 Buenos Aires, Argentina, www.argentores.org.ar.

Associated University Presses
440 Forsgate Drive
Cranbury, NJ 08512

Associated University Presses
16 Barter Street
London WC1A 2AH, England

Associated University Presses
All rights reserved.
P.O. Box 338, Port Credit
Mississauga, Ontario
Canada L5G 4L8

The paper used in this publication meets the requirements of the American National Standard for Permanence of Paper for Printed Library Materials Z39.48-198.

Library of Congress Cataloging-in-Publication Data

Raznovich, Diana
    Defiant acts: four plays / by Diana Raznovich ; edited by Diana Taylor and Victoria Martinez ; drawings by Diana Raznovich = Actos desafiantes ; cuatro obras de Diana Raznovich
    p. cm.
    Contents: Disconcerted -- Inner gardens -- MaTRIX, Inc.-- Rear entry.
    ISBN 0-8387-5479-1 (alk. Paper)
    1. Raznovich, Diana -- Translations into English. I. Title: Actos desafiantes. II. Taylor, Diana, 1950 – III. Martínez, Victoria. IV. Title.

PQ7798.28.A96 A77 2002
862.64—dc21

                                                                                          2001035085

PRINTED IN THE UNITED STATES OF AMERICA

Contents

PLAYS
AND
DRAWINGS:
DiANA RAZNOVICH

Agradecimientos

Este libro que alberga cuatro de mis obras teatrales contiene sin embargo, el imaginario de una persistente unidad. En toda agrupación opera una comprensión implícita de esa búsqueda de un estilo que, en la mitología escritural del teatro, se escapa por las tangentes y se reencuentra en los apagones. Sólo una sensibilidad privilegiada y una mente tan apasionada y brillante como la de Diana Taylor puede haber tramado esa *otra obra* teatral que se desplaza del *Desconcierto* a *Jardín de Otoño*, esa intertextualidad que enlaza a Dolly de *De Atrás para Adelante* con la Madre Diva de *Casa Matriz*. Así que, si bien las obras han sido escritas por separado, el hecho performativo de que se encuentren en este libro proviene de su estrategia crítica y crea, entre las cuatro, un nuevo intertexto del que la considero autora.

Asimismo entiendo que su propuesta de que mis dibujos intercambien complicidades y desafíos con los textos, hace del libro un hecho específico, una novedad creada a propósito de este evento y no una mera sumatoria de obras.

Si se leen sus libros y se percibe como en ellos juegan activamente las letras y la gráfica, se comprenderá por qué le agradezco esa particular "puesta en escena" de estas páginas. Por eso se me ocurre que este libro es el producto de diversos encuentros, pero en su principio generador está el encuentro ininterrumpido entre estas dos Dianas (Taylor y Raznovich) que tuvo su primer chispazo en los años 90 en la Universidad de Kansas, en los hospitalarios predios del Profesor George Woodyard. Como creo que a la domesticación del azar se la llama destino, quiero agradecer a la Vida la fecundidad de ese encuentro con variados destinos, encuentro al que entre ambas hemos llamado *Di & Di Producciones*. Digamos, que aunque tengamos otras obras en "vías de desarrollo" esta es el primer *Di & Di* auténtico que damos a conocer al público.

Quiero agradecerle también a Diana Taylor su decisión de producir este libro y de introducirme en los Estados Unidos de America. Para mí es un privilegio entrar por la generosa puerta que me abre su Prefacio, así como haber asistido a las contínuas reescrituras de las traducciones al inglés, buscando que el pasaje de una lengua a la otra no violente las promesas virtuales que ofrecen ambos códigos lingüísticos, y capitalicen un deliberado entendimiento estilístico. El lenguaje teatral es privado y coloquial, tiene la impúdica y simulada intimidad del escenario y la textualidad de los cuerpos.

Por eso quiero agradecer a Victoria Martínez y a Lidia Ramírez sus denodados esfuerzos para que el viaje de una lengua a otra no rompa los encantamientos, los ritmos interiores, ni la imprevisible sutileza del humor de los textos y permita que los actores y las actrices se encuentren albergados en las traducciones como si fueran originales. Se que el tiempo tomado para que esa magia se produzca estuvo claramente expresada en una lectura para mi inolvidable que se hizo de *Jardín de Otoño, Inner Gardens,* en inglés en el King Juan Carlos I of Spain Center en NYU el martes 22 de septiembre de 1998 en la ciudad de New York. La magia del deslinde topológico hace que el primer acto de *Inner Gardens* transcurra en la noche que va del 21 al 22 de septiembre, coincidiendo con el día de su lectura en Nueva York. Y que un 22 de septiembre, 22 años antes de ese 22 de septiembre Marcos Raznovich, mi papá haya abandonado este mundo en búsqueda de alguna otra opción. *Jardín de Otoño* estuvo desde siempre dedicada a la memoria de mi padre a quien quiero agradecerle el humor y la frescura con que encaró su breve y generosa vida.

Quiero agradecer a las actrices y actores, Novella Nelson, Mary Beth Peil, Jay Goede, Patricia Dalen, William Meisle y Robin Miles así como a Daniel Banks que dirigió esa lectura. Fue un evento que confirma la calidad de esta tarea.

La idea de un texto bilingüe me entusiasma particularmente porque genera una nueva teatralidad que rompe los encadenamientos literales para generar líneas de captación lúdicas entre un idioma y el otro. Agradezco a los editores que hayan aceptado esta propuesta.

Quiero agradecerle a Marina Manheimer-Taylor el haber dibujado a mi lado en una mesa en New Hampshire un desborde de tintas y papeles casi febril. De ese estado festivo salieron los primeros dibujos de este libro, que luego completé en Nueva York en su departamento del Village, en otro arrebato igualmente creativo y compartido. Me parece que sus dibujos, que fueron acompañando a los míos merecerían publicarse aquí. Que al menos quede constancia de lo feliz que me siento por ese inspirado trance de creatividad que nos dio a las dos. A Eric Manheimer quiero darle las muchas gracias por sus comentarios, su amistad entrañable y su abundante sopa judía que abrigó mis estadías en su hogar. Sin el combustible de esa sopa todo hubiera sido más difícil-pero en especial quiero darle las gracias por nuestras caminatas y conversaciones que en momentos muy claves me ayudaron muchísmo.

Quiero agradecerle a Marsha Gall sus valiosas reflexiones sobre la escritura de *De atrás para adelante* y de mis últimos textos, incluidos los que están en proceso de desarrollo. De una contínua zona de conversaciones con ella, derivamos siempre en un precioso paraje donde las cosas adquieren velocidad y en las que surgen tramas apasionantes que benefician no sólo a mis textos sino a mi persona toda.

Quiero agradecerle a Roselyn Costantino sus comentarios sobre *Casa Matriz* que me ayudaron a entender ciertos códigos culturales para la obra en los Estados Unidos.

Quiero agradecer a Nora Glickman y a Gloria Waldman el haber incluido en el libro *Argentine Jewish Theater* mi obra *Lost Belongings*. Fue mi primer texto que se publicó en Estados Unidos en inglés y la siento un antecedente de este volúmen.

Durante la reescritura de *Casa Matriz* recibí la Beca de la Fundación Guggenheim, cuyo aporte agradezco especialmente ya que me dio la oportunidad de resignificar el texto dándole el desarrollo que necesitaba. Eso hizo que se montara en Buenos Aires en la versión definitiva que hoy se publica en este libro.

A Berta Schrager, mi mamá quiero agradecerle su apoyo y sus observaciones. El apoyo fue clave para que decidiera muy tempranamente ser fiel a mi vocación. A sus observaciones—que provocaron mis rebeldías adolescentes—hoy las encuentro muy encantadoras.

A mis amigos, gracias por la gentileza y la contención, las risas y las lágrimas, la intimidad compartida y los días vividos. No quiero dejar a nadie afuera, por eso me resisto a las enumeraciones. Cerrando los ojos, con una mano en el corazón, todos ellos saben lo que me dieron y lo que les estoy agradeciendo. Sabiendo que el Amor no se agradece sino que se vive intensamente, quiero sin embargo agradecer el que recibo cada día y que hace tanto más habitable este mundo en el que me tocó escribir y para colmo vivir.

Diana Raznovich. Buenos Aires. 2000

Acknowledgments

Many, many thanks to the people who made this volume possible: to Diana Raznovich and Victoria Martinez most particularly. Thanks also to Lidia Ramirez, who helped in the always difficult process of making translated texts stage-worthy. In order to fully test the translations, Daniel Banks directed the following actors in a wonderful stage reading of *Inner Gardens*: Novella Nelson, Mary Beth Peil, Jay Goede, Patricia Dalen, William Meisle, Robin Miles. Thanks to all of them and to New York University's International Visitor's Office and James Fernández, Director of the King Juan Carlos of Spain Center at NYU for making this possible. And finally, my thanks to Gisela Cárdenas for her help putting together the final manuscript.

Diana Taylor

* * *

I wish to express my heartfelt thanks to Diana Raznovich and Diana Taylor for extending me the opportunity to translate these wonderful plays. My thanks also to Joanna Tai for word-processing assistance, and to Mary Parlett for her considerable technological guidance.

Victoria Martinez

TRANSLATED BY VICTORIA MARTINEZ

IN COLLABORATION
WITH
LIDIA RAMIREZ

DEFIANT ACTS

FIGHTING FIRE WITH FRIVOLITY:
Diana Raznovich's Defiant Acts

Diana Taylor

Diana Raznovich's trajectory as a playwright, which began in Buenos Aires when her first play won a theater contest in 1967, has been characterized by humor, intelligence, and unwavering defiance of delimiting social systems—whether those systems be authoritarian military dictatorships, coercive economic systems, or the far subtler but nonetheless restrictive systems of gender and sexual formation. Throughout her work, she indicates how the various systems interconnect in creating and manipulating desire even as they define, position, and control desiring bodies. Identities are shaped and bodies are molded into acceptable forms through the constant pressure of socialization. Raznovich's plays represent not only a culture of reproduction (along the lines of Marx's commodity fetishism) but also culture as reproduction, as a desiring machine that generates a series of repetitions and enactments with no original, (somewhat akin to Baudrillard's concept of the "hyper-real").[1] As a playwright and a cartoonist, she uses her artistic systems to critique and transgress the restrictions imposed by her society, which have been considerable to say the least, for a Jewish, bisexual, Oscar Wildesque woman coming of age during the time of the Dirty War (1976–83).

Early in her career, Raznovich began defying Argentine theatrical norms. She rejected the ponderous realistic style so popular among her fellow dramatists. Plaza hay una sola, her second production, was a performance piece comprised of eight different scenes taking place simultaneously in a public park. The audience walked around, encountering a series of situations—a person about to commit suicide, another person giving a speech from a soapbox and so on. Since then, her work both as a cartoonist and in the theater has been marked by her sense of humor and her love of disruption, inversion, and the unexpected.

But her career as a playwright was stalled when repeated threats on her life by the Armed Forces pressured Raznovich into exile in 1975, shortly before the military coup that initiated the Dirty War. She lived and worked in Spain, teaching dramaturgy in an independent theater school until she returned to Argentina in 1981 to participate in the Teatro abierto (Open Theater) festival.

Teatro abierto brought together dramatists, directors, actors, and technicians—all of them blacklisted and fearing for their safety—to produce a cycle of one-act plays that demonstrated that Argentina's artists had not succumbed to the dictatorship's silencing tactics. How could she resist such an important act of collective defiance? Still, even this act of oppositional solidarity sought to control the range of "acceptable" defiance—for several of the other committed playwrights found her contribution (the one-act, one-woman play El desconcierto/ Disconcerted) to the "open" and contestatory theater cycle inappropriate. Who could possibly be interested in a play about a female pianist who can't make sound come out of a piano in the context of the censorship and general silencing of the Dirty War? While Raznovich's intentions were (and are) always to challenge and transgress repressive limits, it was not always in a manner that her more openly political colleagues could always understand or appreciate. Though she was asked to withdraw the play and submit another, she refused.[2] The military reacted more violently not just to her work but to the entire project, burning down the Picadero on the night that Teatro abierto was being staged.[3] Teatro abierto moved to another locale, and continued to stage its productions in the face of growing governmental opposition and growing popular support. Yet, some of her fellow artists "started saying that I was frivolous. I took it as a compliment. There was no permission for my stance or style, and I found it wonderfully transgressive."[4]

Disconcerted, far from being frivolous, depicts a society caught up in the active production of national fictions—fictions that ultimately render all members of the population silent and complicitous. The pianist, Irene della Porta, is paid handsomely by her manager to play Beethoven's Patetique on a piano that emits no sound. The audience buys tickets to watch Irene wrench sounds out of nothingness: "It is as if the woman and the audience, although knowing that the Beethoven Sonata cannot be heard, were mysteriously capable of composing 'this other non-existent concert'" reads the opening stage directions.[5] At the end of the play, the piano regains its sound as if by magic. But after so many silent concerts, Irene della Porta no longer knows how to make "real" music.

Desensitized fingers produce harsh, discordant notes. Shocked and defeated by her ultimate failure as an artist, she rejoices when the piano once again becomes mute.

On the most obvious level, Disconcerted is a critique of Argentine artists and audiences alike who were willing to go along with the censorship imposed by the military dictatorship, convincing themselves that, in fact, they were engaging in meaningful communication. What draws the members of the audience into the theater night after night is, in part, a sharing of collective complicity that they can interpret as "resistance." Although they produce no sound, the reasoning seems to be that by their presence alone, audience members defy those who impose censorship and self-censorship. [6] The idea that public presence at a theatrical event functioned as an act of resistance in part underlay the entire Teatro abierto project. The fact that thousands of people lined up to see plays bajo vigilancia [7] (under surveillance) was interpreted by the military leaders and by the population at large as an oppositional move.

Disconcerted, however, seems directed at those Argentines who were complicitous with the dictatorship and whose passivity in the face of governmental brutality made a new social order—the culture of terror— possible. The "show," far from being oppositional, is produced by the powerbrokers themselves. By their very presence and willingness to be part of the performance, the spectators contribute to the construction of a new community, one that is grounded in fictions. But the spectators do not recognize themselves in the scenario—they are blinded to their situation and think that the drama (which seemingly eludes them as the sound eludes Irene) is taking place someplace else. Yet this silencing and displacement was precisely what the Dirty War was all about.

The performative process of communal binding/blinding depicted by Raznovich points to two forms of gender violence. On one level, "femininity" is a performance that Irene enacts on a daily basis. Clad in her low-cut, tight red gown and dripping with jewels she becomes the Other that the audience pays to see. She even speaks of herself in the third person, as Irene della Porta, as a commodity who has agreed to play along with her objectification and degradation because she gets some tangible benefits out of it: "Endless years of comfort by agreeing to be Irene della Porta playing silently" (569). Raznovich presents gender as performative, much along the lines developed by Judith Butler: "gender is an act which has been rehearsed, much as a script survives the particular actors who make use of it, but which requires individual actors in order to be actualized and reproduced as reality once again."[8] Few roles available to women in patriarchy offer any visibility—the "star" being one of them. But the "star," as Irene explicitly notes, embodies the male spectators' desires. It is "Woman" as a projection of patriarchal fantasies that performs on-stage. She no longer recognizes herself in the mirror—there is no "self" to recognize.

On another level, the project of community building undertaken by the junta is also gendered. From the beginning, the junta made explicit that state formation was inextricable from gender formation. In its first pronouncement, published in La Nación on the day of the military golpe on 24 March, 1976, the Junta declared itself the "supreme organ of the Nation" ready to "fill the void of power" embodied by Perón's widow, "Isabelita," Argentina's constitutional president. In their effort to transform the "infirm," inert Argentine masses into an authentic "national being," the junta undertook to eliminate the toxic elements (or subversives) from the social "body." The war was being fought in the interstices of the Mother Patria, in her bleeding entrails; it was thus transgressive, hidden, dirty. The maternal image of Patria was both the justification for and the physical site of violent politics. The very term "Patria," which comes from Padre or father does not mean fatherland in Spanish but rather the image of motherland framed through patriarchy. There is no woman behind the maternal mage invoked by the military. Yet the feminine image (Patria, Irene della Porta) serves a real function in community building by uniting all those who imagine themselves bound or loyal to her. However, the "feminine" is only useful to the power brokers as long as she remains an image without real agency. As such, "she" gives the spectators their identity. Just as the Armed Forces defined "true" Argentines by virtue of their loyalty to the Patria (and by extension, to the Armed Forces as her defenders), Irene della Porta's fans form a group (an "imagined community" in the words of Benedict Anderson) [9] because of their relationship to her: "Who am I? Who are you?" The nature of this community building is circular—the feminine image is the creation of the patriarchal order, but "she," in turn, gives birth to the nation's image of itself. So too, Irene della Porta candidly admits that she is the creation of her fans: "[they] have made me what I am today. But, who am I?" And yet, her tenuous, rehearsed "identity" unites the audience.

While the woman "disappears" in the image of Patria, Raznovich will not allow her audience to overlook the misogynist violence of this community-building discourse. Her character makes it clear that what draws the audience to the theater is also the "show" of public humiliation that Irene della Porta performs on a nightly basis. The themes of collective complicity, silencing, and disempowerment are played out on the exposed and humiliated body of "Woman": "What do you want of me? (Suddenly she opens her dress and begins to disrobe.) Do you want to unravel hidden truths? Do you want to see me without any more disguises? (She disrobes down to her underclothes.) Now that you see me this way, stripped down to my teeth, do you know more about me than before? Does my nakedness bring success? What is a naked woman? A skeleton out in the open covered with a fragile vital membrane?" As a feminist, Diana Raznovich understood an aspect of the cultural production of community and silencing that other playwrights reproduced but failed to recognize—that the social pact between power brokers and complicitous audiences is being negotiated (both in the military discourse and in "art") on the body of "Woman." The audience searches for its identity in her bodily interstices and looks for "truth" on her naked flesh. Her body functions as a text on which the community's fate is inscribed.

Disconcerted paradoxically signals both the failure and power of art in the context of the Dirty War. The play's presentation of Irene della Porta's body as exposed rather than naked and the grotesque sounds emanating from the piano defies the aesthetization of violence and the commodification of culture even as it portrays it. Raznovich decries the fetishizing even as Irene della Porta succumbs to it. Her play is a work of "committed art" even as it laments the non-existence of such a thing. As Theodor Adorno noted in the late 1960s, "A work of art that is committed strips the magic from a work of art that is content to be a fetish, an idle pastime for those who would like to sleep through the deluge that threatens them, in an apoliticism that is in fact deeply political."[10] Diana Raznovich makes clear that noncommitted, evasive art during periods of social catastrophe helps constitute and cement a culture of terror in which people ultimately lose their capacity for real insight. Even if restrictions were suddenly lifted, and the piano magically regained its sound, those involved in the production of fiction would not be able to reestablish real communication.

Diana Raznovich's opposition to the limits imposed by the oppositional "left" itself, however, went beyond issues of her personal dramatic style. As a feminist, she objected to what she saw as the all-male nature of Teatro abierto, made evident not only in the content of the almost entirely male authored and directed plays, but in the decision to stage Teatro abierto at Tabarís after the burning of the Picadero. As before, Teatro

abierto started early, at 6:30 pm.   At night, the Tabarís continued its
regular programming—a cabaret featuring scantily dressed showgirls and
livened up with misogynist jokes.   When women in Teatro abierto
complained about housing their politically "progressive" and
oppositional theater event in that location, they were overruled.   The
argument was that Teatro abierto would "subvert" the space and give it
new meaning.   But rather than "subvert" the space of feminine
degradation, Teatro abierto decided to exploit it to ensure its own
survival and continuity. The military males, who frequented the cabaret
during its regular hours, would be less likely to destroy a space they
associated with their own pleasure. This strategy of protecting political
content behind or within the context of female sexual exploitation was
not new to the period.[11]   But the consequence, of course, was that gender
inequality and female sexual exploitation could never be the topic of
analysis since the transmission of the political message was seen as
contingent on their continuing exploitation. Thus, Teatro abierto set up a
situation in which theatergoers, prepared to find a critique of their
repressive society, would have to walk past the posters of seminaked
women to get into the theater. The juxtaposition of the political event
against the seminude female body reproduced the visual strategies used
by pro-military magazines (such as Gente) that superimposed headlines
of the atrocious events of the Dirty War on the female bodies in bikinis
that graced half of their covers. Again, the female was reduced to pure
body and backgrounded as the site of violence and political conflict. The
female subject could lay no claim to political participation or to non-
exploitative representation—she served as the scenario on which the
struggle between men—political agents—could take place.
The struggle for a feminist playwright in Argentina during the Dirty War,
then, was far more complicated than taking an antimilitary stand—
dangerous and heroic though that was in itself. It meant taking on not
just the brutal regime but the Argentine imaginary, that imagined sense
of community that defines "Argentine-ness" as a struggle between
men—fought on and over the "feminine" (be it the symbolic body of the
Patria or Motherland, Irene della Porta, or the physical body of a
woman). The violence against women, both in fact and in representation,
went beyond a straightforward "left"/ "right" divide. Thus this meant
taking on the "progressive" authors of the opposition who themselves
depicted the construction of national identity as predicated on female
destruction (as in Ricardo Monti's work, or Eduardo Pavlovsky's). The
leftist critique of the military too often continued to participate in the

military's misogyny. In the struggle to define and claim the "authentic" national identity, both the military and progressive males were fighting to occupy the "masculine" position while emasculating, feminizing, and marginalizing the "other." Even plays that were intended as a critique of the macho military male by a male intellectual (Monti's La cortina de abalorios) still needed the woman's naked body to express its objections and engage its audience.

In one of those examples of ironic inversions that Diana Raznovich is so fond of, the Dirty War ended, the military was more or less chastened, the rulers changed, and she still had plenty to be defiant about. Unlike several important Argentine dramatists who could identify and address the evils of military dictatorship but who did not understand that the coercive system (not just the leaders) had to change, Raznovich had just begun to write about issues of gender and sexuality that had so totally eluded most of her colleagues. Her brilliant plays, Inner Gardens (Jardin de otoño,1983), MaTRIX, Inc. (Casa Matriz,1991) and Rear Entry (De atrás para adelante,1995), continue to explore the feminist premise that desire is created and constrained through the scopic and economic systems that supposedly only represent it, that gender and sexuality are performative, and that subjectivity is socially constructed. Women aren't born women, as Simone de Beauvoir observed decades ago—they become women through the process of socialization. Just as the star role enacted by Irene della Porta was a product of a patriarchal system that profited both economically and politically from her ability to make a spectacle of her humiliation, the other roles and sexual choices available to women were similarly produced.

In Inner Gardens, Raznovich shifts her examination of these constraining systems of gender and sexual formation to the telenovela or soap opera so popular in Latin America. Soap operas, too, of course, are in the business of producing fictions. Like the silent concert staged by Irene della Porta's manager, the telenovela is controlled by the power-broker behind the scenes—here the odious Gaspar Mendez Paz. The consumers of these fictions, like the audience in Disconcerted, live with the fantasy that they are actually opposing those in authority by participating in some romantic battle against the status quo, even as they submissively surrender themselves to the tiny screen. The two main characters of the play—two middle-aged women who have lived together for twenty years named Griselda and Rosalia—spend every afternoon in front of the television passionately involved in the ups and downs of their adored hero, Marcelo-the-mechanic. Though lowly, rough speaking, and

dressed in greasy overalls, he challenges the social barriers that separate
him from the lovely, upper class, and engaged-to-another Valeria, the girl
of his dreams. And the women live the drama with him, consumed with
passionate intensity. Will the girl's father have him thrown in jail? Will
he end up dying there? This, as one of the women points out, is a
"modern" soap opera, which means that things could turn out badly for
the hero—no happy endings guaranteed. The telenovela, like the silent
concert, provides these spectators with the fiction that they are
participating in an erotic life that eludes their grasp.

On one level, though perhaps not the principal one, the play engages the
debates surrounding the political dimension of popular culture. Do the
soaps, one of the best examples of popular culture on a massive level of
production and consumption, instill an antipopular ideology in its
audiences, making them desire values and worldviews that reflect the
industry's interests rather than their own class interests? While the
telenovelas might not overtly intend to control its audience (unlike the
concert in Disconcerted), the product bears the ideological stamp of its
producers. As John Fiske puts it, "every commodity reproduces the
ideology of the system that produced it: a commodity is ideology made
material."[12] The simple David versus Goliath plot of the soap opera
seemingly confronts social bias (specifically class conflict). While the
women cheer their idol on to triumph, and hope that social barriers will
simply evaporate, they certainly are not going to do anything about the
problem. They may not even be aware of class conflict as a social
problem, especially when they personalize it by concluding that the rich
girl's Daddy is a "rotten old man" and that the rude producer "hates the
viewers." The most they can do is call the producer and, as loyal
viewers, demand that those in charge work out a satisfactory ending.
Thus, the antisoap argument goes, these programs encourage the working
classes (who make up the bulk of the viewing audience for these shows)
to dream about triumphing in a social structure that, in fact, is predicated
on their exclusion.

Inner Gardens does not endorse this "antipopular" position outright.
There is an element of playfulness in the way the women participate in
the drama that supports Carlos Monsivais's contention (shared by other
analysts of popular culture such as Fiske, Rowe, and Schelling) that
popular audiences find a way to resemanticize cultural materials
provided from above. Monsivais argues that "collectivities without
political power or social representation sexualize melodrama, extract
satirical threads from black humor, enjoy themselves and are moved

emotionally without changing ideologically. The subaltern classes accept, because they have no alternative, a vulgar and pedestrian industry, and indisputably transform it into self-indulgence and degradation, but also into joyful and combative identity."[13]

Monsivais's contention that the subaltern viewers can engage "emotionally" without "changing ideologically" is the problematic crux of the issue—and the one the play most lucidly dismantles. But, in order to argue this point, I need to provide some more plot summary. Griselda and Rosalia, the two "old maid" types, desire, long for, love, and feel intensely, but they have no adequate outlet for this love. Griselda writes poetry and talks to her plants, and Rosalia goes to the fortune-teller, hoping against hope that some handsome man will appear in her future. Meanwhile, they spend the afternoons lusting for Marcelo-the-mechanic, kissing the screen and wishing they were the adored women in the picture. One day, they decide to kidnap Marcelo and live out their fantasy, even if they have to die afterward. So they do, and the play goes on to show their increased frustration as the star disappoints them. He is not the simple, good, honest, hardworking boy they've grown to love on the series. He is charming and nice, but far more complicated than they anticipated. He can't make passionate love to them, as they had dreamed, though the women can't seem to figure out why. Maybe he's impotent, they ask each other, maybe he's gay. Well, maybe he's not gay but rather homosexual. What's the difference, they wonder, though they sense there probably must be some. And on they go until they discover he lightens and perms his hair and that he uses make-up. The "real" man is more artificial, they conclude, than the "real" Marcelo on TV. So they turn the soap opera back on and let the actor find his own way home. The "real" is a poor substitute for fantasy. They seem comfortable back in their world of safe, predictable, honest, "real" illusion. So, this apparently illustrates Monsivais's point that the viewers can engage emotionally and disengage ideologically.

However, it seems to me that Inner Gardens is specifically concerned with the constraints imposed on emotional and sexual expression by dominant systems of representation that not only reproduce scenes of desire (Marcelo and Valeria) but demarcate their limits. These systems of signification (for soap operas are not just products but systems) do not, I believe, offer as much space for resemanticization as one might like to believe. The "real" love story going on here is not between Marcelo and Valeria but between Griselda and Rosalia. They live together; they love each other; they share a rich, funny, tumultuous domestic relationship; they cannot imagine life without each other. Yet, they have never been permitted to envision their relationship as anything beyond the banal labels that they have available: "my friend, my housemate—my tenant let's say." The idealized male soap-opera star serves to channel and contain the love and desire between them. Their desire circulates through him. Griselda's most acute sensation when she is watching "the best episode of the year," the one in which Marcelo kisses Valeria and admits he's "got it bad" for her, is the feeling of disappointment that Rosalia is not there to watch it with her. This love on the screen is to be shared by them, even though they have momentary snits when each claims the divine Marcelo as her own. Thus, the soaps, as a dominant system of signification validate certain forms of love while making others unthinkable. Class barriers might be the subject matter of the telenovela, but it cannot (yet) question the barriers that make heterosexual love the norm. Griselda and Rosalia, not surprisingly, are as blind to the nature of their desire as the society that created them. They can tell each other they love each other, they can look at each other intently, hold each other and admit they cannot live apart, but only the fantasy of heterosexual passion allows them to do so without assuming the weight and shame too often ascribed to homosexuality. The women simply displace their passion onto the handsome movie star. The story of their lives isn't theirs—it's taking place on TV; their love for each other (which they allude to repeatedly) isn't theirs—it's happening between Marcelo-the-mechanic and the lovely, rich, engaged-to-another Valeria. The women can own their passionate intensity every afternoon precisely because they don't have to recognize it as theirs. Towards the end of Act One, in one of the saddest moments of the play, the women pray for forgiveness for the life they haven't lived:

Forgive me for what I haven't done.
Forgive me for what I haven't had.
Forgive me for what I haven't taken.
Forgive me for what I haven't felt.
Forgive me for not laughing enough.
Forgive me for not using my tears.

The plot of Inner Gardens, I am suggesting, illustrates that emotionally, as well as ideologically, social subjects are produced and delimited by the very systems that, in theory, are there to excite desire. But the play also inverts the paradigm that positions the "feminine" as the object of desire that serves to stabilize a male-dominated community that Raznovich depicted in Disconcerted. In that play, the audience becomes a "community" as it comes together to applaud Irene della Porta. In Inner Gardens, however, there is a more explicit sexual dimension to the mediation that, I have argued, is central to Argentina's social imaginary. Again, we see the case of the triangulation of desire—channeling of erotic intensity through a safe symbol of either feminine or masculine sexuality that allows for proximity without incurring the stigma of a society as homophobic as the Argentine one. Yet, that triangulation is pivotal, both to the lives of these two spinsters as to the gendering of the nation as a whole. As I submitted in Disappearing Acts: Spectacles Gender and Nationalism in Argentina's "Dirty War," "The feminine nation, or Patria, mediated the autoeroticism of the military's performance. The armed forces obsessively conjured up the symbolic Woman to keep their homosocial society from becoming a homosexual one. The military men came together in the heterosexual language of "love" of the Patria" (68–69).[14] Whether it's the Patria, Irene della Porta, or Marcelo-the-mechanic, the discourse of passion circulates through a rigidly monitored economy of heterosexual love.

In her next play, Diana Raznovich extends her exploration of the "substitute" and the supposedly "real" (is Marcelo any more or less "real" to these women than the actor who plays him?) to the social enactment of roles in general. Coming as she does from a society that values the "mother" almost to the exclusion of all other women, it seems inevitable that she would choose that one. MaTRIX, Inc, a full length one-act play, depicts a "daughter," Gloria, who hires a "mother" from an agency specializing in that service. The two women rehearse a series of roles. They range from the traditional long-suffering mother so popular in Latin American literature, to the professional mother who travels around the world; from the cold, rejecting mother, to the transgressive one who vies with her daughter for the lesbian lover. Each "mother," of course, elicits a different "daughter," and Gloria undergoes a series of transformations as she pouts, demands satisfaction, cries, begs for love, and orders the substitute mother to give her money back. Motherhood, so long essentialized as the natural condition that alone justifies the existence of women in Latin America is exposed as not only as a patriarchal construct, but as a commercial one as well. When the substitute mother is asked to play "the long-suffering mother," for example, she states that this is her most sought-after role: "Everyone, absolutely everyone needs to see me in the most menial state of servitude." The show of female submission, just as in Disconcerted, continues to be a bestseller. Yet, the brilliance of the play lies in the performative distance that Raznovich establishes between the enactment and that absent referent that one supposes to be "the real." But even "the real" is destabilized through the highly theatrical nature of the iterations. As the substitute mother makes a show of crying that produces "real" tears, she asks her "daughter" to touch them: "You could not ask for a more tragic effect. I am the Suffering Mother par excellence. Dressed in black, cleaning, crying. Look at these enormous tears!" Thus, the idea of "the real" only lends weight to the representation—and not the other way around. That is, the show does not "represent" the real—as in Aristotelian logic. Rather, "the real" is produced through these constant enactments. So, too, the "substitute mother" signals the constructed quality of the "real" mother, that woman whose claim to identity and visibility depends on her ability to be a quick-change artist—to be all things to all people. The motherhood role so lucidly deconstructed by Raznovich is crucial because it has both severely limited and afforded visibility to Argentine women as different as Evita (the "mother" of the Argentine homeland), and the Mothers of the Plaza de Mayo. As women they had no claim to power or redress but as mothers, symbolic or political, they launched the most visible political movements headed by women of their times. Only as mothers could they speak in a way that their fellow citizens could hear them. But the reality lies in the act itself—Evita never had children; the Madres, privately accepting the death of their own children, claimed to be the mothers of all the disappeared. Motherhood, thus, shifts from the realm of the biological to that of the sociopolitical. The efficacy of the role, then, lies not in its "natural" essence but in its performance. And, in the very public seclusion of the rental agency, Gloria pays the "substitute" to produce real anguish and tears.

The economy of the "substitute" normally serves to bolster the "real," for what would a "substitute" mean, what possible function could it have if it did not replace, stand in for or somehow link up with the "real"? But the notion of the real, so privileged by the deployment of the "substitute" is exactly what becomes shaken in this enactment. The "real," rather, is produced through the capitalist market system that trades in desires and emotions. Rather than allowing us to buy into the seemingly natural Mother/Daughter experience, to idealize it or psychologize it, Raznovich leaves all the performative strings showing. The scene of the natural is highly produced.

Nowhere is the complicated interconnection between the "act" and the "real," between the performative and the so-called "natural," more highlighted than in Raznovich's Rear Entry. Structured as a more conventional three-act comedy, this play is about a wealthy Jewish businessman, Simon Goldberg, who comes on hard times as his bathroom and plumbing industry goes bankrupt. Everyone is in a tizzy—the young wife, the married daughter, the son-in-law—as the business and the fortune seem, literally, to be going down the drain. Simon, who cannot bear strong doses of reality, crumples in a faint/feint. Mariana, the daughter, insists they contact Javier, her wealthy brother whom Simon threw out of the house a decade ago when he found him in bed with Mariana's fiancé. Help comes but, as always with Raznovich, not in the way that one recognizes or expects. Onstage comes the lovely Dolly, previously Javier, now a gorgeous and loving woman with a husband and three daughters. Dolly saves the business by convincing Argentines that they love colored toilet paper (and that their bottoms deserve no less), but she has more trouble convincing her homophobic father that she deserves his love and support as his transsexual son/daughter, Dolly—not as Dolly, whom Simon is prepared to adore but only if she pretends to be Javier's wife.

Clearly, the issues posed here go far beyond the ideas of gender as performative posited both by Disconcerted and MaTRIX, Inc. Gender, of course, is still performative, still an "act" that the body learns to perform over time, through the rigorous course of socialization. But the figure of the transsexual challenges the notion that sex (male/female) is ever a stable marker. What sex is Javier/Dolly? How can we even begin to think about, let alone define, sexual difference? Does "difference" lie in the reproductive organs (so that Javier "dies" as Dolly comes to life)? Or does it lie in the hormones, or in the DNA? How can we think about gender difference is a system that denies women subjectivity? Are women (as in the Dirty War) no more than the "enemy" or "dangerous" other in a binary system founded on the sexual divide, part of a male/female dialectic as thinkers such as Simone de Beauvoir suggest? Or, as the figure of Irene della Porta implies, are women simply the projection of masculinist fantasies and prohibitions in a closed system whose only referent is male, a monologic system or singular phallic order that denies that there even is an other? If so, female subjects are forever linguistically absent and unrepresentable. Does this absence signal the limits of discursive formations themselves and suggest perhaps the possibility of a negotiated existence between discourses, in the margins and fractures? Or does it put in doubt the material existence of real historical beings, situated in discursive formations that erase them?

If subjectivity is produced by the entry into culture, as theorists such as de Beauvoir, Foucault, de Lauretis and Butler have argued,[15] then it is gendered and, more specifically gendered from the monologic male position in a closed system of self-reference. There are many absences here—the discursive absence of the "feminine" in a masculinist imaginary; the absence of real, historical women in protagonistic roles in Argentina; the absence of the material bodies of the women who were permanently "disappeared" from the political landscape.

The disappearance of Javier inverts the system that erases women as linguistic and protagonistic subjects. Dolly becomes visible—and so does the seeming cultural impossibility: a man socialized in a masculinist society like Argentina's may in fact choose to be a "woman." Sex is not a static given. Javier will always be a part of Dolly, as perhaps Dolly was always a part of Javier. Sexual identity isn't simply an either/or—mark the M or the F. As Mariana says after she and Dolly go through their old costume box and perform some of the routines they acted out as children, "I think there are three of us, Mariana, Javier and Dolly." There is no immutable "real" that engenders a series of acts—but a series of acts that construct the "real." These performances including those linguistic performances that J. Austin refers to when he writes about speech acts that effect change.[16] Social systems only give permission for two acceptable performances of gender to be seen, and these are marked as dominant (masculine) and subordinate (feminine) in myriad ways. Language (in this case Spanish) also genders all nouns, and also subsumes the subordinate into the dominant. The duo, made up of Mariana and Javier, was called "Los hermanos Goldberg" (the Goldberg Brothers), a name that erased distinctions between the two. Now, the male Javier has disappeared behind the feminine Dolly, erasing all visual traces of his presence in her as the "Goldberg Brothers" erased the presence of Mariana. Thus, identities disappear and reappear (more or less violently) through a whole series of systems—be they political and linguistic disappearances or through systems that dictate the appropriate enactments of gender and sexuality.

Appropriate. Perhaps that word sums up the normalizing code of admissible behavior that Diana Raznovich so riles, jokes, and warns against. The military junta imposed and enforced rules governing appropriate behavior; the opposition dictated the terms of appropriate resistance. Society demands that citizens act their gender and sex appropriately. Economic systems—television, advertising, and so forth— tell us what sells and what doesn't, what cultural products can enter the market and which will be excluded (no censorship here, they say, they just aren't "marketable"). And the way the appropriate becomes the normalized relates to desire. One of the challenges that face authoritarian governments is that they must teach the population to desire a nebulous higher good (national unity, or a passionate defense of the motherland, for example) so that people will accept civil restrictions (i.e., loss of personal liberties—the right to vote, organize, strike, protest, etc.). Those who refuse to desire what they've been asked to are figuratively or literally "disappeared" as citizens. Capitalist economic systems not only create desire and fulfill it by supplying the desired commodity but, as Marx argued, they erase the human labor that went into production. The worker disappears, leaving only the object whose worth lies not in its production value, but in its exchange value. Gender and sexual identities are produced and reproduced in similar economies. The male occupies the position of producer and consumer while the female's worth rests in her exchange value—as star, she embodies the male fantasy to the mutual benefit of producer and consumer. As the ideal mother, she performs her act of servitude—an act, Raznovich observes, that is greatly in demand. The efficacy of these enactments, of course, depends on their naturalization—that is, on people's willingness to see them as both normative and desirable. Those who fail to participate in the desirability of this socially constructed desire also disappear into some other category reserved for the "deviants" and gender benders. And what is more violent, Diana Raznovich seems to ask in her humorous, provocative work—the self-inflicted violence of the one who tries to squeeze into appropriate norms? Or the other-inflicted violence (ranging from disappearance to ostracism) visited on those who fail to comply? There are different kinds of violence, different kinds of repression. A playwright like Diana Raznovich who sees the interconnection between the different kinds of systemic violence has her work cut out for her. However, to invert the normative, she turns to comedy. Humor is subversive; it is capable of challenging and unsettling the norm. "I wish people understood how subversive humor really is," Raznovich says. "You can say a lot more with laughter than with tragedy." So she goes on being "frivolous," defiant, transgressive, and never altogether appropriate.

Notes

1. See Karl Marx, Capital, vol. 1 (Moscow: Foreign Languages Publishing House, 1961) and Jean Baudrillard, Simulations (New York: Semiotexte, 1983).
2. Raznovich-Taylor Interview, Dartmouth College, September 1994.
3. Juana A. Arancibia and Zulema Mirkin, "Introducción" to Teatro Argentino durante el proceso, (Buenos Aires: Instituto Literario y Cultural Hispánico, 1992), 21.
4. Raznovich/Taylor Interview, Buenos Aires, 1994.
5. All translations from Raznovich's plays are by Victoria Martínez, unless otherwise noted. El Desconcierto was published as Disconcerted in The Literary Review 32. 4 (1989): 568-572.
6. It is interesting to note that muteness and public silence was interpreted both as an act of complicity and an act of resistance during the Dirty War. On the one hand, those who did not speak out against government brutality enabled the criminal practices of abduction, disappearance, and torture to continue. However, not speaking was also seen as a heroic defiance against a system that demanded conformity, just as it was seen as defiance against the torturer who demanded "information" during the act of torture.
7. This is the term used by Miguel Angel Giella to describe Teatro abierto in his study/anthology: Teatro abierto, 1981: Teatro Argentino Bajo Vigilancia (Buenos Aires: Corregidor 1991).
8. Judith Butler, "Performative Acts and Gender Construction" in Performing Feminisms: Feminist Critical Theory and Theatre, edited by Sue-Ellen Case (Baltimore: Johns Hopkins University Press, 1990), 277. See also Gender Trouble (New York: Routledge, 1990), and Bodies That Matter (New York: Routledge, 1993).
9. Benedict Anderson, Imagined Communities (London: Verso, 1983).
10. Theodor Adorno, "Commitment" in Aesthetics and Politics, (London: Verso, 1977), 177.
11. The eminent film maker Adolfo Aristarain, who directed Time for Revenge in 1981, admitted to doing the same. He included long and unnecessary sexual scenes in the film, he explained in an interview with Annette Insdorf, "'so the censors took five days and questioned things—not politics or ideology, but sex. All I had to do was cut a few frames at the end of some scenes, like one of a strip-tease. It doesn't hurt the scenes—especially if you made them longer than they should have been,' he said with a knowing smile." Annette Insdorf, "Time for Revenge: A Discussion with Adolfo Aristarain," Cineaste (1983): 17.
12. John Fiske, Understanding Popular Culture (London, New York: Routledge, 1989).
13. Quoted in William Rowe and Vivian Schelling, Memory and Modernity: Popular Culture in Latin America (London: Verso, 1991).

14. Diana Taylor, <u>Disappearing Acts: Spectacles of Gender and Nationalism in Argentina's 'Dirty War</u>.' (Durham: Duke University Press, 1997).

15. See Michel Foucault, <u>The History of Sexuality</u>, vol. 1 (New York: Vintage, 1980) <u>Discipline and Punish</u> (New York: Vintage, 1979), and Simone de Beauvoir, <u>The Second Sex</u> (Harmondsworth: Penguin, 1984).

16. J. L. Austin, <u>How To Do Things With Words</u> (Cambridge: Harvard University Press, 1962).

THE PLAYS

DIANA RAZNOVIG

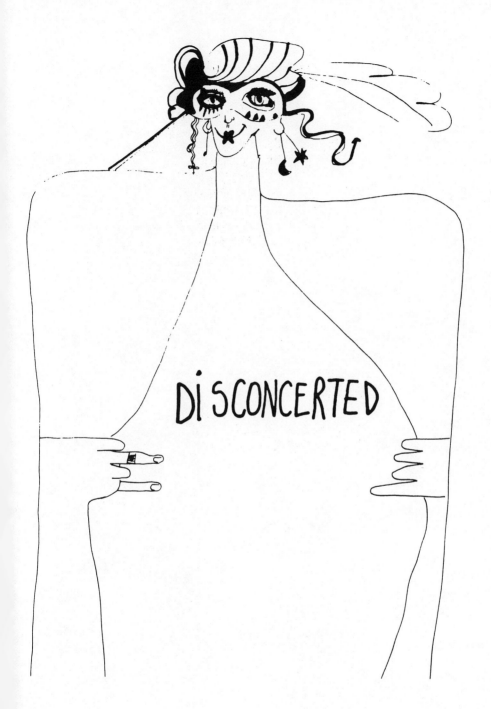

DISCONCERTED

Translated by Victoria Martinez

Character
Irene della Porta: The Pianist

Setting
(A piano sits on the empty stage. After a pause a woman dressed in a long red dress embellished with jewels greets the audience and begins to play. She pounds with vehemence. The piano does not make a sound. Silence fills the concert hall. It is a silence without sound; the unexpected silence of a piano vigorously pounded by the woman. A silence that for some moments seems to want to hide or destroy through its vehement execution. It is as if the woman and the audience, knowing that the Beethoven Sonata cannot be heard, were mysteriously capable of composing "this other non-existent concert." After the pause created by the woman silently playing, she gets up unexpectedly from the keyboard and, visibly displeased, addresses the audience.)

Pianist Ladies and gentlemen: Here's yet another episode of sabotage in the long line of episodes that plague me whenever you and I try to put on this concert. You have been following me faithfully, and I have been playing for you in spite of everything. Well, not exactly everything, no! In spite of a manager who vents his fury by making sure that no concert of mine is possible! *(She begins to play the piano and again it emits no sound. She returns to the audience.)* The world of my admirers (as I know, unfortunately) is quite divided. I wish to thank all of you, my old fans and my new ones for all your support. I wouldn't know how to go on living without you. Without your help, Irene della Porta wouldn't know who she was. I thank my old fans because they beg me to return to the concert stage. I thank my current fans because they ask me to continue playing these silent concerts that have enjoyed so much success.

They're all justified. Your inspiring presence has made me what I am today. But, just who am I? Tell me that? Does my manager know who I am? Do my fans know who I am? Do I myself know who I am? Am I me, or some other pianist who doesn't play? And the one who plays, when did she stop playing? *(She laughs.)* My manager tells me not to ask so many questions. We are crowned by success, the audience applauds, the concert hall fills up and your personality radiates a powerful magnetic soundless pulse. Maybe he's right. Maybe we're all right. Perhaps you, by attending this humiliating performance, feel that the truth attends with you. *(Pause. She returns to the piano. She tries again to concentrate and play, but the piano does not emit a sound.)* Ah! When will this piano ever make a sound? When will the notes fall upon the center of the world like holy water from my fingers? When will I play again? When will you set me free from this duty to satisfy your curiosity with useless anecdotes about my life? What more do you want to know? What are you waiting to find out? Why do you come to all these functions? Why do you fill up this room and wait for me to confess everything? But, what do I have to confess? What can I tell you about myself that you haven't already read in the newspapers? Well, what does it matter if you know everything, if you know all about my pact with mediocrity up to the last desperate details. *(Pause. She returns to the piano. Suddenly she rises.)* Okay. So I've compromised. Mediocrity offered me warm protection. Agreeing to be Irene della Porta playing silently gave me endless years of comfort. "Lots of pianists play like you," my manager told me. "But Irene della Porta not playing will be sheer genius. The one and only." In every life there's one moment that makes the difference, one secret instant that destroys everything that came before, that destroys all real honesty. In one instant you agree to lose, but keep believing you're going to win. What was my blindness? Who blinded me? Was I really blind? When did I begin to accept it? Did I accept it long before I admitted it? And by admitting it now, much later, do I still deny it? *(Pause. She laughs.)* Who needs excuses when here I am, bound before you and you celebrate my bondage? This is a triumph. Irene della Porta earns a lot of money doing this. My manager celebrates the triumph night after night. And with you, it's the same old story, the same habits, the same faces reflected in the mirror. Then you come running to the theater and pay so that I can pull this marvelous nonexistent scale out of the intangible darkness; this nonexistent re-do-so-fa-la-mi-re-ti-do. And everything falls into mirror-like stagnation, into this incredible parcel of universe that drills memories of endless caresses into our ears, long oceanic tongues, outlines of other lives that don't concern us, unknown loves that we'll never know, great passions that all of us will carry inside in order to surrender ourselves to someone far away who doesn't know us, someone who also searches for us: do-re-so-mi-la-fa-do-ti-ti-ti-fa-re-mi-do-so. Destiny, that useless font of holy water, that fiction is only an idiotic covenant with a God who only emerges at this moment in a mi-so-do-re-fa-mi-re-do-do-do that although it may not exist, is infinite. *(She rises. Agitated. Mystically she opens her fingers.)* What do you want from me? *(Suddenly she opens her dress and begins to undress.)* Do you want to unravel hidden truths? Do you want to see me without any more disguises? *(She undresses down to her underclothes.)* Do you know any more now about this Irene della Porta than before? Now that you see me this way, stripped down to my teeth, do you know more about me now than before? What is a person? Who am I? Who are you? What is success? Does my nakedness bring success? What is a naked woman? A skeleton out in the open covered with a fragile living membrane? What is a piano if it does not play? *(Half-dressed, she returns to the soundless piano and plays it ardently.)* Tonight you consecrate me. Roses rain upon my head. A chilled bottle of champagne is waiting for me in my dressing room. Murmurs float through the air whispering my name. *(To the audience.)* Are you the same people who came to see my other concerts? Or are you other people? *(To one spectator.)* You, sir. You who used to come to all my concerts. You who still follow me. You who have that secret, profound look on your face. You who have been sending me roses for years. Why do you come here? Does my downfall amuse you? Does this show, all put together so that my concert will take place, amuse you? And they say, "What a disgrace, a pianist of her caliber. She used to play so well." They make their comments while they eat, and I see them talking and laughing, and buying tickets and packing the house while I attend my own suicide. And that's a disgrace too. You're killing me. You've already killed me. I'm nothing more than a cadaver promenading around this dead stage playing always the same thing, its own death, its mummification and its destruction. *(She laughs.)* I'm going back to the piano. I am going to open it and pull out a revolver. *(She laughs and does what she said she would do.)* You already know this part of the show. Is this what brings you in? I talk about my mummification and my destruction and I take out the revolver and I point it at you. *(She points it at a member of the audience.)* You all know that this revolver is loaded, but you're not afraid. You've seen me point this at you before and nothing ever happens. *(She laughs.)* You've also hoped that I would line this up and point it at my own head. *(She does it.)* And you have seen how, in spite of the suspense *(She creates suspense.)* I finish by lowering the weapon and pointing it. Tonight you won't see me fall, and you won't cry for me or cover the inert body with flowers. The body of she who once was Irene della Porta *(She laughs. She holds the weapon. Again she sits at the piano. An executory silence. She adopts a confessional, hallucinatory tone of voice.)* I'm happy, I'm happy not to perform this concert for you. Happy to execute this nonsonata by Beethoven for you. Thank you for being here tonight. Thanks to you I have learned something about art. Art doesn't lie in the sounds. Music doesn't lie in the chords. Now you should allow a trembling current of water to carve secret canyons into your chests. Allow something, a B flat or a chill, to raise you seductively from the isolated confines of your seats, allow something to urge you along toward a sustained chord that sparkles like a precious jewel bringing out the best in all of us; something that is not a chord in D major. It makes you forget that you are there, sitting in the silence of this concert hall, asking me to separate you from that pathetic fragment of reality that make you the same every day, that makes you wake up with the same mother. Why do you all come here? *(She gets dressed.)* My contract ends soon. And then I'll play again. I have to become Irene della Porta again. Will you come? Will you come with me, or will you leave me playing Beethoven's *Pathétique* alone in an enormous concert hall? *(She becomes emotional.)* This has to end. This is like a wonderful vacation on a desert island. This has been a pleasant break. A white wind that has filled me up. A storm that has yanked the piano bench out from under me. And now where I have stopped? I am at the peak of my success. We have a packed hall. We have earned a lot of money. What a beautiful desert. At times it makes you want to stay, never to return. At times it makes you want the comfortable moment to pass. At times it makes me want to stay here inside with all of you. *(She weeps disconsolately.)* Sometime in front of an opaque mirror my own face, erased by time will ask me, "Why?" It will ask me, "How?" And I will offer useless explanations about original intentions, explanations about the blue bird of happiness. *(She laughs.)* How easy it is to make excuses to a mirror. *(She laughs.)* Mirror, mirror on the wall, who is the fairest of them all? And the most talented? And the most intelligent? And the prettiest? *(She laughs.)* Mirror, Mirror, who is the most talented woman in the world? *(She laughs. Content, she returns to the piano and plays in silence. As if at her own party, she laughs happily and plays.)*

You're probably right, I would come here too. I too would pay to see this spectacle that I offer every night. I too would fill up this hall every night and I would shout, "Bravo." And at the end I would throw roses randomly to you. *(She takes a long-stemmed rose and throws it into the orchestra pit.)* Roses, roses to celebrate the triumph of such an unusual performance. Roses falling upon a sea of applause, roses dreaming about other roses in an immense field open to the light of memory. Roses for remembering, roses to breathe in the night that shuts in every petal. *(She finishes distributing the roses. She explodes, totally possessed by profound emotion.)* Oh, how I would love to play *La Pathétique* at this moment! Ludwig von Beethoven, how I would like to meet the torments of your generous soul. How I would like to nourish myself in your fertile and generous water-filled canyon, to drown myself in those waters that I still hold inside myself! I'm happy enough to look inside and see you, Beethoven, making your *Pathétique* reverberate constantly inside me. I die and I am reborn daily inside your waters. Beethoven, my friend, I secretly move you from my soul to my hand, and I feel you in my hand like a precious jewel. Oh, if only I could play. If only I could bring you out from inside of me so you wouldn't be just a flooded landscape anymore. Am I an errant soul or a body in limbo? Oh, how I would like to break these cyclical, empty days, and show myself what is truly alive. *(She returns to the piano in this state of exaltation. Suddenly the piano sounds. She remains paralyzed. She cannot believe it. She plays again, testing different keys, and the piano plays. She looks at the bewildered audience and shows them again that the piano plays.)* What's this? We didn't agree to this. *(Pause)* This is not in my contract. *(She tests the piano and it plays. She shouts out.)* It plays! Sound is coming out now. *(She tries it.)* It plays now. *(She laughs.)* Ladies and gentlemen, you did not pay for . . . *(She laughs. She cries and tries the notes on the piano.)* It's been so long . . . It's been centuries of unlived life since I've heard these sounds. It's been ages inside ages since the last innocent note has sounded from my fingers. *(She plays amid laughs.)* The beautiful F note destroys the laws of gravity. *(She laughs. She addresses the audience.)* Ladies and gentlemen. I wonder if this unexpected night was on the calendar. Could it be true that I again have the chance to play *La Pathétique* by Ludwig von Beethoven? Could you be my first witnesses? *(She laughs and returns to the piano.)* Beethoven. Hello, Beethoven. *(She throws herself into playing with profound emotion. She has forgotten everything. She tries to play* La Pathétique *but her fingers, stiffened by the long period of inactivity, do not respond. She desperately tries to recover the possibility of playing like before, like she used to; but the harder she tries the more she fails, and horrible sounds come out from her fingers as she plays the music so poorly that it grates the ears. She hits the keys with her fists. She burns with fury and impotence. She bangs her head against the keyboard as if she could pull the sounds that the piano holds inside out by the entrails. Then the sound stops and there is a long pause in which she tries to collect herself. She tests the piano to no avail. She returns to the audience and makes a small and dignified bow; then she sits down again at the bench, pathetically silent, and she plays the silent piano with dignity. The play ends with the spot on her playing nothing until it goes out and the stage is dark.)*

INNER GARDENS

Translated by Nora Glickman and Victoria Martinez in collaboration
with Lidia Ramirez

Characters
Rosalia *A middle-aged, unmarried woman.*
Griselda *Same age and marital status as Rosalia. She has rented a
room in Roaslia's house for the last twenty years.*
Mariano Rivas *A soap-opera star. He plays the role of Marcelo.*

Characters on "Marcelo the Mechanic"
Valeria *Marcelo's love interest*
Father *Valeria's father*
Tachuela *Marcelo's assistant in the garage*

Setting
*The play takes place in Rosalia's living room. The room and the house
give the impression of a middle-class setting in a house that Rosalia
inherited. It's a high-ceilinged room with numerous doors that lead to
other parts of the house. Rosalia makes her living by renting a room to
Griselda. The two have built a life together here. There is solarium, full
of plants, open to the living room at the back of the scene. This glass
room adds transparency and dimension to the scene. Throughout the
play, different light filters in through the glass, moonlight, rain, and the
violet lights of dawn, and times phantasmal, a light that reflects the
illusory nature of their lives.*

*The living room is furnished with massive antiques. There is a dining
table with four chairs and a number of chairs aged with use. There could
be sepia-colored photographs of Rosalia's family on the walls, or there
could be darker spaces where photos used to hang. There is a large*

chest where Griselda keeps her hats and perhaps an old sewing machine
that she still uses. There is an ashen patina of neglect due to Rosalia's
lack of money or interest in renovation. Facing the audience, in the
middle of the room is a television with a gigantic screen, the only object
with color in the shabbiness. This disproportionately sized TV is the
center of their lives; the chairs are placed around it, always ready for the
two to engross themselves. The TV is a sort of religious altar that
Griselda and Rosalia tend to daily, placing vases of fresh flowers,
pictures of Mariano Rivas, and a variety of saints and candles. It is their
sanctuary, where they spend their lives following the soap operas
featuring their beloved hero, Mariano Rivas. The size of the screen
allows the audience to watch the episodes included in the play. The TV
allows the audience to see Marcelo the mechanic (Mariano Rivas) in his
role on screen in the first act, before seeing him live in the second.

The scenery changes in the second act. The two women decorate for a
party and these changes should be evident in all the details. The room is
cleaned, the table is set with good china, the furniture is rearranged, and
all is spruced up to welcome the man that Rosalia and Griselda love.

ACT ONE

Scene 1

(Frightened by her own dream, Rosalia wakes up with a scream. She
gets up abruptly, turns off the television. She settles down again and
watches Griselda sleep.)

Rosalia Didn't we decide to do something tonight? (*Griselda continues*
to sleep soundly. Rosalia tries to remain calm. Sitting up, she pauses.
She stands up and opens the window.) Look at that moon! Just for us.
But what do you know about the moon? You don't have the strength to
stay awake. But I knew that, and besides, I'm used to it. If I could only
sleep like that, with my body, and hands so relaxed. (*Stroking*
Griselda's head) Like a child exhausted from playing that has fallen
asleep after eating her pudding. You never even say goodnight to me.
Not even a goodnight. Well, I probably wouldn't say "goodnight" either.
(*She goes back to the window and looks out at the moon. She's silent for*
a couple of beats.) The moon is dying of laughter tonight. She's
laughing at you, you who were going to stay up all night. Didn't you

stay up all night during Carnival?

Griselda Is it Carnival tonight?

Rosalia You have no idea how much you're missing.

Griselda What time is it?

Rosalia If I tell you it's one o'clock, if I tell you it's two, or three, or four...

Griselda It's four o'clock! *(She sits up, alarmed by the time.)*

Rosalia These are hours you know nothing about.

Griselda Because I don't suffer from insomnia.

Rosalia Insomnia. What a word. Insomnia. Somnia. I have insomnia. And you have somnia.

Griselda I have somnia? There's no such word. Stop babbling. It's four a.m., dear.

Rosalia It's not four. It's twelve thirty.

Griselda And is it Carnival?

Rosalia It's Thursday, September 22nd. Last month I asked a friend, my roommate, my boarder, let's say, to stay awake all night with me.

Griselda You' re right. Forgive me. I fell asleep. Tell me what to do. What do you drink in your nights of insomnia?

Rosalia Milk.

Griselda Milk?

Rosalia Whiskey.

Griselda Imported?

Rosalia You'll have to settle for domestic.

Griselda It's got to be imported!

(Rosalia leaves the room. Griselda falls asleep again. Rosalia comes back finding Griselda sleeping, pours her whiskey and wakes her up.)

Rosalia I have an appointment with Felix.

Griselda You always have an appointment with Felix.

Rosalia But this time it's different.

Griselda At what time?

Rosalia At three thirty.

Griselda You'll miss the soap opera.

Rosalia I'll be back in time. You'll see. I have to see Felix. Jupiter was not aligned with my moon, but this week he has set me free. I've decided to become a new person.

Griselda Me too. Give me more whiskey. *(Rosalia pours her another. Griselda falls asleep immediately.*

Rosalia Tell me something. Something personal.

Griselda *(Waking up, somewhat woozy.)* Ok. Ok. Did I ever tell you about Daniel?

Rosalia Who is he?

Griselda An old boyfriend. I was studying literature, something my mother didn't like at all. She used to ask me, "Where are you going to go with a literature degree? "To poetry, mother. To poetry." Everything goes round. And round everything goes. The planets go round. The moon.

Rosalia Yes! You have to come with me to Felix's.

Griselda No Rosalia. No! I have principles. And beliefs. I've lived in your house for twenty years, tolerating but not approving. Do you want me to fix you something to eat?

Rosalia No!

Griselda I'll sing for you.

Rosalia Ok. Something Spanish. *(Griselda begins to sing flamenco.)* And what happened with Daniel?

Griselda He lied to me. He read obscure poets, ones that I didn't know; and one day he brought me a poem by an obscure poet, but he told me the poem was his. And I believed him. I fell even deeper in love thinking that the poem was his.

> "In our darkest waters
> A steady splendor shines
> A bride's ring
> Or God's watchful eye."

Rosalia He obviously wanted to marry you.

Griselda But the poem was written by someone else, Gabriel Celaya. *(She falls asleep.)*

Rosalia I wouldn't say goodnight either, if I could fall asleep like that. Just like that. From one minute to the next. Out like a light. *(She tries to do it but cannot.)* A bride's ring, or God's watchful eye. *(Tries to make believe she's sleeping. She opens one eye.)* God's watchful eye. That's insomnia! So what if the poem wasn't his? *(She shakes Griselda and shouts.)* God's watchful eye, Griselda! I would've forgiven him, you know.

Griselda A bride's ring or God's watchful eye. *(She suddenly begins to cry.)* Today, I would've forgiven him too.

Lights fade to black.

Scene 2

(In total darkness the sound of dialogue from the television can be heard.

It's a conversation between the characters of a soap opera, Marcelo and Valeria. Marcelo is a car mechanic and his speech is working class, non-educated. Valeria is a young woman, upper middle class. The television lights up Griselda's face, she is wearing a blue floral dress. As she watches the program, she eats voraciously from an enormous tin can of crackers.)

Marcelo Was your boyfriend happy with his car?
Valeria Yes! You did a great job... Thank you.
Marcelo Tell your boyfriend to come by whenever he wants. It's good to give the car a check up every once in a while...can you also tell him... *(He stops himself.)* Man, I almost put my foot in my mouth.
Valeria Why?
Marcelo Because I was going to send your boyfriend a message, that would sit in his gut like a dumpling in a simmering pot.
(Valeria laughs.)
Griselda *(Melting)* You're divine! I could eat you up. Ay, Rosalia, what you're missing. You just had to see Felix today. What a shame!
Valeria And exactly what message were you going to send my boyfriend?
Marcelo No way! I can't tell you...
Griselda I bet he'll tell her! Shoot Rosalia, you're missing all this for that damn Felix! This is the best episode of the year.
Valeria Is it something about the car?
Marcelo It's something about you. *(Suspense music)*
Valeria *(Nervous)* Well, I have to go now.
Marcelo *(Looking closely at her, examining her face.)* I like that.
Valeria What?
Marcelo The way your cheeks turn red when you get nervous...
Griselda How sweet! I could die...
Valeria You're terrible.
Marcelo Here's the message I would have given him. Flaco, your girlfriend's got a mouth like a tiny strawberry.
Griselda Now this means trouble! I bet there's going to be trouble!
Valeria Marcelo...
Marcelo And you know something else, buddy, I've got it bad for your girlfriend...real bad...
Griselda *(Jumping up in her chair)* Kiss her, kiss her! It's now or never! Kiss her with all you've got!
Valeria Marcelo...I...I. *(Almost crying)* I've got it bad for you too...

(They fall into each other's arms. Music in the background.) Real
bad...like...like you...said... *(They kiss.)*

Griselda Rosalia, you're missing the best episode of the year. How
well you kiss, my love, my life!

Marcelo I know you think I'm a loser, that my hands are always
covered with grease, and these overalls that walk by
themselves...really...they walk all by themselves...the other day I took
Juan's kid to the zoo, and I got really dressed up...and when we got to
the hippopotamus' cage, we saw that my overalls had been following us
for over a half an hour. Don't laugh. I believe I was born with my
overalls on and I'm going to die with my overalls on. The day I marry
you, I'm wearin' 'em. So you won't forget you're marrying a working
man, the kind those snobs in your family look down on 'cause we're low
class, or 'cause we make too much noise when we bite down on an
apple. *(Taking an apple out of his pocket)...* The day that you bite this
apple is the day you lose forever... *(He bites it.)* That's why you don't
wanna bite it...'cause you know that this apple's more dangerous for you
than all the caviar and lobster your prune-faced butler gives you for
breakfast to start your day. You know how I'm gonna start off your
days?

Valeria How?

Marcelo Like this. *(He kisses her passionately.)* And this.

Griselda One more kiss! Ooooh! How I'd like you to kiss me like that!
(She kisses the screen. The titles come up.) AAAhhhh! It's over. It's
over and you've missed the whole thing. *(She turns off the television.)*
Deep down, I'm glad that you were all mine today. I believe it was
destiny. I believe certain things happen when you don't expect them.
Like this sudden kiss. *(Kisses one of the plants.)* That woman has no
sense. Don't you agree Begonia? She has no sense... *(She fixes it.)*
Come, I'll pour you a little water. In this house if I don't take care of
you no one will. *(As she waters the plant, she speaks to it tenderly.)* Do
you like it, Begonia? Fresh water, huh? *(She drinks some water.)* It
tastes good. Look at the episode she just missed...what can that fortune-
teller tell her that she doesn't already know? *(Grabs another plant.)*
What can he say that's new, my dear Alpine Violet? You're thirsty too?
It's the heat. You understand, don't you, little Violet? When I worked at
Madam Rifau's I had my own office, and there the window was always
open, winter and summer; always, as the air knows no season. If you
block the path of air, it abandons you; it leaves your side. It cares for
others. The plants I had in that window grew like tropical bushes. And I

didn't have asthma then. *(Pause)* Well, at least I didn't have this kind of asthma that comes from the heat. How happy you'd have been at that window, my dear Violetita of the Alps...! How happy! Happy, just like Valeria in Marcelo's arms. Happy... *(After watering the violet plant she picks up a fern.)* And you, Mr. Fern, how droopy you've become! Come over here don't play shy! *(She waters it.)* With that green mane of hair... all spread out, like a soap opera star. *(She tidies up the fern and hugs it, as if it were Marcelo.)* What's wrong? Let's see. Tell me. Are you out of air? Someday I'll leave this house and take all of you. I'm just waiting for the problem with the lawyers of my uncle's inheritance to be solved and then I'll take you all far away to a place without heaters. When all is said and done, I'm giving up my life to pay for this room! I'm taking you all to a house on the ocean. I'd love to live by the sea, like Alfonsina Storni.
(Walks mystically, still holding the fern in her hand.)
> "I'd like, on a divine October afternoon,
> to stroll on the faraway shore of the sea."

I always wanted to be Alfonsina Storni. I meet all the requirements to be her.
> "So the golden sand and the summer waters
> and the pure skies could watch me go by."

But I was not Alfonsina Storni, so here I am, locked up, sewing for the fat woman next door.
> "I'd like to be tall, perfect, to be majestic
> like a Roman, to merge with"

I have worked for Madam Rifau; I, who have created her best designs, my dear Mr. Fern.
> "With tall waves and dead rocks
> and the wide beaches that bind the sea."

(At this point Rosalia comes in from the street, agitated. She has been running, in order not to miss today's episode.)

Rosalia Is it over yet? *(Griselda, still holding the fern in her hand, does not answer.)* Did they see each other?

Griselda *(Referring to the packages)* What did you buy?

Rosalia They didn't see each other?

Griselda *(Opening packages)* How lovely! You bought a lamp just like the one in the soap. Where did you get it?

Rosalia That man almost drove me crazy. I had to buy something for myself. When I left his house I had a n attack. No one could stop me. It was fantastic. You can't imagine the things he told me. *(Pause. Goes on*

GRISELDA
as
ALFONSINA
STORNI

talking about the fortuneteller.) Everything's going to happen this year! There's a man in my future. Can you believe it? I sat down; he looked into my eyes. What eyes he has, they're almost yellow. I've never seen such horribly colored eyes. But they can see right through you. I could feel his eyes at the center of my soul. "There's a man," he said. "It's inevitable." That's what he said. I swear to you. "A young man." Then soon after, he threw the cards. They came up trumps all over the place. And love, love! "Felix." I said to him, "you're joking with me." He didn't answer, but if looks could kill. He didn't like what I said at all. *(Pause)* I must have missed a great episode. I wanted to make it, but I saw the lamp and lost track of time. You see? It's exactly the same as the one on Valeria's father's desk. *(Going back to the previous topic)* He didn't like it a bit; and then he said to me: "You just ask the questions." "Felix, don't get angry." I said, "it's just that things look so good, that it's hard to believe." "Just ask me questions," he said. He killed me. "What man?" I asked him. "The one you want most," he answered. The one you want most. "But I'm in love with a soap opera star." I said. He didn't answer but he threw two more cards and they came up trumps. Believe it or not. One card after another. "Ask me another question," he said. So I asked him about you. He threw two more cards and the same thing happened.

(In the meantime, Griselda has found a place for the lamp. She has put in a light bulb and turned it on.)

Griselda What do you mean "the same thing"?

Rosalia Did they or didn't they see each other? I did everything I could to get here on time. I swear.

Griselda What do you mean, "the same thing"?

Rosalia A man!

Griselda What man?

Rosalia Trumps. You had three trumps in a row.

Griselda Me?

Rosalia Any man you want, "She's also in love with a soap star," I told him.

Griselda And?

Rosalia Yellow eyes said nothing. "Just like me," I told him.

Griselda And?

Rosalia Nothing. "Isn't that bad for our friendship?" I asked.

Griselda And?

Rosalia He threw the cards once more.

Griselda And?

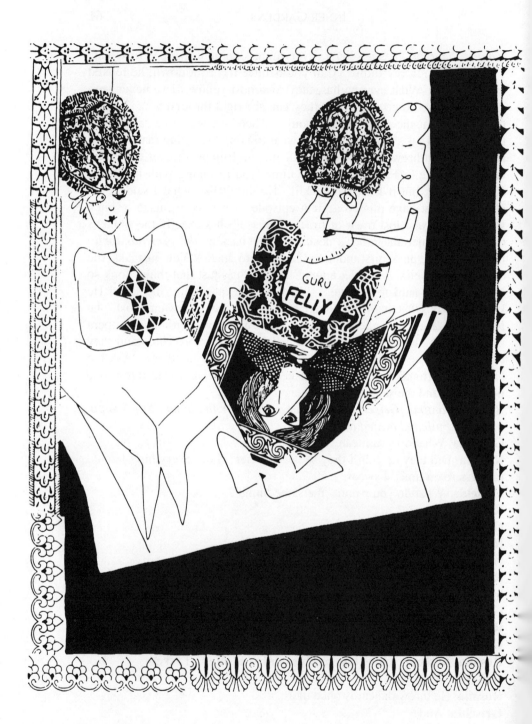

Rosalia Trumps. Trumps all over the place. I paid him and left. When I reached the street I didn't know what to do with myself. It's the first time he's ever told me anything good. Something so certain. Sometimes he's given me hope; he's given me something to look forward to... But today... Did Valeria and Marcelo see each other or not?

Griselda Yes.

Rosalia What happened?

Griselda Shall I pour the tea?

Rosalia Did he say something to her?

Griselda Everything.

Rosalia Everything? What everything?

Griselda He was marvelous. You could eat him up. With the charm he has when he speaks...so tough. *(Laughs while Rosalia looks at her, seriously.)*

Rosalia What did he say to her?

Griselda He said everything to her, and then he kissed her.

Rosalia Don't tell me he kissed her. *(Upset)* We've been waiting three months for him to kiss her. How did he kiss her?

Griselda On the mouth.

Rosalia *(Very upset)* What did he say? Tell me how it was.

Griselda I'm telling you, Rosalia.

Rosalia You're not telling me a thing. It's too general. This is nonsense. I don't understand. I don't believe he really kissed her.

Griselda I don't remember everything word for word. I'm telling you what I remember.

Rosalia He kissed her. Swear it. You're not just saying this on purpose to make me suffer. The problem is you don't like me to see Felix. He didn't kiss her at all. You're putting me on. *(Griselda goes to the kitchen.)* Where are you going?

Griselda Tea is ready.

(Rosalia sits down by herself after taking off her jacket.)

Rosalia Nothing happened. I know her very well. She's doing this to me on purpose.

Griselda *(Comes in with the tea on a tray.)* I'm not doing it on purpose.

Rosalia Then I've missed the best episode.

Griselda The best.

Rosalia And how did he kiss her?

Griselda He held her face with both hands and gave her a long, long, long kiss.

Rosalia How long?

Griselda Very long.

Rosalia How many minutes?

Griselda I don't know. I didn't time it; but it was long enough.

Rosalia And then?

Griselda Then he told her he loved her.

Rosalia What about her boyfriend?

Griselda Nothing happened with him, dear. Marcelo told Valeria that he loved her and he kissed her again.

Rosalia A long one?

Griselda Longer than the first one. *(Pause)* If you could only see how well he kisses! And those overalls! All stained with grease; and those big dirty hands. He grabbed her face and she began to tremble. You've seen how she is, so fragile, she looks like she could fall apart.

Rosalia What do you mean fall apart? She's a tightly wound spring.

Griselda And he spoke to her in that way of his.

Rosalia What way?

Griselda That tough way that drives me out of my mind. He spoke to her, and he looked at her, and she began to melt, and he told her, "I've got it bad for you. This is like a scene from a soap opera." And something about dumplings simmering in a pot.

Rosalia Dumplings simmering in a pot?

Griselda I can't remember. I think he was hungry. Something about dumplings in a simmering pot. And that he had put his foot in it.

Rosalia Where did he put his foot?

Griselda I don't remember. But then he kissed her.

Rosalia You see how bad you tell it.

Griselda I was watching how he kissed her the whole time. I was watching him, and how that lock of hair falls on his forehead. And how good looking he is, so tough, and I couldn't concentrate on anything else, he's so cute with that strong nose, I don't know, he makes me happy just looking at him, and I get lost in his voice, and what a voice he has. Where did he get it? It's so sweet, but at the same time so manly, he drives me crazy.

Rosalia Whatever did his mother do to have such a beautiful son?

Griselda Well…maybe she was very pretty.

Rosalia Or maybe the father was.

Griselda Or both. Can you imagine? The mother, the father and the three brothers, all of them handsome.

Rosalia They couldn't be all as handsome as he, then they'd all be famous.

Griselda   That lock of hair! When it falls over his forehead and he lifts it up like this, with that filthy hand.
Rosalia   Greasy, not filthy.
Griselda   Filthy with grease.
Rosalia   Grease isn't filth. It's work.
Griselda   And that hair...
Rosalia   You've already told me about the hair.
Griselda   I like to talk about it. It's not like any other man's hair.
Rosalia   What other men?
Griselda   Others.
Rosalia   You're not talking about your boyfriend the vet; he was bald.
Griselda   You can't compare. That one was skinny, wore glasses, stuttered and was half lame. That's a man? This one is tall, has a piercing look, eyes that see right through you. I don't know... there's something cuddly in him that drives me crazy. Ooooo! I feel like reciting the poem I wrote for him. All of a sudden, I have this urge. I don't know... *(Moved)* I feel inspired.
Rosalia   I'm listening. What else can I do but listen to you?
Griselda

> "If you only knew, my love,
> if you only knew,
> from where my passion springs
> it comes from the very depths of my bosom.
> It goes from my heart to your heart."

(She paces about, carried away by her poetry.)

> "The closer I am to you,
> the more elusive,
> the farther you are from my illusions.
> I would want you with me,
> yet you live inside a television set."

(Lifting the television in her arms)

> "Oh, foul machine that creates an abyss
> that raises a dagger to my pain.
> But still, it's a friend
> to my disconsolate heart.
> I'd throw you to the ground
> and break you into a thousand smithereens!"

Rosalia   *(Shouting)* NO!
Griselda

> "But a voice from within cries out 'No!'

because then, my love, what would remain
of so many long afternoons of illusions."
(During the last scene, the lights have been dimming, until all is dark.)

Scene 3

(Lights come up. Griselda is surrounded by her plants, dressed in an Oriental-style white robe, doing very slow breathing exercises, concentrated and harmonious. Meanwhile, Rosalia sweeps the floor in a frenzy.)

Griselda We raise our arms toward the sky. We hold our spine straight and the center of our energy now falls on our lower back; the lower back is what supports the body. In this position we turn toward the East to greet the sun. And in this position we turn toward the West to greet the moon. *(She stops.)* Can't you do something else? Iron, cook... *(Rosalia continues sweeping Griselda tries to resume her exercises.)* We inhale with open lungs the air that envelops us. *(She breathes in and then coughs.)*

Rosalia There are plazas. There are public gardens. There are rehabilitation centers for asthmatics. There are large open spaces.

Griselda There are evil people. There are all kinds.

Rosalia There are inopportune people. There are all kinds.

(Rosalia continues to sweep; Griselda goes back to her exercises.)

Griselda We stretch our hands up trying to reach the sun.

(Rosalia breaks up laughing. Griselda's eyes fill up with tears of anger. Rosalia represses her laughter and goes on sweeping.)

Griselda   Trying to reach the sun, maintaining the position on our tiptoes so our bodies get a full stretch, its maximum possibility. *(She holds that position. Rosalia continues to sweep but comes very close to her. Griselda stops, very upset.)* This is the last straw. I'm leaving at the end of the month.

Rosalia I'm renting you a room, not a gym.

Griselda And I'm a person, get it? A person.

Rosalia A sick person. I've had it with sicknesses. I want a bit of health.

Griselda That's why I do gymnastics. To cure myself.

Rosalia *(Laughing)* Gymnastics! Don't you realize that Samatra is not Hindu? Don't you realize that this is not gymnastics? Don't you see he's taking you for your money? Like an idiot. Don't you understand anything in this life?

(Rosalia continues sweeping; Griselda grabs another broom and sweeps in the opposite direction. They create a kind of "battle of the brooms" as they sweep frantically.)

Griselda You want cleaning? Here's cleaning.

Rosalia You're messing up what I've already swept.

Griselda And you're ruining my life.

Rosalia Oh, if your dear Mariano Rivas could see you. If he could only see you now!

Griselda I think it would be much worse if he could see you. He couldn't bear it.

Rosalia *(Tearing the broom from Griselda)* Stop sweeping!

Griselda That's my broom. Give it back to me.

(They fight over the broom.)

Rosalia The broom may be yours, but the floor is mine.

Griselda Then I'll sweep this armchair because it's mine. My armchair. My broom. My Mariano Rivas. Mine. Mine. What's mine is mine. My gymnastics. My asthma. *(She sweeps the armchair frantically.)*

Rosalia Do I have to wait until the end of the month before you leave? Can't we move that date forward a bit?

Griselda Yes we can. I'm leaving right away. I'm fed up with your evil doings. I'm fed up with seeing that face of yours.

Rosalia *(Holding on to her)* My face? What do you have against my face?

Griselda Your face. Your hair. Your hands. The way you walk... your little quirks and your jealousy.

Rosalia *(Laughing)* Me, jealous of you? How can you believe you have anything worth being jealous of? What can I envy in a weak, run-down person who greets the sun by raising her arms to the East? What envy can I feel for an asthmatic without a past or a future, a woman who doesn't have a place to drop dead in? Maybe you think Mariano Rivas would notice you. Do you think he'd look at you for even a second?

Griselda Don't get Mariano Rivas mixed up in all this. He has nothing to do with this. Don't get him involved, understand?

Rosalia I'll involve Mariano Rivas if I choose to because Mariano Rivas is mine. *(Pause)* Or at least I have the right to think he's mine. *(She lets go of her. Griselda looks at her silently.)*

Griselda *(Raising her arms)* We greet Rosalia from the North and after twenty years of nonsense, we search for the sun elsewhere. We greet the house from the South and we leave the owner alone to enjoy all her sweet belongings. *(She exits. Rosalia remains on stage, sweeping. Griselda comes out with a suitcase ready to leave.)* I'll ask my cousin to bring his van to pick up my plants. I'm leaving you the rest. *(She pays Rosalia her rent.)* I'm paying you for the entire month. It's almost the end of the month anyway and you could use the money. *(Rosalia tears up the money. Then she grabs Griselda's suitcase, opens it up and spills its contents. Some clothes and many poems fall out. There is a heavy silence. Then Rosalia begins to pick up everything.)*

Rosalia Stay.

Griselda I can't. I have to go.

Rosalia Where will you go?

Griselda I don't know. I'll find myself a place with a yard. I'm asthmatic. I need a yard.

Rosalia And I'm alone. I need you.

Griselda No. You don't need me. You need Mariano Rivas. Not me. I'm a nuisance to you.

Rosalia Stay. I can give you one more room. The one in the back, you can set up a gym.

Griselda I can't afford it.

Rosalia It's a gift... I can't imagine this place without you. I'd be looking for you all the time.

Griselda Don't you realize I can't stay?

Rosalia Don't you realize you can't leave? *(Pause. They finally embrace.)* I'm sorry.

Griselda No, I'm sorry.

Rosalia You're the best person I know. You're the only one who truly loves me. You're my friend. Please forgive me, Griselda.

Griselda No, forgive me. Forgive my asthma.

Rosalia *(Laughing)* Your asthma is marvelous. *(They both laugh.)* Mariano Rivas probably likes asthmatic women. They need people to take care of them. They make you feel needed.

Griselda Mariano Rivas probably loves vivacious women like you. Women who are ready for anything.

Rosalia I think he needs both of us.

Griselda Ah, if he only knew it. If he only knew how he needs us both.

Rosalia Someday he'll know.

Griselda Someday, someday, someday, someday...

Rosalia Yes, Griselda. Someday we'll be happy; someday we'll be youn, someday Mariano Rivas will fall in love with us, dressed like Marcelo the mechanic, covererd in the grease that looks so good on him,

he'll kiss us on the mouth, and he'll call us "my girls."
Griselda and Rosalia Someday…someday…someday…someday…

Blackout

Scene 4

(When the lights come up we can see Griselda and Rosalia lying down in their armchairs. They are giving themselves facials. Rosalia's face is covered with orange slices and Griselda's with tomato slices. Rosalia is laughing heartily. Griselda is silent.)
Rosalia How funny! *(She's laughing.)* How funny!
Griselda What? What?
Rosalia *(Serious)* I was thinking about death.
(Both pause and become serious. Then Griselda begins to laugh alone. The laugh is contagious, Rosalia joins her. There is a touch of anxiety and fear in this laughter, but it is still happy.)
Rosalia How do you imagine death?
Griselda Oh! Can anyone imagine death?
Rosalia *(Amidst another burst of laughter)* I can.
Griselda *(Laughing)* Me too. I always imagine it.
Rosalia I believe death wears shiny shoes. She is neither white nor black. She is a color that does not exist. She looks at me and says, "C'mon, girl."
Griselda Is that how death talks?
Rosalia
C'mon girl, you're out of time. *(Silence)* Is your asthma coming back?
Griselda No! On the contrary. I'm having a good time. Death is a tango!
Rosalia Death speaks like Marcelo in the soap opera. She's very fat, with phosphorescent hair and a tongue like a rag.
Griselda *(Laughing)* Yes, yes. A rag tongue to wrap me in. *(Griselda ceremoniously removes the tomatoes from her face. She puts them carefully on the table.)* Time is up. Now comes the vegetable facial mask. *(Griselda removes the oranges from her face. Griselda takes a plate with strips of different green vegetables, and places them carefully on Rosalia's face.)*
Rosalia What's next?
Griselda Blood circulation. It's the time for the slaps. *(She slaps herself in the face)* To me death is a very tall man who asks me

questions. *(At each question she slaps herself harder.)* What is your shoe size? What was your favorite food? How many times did you go to bed with a man? What's the widest river in the world? What countries have you visited? Were you afraid of thunderstorms? When did you stop believing in storks? Did you ever bet your life on anything? Did you also believe that Argentina was going to win the Falkland War? Were you ever happy for more than half an hour? Would you have wanted three children? Do you wish you had published a book of poetry?

(She's hit her face so hard that tears come to her eyes. She approaches Rosalia and removes the vegetables from her face. They look at each other intensely without saying a word. Griselda tries to compose herself: Rosalia turns on the television.)

Valeria *(Happily)* Daddy, daddy, daddy! (She covers him with kisses and sits on his lap.)

Father You're making me nervous. *(Laughing)* You're about to ask me for something aren't you?

Valeria Not at all. I'm happy... that's all.

Father *(Embracing her)* Then I'm happy too.

Valeria I need you.

Father I'm all yours.

Valeria I'm in love. I've never been in love before. Were you ever madly in love?

Father Sometimes. Sometimes I've been. *(Pause. He kisses her.)* Javier Ugarte is a serious boy. It's hard for me not to be jealous, but I trust Javier. I like him. He's got integrity. He's a proper young man. A young man with his feet on the ground. Who stands tall. He's full of life, full of possibilities. I wish you every happiness, my daughter. I hope you're very happy. *(Moved)* As happy as I want you to be.

Valeria I'm not in love with Javier Ugarte.

Father *(Her father looks at her in complete astonishment.)* What?

Valeria I know you'll understand. That's the way love is. It just happens. *(Pause)* You'll help me Daddy, won't you?

Father *(Distrustful)* Help you how? What?

Valeria Daddy, I'm in love with someone else. A marvelous person. A person with a huge heart and strong working hands.

Father But the preparations are under way for your wedding with Javier Ugarte... How can you go back on your word now? How can a daughter of mine do such a thing? Who are you in love with? Who's the low life who seduced you?

Valeria Don't speak that way Daddy...

Father I speak as I choose... Who are you in love with?
Valeria With... with Marcelo... Marcelo the mechanic.
(The father slaps her face. She cries. The scene ends.)
Griselda What a rotten old man!
Rosalia I swear he can crush Marcelo, if he wants to.
(A new scene at Marcelo's shop. He is singing and working.)
Rosalia Just look at him! How divine!
Griselda How can I see him, when you're blocking me?
Rosalia Listen. I want to see him too. Or is he all yours? *(They fight for the best place. Then they settle down.)* What a perfect little nose he has.
Griselda Just look at his hair. Today it's nicer than ever...
Rosalia There's a man in my life. That's what Felix said. I can see him coming. *(Kisses the television.)*
Griselda Move your head!
Marcelo Pass me the hinge, Tachuela, will ya?
Tachuela What hinge, Marcelo?
Marcelo The one on the window.
Griselda Just look how he puts the bolts in his mouth.
Rosalia He has teeth like a cannibal. Did you see how he chews? I love to see him eat especially when he bites into his apples.
Griselda Shut up, I can't hear.
Rosalia I'd have him eat apples all day. I bet that's the way he kisses, with big bites.
(A bell rings on the soap opera.)
Marcelo Tachuela, answer that.
Policeman's Voice Good afternoon. I'm Officer Ramirez. I have a warrant for the arrest of Mr. Marcelo Bragante. Is he in?
(Suspense music and soap opera theme. Rosalia turns off the television.)
Griselda How do you know it's over?
Rosalia Didn't you see the credits? It's over.
Griselda I bet they drag him off to jail.
Rosalia Of course, her father sent the police. He's a pretty powerful man; I told you he'd crush him like a fly.
Griselda Poor thing! What will we do now?
Rosalia Well, just imagine what would happen if anything happened to Marcelo. The show would be over. So it can't happen.
Griselda But these are modern soaps. Some end badly. Remember last year that show "My Friendly Teen" ended with her dying. Yup, this is a modern one that will end badly. Marcelo is going to jail now, and the

father will hire someone to kill him. It'll look like an accident and he'll spend a lot of money to cover up the whole thing.

Rosalia It can also end well. Marcelo will marry Valeria and Javier will admit his mistakes and leave the country.

Griselda And where does the father fit in all this? No, no, dear. Here's a "daddy" who's a very important character and who'll stop at nothing. Don't you see? He's sent the police to Marcelo's place. Marcelo is going to jail and there'll be a lot of episodes with Marcelo and Valeria suffering because they're separated.

Rosalia How can he go to jail? He hasn't done anything wrong.

Griselda What does that have to do with anything? Do you really believe only guilty people go to jail?

Rosalia We can't stand here and let this happen. We've been following Mariano Rivera in the soaps for four years. Remember last year's "The Wild Guy?" How much we suffered. We never knew whether he'd live or die.

Griselda But "Marcelo the Mechanic" is much more modern. Can't you tell? He's going to die in jail. It's a soap opera with a tragic ending. Listen to what I'm telling you.

Rosalia Give me the phone. *(Griselda gives her the phone.)* What's the station's number?

(Griselda finds the number in the phone book. Rosalia dials.)

Griselda Who are you calling?

Rosalia The writer of the soap of course. *(Someone answers.)* Hello. Good afternoon. I'd like to speak to Mr. Gaspar Mendez Paz. *(Pause)* Hello, yes, Lolita Torres. *(Pause)* Hello, yes, no, I'm not Lolita Torres but I said I was because if I hadn't, you wouldn't help me. I'm Rosalia Echague, I've always been a passionate fan of your soaps. Now I'm calling to find out if the soap is going to have a tragic ending, and to ask you to please not put Marcelo in jail. He's suffered enough for Valeria's love, and now that he has finally gotten it, you are going to ruin it for him. *(Pause)* He hung up on me. *(She calls again.)* May I speak to Mr. Gaspar Mendez Paz? Tell him Susana Gimenez. *(Pause)* Hello, it's Rosalia Echague again. *(Short pause)* Oh my God! *(She hangs up.)*

Griselda What did he say?

Rosalia He swore at me. That man has a foul mouth. And to think that the life of Marcelo the mechanic depends on people like him. I'm telling you, he's going to destroy Marcelo. Even if it's just to spite me. I should've asked him to put Marcelo in jail. That way he would set him free. That man hates me.

Griselda That man doesn't even know you.

Rosalia That man hates the viewers, and I'm a viewer.

Griselda Then he hates me too.

Rosalia Yes, but he hates me more, because I dared to confront him. I called him. *(Pause)* Poor Marcelo, because of me he's going to suffer even more.

Griselda Stop talking nonsense. One thing has nothing to do with the other.

Rosalia *(Hysterical)* It's got everything to do with it. Felix told me so. He told me my life was going to change at this time. And I'm not alone. Yours will change, too. There's a man. And we have to do something.

Griselda What?

Rosalia I don t know. Something definite. Something that will show Mariano Rivas how we feel about him. Understand?

Griselda Yes, but what?

Rosalia He has to know we exist. He has to come into our life. That's what Felix said. It's all a question of daring.

Griselda But what can we do?

Rosalia Something that will plunge us into real life. Something that will shake us from the root and flip us upside down. A point of no return. Do you understand? *(As if she were hallucinating)* I feel big changes Griselda. I'm sick of our trivial lives. Tired of putting tomatoes on our faces to hold back time. Time passes anyway, Griselda. We have been taking too much care of ourselves. But for whom are we taking care of ourselves? For God.

Griselda *(Very frightened)* Oh, my God.

Rosalia God created life to be lived. God will forgive us. Kneel down Griselda. Let s ask for forgiveness.

Griselda Forgiveness? But we haven't done anything wrong.

Rosalia

> Forgive me for what I haven't done.
> Forgive me for what I haven't had.
> Forgive me for what I haven't taken.
> Forgive me for what I haven't felt.
> Forgive me for not laughing enough.
> Forgive me for not using my tears.

(Suddenly Griselda starts laughing Rosalia look at her seriously.)

Griselda I'm sorry.

Rosalia Don't ask me for forgiveness. Ask God.

Blackout

Scene 5

(It is night. A violet light broken by bolts of lightning spreads over the empty stage. It is raining heavily, and for a few seconds the open windows bang uninterruptedly on the parrot's cage, which shakes with the wind. Rosalia, furious and disheveled, comes in. Her hair is very wild, her face is covered with white cream. She walks barefoot and wears a loose, graceless nightgown. She looks like a ghost.)

Rosalia The window's open, again! What's in your head? The house could fall apart and you go on sleeping as if nothing's happening. You're going to kill us! *(She closes the window furiously meeting the resistance of the wind.)* For twenty years you've been opening the windows that I've closed. *(An uncontrollable hatred takes her over she paces about the stage as if she were looking for prey to kill. Finally she takes hold of a fern.)* For the last twenty years I've been living with vegetables. Twenty years I've been listening to you talk to Begonia, asking her to chase away the evil eye, and asking Violetita of the Alps to cure our colds, and asking my Mr. "Macho" fern to find a boyfriend. *(She raises the fern as if making an offering.)*
"Mr. Fern, give me love,
I will take care of you.
Give me joy
take away my loneliness."
(She lowers the fern and slowly rips off its leaves.) See how I take away your loneliness. Don't you feel better now? I'm not waiting any longer Griselda. Don't you see? I can't take anymore. No begonias, no hydrangea, no geraniums, no carnations...what we need in this house is a man! A man, not plants! *(She leaves the fern, removes the parakeets from the cage, violently, and throws them out the window. Then. with difficulty she closes the window again.)* Fly, boys, fly! No one needs you in this house! Take away my loneliness. *(After closing the window she walks around the winter garden, as if looking for something.)* I'm going to bring a man to this house. And you're going to help me Griselda. Wake up. *(She climbs up a ladder and searches for an iron box hidden in a chest. Still up there, she takes out a gun. She looks at it frightened, almost astounded.)* Take away my loneliness! Take away my loneliness. *(At this moment Griselda enters. She is also unkempt. She is wearing a nightgown and has cream on her face like a mask. Rosalia looks at her from above and points at her with the gun.)*

Griselda Rosalia... *(Trembling)*

Rosalia So you see, I'm not a sleepwalker. I'm awake. My eyes are open. Much more open than yours. *(Griselda breathes with fatigue.)* Once you tried to use this gun to stop your suffering. Do you remember? *(Griselda does not answer.)* You had left me a letter and everything. Do you remember? *(Pause)* Do you remember?

Griselda Yes.

Rosalia The male vet left with the female vet, and Griselda was left with Mr. Macho Fern. Do you remember?

Griselda Yes.

Rosalia You used to sing every night to Mr. Macho Fern. Remember?

Griselda Yes.

Rosalia But Mr. Macho Fern did not cure your loneliness.

Griselda No.

Rosalia Repeat after me: Mr. Macho Fern did not cure my loneliness.

Griselda No.

Rosalia Repeat after me: Mr. Macho Fern did not cure my loneliness.

Griselda No.

Rosalia Repeat it or I'll shoot. *(Pointing the gun)*

Griselda Mr. Fern didn't...didn't...didn't cure my loneliness.

Rosalia I'll cure it for you. Do you understand?

Griselda Yes.

Rosalia I'll cure it with this. *(Referring to the gun)*

Griselda *(Trembling, she thinks Rosalia is about to kill her.)* Yes...

Rosalia We're going to bring Mariano Rivas to this house. You and I, with this.

Griselda *(Relieved)* We are?

Rosalia Just for the two of us. *(She laughs. Griselda puts on a smile.)*

Griselda *(Almost in tears)* Yes.

Rosalia Repeat it.

Griselda Just for the two of us.

Rosalia Even if it's just for a few hours.

Griselda Just for the two of us. *(Laughs.)*

Rosalia We'll make him happy.

Griselda *(Laughing harder)* Just for the two of us.

Rosalia Marcelo the mechanic is coming to our house. *(They laugh.)*

Griselda I'm going to do it Rosalia. I'm going to do it. I know that I'm going to do it!

(Rosalia climbs down the ladder, revolver in hand.)

Rosalia At first, he won't want to come.

Griselda But we'll bring him anyway.

Rosalia And then he won't want to leave. *(They laugh.)*

Griselda We'll prepare everything. Detail by detail. For a few hours no one will notice.

Rosalia Marcelo the mechanic at our house! *(They fall into each other's arms.)* I love you so much, so much.

Griselda Me, too.

Rosalia You're all I have in this world.

Griselda You are all that I have in this world. *(They kiss very affectionately.)*

Rosalia For at least an hour we'll be happy.

Griselda Like Cinderella.

Rosalia Enough with the soaps! Now Marcelo the mechanic will be here at our house.

Griselda Yes, yes! Enough soap operas! Now the soap opera is us!

Rosalia The best story line ever! Our story!

Griselda The greatest soap opera of our life!

Rosalia *(Opens the closet and gets inside.)* I knew it... I knew that great moments were coming our way! I told you, Griselda, that some day...

Griselda *(Laughing)* Today's the day, Rosalia! Today is our day! Now it's our turn to live! Now it's finally our turn to experience our greatest love!!! Now!

Rosalia Now, yes...now.

Griselda Now. Now, now.

Rosalia Now, and here.

Griselda Bring him...touch him....savor him.

Rosalia Look at him....feel him....take care of him.

Griselda Mariano Rivas with us, here.

Rosalia Marcelo, our mechanic, will repair all the cars we want him to.

Griselda Love now, love...I love you!

Rosalia We're going to bite the apple...the big apple of happiness!

Blackout

ACT TWO

Scene 1

(The set is the same, but it has been carefully arranged to welcome Mariano Rivas. It is very festive. On the table there is a metal bucket

*with a bottle of champagne and three glasses. The chest in a privileged
spot now, and so is the mirror. Everything has been polished. From the
opening of the act, the women run around arranging and rearranging the
scene. They are trying to reestablish calm, trying not to spoil the mood.
When the scene opens, a violent movement from inside can be heard.
Mariano is resisting like a mad horse. They try desperately to appease
him. They fight violently, but without harming one another. At times it
looks like he is going to escape. But the two women exhibit unbelievable
strength. They finally surround him. But he still resists fiercely, and
finally Rosalia gets the revolver and points. Mariano is paralyzed by the
sight. He does not struggle anymore. He takes some steps. He's
surrounded. Very angry, he sits on a tall bench, his arms crossed.
There's a long pause. Rosalia still pointing the revolver.)*

Mariano I'm not moving. Don't you see that I'm not moving?
Rosalia At any moment you could jump again.
Mariano No. No, I won't jump up. *(Containing his anger)* Not
anymore. *(Pause)* Can you please point that in another direction? *(He
points towards Griselda.)* Don't kill me…
Rosalia I don't intend to kill anybody.
Mariano So what's the weapon for?
Griselda Mariano, do we look like murderers?
Mariano Oh, that's really a cliché. Nowadays murderers look like
angels. And you've go to watch your back with angels. It's not like
when I was a kid, when the bad guy looked like a bad guy, and you could
tell the good guy by the way he walked. Who could guess, for example,
that you two are going to kill me?
Griselda We're not murderers
Mariano Not yet, but in a few moments you could turn into one.
Griselda *(Desperately to Rosalia)* Look at what we're getting out of this.
Look at what he thinks of us Rosalia.
Rosalia Stop it.
Mariano What's a revolver for? Eh?
Rosalia Stop it!
Mariano What's it for? Answer me!!!
Rosalia To kill!
Griselda Honestly, this gun is not important. You give it more
importance that it has. What is important is that you are here in this
house with us.
Mariano Look; I'm here thanks to that revolver. And because life…at

least for me, is important. What do you want me to talk about? About how stupid I was to leave my car open so you could get inside? It's too late to talk about that now. Now you have me here. I talk about the gun because I wouldn't be here if it weren't for that gun.

Rosalia *(In a burst of hysterical laughter)* Do you realize what it means to us to have you here today? Have you ever read "Mirages in the Desert?" Looking at you every day on screen was a mirage and this house was a desert, and now you're here. *(Laughs.)* Even the plants have perked up. You don't understand. That's why you think I'm going to kill you. Do you think I'm going to shoot the thing I love most? *(Laughs.)* It's a moment…you have no idea what you wake up in me.

Mariano *(Harshly)* All right then. If you're not going to kill me I'm leaving. *(Stands up, getting ready to leave.)* It was a pleasure meeting you.

Rosalia Stay where you are, honey. *(She points the gun at him implacably.)*

Mariano Ah, so now we're getting intimate. The weapon brings us closer, huh? So you weren't going to kill me? *(Laughs.)*

Rosalia What's so funny?

Mariano Me, of course. You two don't make me laugh at all, as you can well imagine.

Griselda Laugh as much as you want. Laughter is a good starting point. Laugh and make believe you wanted to visit us. You'll feel entirely different. Do as I say, give it a try…that you came because you wanted to see us, because you missed us. You're a great actor. If you put your mind to it, you'll be able to believe it. Don't you manage to make us believe every afternoon that you're Marcelo the mechanic? If you concentrate, you'll forget the bad moments we've just experienced. Let's not waste time on nonsense. Let's not waste time today, dear. *(She is very moved when she says the last words.)* You're not laughing anymore? C'mon laugh!!! Don't you want to laugh with me? *(She laughs to make him laugh.)*

Mariano *(Harshly)* How much do you want?

Rosalia *(Disconsolate)* What?

Mariano I'm a successful actor and I'm employed, which doesn't mean I'm a millionaire; so I'm not about to pay outrageous sums to be left alone. I want to tell you that beforehand. How much do you want?

Rosalia Hush! No one's going to take money from you here. Don't humiliate us that way. You don't know who you're dealing with. You're totally mistaken. We're not going to kill you, or take your money. Who do you think we are?

Mariano Let's call a spade a spade. People who deprive a man of his freedom and take him away are called kidnappers. And people who threaten other people with a weapon are called assassins, although they may have not killed anyone yet. Let's call things by their names.

(Pause. They are very shaken by what he just said.)

Griselda *(Impulsively she moves in front of him.)* Look me in the eye. What do you see?

Mariano What do I see?

Griselda Do you see someone who is about to kill you?

Mariano No.

Griselda Do you see someone who wants to take your money?

Mariano No.

Rosalia I love watching him look. *(Tenderly)* Finally he's beginning to look like Marcelo the mechanic.

(Rosalia gets Mariano's attention. He fixes his eyes on her. Jealous Griselda turns Mariano's head so that he keeps looking at her.)

Griselda What do you see in my eyes? Way, way back? You know how to see inside of me. Your eyes drill into me. *(He looks at her as if he were hypnotizing in her.)* What do you see? Smoke? Fear? A storm?

Mariano No.

Griselda Do you see desire?

Mariano Yes.

Griselda Doesn't looking at me calm you down?

Mariano Yes.

Griselda Why?

Mariano I don't know.

Griselda Yes, you do. You always knew it. From the moment you came in that door. Do you want to know when I fell in love with you? Almost three years ago, on a Thursday. You scratched your head; a small, unimportant gesture, like any other. It was a very cold day and I was drinking hot chocolate because it was my birthday. Rosalia had gone to the beach. And you scratched your head in that innocent way of yours. That mischievous way you have... Could you scratch your head like that now? Could you give me that gift again?

Mariano I want to go.

Rosalia Do you see? Do you see what you just did? Now he wants to leave. Don 't pay any attention to her. She needs to talk constantly. I've been listening to her for twenty years. The best thing to do is not to pay attention to her. Look at me. *(She grabs his head.)*

Mariano I want to go.

Griselda Look at her. Look at her, too. Isn't there a woman deep inside? Is that a woman who could hurt you?

Mariano I want to leave! The only thing I want to do is leave! *(He bursts out crying to achieve his goal.)* They are waiting for me. I have to go. It's late. Don't you see?

Rosalia Not anymore. If they were waiting for you, they aren't any longer—you never showed up.

Mariano What do you want from me?

Rosalia Who was waiting for you?

Mariano What do you care?

Rosalia It's important, it's important. You know? It means a lot to me.

Mariano What do you want from me?

Griselda *(Smelling him)* To smell you. Just to smell you.

(He begins to cry.) Why are you crying, my dear? Why are you crying?

Mariano Why are you smelling me? *(Crying. Tries to control himself.)*

Rosalia Don't you see he doesn't want you to smell him? Don't you see that you're bothering him? Don't you see that he's unhappier by the minute? He couldn't care less about us. He wants to leave. All he wants is to leave. And we're not going to stop him. If he's not happy here, inside, with us, we'll have to let him go. *(He cannot stop crying.)* We're going to let him go so he can return to his own life. We can't keep him here with this nonsense. He's a thoroughbred. He needs freedom. Isn't that so, my love? Don't you cry anymore; we'll let you go... *(She protects him; she strokes him.)*

Griselda No! I won't let him leave like this! We didn't do all this to let him go just like that. No, Rosalia, no. You should have thought about that earlier, because it's too late now. *(She grabs the gun.)* Now he's going to stay here till the end. Understand, Rosalia? He's here until the end.

Blackout

Scene 2

(When the lights go up, it becomes obvious that the mood has changed. The three are seated around the table, eating the cold dinner that was as prepared earlier for Mariano's welcome. The three are relaxed, amused, and connected with each other.)

Mariano And then the producer pretended to be difficult, and he threatened to replace me with Julian Iraola if I didn't lower my salary demands. But I stuck to my guns and told my agent that we were not going to let him shake us up. We had to hold on tight.
Rosalia That's right! Hold on tight when the earth is shaking!
Griselda I lived through the San Juan earthquake.
Mariano And I was in the Canal seaquake. *(They laugh.)* I killed them with my indifference...holding on tight. Without budging. But, what the producer didn't know was that I knew he would have to come crawling to my house to beg me to do the role. And they had to pay me everything I asked, peso for peso. Because I knew that Julian Iraola had already signed a contract with another station. *(Laughing)* I got that information from Julian himself, who just happened to be my friend, and not theirs. They came to me with their tail between their legs.
Rosalia And they paid you everything you demanded?
Mariano Every penny.
Rosalia And thanks to that, there's a full moon tonight. *(They laugh.)* And with that money I was able to cook my famous truffle pate tonight.
Mariano May I have a little more please?
Rosalia Why certainly you may have it all. *(She serves him what's left.)* I made it just for you.
Mariano It's the best truffle pate I've had in all of my kidnappings. All I got in the others was bread and water. But you... truffle pate and champagne.
(They laugh.)
Griselda But you've never been kidnapped before! Don't be such a liar. It's obvious that you're a virgin in the kidnapping department.
Mariano Yes, I am. But only in that department.
Rosalia We, on the other hand, are in a lot of departments.
Mariano And that's why I'm here.
Griselda All right, let's not get so demanding.
Mariano Ah, but I will. Next time you kidnap me I want duck a l'orange. And the third time, boar basted in cognac and sugar flambé. I'll spread the word, "If you're looking for a good restaurant, get yourself kidnapped by Rosalia and Griselda."
Griselda He's making fun of us.
Mariano I'm a cruel boy. *(Pause)* And that drives you crazy. No? The meaner I am the crazier you get. The days that I'm good, the girls change the station. *(He roughly grabs Griselda's face.)* You like to be

held tight, don't you? You like it. Go ahead, confess. No one is listening.

Griselda Yes, yes. *(Very nervous.)* That's what I like.

Mariano You like it when I make you suffer, when I corner you, when I press up against you a bit. Your eyes sparkle. Now you look like a cat. You like it when I make you move to the rhythm of fear. *(Laughing at Rosalia)* Come, come, you too. *(Grabbing Rosalia too.)* Don 't be afraid Nothing's going to happen to you.

Rosalia I'm not afraid.

Mariano Look, look how you're shaking. I have you like this every afternoon. I have a million women like this every afternoon. Just like you are now.

Griselda A million?

Mariano Tall, fat, short, ugly, housewives, maids, mothers, working women. They all tremble for me half an hour every day!

Rosalia How does it feel?

Mariano It feels like this, what I feel now. *(Laughing)* And this is success. When you feel like this, it means you've made the big leagues.

Rosalia Success makes you laugh?

Mariano My life makes me laugh. *(Letting go of them)* I used to build towers when I was a kid. My dad was a carpenter, and he'd leave me the left over pieces of wood, and I'd make towers that reached the ceiling. And then I'd try to climb to the top, but the wooden sticks couldn't hold me. They'd break, and I'd fall on the ground and hurt my back. But I never gave up. I'd build another tower, stronger. I'd put rivets all over it and I'd prop it up with special crossbars. I'd be hammering nails all over the place. And then I'd try again. But the tower would break and I'd fall again. Until one day...February...I remember because it was my birthday. My eleventh birthday...I made the strongest tower of my life. I told myself that I would celebrate my birthday up there. I put on a white pair of shorts and a new shirt that Ines had given me. I climbed and climbed and climbed *(He climbs up on the furniture until he reaches the chest.)* And this time the tower did not break. I spent the entire day there. Then I decided to live there forever. *(Pause)* And I'm still there. Blowing out the candles. And now I'm afraid to come down. Because I don't know anything about life down there.

Rosalia Sad and ugly things happen down here. You 're better off staying up there. Having birthdays without getting any older. Someone has to be up there.

Mariano Ugly and sad things happen up here, too.

Griselda You can't see it. You can't see it from down here.

Mariano Well, up here sadder and uglier things happen than down there because we don t notice. *(He laughs.)* If you only knew what we have to do to stay up here. *(They laugh.)* If you knew the things I had to do to keep from falling from the tower…if you knew what it feels like inside this body, inside this face. If you knew what it was like to have a face like this… *(He slaps his face.)* Man, if I were to tell you what the world looks like from this rotten tower! A rotten tower in a rotten world! And up here, at the top, a rotten star! *(Pause)* But no one's going to move me. No one, the star says to himself. No one, and one day…boom! *(He throws himself on the ground.)* He falls. He falls with everything. *(He gets up and looks at them.)* Who threw him off? No one knows. I don't want to know. He can't waste time. He asks for an apple. *(Shouting.)* An apple! I need an apple! *(Rosalia turns and gets him a perfect red apple.)* My teeth. I have to show my teeth. A good bite is full of promises. *(He climbs up again.)* And this is how I began to bite the apple. It was the key to my success. *(Laughing)* The original sin. I signed a contract stipulating that I eat one apple per episode.

Griselda Apples are so good for you! It's an extraordinary gesture! It's the best campaign against drug addiction that I know.

(Mariano jumps up and offers them one. They look at him in ecstasy.)

Mariano It's another kind of addiction.

Rosalia Bite it, go ahead, bite it.

Griselda We've spent years watching you bite apples on television.

Rosalia We don't eat any other fruit around here.

Mariano *(Laughing)* But I cheat on everyone. It's not the only kind of fruit I eat. Because although my contract doesn't allow me to eat any other fruit, my mother buys me tangerines, and I eat them under the sheets before I go to sleep.

Rosalia *(Covering her ears)* I don't want to hear about those things.

Griselda We didn't bring you here for this.

Mariano You brought me here so that I could eat an apple right in front of you. Isn't that so? This is what you're looking for, right?

Griselda I've looked for that all my life. That's the only thing I've ever wanted. *(Her eyes fill with tears.)* That's all I've searched for.

(He tosses the apple in the air juggling it, like a magician in a circus. He threatens to bite it, but doesn't. He offers them the apple and takes it away from them just when they're about to eat it.)

Mariano That 's what brought on the downfall of humanity. Because of a little apple. If Adam hadn't taken a bite from it we'd be immortal. But

he couldn't help biting it, he couldn't, he couldn't, he couldn't! *(He tosses it into the air again, toying with their fantasies.)*
Rosalia Even if it was a sin.
Griselda Even if it was a sin.
Mariano *(Amused)* He couldn't. And then… then he brought the apple to his mouth and… *(He bites the apple very sensuously. They watch him mad with desire. He feels he has them in his grip. He bites voraciously. And takes another bite. They scream excitedly. He offers them the apple.)* He couldn't say no. *(He provokes them with the apple. They follow him. He lifts up the apple.)* He couldn't say no. Poor Adam. How could he say no, if he couldn't. *(Finally he lets them take a bite from the apple and, suddenly, he slaps them to bring them back to reality.)* And that was his sin. The sin of all humanity. Because if he had been able to say no, he'd have been saved, and we'd all have been saved. *(He has grabbed both of them. Rosalia has the apple in her mouth. They try desperately to get away. He drags them through the room towards the door. They resist and hit him. There is a very violent struggle. Griselda bites him.)*
Mariano Not me. The apple!
(Griselda bites him harder and this forces him to let go of her. Griselda falls and immediately grabs the gun. He grabs Rosalia as a hostage and protects himself behind her. There is a tense pause. Rosalia tries to break loose in a panic. Griselda aims steadily at Rosalia, but nervously.)
Griselda I have to do it. I have to do it.
Rosalia Griselda, this is getting out of hand.
Griselda I'm holding a weapon. Be careful what you say. *(Griselda aims almost straight at her.)*
Rosalia I love you, Griselda.
Griselda What does that matter? After you've crossed a certain line, you can't go back.
Rosalia This is the first time I've ever seen you like this.
Griselda I was someone else before.
Rosalia I've tried to help you, but it's gone wrong. Look how wrong it's gone. Look how wrong.
Mariano Are you going to shoot or aren't you?
Griselda Yes. *(Shoots into the air. Rosalia falls down. She turns around and hits Mariano with great anger.)*
Rosalia Why did you betray us?
Griselda Leave him alone. Leave him alone. *(Rosalia stops hitting*

him.) Leave the boy in peace.

Mariano *(Frightened, Mariano stands up. Pause)*You said you weren't going to kill me.

Rosalia But you didn't believe us.

Griselda *(Laughing)* I shot the gun. Did you see that, Rosalia? I shot it!

Mariano Yes. I believed you. I believed you. I still believe you. *(His eyes fill with tears, but he laughs.)* I still believe you. See?

·**Rosalia** You do well to believe us. But I don't know if it matters anymore.

Griselda *(Still aiming at him)* Grab the apple! *(He grabs an apple.)* Hold it tight like before. *(Does as he's told.)* Good. You know how to hold it. *(He grabs it more energetically, using the same gestures as before.)* Bite it.

Rosalia With desire, like when you get paid. With passion.

(Mariano bites the apple with passion.)

Rosalia With more passion. Sink your teeth into it.

(He sinks his teeth into the apple.)

Griselda Now give Rosalia a bite. *(He hesitates.)* Give her a bite. *(He gives Rosalia a bite.)*

Rosalia *(Rosalia bites it and laughs. She bites more of it and laughs.)*It's the sweetest apple I've ever eaten. Really it's the only apple I've ever eaten in my whole life. *(She takes more bites.)* The others were not apples. They were tangerines.

Griselda Climb on your tower. Take your shoes off. *(He does so, climbing on to the large chest that was his tower.)* Your sweater. *(He takes off his sweater. She takes it, smells it. Then she circles him as one who walks around a statue.)* Your pants. *(He takes off his pants.)*

Rosalia *(Crying, sobbing)* It's the first time I see a man naked... I never even saw my father. He was so straight...so straight-laced.

Griselda Take everything off.

Blackout

Scene 3

(When the lights go up again, it is apparent that no time has passed. Mariano is about to act out the soap opera for the two women. There is a tense silence. Mariano appears strongly lit by two lights, as if he were in a television studio. Mariano stands alone in the middle of the stage. The two women watch him dumbstruck. Mariano slowly dresses up like

*Marcelo, the mechanic.   He puts on overalls, leaving the zipper quite
open. His tools are inside the large chest, he distributes them throughout
his pockets.)*

Rosalia   Wait a minute.   Wait a minute.   *(Finds a camera with a flash.)*
Take a picture of me, of me with him.   Take it, Griselda, take a picture of
me with him.   Hold me in your arms. my dear mechanic.   *(He lifts her in
his arms.   She smiles.   Griselda photographs them.)*   I'm going to make
two hundred thousand copies and I'll distribute them all over the Buenos
Aires subways.
Mariano   Good.   It will make it easier for the police to find you.
Rosalia   And what can the police do to me for having been happy?   Or
do they put people in jail for being happy?   *(She laughs.   He puts her
down.   She suddenly kisses him on the mouth.)*   Now let them take me to
jail till the end of my days!   Now I have memories...   I have memories...
(Her eyes fill with tears.   Griselda pulls away.)   He kissed me!   Did you
see how he kissed me?   He's crazy about me.
Griselda   *(To Mariano)*   If you could only concentrate and begin... it
would be so good.   *(She uses her inhaler because she has the beginning
of an asthma attack.)*   Before either one of us loses control or can't even
answer for ourselves...if you could just calm us with your tenderness.
Like it has calmed us for the last three years...every lousy afternoon of
our damned lives   *(She breathes into the inhaler.)*   Neither of us cares if
we die after today, you know. *(Pause)* Nothing has ever happened to her
in her whole life.   And not to me either.   And suddenly in an instant
everything happened. *(She hugs Rosalia.)*   And there's no more fear.   No
ghosts.   We're lost in some lost corner of the planet.
(Mariano begins to act out the soap opera. They look at him in ecstasy.)
Marcelo   I know you think I'm a loser, that my hands are always
covered with grease and these overalls walk by themselves...really...
they walk all by themselves...the other day I took Juan's kid to the zoo,
and I got really dressed up...and when we got to the hippopotamus'
cage, we saw that my overalls had been following us for over a half an
hour.   Don't laugh...I believe I was born with my overalls on and I'll die
with my overalls on.   The day I marry you, I m marrying you with my
overalls on.   So you won't forget you're marrying a working man, the
kind those snobs in your family look down on 'cause we're low class, or
'cause we make too much noise when we bite down on an apple.
(Taking an apple out of his pocket) The day that you bite this apple is
the day you lose forever...*(He bites it.)* That's why you don't wanna bite

it…'cause you know that this apple's more dangerous for you than all the caviar and lobster your prune-faced butler gives you for breakfast to start your day. You know how I'm gonna start off your days?

Griselda *(Performing the role of Valeria)* How?

Mariano Like this. *(He kisses her passionately.)* Like this.

Griselda *(To Rosalia)* You see? This is precisely the part you missed. Did your see how he kissed her? Did you see it was true he kissed her? Kiss me again.

Mariano No.

Rosalia Again. The last part again.

Mariano No.

Griselda Just the part about how you'll start your day. That little part, that's all.

Mariano *(Gives in but acts it badly.)* Cause you know that this apple's more dangerous for you than all the caviar and lobster your prune-faced butler gives you for breakfast to start your day. You know how I'm gonna start off your days?

Rosalia *(Pushing Griselda away)* How?

Mariano Like this. *(He slaps her face.)* Like this. *(He slaps her again.)* Like this. *(He slaps her once more.)*

Rosalia I still like you. I still like you. Even if you slap me. *(She straightens up.)* I never loved anyone so much. Do you know? I love you more than I love myself. I love you more than I love my brother up North. And even if you rebel, if you slap me because your attraction to me makes you angry. You're upset that this woman drives you out of your mind, aren't you? You're going to do the scene over again. *(Pause)*

Mariano Cause you know that this apple's more dangerous for you than all the caviar and lobster your…*(His eyes fill with tears.)* than all the caviar and lobster your prune-faced butler gives you for breakfast to start your day. *(He is overcome by anguish and despair.)* Mama, how did I end up here? *(Tries to overcome his feelings.)*…the caviar and lobster your prune-faced butler gives you for breakfast to start your day… *(Forcing himself not to cry)* I only wanted to live in a tower… *(Continues playing the same scene.)* For breakfast every morning mama in the tower everyday that butler…I never had a butler mama…nobody has a butler with a face like a prune who starts off your day. Do you know how I'll start off your day? *(Crying, chiding her with his screams)* Do you know how I'll start off your day? *(Falls on his knees. His despair leaves the women both perplexed and desolate.)*

Blackout

Scene 4

(As the lights come up we can see the atmosphere has calmed down. Mariano is sleeping on the sofa, exhausted, overcome by the emotional experiences. A bluish light tints the scene. Rosalia has placed herself in front of him and watches him tenderly as he sleeps... Griselda looks through the chest and finds a very old cap and shawl which, she puts on. She searches among her poems kept in a huge box.)

Rosalia Who is he dreaming about?

Griselda About me, of course. About me. He couldn't be dreaming about you.

Rosalia   Maybe he isn't dreaming about either of us. *(Pause)* His nostrils are moving. Maybe he's dreaming about the perfume on the neck of a very beautiful woman. It looks like he's smiling. Maybe he's reached the top of his tower. And up there, the moon is full, the night is warm, and someone is waiting for him.

Griselda I'm waiting for him don't you see?

Rosalia Why did you put that on?

Griselda I should never have taken it off. I was born to be wrapped in mist. My big mistake was to enter into the everyday routine. I march in the beat of a different drummer. I am not shackled by the laws of convention, or by the code of the market around the corner. *(Pause)* You always send me to that market. That's why I put it on. That's why.

Rosalia Well, you just try going out like that.

Griselda I've already suffered a host of humiliations by trying to adapt to this suffocating world. But he has unleashed my spirit. And I don't care about anything anymore. Now I'm possessed by dark truths. Can't you see how I have changed? See how pale my hands are? *(She shows Rosalia her hands.)*

Rosalia You're going to wake him up... don't you see that he needs rest? That he needs to dream?

Griselda He's dreaming about me. I am walking in a blue room flinging my pack of poems around the room. *(Reciting toward Mariano)*

> Although you do not understand me my love
> my endless loneliness, not even my sadness
> filled with longing for the summer
> we did not even see each other,

longing, my love, longing.
(She strolls full of melancholy.)

Longing, my love, longing
for what could have been
and my sadness is so deep and so sad
that although it's summer my sweetness.
although it's summer
I still feel cold.

(Pauses. Toward the end of the poem, Mariano opens his eyes and looks at her as if she were a ghost.)

Rosalia *(To Mariano)* It's a dream...you're dreaming. *(She laughs.)* It's a marvelous dream.

Griselda I have spent the last few years writing poems. I've poured everything that I feel for you into these pages. Do you care? Does it move you at all? Does any of this brush your heart?

Mariano my suffering love
My fictional love
My uncertain dream
My barrio mechanic, my Marcelo

(Mariano does not dare react.)

Rosalia That's what dreams are, Mariano. Everything here is possible. We are free to untie the knots that bind us. We are much more real, my love.

Mariano *(Panicking)* What are you going to do to me?

Rosalia What do you mean what are we going to do to you? What are you going to do to us? *(Searching among her papers.)*

Griselda

Do with me as you please
I want to be the piece that your hands sculpt
I want to be the wood
Where you carve your ideas.
Of all your whims
I want to be your prisoner.

Mariano I believe... believe the time has come for me to leave... *(He unfastens his overalls.)*

Rosalia He wants to get undressed. *(Impulsively she helps him unfasten hits overalls.)* I'll help you get naked.

Griselda

I care not about the flesh; I want the soul

especially since the flesh comes and devours us
the soul will yield its ephemeral place
because it is the soul that remains
while the flesh vanishes.

Rosalia   Help me. I won't be able to take these off by myself. *(She grabs him from behind to hold him. He defends himself and kicks).*

Griselda   *(As she's attempting to remove his overalls)* He's upset.

Rosalia   He's a man.

Mariano   *(Panicking)* Please! Let me go now! Don't mess with me! Leave me alone, please! What are you doing to me? Let me leave now, please. I'll give you whatever you want.

(They both throw him on the floor and climb on him.)

Rosalia   He has surrendered, surrendered like a diver who jumps into the depths of the sea. Surrendered, like a sailor, by the sea. With wild abandon, love, surrendered.

Mariano   I'll do whatever you want. I swear to you that no one will find out that you kidnapped me. I promise that no one will find out. I promise I won't say a word. *(They begin to touch him inappropriately.)* Please, no? What are you doing? Oh, no, no, no, no, no. Don't touch me please.

Rosalia   Well... go on Griselda. Or don't you know how to make love?

Griselda   Why wouldn't I know? It's just that he isn't cooperating at all. And I was always told that the man played the active role.

Rosalia   Don't start with your preconceived ideas now.

Griselda   They're not preconceived, they're conceived.

Mariano   Let me go! Let me go, please. I swear that I'll do anything you ask. I promise to come see you every day. Please.

Griselda   But nothing's going to happen to you. It's a question of showing a little good will. We're not asking for much more. My love.

Mariano   I can't. Don't you understand that I can't?

Griselda   Never?

Mariano   I can't now.

Griselda   A man always can.

Mariano   That's not true.

Griselda   Are you sick?

Mariano   No I'm not.

Griselda   Then, we're two angels in heaven. *(Throwing herself at him, Griselda showers him with kisses. He resists her as much as he can. Rosalia holds him.)*

Rosalia   I think he's gay.

Mariano I'm not gay. I'm not. *(He tries to get away, but he cannot.)*
Rosalia He must be a little gay, because with two women like us smothering him with love...something should have happened by now. I'm not saying that we should be pregnant by now...but something... Something a little more intense. *(She kisses him passionately and he rejects her. He bites her. She hits him, then kisses him again.)*
Griselda Maybe he's impotent.
Mariano I'm not impotent!
Rosalia Well then, he's both. Gay on the one hand, and impotent on the other.
Mariano No, no. I can assure you that I'm not. I can assure you.
Griselda Here it's not a question of assurances, my dear, here it's a question of doing something.
Mariano If you both...if you both help me, perhaps...
(Pause. They both look at him.)
Griselda Ask us whatever you want. Whatever you need.
Mariano I need a little space.
Griselda What a weird request... I always thought that erotic feelings arose from physical proximity. But, of course. I'm from an older generation... not so old, but older. Now they like a little distance.
(The two women move away from him. A pause.)
Rosalia And?
Griselda You can start with either one of us. We've agreed not to be jealous.
(He looks at them. He makes an effort to want them.)
Mariano *(Laughing heartily)* How ridiculous! My God! How ridiculous! *(He laughs almost to the point of despair)*
Rosalia He's not gay, but he's probably homosexual.
Griselda What's the difference?
Rosalia I'll explain later.
(He looks at them almost with pity.)
Griselda Are you going to keep this up for the rest of the night?
Mariano Griselda ... *(He laughs.)* I had a teacher once named Griselda...she was very pretty...very dark...she had long hair that hung over her white apron...she was my sixth grade teacher. She had enormous breasts that moved under her apron. At twelve years old those tits meant the world to me Griselda...and your breasts now...
Griselda Mine... mine aren't like that.
Mariano But the name.
Griselda Ah. yes. The name.

Mariano Come over here. *(Touching her breasts)* No, no. I can't.
Please, move away again. I was beginning to feel something. Move
away again…*(Griselda moves away once more.)*
Rosalia   And didn't you have an aunt named Rosalia? Or a friend of
your mother's?
Mariano No. *(He laughs.)* But I did have a filly, a little blue filly.
Rosalia Blue.
Mariano Blue. *(Pulls her towards him.)* And I liked to ride her, and
make her gallop and jump fences, and whip her until it hurt. *(He slaps
her buttocks.)* I can't! It's not that I don't want to, it's just that I can't. I
can't! I can't! Do you understand? I can't!
Griselda Are you having trouble? I mean…that kind of trouble?
Mariano I don't have trouble with women. I can have any woman I
want. I like women a lot. *(He laughs.)*
Griselda *(Laughing too)* So then?
Rosalia *(Approaching him. She caresses him.)* You need to get in the
mood. Let me help you. Let yourself go, close your eyes and think of an
immense sea, and my body is the waves and you jump in to swim.
Griselda And along comes a shark! *(She bites him on the ear. He
screams.)* The sharks bite, but you go on swimming. You dive in.
Rosalia See how generous the sea is. It's all for you.
*(He feels like the two women are drowning him. He desperately tries to
throw them off him. They are dissatisfied, frustrated, and they look at
him resentfully.)*
Griselda We've done everything we can to help you. We've tried to get
to the root of your problem. If you show us the way, we'd get to our
destination faster and we'd all be happier.
Rosalia Maybe we've overwhelmed you. *(Stroking his hair.)* For me.
just stroking your hair is like touching heaven with my hands, you
know…
Mariano Yes.
Rosalia May I stroke you?
Mariano Yes. *(He gives her his head.)*
Rosalia Griselda, look. *(Griselda comes over.)*
Griselda *(Anguished laughter)* It's a perm. I'm sure he's had a perm.
Rosalia His curls are not natural.
Griselda How long have you had it permed?
Mariano When I began acting they advised me to lighten my hair and
have it permed… people like it a lot…don't they?
Griselda And is that your nose?

Mariano Yes, the nose is... *(He laughs.)* The nose is mine.

Rosalia He's wearing makeup. *(Touches his face.)*

Griselda Do you always wear make-up? Do you always wear rouge? And mascara on your eyelashes? And lipstick on your mouth? *(Kissing him on the mouth)* Hmmm, hmmmm, hmmmm...you wear the same lipstick I do.

Mariano You grabbed me just as I was leaving the station. All actors wear make up on TV.

Rosalia I don't want to know about it. I don't want to know any more. I'm sorry. I've made such a big mistake...I'm sorry for Griselda. Sorry for myself. Sorry.

Griselda *(Exploding)* My hair, my beloved hair...the hair that I take to bed with me, the disheveled hair that inspires my poems. The only desire I ever had was to run my fingers into that hair...like putting your hand into the earth to feel one's own roots. That's how your hair called me, and when I'd see you throw yourself on the ground between the wheels of a car I would suffer thinking your hair would get dirty...and I imagined you showering and filling your head with soap...that blonde hair, so shiny and thick... How could you do this to me?

Rosalia Answer her. Say something. Defend yourself. Say something to show that you're worth it. There must be something inside that fake head and behind that thick make up.

Mariano You're confused...everyone...

Rosalia Everyone. To hell with everyone! I don't want to know about everyone. I've had enough with what you've shown me. *(Agonizing)* You know? I've never gone so far for anyone. I never fell so hard. I keep falling and falling. Nothing matters to me now. *(She pauses.)* But there is one thing that makes me happy. You don't exist. But we do. We are alive. *(Griselda opens the doors and windows. Mariano looks at everything.)*

Griselda What are you waiting for? You should be running out of here now. Your car is parked around the corner, and your life is waiting for you, and we are no longer holding you. *(A wave of despair hits her.)* A perm, and dye, and make-up, and gay. You're not missing anything, are you?

Mariano But what kind of joke is this? You are very much mistaken.

Griselda We were very much mistaken. *(Furious)* Very much mistaken, too mistaken. But who caused the mistake?

Mariano Naturally, I couldn't do it, but now I believe I can. I'm sorry. I'm truly sorry. *(Grabbing Griselda)* I think that you're prettier than my

sixth grade teacher. And furthermore, I'm not twelve years old anymore,
and I can show you how I feel!

(Griselda pushes him away violently)

Griselda Get this mannequin off of me! *(To Rosalia)* Why are you
letting him touch me?

Rosalia Go on. We...we're not going to tell anyone about what we
saw... no one...don't worry... it's enough for us that we know.

Mariano I am a man. I'm a great guy. Everyone loves me. Women...

Rosalia Go, go with the women that are waiting to get your autograph.
Go!

Mariano I want to stay. Don't you understand that I want to stay? You
have to let me, let me stay... I need you to let me stay.

Griselda Look, you can't stay. You can't. *(She throws his clothes on top
of him.)* You can't stay. We don't want you.

(He stays on his knees, destroyed.)

Rosalia Besides, it's time for the soap opera. And I'm not going to
miss an episode for you....

Griselda *(Turning on the television)* That's all we need... *(Laughing)*
To miss an episode on top of everything else.

*(The three are watching the program. Mariano slowly gathers his things
and prepares to leave. The women are so completely wrapped up in the
action on the television that they don't see him. Meanwhile Mariano
has tried to get them to listen to him.)*

Mariano I am a man, and I'm going to prove it to you. That's me! I'm
him, I'm him, I'm him.

*(The following scene takes place on the television. Marcelo is seen
leaving the jail. He is met by Valeria who embraces him.)*

Valeria My love...you're out...they let you go.

Marcelo They had nothing on me. I'm an honest guy who works hard
for a living. What can they accuse me of?

Valeria They can accuse you of having curly blonde hair. *(She runs her
fingers through his hair.)* And of having the most transparent smile on
earth. *(He smiles and he hugs her. He picks her up in his arms and
spins her around.)* They can accuse you of being happy...

Marcelo I love you. *(They give each other a long kiss.)*

Valeria Look what I brought you. *(She hands him an apple. He toasts
as if it were a glass of champagne.)*

Marcelo Hmmm, delicious. This is the best apple I've ever eaten in my
life. Because it's the apple of happiness. *(They laugh and he eats the
apple.)*

Mariano That's me! I'm him, I'm him, I'm him. It's me, it's me!
(The women cling to the television until the lights fade out.)

The End

MaTRIX, Inc.

Translated by Victoria Martinez in collaboration with Lidia Ramirez

A play in one act

Characters
Gloria: *Thirty years old. Very attractive, sensual, and pleasant; however she has a tendency to be moody, somber, and irascible. She adapts easily to each different daughter that she must play.*
Substitute Mother: *Of indeterminate age, perhaps around forty years old. There should not be a marked difference between her and her client. The two could even be the same age since the Substitute Mother is only a substitute, not her client's real mother. She has fine, beautiful features. She is exceedingly dramatic, agreeable, an excellent actress (every Substitute Mother is), and fully capable of shedding the role of one mother and putting herself in the skin of another.*

Setting
The play takes place in one of the studios at the MaTRIX, Inc. agency. The studio is set up like a room in a single woman's apartment. The room is strategically designed and decorated so that its belongings can easily be transformed or removed. The characters as well as the room need to be able to change according to the needs of each scene. There are two doors onstage; one within the scenery representing Barbara's door, and the second representing the stage door.
There is a metal clothes rack full of clothing for the changes of the different mother and daughter roles to be played out. There should also be a bar with drinks, chairs, and a table when needed in the scenes. The lights alternate between warm and cold colors, depending upon the mood of the scene or the breakdown in negotiations between Gloria and the Substitute Mother and/or the daughter and mother.

The Substitute Mother has a suitcase. She uses that during the play to pull out various props and costumes.

(Gloria, wearing a salmon colored silk outfit, stands on the bed, her back to the audience. She is "conducting" Bach's "Magnificat." The doorbell rings. She doesn't hear it. She is absorbed in the music that fills the room. The doorbell rings persistently. She keeps "conducting" until, in a sudden fit of anger, she breaks the baton; and magically, the music stops.)

Gloria   This was a transcendental personal moment!   Just when I had almost reached the point that someday I would call "my happiness!" *(Impatiently opening the door)* And you of course, can't stand the change one feels reaching a point of pleasure.
(As the door opens, Indian music begins to play and a strong light shines on the Substitute Mother. She enters, dressed in a sari.)
Substitute Mother   I never should have believed him! He was too young, too beautiful, and too dark.   We made love six or seven times a day. Always on incredible white elephants, under a rainbow of glorious sacred music. He loved to see me smile… Daughter of my soul, have you ever had a solar orgasm? Or have yours only been lunar? I know that mothers don't normally ask these types of questions, but our relationship has always been so loving and affectionate, so intense. If I ever commit suicide, I'll do it in your house. And you'll understand that it's an act of love. I have taught you the difference between love and passion from a very early age. I have learned too late the difference between love and passion. India's a good place to lose oneself forever. I've loved him! I don't think I could live without him.   It's too much. Why aren't you consoling me, my daughter? You're all that I have left. I'm a mere shadow of my former self, the forgotten footprint in the moving sands of nothing. He left me without a word. And the next day I saw him go by on a white elephant with another woman. I'm going to die of sadness. Do something for your mother, darling. Help me die with dignity.
Gloria   That suit looks wonderful on you, Mother. *(She kisses her coldly.)* Chanel? How was your trip? I'm sorry I didn't pick you up at the airport, but…
(Substitute Mother stopping the scene. In her role as an employee of MaTRIX, Inc., she seems somewhat lost because she is trying to remember the details of the type of mother she is supposed to play.)
Gloria   Paris. You have a huge home in Paris, mother. You spend a lot of time there. You stay as far from your children as you can. *(She goes over*

to the bar.) It's been a year since we've seen each other. And I have to accept the fact that I'm an unwanted daughter. *(She takes a drink.)* And to think that I've spent the last year waiting for one miserable postcard from my mother. *(Drinks whisky.)* But, didn't they tell you all this at MaTRIX?

Substitute Mother Paris? And not even a postcard? Didn't I just arrive from India? Aren't you the one who asked for the mother whose addicted to riding on elephants, dressed in white, and has a black lover?

Gloria *(Upset by inefficiency in a service that costs so much.)* I never asked for that scenario! That entrance doesn't do a thing for me. Listen, I'm not going to waste my time and my money with a mother who's distraught because her lover dumped her! I paid for a cold and inconsiderate mother so I could be the rejected daughter!

Substitute Mother *(Grandiloquently)* So! That's how you treat my grand operatic entrance. Instead of applauding me, you humiliate me! I really should be on Broadway. This is not the place for me. I should be a star on Broadway!

Gloria As much as I appreciate your Shakespearean performance, put yourself in my shoes! Just imagine that you pay to break the sound barrier of emotions and nothing like that happens.

Substitute Mother *(Upset by her professional gaffe.)* You're right. I got mixed up. It happens to the best of us, listen, I could tell you about some big mistakes that Madonna and Meryl Streep have made, among others.

Gloria Mixed up? And you're so casual about it? Here I am, waiting for my heartless mother from Paris who will destroy my heart and here appears a woman from India whose had her heart broken, who I have to take care of?

Substitute Mother *(Disturbed by her mistake the Substitute Mother puts on her glasses and looks through some papers from MaTRIX, Inc.. She laughs at herself.)* Oh, yes! Here it is! *(Reading)* "Arrive in disgrace from India. Try to commit suicide by jumping out the window of your son's house. He saves you." I confused you with a client hooked on suffering. I'm supposed to see him tomorrow. Here's the mistake. See? *(She shows Gloria the calendar.)* I'm sorry. I'm inundated with work. I'm one substitute mother in great demand. Sometimes I get mixed up.

Gloria You were going to commit suicide, right in front of me? Right after you arrived?

Substitute Mother It says here, you were going to save me.

Gloria What a beginning! A suicide right under my nose! And to top it off, a mistaken suicide!

Substitute Mother We stopped in time; no real damage was done. You felt some emotion and we work to produce emotions, although they might be incorrect ones. Just to make sure: Did you sign up for the "Be In" plan or the "Hello Little Princess"?

Gloria *(Beside herself with anger-she paces up and down the stage.)* Oh, no you don't! This is ridiculous! Inhumane! You come in as the mother you're going to play tomorrow. Then you ask me what plan I signed up for? I saved up for a year for this moment. I saved every penny to have you here with me. Coming to MaTRIX isn't for some one like me. And if I decided to do this it's because...

Substitute Mother *(Interrupting abruptly)* Don't tell me why you signed up for the service. It's none of my business! Imagine if I listened to the confessions of all my clients. Go to a psychiatrist, a rabbi, or a priest. I'm here to do a good job. Now let's concentrate!

Gloria *(Furious)* Now you're telling me what to do?

Substitute Mother I want to make sure you know the rules.

Gloria I'm the one who gives the orders around here! You belong to me, and I don't mean that figuratively!

Substitute Mother How do you mean it, then?

Gloria I mean it literally. And I have grounds to mean it that way!

Substitute Mother *(She laughs at Gloria in a hurtful way.)* I think any ground you have is a bit shaky.

Gloria *(Furious)* What are you laughing at?

Substitute Mother I want you to understand that I belong as much to you as I do to the others.

Gloria I paid for you to belong to me. I don't want to be crass, but let's just say I "acquired" you.

Substitute Mother I don't want to disappoint you, but eight people have "acquired" me today.

Gloria Eight!

Substitute Mother Look see for yourself *(She shows her agenda.)* Look at today's date, eight.

Gloria You can't tell me that you're seeing seven other people today!

Substitute Mother It's all in a day's work. The same as always. Eight clients.

Gloria *(She reacts indignantly.)* Did I ask you for that information? Doesn't it seem a bit promiscuous telling me how many clients are paying you to be their mother? Who asked for those types of details?

Substitute Mother No one asked me. I just thought that.

Gloria *(Furious)* Why are you giving me that information? In what part of our contract, in what clause, on what line does it say that I wanted to know the number of clients that you planned to see today?

Substitute Mother Nowhere. I didn't say it was part of the contract. I said it because you bragged about being my exclusive client. And on top of that, my owner! You said you owned me!

Gloria OK, I'll admit that! But while you're here, you're mine, mine, mine! Whether you like it or not. Mine. You're MY substitute mother! Do you understand?

Substitute Mother If you're so sure of this so-called ownership, why does it bother you that I'll see others today?

Gloria It doesn't bother me. I'm just not interested that's all.

Substitute Mother Are you sure that's all?

Gloria I'm totally indifferent. They don't exist for me.

Substitute Mother Well, they do for me… Not only them, but eight more clients tomorrow, and eight the day after, and so on and so forth. Multiply eight by thirty and you get two hundred and forty per month. Can you imagine satisfying the whims of two hundred and forty children per month? Do you realize how much patience I need to have? Can you imagine how many different mothers I have to play? Can you imagine all the crazy stipulations and obligations I need to fulfill?

Gloria Look, at the moment I can't imagine anything because you haven't even satisfied my most minimal demands. And you're trying to make me feel pity for you because you're really nothing but a... *(She's at the point of saying, "prostitute.")* a...a...

Substitute Mother A what?

Gloria A substitute mother who is so, so...distributed. *(Her voice breaks with emotion.)* Do you want to know the truth? The others do matter to me! I hate them. I want to be the only one. If I had the money, I would buy the other two hundred and thirty nine hours a month.

Substitute Mother You're not the only one with this insatiable need. I am booked for the rest of the year. There's an addict like yourself who's going to take me on vacation with her in the Caribbean so I can play thousands of substitute mothers. There's a famous actress who spends everything she earns to hire me so that I can assure her that she's my favorite daughter. There's a senator who pays triple on Thursdays so that I can give him my undivided attention. There's an obese woman who pays me only to cook her favorite raviolis and... *(Interrupting herself)* But why am I telling you all this? What do you care? You chose my photo from thousands of others. I'm not having a good day, obviously. Why am I telling you about myself when you contracted a substitute mother? None of my clients want to know anything about me.

Gloria Don't compare me to those perverts. I'm different.

Substitute Mother Different, how? Just like the rest you would contract me 365 days, if you had the money? Or did I misunderstand?

Gloria You understood me very well. I must admit that you managed to awaken extreme feelings of jealousy and exclusion in me. You are a fascinating woman. You're enchanting. I chose well. Although you make mistakes and talk about the others.

Substitute Mother Lately I have awakened great passions in my clients. Shall I describe some? There's a jazz musician, very young, gay, fabulous, that while we dance he...

Gloria No! No! No! Don't describe other passions. Don't talk to me about other clients. I don't even want to know their names! Imagine if I ever met one of them!

Substitute Mother Of course you know some of them. On Friday I have to visit a guy named Manuel. He's your ex-husband, isn't he? (*Gloria throws herself on the woman and puts her hand over her mouth. They struggle and fall to the floor. Gloria straddles the Substitute Mother and grasps her violently by the throat.*) Let go! You're choking me. Look if you injure me you're going to have to pay a lot of money to MaTRIX. (*This frightens Gloria. The Substitute Mother defends herself and dominates the situation. It's obvious she has martial arts training. She flips Gloria in the air and surprises her with a Judo move that keeps Gloria from defending herself. Gloria is immobilized by this move. Controlling the situation*) Is the crisis over, dear?

Gloria You appear to be well trained.

Substitute Mother It's part of our preparation. We receive training in defense in addition to acting, dancing, and singing. We have to be ready for anything. We don't want to be caught off guard. (*Gloria calms down. She tries to compose herself.*)

Gloria Don't mention my ex again.

Substitute Mother All right. But, didn't you want to feel jealous? The combination of a wrong entrance and the mention of other clients usually work wonderfully to invoke jealousy! Didn't I drive you to the brink?

Gloria You want me to believe that your mistake was intentional?

Substitute Mother Don't tell me you think I really made a mistake! O.k., o.k., if that's what you want to believe. I made a mistake.

Gloria And the other clients?

Substitute Mother You just made me promise not to mention them again.

Gloria Well, I take it back. Now, tell me if my ex-husband hired you or if that was one of your strategies for making me really jealous!

Substitute Mother Imagine whatever you want. Imagining is a good exercise when your sense of reality has been lost.... *(Gloria slaps the Substitute Mother, and the latter returns the blow.)* You slapped me too soon, that was supposed to come later.

Gloria Hey! You did the entrance that someone else paid for. What are you going to do for the next client, the entrance I paid for?

Substitute Mother Oh no. I might do the same thing again. That character attracts me. Mothers with black lovers who've just arrived from India. Clients rarely request it! The entrance that you paid for is such a cliché.

Gloria I rented a cold mother for the entrance, one who would keep me waiting. I asked to have time for the haunting feeling of restlessness to build. You gave me no time for doubting. I needed to doubt you. I paid for the uncertainty. I wasn't supposed to know if my mother would come or not. But you came in sooner than you should've. *(A slight pause)* Do you have to work after this?

Substitute Mother Don't worry about me. I have plenty of work. *(Worried)* Weren't you the least bit anxious?

Gloria A little. If you had waited five minutes longer and had not mixed up your clients your entrance would have been a success.

Substitute Mother A success? It was unforgettable! It was an exercise in technique. The rift between that mother and that daughter was like a volcano erupting. But you can claim your entrance. Do you want the entrance you paid for?

Gloria Of course I want the entrance I paid for! I demand that our contract be fulfilled.

Substitute Mother But first, let's clarify exactly what type of mother you want. *(She takes out a tablet and prepares to take notes.)*

Gloria *(Looking for the right words)* I want a mother that makes me tremble with anxiety. A mother as cold as ice.

Substitute Mother The things they ask us to do!

Gloria *(Inspired)* Distant, unreadable, illusive, bad. Evil.

Substitute Mother A delicious character!

Gloria I paid to wait. I paid to suffer. I want to doubt! I've wanted to wait for my mother for such a long time! I paid for a mother that would make me suffer for her continuous lack of respect for our scheduled visits.

Substitute Mother *(She reads her notes and memorizes them.)* O.K. I'll satisfy you. Let's make believe I haven't arrived yet. Goodbye Gloria.

Gloria Goodbye. *(The Substitute Mother exits. The lights fade to half. Gloria tries to recuperate the same atmosphere as in the beginning. She*

puts on Bach's "Magnificat." Gloria holds the conductor's baton and tries to direct the orchestra. She realizes she can't go back to the beginning as if she hasn't done it before. She stops the music.) We're making a mistake trying to start from scratch. I already know her. I'm deceiving myself. This fake entrance isn't worth it. Come back immediately and let's continue with the mother I already got. *(She walks around the set anxiously.)* Maybe she got sick of me? This is unacceptable. She can't make me wait like this. We're wasting precious time. *(She opens the door assuming that the substitute mother will be there. She's not.)* We're wasting precious time. I admit I wasn't very nice. It was all my fault. She's got her limits and I was harsh on her. I humiliated her and now she's gone. She was a really good actress. That was a marvelous wrong entrance. She's really unique. Why couldn't I have told her that? *(The Substitute Mother enters wearing a very elegant outfit. She wears a pillbox hat and gloves, which she does not remove during the scene.)*
Mama! Oh! A whole year without seeing each other! *(She hugs her.)*

Substitute Mother *(Cold and distant; pushing Gloria away. She sits down.)* Save the effusiveness, please. I see you're still slathering people with kisses.

Gloria I'm sorry, Mama. It's just that it's been such a long time. Come in, come in, I've wanted you so much to see my house.

(The Substitute Mother does not look at the house; she sits at the edge of a chair, and she's very tense. She takes out a mirror from her purse to check her makeup. She tries to remove Gloria's kiss marks from her cheeks.)

Substitute Mother Look how you messed up my cheek.

Gloria You look wonderful, Mama. How was Paris? Why didn't you write to me at all? Was there ever a moment that you missed me? Did you ever think about me? Why didn't you call me for Christmas or New Year's?

Substitute Mother I can't answer all of those questions at once, Maria. I don't even know what you're asking.

Gloria I'm not Maria, Mama. I'm Gloria.

Substitute Mother *(Takes out a gift from her purse.)* I brought you your favorite perfume. Eau Savage for men. *(She gives it to her.)*

Gloria Eau Savage is Guillermo's favorite. My favorite is Samsara by Guerlain.

Substitute Mother What an ungrateful daughter! Maria, I came all the way across the Atlantic to bring you your favorite perfume and you tell me I've confused you with your siblings.

Gloria *(Hurt.)* Mama, look me in the eye. I am your daughter, Gloria. I love you; I love you very much. I'm very happy you came to see me. I waited a long time for the privilege of being alone with you. *(Gloria takes her mother's hand but her mother is agitated by the physical contact.)*

Substitute Mother All this touching makes me nervous. Can you avoid it? So you've wanted to be alone with me. Why?

Gloria *(Affectionately taking her mother's hands. The Substitute Mother stiffens but tries not to yank her hands away.)* I wanted to tell you that I love you very much. *(Her eyes fill with tears.)* It's important to me that you know that. I love you.

Substitute Mother O. K. now I know. I know that you love me, Maria. *(She takes her hands away moves away from her daughter.)*

Gloria Don't call me Maria! Maria is my sister. I'm Gloria, Mama.

Substitute Mother I know that. There's no doubt in my mind you're not Maria. Maria would have never sat me down on a chair to tell me all this foolishness. *(Sarcastic and cruel)* "I love you mamita and it's important to me that you know that, etc., etc., etc.," Maria would never hold my hands. Never! She knows that I don't think all that touching is hygienic. *(Standing up)* Maria would never kiss me that way. Is there anything less elegant than pursing your lips and pressing them upon the person next to you, and making that disagreeable sound? *(She makes a kissing sound.)* Give me back the perfume. I'm giving it to Guillermo. I promise to get it right when I visit you next year.

Gloria *(Giving back the perfume)* Mama, this is the first time you've remembered to bring me a birthday gift, and you got it wrong. You always get it wrong. You always give me the gifts intended for Guillermo. And you give him the gifts for Maria, and Maria the gifts for Genoveva.

Substitute Mother *(Amused)* I do that? How amusing! I find my distractions charming.

Gloria Mama, I changed all the colors in the house especially for you. At least look at my home since you can't look at me.

Substitute Mother *(Without looking)* The place looks great, Maria.

Gloria Gloria.

Substitute Mother The place looks glorious, Maria.

Gloria No, no, no! *(Getting out of character and demanding as the client.)* I told you twenty times that my name is Gloria. I don't mean to be harsh with you, but more than being cold, you seem to have amnesia!

Substitute Mother I have emotional amnesia! I don't know whom I love.

Gloria Then you don't know if you love me?

Substitute Mother Me? Love you? I love you?

Gloria Excellent! Well, you've done it. I've never felt worse.

COLD
MOTHER
WHO CAN'T
REMEMBER
YOUR
NAME.

Substitute Mother Isn't that what you wanted?

Gloria Yes, yes. Thank you. I've never felt so good feeling so bad.

Substitute Mother Did you feel like the daughter of a cold-hearted woman?

Gloria I felt that you were cruel, cold, evil.

Substitute Mother I can be a lot more evil. One must have a certain grandeur to be evil and I have what it takes. *(She takes her belt and uses it like a whip.)* I love playing demonic mothers.

Gloria It was enough for me. I don't need any more cruelty.

Substitute Mother Too bad you don't want to get to the depth of evil. I love the sadistic mother.

Gloria Enough!

Substitute Mother Have you reached the point of desperation you wanted?

Gloria Now you're supposed to criticize me for not having been "glorious" enough.

Substitute Mother Oh, this part's for another mother. *(The Substitute Mother exits. We can hear Neapolitan music. The set is humble, with a rope to hang wash and a terrace that makes it look like an Italian immigrant slum. Gloria adapts to the scene by putting a pillow under her skirt so that she looks pregnant. She changes her demeanor to one of a poor pregnant girl from the slums with a mother that humiliates her. The Substitute Mother enters with wash and starts to hang it on the line. Gloria helps her. The Substitute Mother speaks with an Italian accent.)* I should've named you Mabelita. That's the way your father wanted it. But I named you Gloria. That name has brought you bad luck. No one in this neighborhood is named Gloria. Gloria is the name of someone refined, successful. Look how successful you are! I curse the day that I named you Gloria!

Gloria I curse it too. You cursed me with the name of failure.

Substitute Mother You could have married that diplomat, the one you met at your upper-class friend's house! Today you would have been "in your glory." But you had to have the runt. All he's given you are children, he doesn't work, and you're all constantly asking me for money. A runt! What did you see in him?

Gloria He was the only one who ever said, "Gloria, you are so glorious." We were swimming and I saw those muscular legs. My God, he looked good! And when he dove into the cold water, oh my God. And when he dried himself off, so slow. Mama, I was his forever.

Substitute Mother And here you are, loaded with kids. He doesn't even look at you, and spends his time complaining that I don't give him enough money for the horses.

Gloria Every time I ask you for money, all you do is tell me about my failures.

Substitute Mother *(Takes out money from her bra.)* Here's another $500. But don't you dare spend it on him. You better spend it on my grandchildren.

Gloria *(Puts it in her bra.)* Thanks, Mama... I can't work 'til I have this baby. I feel so alone.

Substitute Mother But you keep on havin' kids with that runt.

Gloria It's just that he still tells me "Gloria, you are so glorious." I'm a goner. How can a man make you so crazy?

Substitute Mother A man? Make me crazy? Me? *(Crosses herself.)* Everyone knows your father never saw me naked. He always left my shirt on when we "did the dirty deed." And we did it because of him. Not because I liked it, the way you do. My God! Losing a diplomat because of that Runt!

Gloria *(The demanding client)* You're treating me like an idiot.

Substitute Mother In your plan you ordered a poor, domineering mother who criticizes you. Now that you have her, you're complaining?

Gloria The mother is great. What doesn't fit in your scenario is the social-economic status. Where could I have met a diplomat? The neighborhood is low class. What diplomat would come to a neighborhood of Sicilian immigrants looking for a girlfriend?

Substitute Mother I said you met him at an upper-class friend's house.

Gloria O.K., but I want you to continue dwelling on how sorry you are for giving me the name Gloria.

(The Substitute Mother goes back into the Italian mother's character.)

Substitute Mother I curse the day that I named you Gloria. You liked to write and now you sell candies. You could've dated a diplomat, but you married that runt. You wanted to be beautiful, but you're crossed-eyed and have bow-legs.

Gloria You're the one with bow-legs. Look how your slippers drag!!!

Substitute Mother You got the legs from me. But those eyes that look like scrambled eggs you got from your father. You inherited the worst from us both.

Gloria Today is my birthday, Mama. How can you treat me like this?

Substitute Mother *(Stops the scene.)* You paid me to treat you like this!

Gloria I was talking to my mother. I wasn't questioning your professionalism.

Substitute Mother Oh, okay. Let's continue. Concentrate. *(Immediately returns to character.)*

Gloria I was playing the scene well. Why did you stop it?

Substitute Mother Your birthday! The day I gave birth to you was the worst day of my life!

Gloria *(She interrupts, the words spilling out quickly.)* I didn't pay you to tell me that! Look over the contract. Today really IS my birthday, Madam. I'm giving myself a MaTRIX service. You're my birthday present to myself.

Substitute Mother A present? Me, a present? *(Appalled with the idea of being a gift object.)* Let's do another mother. This one's lower back hurts. *(The Substitute Mother exits with the rest of the laundry. The clothesline disappears from the scene. Gloria removes the pillow from underneath her skirt. She puts on a raincoat, takes an umbrella and opens it. She picks up some books and puts on glasses to look like an intellectual. She adapts her character to the changes. The lights are changed to give a sensation of a train station. Off-stage we can hear the mother. She's an "Idische Mame," a typical Jewish mother with a Russian accent. Gloria closes the umbrella, takes out a letter and finds a corner in the train station. She reads the letter. Gloria does not see the Substitute Mother make her entrance.)*

Gloria *(Reading aloud)* My darling little girl: It's been so long since I've heard anything from you. But now I don't have to make you feel guilty about my need to see you. This is the last letter I'll write before we see each other. Well, tomorrow I'll arrive at the City. I beg you to meet me at the station. I know that this will cause you trouble but I have something very important to tell you, and I'd rather tell you personally. I will be arriving on the 9:00 p.m. train. Adoringly, Your Mother. *(We can hear the sound of a train arriving. Behind Gloria the mother enters in a wheel chair, every part of her body wrapped in a cast, except part of her face. When Gloria finally sees her she's shocked. She throws down her books and letters and runs to her mother. She hugs her mother's knees.)* Mama! Mama! What happened to you? Oh, Mama!

Substitute Mother *(Lifts her face so Gloria can kiss the only little un-bandaged spot.)* Nothing much. How are your studies?

Gloria *(Extremely upset)* Why didn't anyone tell me about this?

Substitute Mother Stand up. Stand up, *shatzele*, I can't see you if you're kneeling. I brought you some bagels. *(She hands her the bag of food the best way she can.)* I didn't make them this time, aunt Sarah did. They're not as good as mine are but they'll do. *(Gloria opens the package and* *eats.)* See? See? You're starving. Even Sarah's bagels are good when you're starving!

Gloria They're delicious. Did you have an accident?

Substitute Mother Who really cares about what happens to me?

Gloria I do, of course!

Substitute Mother Let's not talk about me. It was a small insignificant fall. Let's talk about something interesting. Let's talk about ontology.

Gloria A small insignificant fall?! Mama, you broke every bone in your body! I want to know how this disaster happened!

Substitute Mother Working.

Gloria In the candy shop!?

Substitute Mother Oh that place closed. I had to get another job to be able to send you money.

Gloria Mama, what kind of job did you get?

Substitute Mother Cleaning windows in an office building. No one wants that kind of work. But I loved it, hanging on the scaffold, in the open air, touching the sky with my hands. I had the wonderful feeling like I was flying. I fell from the third floor. It's not important. I did it for your doctorate in ontology! As I cleaned, I thought of you being a doctor of ontology thanks to my cleaning. My Gloria, a doctor of ontology.

Gloria Since when do you clean the windows of skyscrapers?

Substitute Mother I knew you'd be upset! That's why I didn't want to tell you!

Gloria Since when have you been endangering your life this way?

Substitute Mother About five years ago. I did it all for your studies. It's not important.

Gloria Cleaning the windows of skyscrapers so I could study? I don't want you to do things like that for me... Mama, I don't want you to send me another cent. You're too good. You're a much better person than I am.

Substitute Mother Oh, let me help you. Gloria, I can lick stamps at the post office. I didn't break my tongue. *(She sticks out her tongue.)* They don't pay much for stamp lickers, but it's better than nothing. *(She takes out a little bag with money.)* I've put together a little money for you, Gloria. It's not much, but the idea that I could help you is enough for me. Don't waste it. A mother in a full body cast that works with her tongue deserves your compassion.

(Gloria accepts the money full of emotion. She kneels and kisses her mothers hands that are in a cast. She leans her head on her mother's lap. The mother sings a popular and well-known Yiddish lullaby. Gloria sings

The
guilt-producing
jewish
mother

along.)

Gloria Mama, I feel so guilty. It's horrible, I feel like I pushed you to the edge.

Substitute Mother Don't worry. It's my pleasure.

Gloria How can I not worry? *(Looks at her, full of guilt.)* Look at you. It's all my fault. I feel guilty, guilty, guilty! Guilty for being born. Guilty for living. *(She starts pushing her mother's wheel chair. The Substitute Mother decides the scene is over. She jumps from the wheel chair. Walks around in full cast.)*

Substitute Mother That was good, as always. The Yiddish mother is one of my best acts. It's very effective. Every time someone wants guilt I perform with great success. Very effective. Look how I've left you! Or are you going to tell me that you didn't feel terribly guilty.

Gloria Terribly guilty.

(The Substitute Mother removes the cast with high energy.)

Substitute Mother Can you help me get the cast off my head?

Gloria That was a guilt trip with no way out.

Substitute Mother Oh, no the "guilt trip with no way out." is coming. You ordered your mother's death, right?

Gloria You can skip this one, if you want.

Substitute Mother Oh no. I love this role. *(She puts on a black scary robe and white makeup. Gloria changes into mourning clothes. She starts to cry.)* It's a sudden death.

Gloria Completely sudden. I need the shock.

(The Substitute Mother prepares her. She suddenly dies holding flowers in her hands. A crucifix appears over the bed. The lights change to whiter hues. Funeral music comes up. Gloria is left alone with the deceased mother. Speaking through a torrent of tears.) Mama, how beautiful you are. Death becomes you. I've always wanted to be the mature one of the two, the more peaceful one. Mama, how I always loved to walk in the rain with you, hand in hand. How I loved your company in the country, riding horseback. Although we always ended up fighting. They weren't deep fights. Isn't that true, Mama? Mama, I never told you... I never told you... I never told you that I loved you. I was never able to kiss you. *(She kisses her.)* I never hugged you and never let you hug me. *(She kisses her again.)* Never, never, never. How could I do that to you? *(She cries disconsolately.)* Answer me. Tell me that you loved me anyway. Let me hear your voice again. Say something. For God's sake! Open your eyes. *(She shakes her vigorously as if she had only fainted instead of being dead.)* Tell me that there's still time, Mama! All I ask is for a little time! Tell me

that we have time! Time! I only ask you for a little time! Mama! Give me more time!

Substitute Mother *(She opens her eyes. She sits up.)* Time for what?

Gloria The dead don't speak, Lady!

Substitute Mother But you keep badgering me with questions, my dear.

Gloria The dead can't answer questions! Now you've profaned the most sacred. You ruined the death of the mother. Everything was going so great! I was experiencing so much emotion that I was falling into the abyss. I had entered my own tragic dimension. You have absolutely no consideration for my deepest feelings! You trivialize everything!

Substitute Mother Look, we've spent a lot of time on the dead mother. Other mothers are waiting, and they're much more entertaining.

Gloria The person that should be entertained here is me. And since this type of entertainment is so expensive, you should fulfill my wishes. Please go back to sleep.

(The Substitute Mother lies back; against her wishes.)

Substitute Mother I'm going to play dead again but don't bombard me with questions.

Gloria Unanswered questions allow us to cross over to the other side. To feel all alone. I'm not asking questions that can be answered. *(The Substitute Mother plays dead. Gloria goes back to her crying.)* Mama... Mama, I need to tell you that... that... *(She stops.)* I have nothing to say. The interruption ruined it!

Substitute Mother Finally. *(She takes off the morbid clothing.)* We experienced death now we must celebrate life. Happy Birthday, Gloria!

(The Substitute Mother exits. A table prepared for a birthday party with treats, candies, and hors d'oeuvres appears. There is a cake with 30 candles. Balloons and a banner that reads "Happy Birthday Gloria" create an atmosphere is very festive in contrast to the earlier one. Gloria puts on a beautiful party dress, very festive. The Mother rings the doorbell. Gloria opens the door with an enormous smile. The Substitute Mother enters she is wearing a polka dot dress, very loud and carrying a birthday gift for Gloria, decorated with big red bow.)

> Happy Birthday to you!
> Happy Birthday to you!
> Happy Birthday, my beautiful Gloria!
> Happy birthday to you!

Gloria Happy Birthday to me! *(Gloria opens her gift and it's a dress identical to the Substitute Mother's.)* Mama, it's beautiful! *(She puts it up against her dress.)* We look like twins! *(They hug. Gloria gets a keyboard* *and they play it together. They sing a love song. Gloria stops and watches her mother sing.)* Mama, it makes me so happy to hear you sing.

Substitute Mother *(Happy with herself.)* I can just imagine!

Gloria Oh, no you don't. I did not pay you to praise yourself!

Substitute Mother I just imagined that you adore me!

Gloria But at the same time, you were praising your own performance. You should never have said, "I can just imagine" when I told you that it made me so happy to hear you sing!

Substitute Mother *(Resolves the problem.)* I'll change my response. Say the line again.

Gloria *(She accepts the solution and returns to the performance.)* Mama, it makes me so happy to hear you sing.

Substitute Mother Gloria, you're the best thing that's ever happened to me!

Gloria *(Stops the scene again.)* You already told me that, and you said it much better before.

Substitute Mother *(Trying not to lose her patience)* Gloria, giving birth to you gave meaning to my life?

Gloria I can just imagine.

Substitute Mother You can't say that either. A daughter feels that her birth has ruined her mother's life!

Gloria Not with a mother like this one! I paid this mother in order to give meaning to my life. It's a little luxury that I want to give myself.

Substitute Mother *(Returns to the charming mother.)* Gloria, light of my life, giving birth to you gave my ephemeral life meaning.

Gloria Your tone is distant, sarcastic; it has a professional ring to it. You're supposed to make me forget that you're doing this for money. Phrase your sentences better, more specific.

Substitute Mother Gloria, you're absolutely irreplaceable.

Gloria Mama, am I really irreplaceable?

Substitute Mother *(Upset about her career as a Substitute Mother.)* Irreplaceable! Not like me, a Substitute Mother. I am absolutely replaceable! *(An awkward pause, the Substitute Mother recovers herself. She hugs Gloria again.)* I'm sorry. *(Back in character again.)* Yes, my love, you are irreplaceable, unique, original; and above all, you are a great person.

Gloria Repeat that! It cost me a lot.

Substitute Mother You're the best person I've ever met in my life.

Gloria Enough! Now I don't even believe it. *(She moves away from her side.)* You do everything a little too excessively, so it's hard to believe.

Substitute Mother We are instructed to do that. Make it extra special. Otherwise no one would contract a Substitute Mother. The client would stick to her own mother. We cannot, we must not try to be like the real mothers of our clients.

Gloria Well then, I can't get what I really need out of you.

Substitute Mother Perhaps the program of mothers that you selected is not adequate, or perhaps I'm not the type who suits your needs.

Gloria *(Regretting what has just happened)* Let's not waste time! Straighten up this room. Get everything in order! Let's not dwell on the past and let's try to save this relationship!

Substitute Mother *(Very tough, consults the plan, furious.)* Everyone, absolutely everyone wants to see me in the most menial state of servitude. I'll never get away from having to clean the house! Frankly, this job of being a Substitute Mother has some degrading stipulations! And we've discussed this in the union meetings. *(Gloria folds her arms. The Substitute mother puts on a disheveled wig with a polka dot handkerchief. She puts on a black dress, black stockings, and slippers. Takes out a duster, broom, and other cleaning supplies out her suitcase. A tango begins to play. The Substitute Mother cleans up the stage in silence. Meanwhile Gloria is brushing her hair in front of a mirror.)* You're going out again with that lowlife?

Gloria Mama, mind your business.

Substitute Mother *(The Substitute Mother is sweeping.)* You're all I have left. My oldest son had to run away because of fraud. Your sister, Beatriz, ran away with a guerrilla fighter in the middle of a military dictatorship! They wouldn't even let me keep a picture so I can mourn her absence. And you…

Gloria Did you iron my fuscia dress? *(The mother solicitously brings her the dress impeccably ironed.)* Didn't I tell you to hurry?

Substitute Mother *(Cowed)* It's just that it looks so much more elegant ironed.

Gloria *(Yells at her.)* I want to look sexy, not elegant, Mama. *(She crumples the dress.)* Mama, you get on my nerves. *(She messes up the bed, the Substitute Mother immediately makes it again.)* Why do you make the bed? Marcelo likes to fuck in an unmade bed. *(Gloria empties out a chest of drawer and throws the clothes all over the floor. In slow motion the Substitute Mother puts everything back in order.)*

Gloria *(Ferociously)* He ran away with your sister, Mama!

Substitute Mother My little baby. Are you eating right? What's wrong? Is there something wrong? *(Lamenting)* If only your father hadn't run out

the back door.

Substitute Mother Well, good. My sister has always been more attractive than me. *(Gloria puts on a pair of tight pants and a revealing tank top. The Substitute mother is very preoccupied.)* You can't go out into the street like that.

Gloria I'll go out any way I like! Or do you want me to dress like you, a cleaning lady? *(The Substitute Mother begins to make the bed again. Gloria pours herself a shot of whisky.)*

Substitute Mother *(Timidly, in a small voice)* Are you drinking again? You told me that you quit.

Gloria *(Confronts her.)* I lied to get you off my back. I enjoy lying to you, you old bag. It's a treat to see you believe all the stories. I'm, I'm pregnant, Mama.

Substitute Mother *(In tears)* My precious little girl, sit down. Don't over exert yourself. And how many months along are you?

Gloria Three.

Substitute Mother But, he's a married man!   How could he do this?

Gloria I don't know if he's the one. I don't know whose child this is.

Substitute Mother So, you've been sleeping with more than one man? *(Trembling)*

Gloria *(Stopping the scene)* It is obvious, Madam that if I say I don't know whom the father is, it's because I am sleeping with more than one man. Anyway you promised to suffer.

Substitute Mother *(Professional)* I'm suffering enormously. Do you want me to show it more?

Gloria Of course I do. It's my birthday. What better present from a mother than to show all her suffering? *(The Substitute Mother begins to cry very loudly. Gloria puts on a hard rock to cover up the sound of her crying.)* I can't stand your crying, Mama. Why the hell are you crying? The one who's screwed up here is me. Why don't you help me find solutions instead of filling my sheets with tears? You made me this way, Mama. Now, deal with this thirty-year old baby who can't seem to grow out of her adolescence and continues to depend on her mother. *(The Substitute Mother cries copiously with real tears. Then she interrupts her act.)*

Substitute Mother *(In a highly professional tone)* You just come over here, missy. *(Gloria approaches her.)* These are real tears. Touch. *(Gloria touches them and tastes them.)* You could not ask for a more tragic effect. I am the suffering Mother par excellence. Dressed in black, cleaning, crying, with an alcoholic, pregnant daughter. I'm the "Greatest Suffering

Mother." I'm the mother the tangos are written about.   Literature has dedicated itself to me.   I'm a biblical mother: "You shall deliver with pain." I am the sainted mother. Look at my tears!

Gloria I know you know this type of mother very well!

Substitute Mother She's in high demand by the clients in MaTRIX. Everyone wants to be a rebellious child! To rebel against such a submissive mother is very easy. *(She speaks defiantly.)* I dare you to rebel against an emancipated mother! Or against a famous intellectual! Or simply against an international diva. *(She turns her suitcase up side down.)* I have everything I need for her. These types of mothers are rarely chosen. Everyone wants the easy route, denigrating. Everyone enjoys seeing me cry, because they feel free, rebellious, young. But no one likes to see me smile. Who pays to see me enjoy myself? No one hires a mother that has a good time. I dare you to rebel against a mother who enjoys life!

(The Substitute Mother exits. The stage is transformed into a playwright's studio. There are books, paintings, a computer, and loose papers. The Substitute Mother enters; she's got keys to the door. She takes off her black dress and she transforms into a cultured woman, one that has traveled, and leads an exciting and divine life. She walks like a model, with rhythm. She's quick with everything, and has great taste and lots of class. Gloria does not change.)

Substitute Mother *(She bursts out.)* That wild style looks fantastic on you. Very chic. Did you have an abortion, or are you going to have the child?

Gloria I lost it. Don't worry, you're not going to be a grandmother. You've just had a face-lift, and the last thing you need is a grandchild.

Substitute Mother You knew from the start that it was a bad move. Anyway, I'm dating a guy who's pretty young. You and I, well… We hate the norm.

Gloria Mama, don't decide for me what I hate.

Substitute Mother Do you have any whisky in this underground lair of yours? *(Gloria gives her some.)* This is the fourth one I've had this morning. This day is a goner. You're going to drink with me, aren't you, my love? You're not going to let me drink by myself? It's been so long since we've seen each other. *(Gloria serves herself and they drink.)* Did you finish your play?

Gloria Which one?

Substitute Mother The one with me as the lead character. How well you recreated me. The scenes that you sent to my office in New York made me fall over laughing. You have me down to a "t". Despotic, malevolent, fascinating, divine. You even had the character wear this capelina and this zorro. Since I read it in your play I don't take them off, even when I travel on an airplane. I find it so theatrical. It gives me new found energy. In the play you had doubts that I was your real mother? Has anyone tried to confuse you, sweetheart?

Gloria Yes, I finished. They're rehearsing it now.

Substitute Mother They couldn't wait. How incredibly exciting! Of course with that fabulous lead character! And who's playing me?

Gloria Glenn Close.

Substitute Mother A wonderful actress. But she's not really the type. What I'm trying to say is, with all due respect, I could show her a few tricks to make her seem more like me. I'm not suggesting that she try to recreate me exactly, because that would be impossible. I think she should reinvent me. But there are certain aspects of my personality…

Gloria I imagine between the actress and the director they will know how to bring the character to life!

Substitute Mother But, the character knows best how to be portrayed! *(She interrupts the scene.)* You're not rebellious enough! Didn't we agree that you were going to rebel? That was the challenge. Come on!

Gloria *(Fed up)* I'm the one who makes the demands. You seem to forget that you are mine. You're very expensive to rent. I paid a lot of money for all your splendor. But you can do better.

Substitute Mother I'm holding you spellbound, darling.

Gloria *(Returning to her role)* You never told me about the adoption.

Substitute Mother This is one of your father's delusions. Tell my ex-husband to stop running all over my favorite spots in New York with fifteen-year-olds, and tell him to admit how passionate and in love we were when we conceived you. Gloria, my love, isn't today your birthday?

Gloria Mama, I'm thirty years old today.

Substitute Mother So much time has passed. You make me feel so old. Can you see your thirty years on me? I don't know what to have lifted next. And you, have you had any "nips and tucks?"

Gloria Do you think I need it? Do I look wrinkled?

Substitute Mother This is the age where they begin to show up. It's a dangerous age. Besides, as a successful playwright, with her picture on the pages of magazines next to young actresses.

Gloria Do you really think so? *(She looks at herself in the mirror.)*

Substitute Mother *(Stops the scene.)* Where's the rebellion? You're at the point of accepting plastic surgery when you have perfect skin!

Gloria Mama, I can't rebel against you! I can't do anything but watch you

pace around like an idiot. Is that why I like women?

Substitute Mother What do you mean, you like women?

Gloria I go to bed with men, but I fall in love with women.

Substitute Mother I can tell that you're wondering what it's like to caress a woman's body. I can see that you're tempted.

Gloria Mama, I'm involved in a passionate relationship now. I already took that leap.

Substitute Mother Splendid. I think it's fantastic that you assumed that responsibility. Down with hypocrisy! And who is the object of your great passion, my daughter?

Gloria Your friend, Lourdes.

Substitute Mother Lourdes! God, help me! How could Lourdes do that to us? She's so moral.

Gloria We both had to rebel against you, Mother. *(She breaks up laughing. She stops the play.)* Did you see how rebellious I was? Did you see how I shit on you, my dear lady?

Substitute Mother I have to admit that the relationship with that Lourdes was ingenious.

Gloria Mama, can I get you some whiskey?

Substitute Mother I don't know. You always have such bad whiskey.

Gloria Lourdes gave it to me.

Substitute Mother Boy, she can't do anything original, can she?

Gloria Has she given you the same whiskey?

Substitute Mother The same whiskey under the same circumstances. She was the first woman in my life. Lourdes is mesmerizing. At least she knew how to get us both.

Gloria *(Furious, she stops the game.)* This is going too far. I didn't pay you to have a past with Lourdes.

Substitute Mother Rebel! I'm not the little mother who takes all the abuse. I don't suffer, dear. How can you rebel against a mother who doesn't suffer?

Gloria You came here to satisfy my whims.

Substitute Mother This is the way this kind of mother satisfies your whims. You're not going to leave me for a loser, sleeping with my best friend!

Gloria And you can't tell me on my birthday that the great love of my life is also your lover. That seems excessive to me.

Substitute Mother I told you that we are trained to be excessive.

Gloria I'm going to kill Lourdes, Mama. *(She puts on Bach's "Magnificat.")*

Substitute Mother Oh no. Write! You can elaborate in your writing. A passionate triangle. If you kill her in your fiction it will alleviate all your anger. One question. Did she give you that top?

Gloria The tanktop, the pants, the paint for this room, and Bach's "Magnificat."

Substitute Mother Bach's "Magnificat" too? Turn it off.

(Gloria holds the conductor's baton and directs an imaginary orchestra.)

Gloria How jealous we are. Now, you're the one who's jealous, Mama. *(She laughs. The Substitute Mother takes away the baton and breaks the record.)*

Substitute Mother This is why you paid MaTRIX, Inc. such a high price. So that you can win some of the games. I have left you guilt free. In the end...this is part of the satisfaction that MaTRIX offers our clients.

Gloria Are you going to breast feed me?

Substitute Mother Not with these clothes, I'm not.

(She puts on a white slip and an enormous round nipple. She sits down and Gloria happily climbs up on her lap. The Substitute Mother takes out the breast full of cream and Gloria sucks on the nipple while a sweet lullaby begins to play.)

Gloria Hummmmmmmmmmmm, humm, hummm.

(The Substitute Mother squeezes the breast and a white stream resembling shaving cream begins to come out completely covering Gloria, who, covered with cream, clings to the mother's neck.)

Gloria This is a finale worthy of an opera. I'm going to hire you next week. *(The Substitute Mother stands up. She takes the breast and puts it away. She dresses herself in the outfit she was wearing at the beginning of the play. Gloria continues to take cream and put it in her mouth with her finger. The Substitute Mother packs her costumes and equipment in her bags.)* I don't want to hear any details. I hate details when I'm being abandoned. Abandon me with all you've got. Leave me destroyed. You could do the mother you should've done from the beginning.

Substitute Mother The one who called you Maria?

Gloria *(Approaches her, begging.)* Mama, aren't you going to give me a kiss?

Substitute Mother You're full of.... you're all spotted with...I'm wearing a Christian Dior suit. *(She looks at Gloria with disgust).*

Gloria I thought it was Chanel.

Substitute Mother Your mistakes are boring me.

Gloria *(Cleaning her self off to please her mother)* What else?

Substitute Mother Your meticulousness.

Gloria Why did you come here, Mama?

Substitute Mother To get the thousand dollars that I lent you.

Gloria I owe you seven hundred dollars. Look at the bill from MaTRIX.

Substitute Mother Breast-feeding is a separate charge. Also, cleaning the room is separate. Look, it's in the contract.

(She shows her the contract. Gloria looks at it. She takes money from a box and gives it to the Substitute Mother.)

Gloria Now we don't owe each other anything.

Substitute Mother I prefer not to see you for a while. You are a very… A very demanding daughter. That's the truth.

Gloria *(Stopping the scene)* If I choose you next week and I pay, you'll have to come back.

Substitute Mother With what money?

Gloria I'll borrow it. There's a series of mothers that I'm interested in your doing for me.

Substitute Mother My vacation is coming up next week. There's going to be someone else. I highly recommend Anita Zavala. She's very versatile and she's fat. That adds an unusual twist.

Gloria But I, I love you. I mean, I don't love you.

Substitute Mother I don't love you either. Here all sentiments are left aside. We leave our feelings on the side. That's why you have your real mother. You do have a real mother?

Gloria Yes. Of course.

Substitute Mother And which mother was closest to yours?

Gloria Why do you care?

Substitute Mother That gave me a flash of real jealousy. That shouldn't happen to me. Goodbye, Gloria. *(She extends her hand.)*

Gloria Do you have children?

Substitute Mother We substitute mothers never answer real questions. That limits one's imagination. Come back to MaTRIX any time you need to.

Gloria *(Takes out her money and gives the mother an extra hundred dollars.)* You deserve a tip, ma'am.

Substitute Mother I deserve royal fees, my dear. We don't accept tips.

(She throws the money down, picks up her bag and leaves.)

Gloria *(Left alone on stage she shouts.)* Mamaaaaaaaaaaa!!!

The End

REAR ENTRY

Translated by Victoria Martinez in collaboration with Lidia Ramirez

Characters

Simon Goldberg: *57 years old. Industrialist. Owner of a plumbing supplies factory (tubs, toilets, bidets, etc.). Widowed and married to Luna for eight years.*
Luna Mantovani: *35 years old. Simon's second wife. Ex-actress.*
Mariana Goldberg: *35 years old. Simon's daughter, close friend of Luna.*
Gregorio Murray: *37 years old. Married to Mariana for six years. Has been working for Simon since then.*
Dolly Goldberg: *30 years old. Simon's daughter. Multi-millionaire; businesswoman. Transsexual. Formerly* **Javier Goldberg.**
Paco Frias, *35 years old. Psychoanalyst. Dolly's husband.*
Moving men and servants in non-speaking roles.

Setting

A hot day in Buenos Aires. It is December close to the New Year. The set is a combined living-dining room in Simon and Luna's apartment. As the curtain rises two moving men are removing expensive paintings, elegant furniture, electrical appliances, etc. The apartment is nearly empty. One of the moving men is carrying out a silver menorah.

ACT ONE

Scene 1

Simon No! Not Grandmother Rebecca's menorah! You can't have any part of her! *(He and the moving man struggle over the menorah. Finally the moving man releases it. Simon hugs the menorah.)*

Luna Simon, they've taken much more valuable things!

Simon Depends on what you call valuable! They can't take my grandmother's menorah! It means the world to me!

(Luna laughs anxiously watching Simon's reaction as the men take everything away. The men pick up two of Simon's golf trophies.)

Simon Listen Mister, I won those playing golf! I don't think they're of any value!

(Luna starts to cry, lost between Simon's childlike behavior and the general stripping of everything she owns.)

Luna This must be a nightmare. I have to wake up! My God! This really can't be happening! *(The men, indifferent, continue moving things out. Finally, the apartment is empty, except for the chairs in which Simon and Luna are seated. The movers give them a paper to sign and they leave. Luna and Simon remain in their chairs, Simon clutching the menorah.)* Everything! They've taken everything! *(She begins to walk around the empty space, totally disheartened.)* How did you let this happen? How come I didn't see this coming? How?

(They walk back and forth in an attempt to come to grips with their total loss. Simon still clutching the menorah.)

Simon I don't understand, something went wrong. I must have done something wrong. Maybe I'm too old. Maybe I'm worthless. I've never been poor, Luna. Now I have nothing. Nothing. Now I can see it from the other side. My grandmother came to Argentina with nothing but this menorah. And now I'm back to square one. I've lost everything.

Luna Well, I was poor once, Simon; and, frankly, the other side is a pretty dreary place.

Simon *(With a philosophical look.)* Dreary...yes...dreary is a good adjective. But it's not only that, it's also lonely. Look at this empty apartment. There's no atmosphere. Isn't the...the atmosphere miserable?

Luna Well, I'd use a less sophisticated word. As far as I'm concerned, the atmosphere is shitty! If we can even call it an atmosphere!

Simon Sure it has atmosphere! The creditors can't take that away! *(Defiantly)* Actually, my love, the more things the creditors take away, the more atmosphere they leave behind!

Luna I married the owner of the country's biggest plumbing supply factory, not the owner of the most miserable atmosphere on the planet!

Simon Well, a catastrophe can change a person. I once produced plumbing supplies, and now I am a philosopher of misery who has discovered that he's the owner of this magnificent atmosphere!!! If my wife could see me now, she wouldn't believe it. She always lived in luxury. Trips, jewels, furs, chauffeur. My wife had everything!

Luna I'm your wife!

Simon I'm referring to Dorita, may she rest in peace. She always lived like a queen. But so have you, since you married me. Could you ever imagine us this way?

Luna No I couldn't, and I never expected this. As a matter of fact when you told me that nothing was selling and that things were in bad shape, I thought you were just kvetching. You didn't sound serious.

Simon I didn't want to worry you, Luna. I thought that Gregorio and I could stop the disaster, but the problems got worse. And now all we have is nothingness.

Luna Don't tell me this experience of going broke is an existential one?

Simon *(Calmly)* I'm telling you that I think I'm having a heart attack.

Luna *(Furious)* A heart attack? You ruined the business, you lost everything that we had, and now to top it off you're going to have a heart attack?

Simon It appears so, my love. *(Inspecting himself for symptoms)* Tell me: do heart attacks start with a tingling tongue?

Luna No, that's an abscess.

Simon Do heart attacks make your jaw stiff?

Luna Listen to me, Simon: where is your heart? In the roof of your mouth?

Simon *(Touching the roof of his mouth.)* It's possible. It's very possible to have your heart in the roof of your mouth. *(He falls to the floor.)*

Luna Listen, you can't die like this! Come on, Simon. This is not a heart attack. Wake up! *(She approaches him and helps him sit up.)*

Simon *(Wistfully)* What do I have to do to have a heart attack, Luna?

Luna What you've done to the business should do it. Except, your heart seems to be pretty strong!

(He stands up.)

Simon Alright, if I'm not going to die, then I better live. I'm ruined, but I still have you. We still have each other, and that's what counts! *(Trying to cheer Luna)* Luna, I love you! We still have our whole lives ahead of us. We can start again from zero! *(He takes her hand and walks her around the empty space.)*

Luna From zero? We're starting from less than zero, because we're in debt! I don't have the strength or desire to start from scratch. I married a powerful man!

Simon *(Clutching his stomach.)* I'm scared. The movers didn't take the toilet, did they? *(He runs to the bathroom. Luna walks around the empty stage.)*

Luna   Why didn't they take me, along with everything else? *(The doorbell rings. She goes to open it. It's Mariana and Gregorio.)* Come in, come in! Make yourselves comfortable!

(Mariana and Gregorio stand frozen in astonishment at the totally empty apartment. For a moment they can't say a word.)

Gregorio   This is unbelievable. I never thought they would do this.

Luna   Well, they did.

(Luna and Mariana embrace.)

Mariana   Couldn't you stop them?

Luna   No! The more I begged them not to take a painting I loved or my CD collection, the more pleasure they got.

Gregorio   What a bunch of leeches! They took everything! I've never seen anything like it!

Mariana   And the piano? My piano?!

Luna   Oh, they loved that! A grand piano, so elegant, with such good sound. I'm sure it was a pleasure to get a hold of that!

Gregorio   *(He walks over to Luna and hugs her.)* Luna, you're both strong, healthy, you have your entire lives ahead of you! They can't destroy Simon so easily. This is just a setback. *(Pulling her against him)*

Luna   Mariana. Can you get your husband off of me? I can't stand snide sarcasm, or idiotic optimism, unless he's got 200,000 dollars.

Gregorio   And where do you think I'm going to come up with 200,000 dollars?

(Mariana looks at Gregorio, annoyed.)

Mariana   Luna, don't worry. We can give you something! We'll give you something to get over this hurdle! You can count on us.

Gregorio   Mariana! Can we talk?

Mariana   *(Giving him a furious look)* Gregorio.

Gregorio   I'm only asking you to consult me first!

Mariana   *(To Luna)* Look, all these years that Gregorio has been working for Papi we've been saving money for a house, but we can give you some.

Gregorio   *(Pale)* Some what?

Mariana   *(She'd like to kill him.)* Don't act stupid Gregorio, especially under these circumstances!

Gregorio   Some what?!

Mariana   I'm not going to let my father and Luna, who have always helped us, live in poverty!

Gregorio You're being unrealistic.

Mariana And you're being ungrateful!

Gregorio Ungrateful? Me? You wouldn't dare say that in front of your father. Where is Simon?

Luna On the toilet. The last Goldberg toilet we have left! He's in a state of grace, meditating. And me, alone.

Mariana You're not alone, Luna.

(Luna hugs Mariana. The women are emotional and Gregorio is furious.)

Luna Mariana, I knew that you wouldn't fail me!

Mariana I love you. And we've always counted on you guys. Papi gave Gregorio work and that helped us get ahead. Now it's our turn to help. *(She pauses. She has difficulty broaching the topic.)* But there's also my brother Javier. We all know that he's very well off.

Gregorio *(Astounded)* Javier?

Mariana Yes, my brother. My only brother. We're on the brink of disaster, so this is no time to be judgmental! Enough with grudges! I'm saying this from the bottom of my heart. Why don't we call him and ask him for help?

Gregorio I hear what you're saying, but I can't believe my ears. Help from your brother Javier! That's the worst thing you could do to your father, and you know it! I'd like to know how you have the guts to confront him after everything that happened. *(Peevish)* Boy, desperate circumstances make people's minds work in strange ways. When people are desperate their souls begin to stink. And people, including my wife, stop being human.

Mariana Or maybe for the first time they realize they are human. Maybe out of desperation they take risks that out of fear they wouldn't have had the guts to do so under normal times.

Gregorio Stop your rhetoric. You turned your back on him ten years ago, just like the rest of your family.

Mariana It's a sad story, but ten years have gone by. Now we can look at everything from a different perspective. We were very young then. Now we're more mature. We can reconcile.

Gregorio It'll be a very, very interesting reconciliation! I don't think your brother will buy it. Maybe if you had called him a year ago. But today, Mariana!

Mariana I've wanted to call him for a long time but I never had the nerve. But now I could do it.

Gregorio And he, no doubt, will be quite ready to tell you to go to hell!

Mariana In these circumstances, he's got to be here. *(Pause)* I'm going to ask him for help.

(As Simon re-enters)

Simon *(Doubling over)* Oh no! Not again! I can't get away from the toilet! Who are you asking for help?

Gregorio Simon! *(He hugs him.)* Simon, you're pale. They didn't leave you anything.

Simon Who are you asking for help?

Gregorio It's not important. It's nonsense.

Luna Of course it's important! It's very important to have a rich son; and he's the one who can bring us back from the brink of disaster!

Simon What? What are you talking about?

Luna Mariana, showing good judgment as always, wants to ask your son for help.

Simon Help from whom? But don't you know that "it" is no longer my son? Mariana, don't you think I've been humiliated enough?

Gregorio *(Intervening on Simon's behalf)* Don't worry, Simon. I won't allow any more humiliations.

Simon He uses my name every time he opens up one of his shops for queers, or a dance club for men only! "Goldberg's Dick Stop!" "Goldberg's Gay Shores!" "Goldberg Colored Condoms!" Using my prestigious name.

Luna Prestigious?

Simon I am a very prestigious man!

Luna You're a very broke man!

Simon *(He pauses. Subdued)* I kicked him out when I found him naked in my bed with Mariana's fiancé. Or have you forgotten, Mariana?

Luna He did that?

Gregorio *(Turning to Mariana)* You never told me the details.

Mariana Details? The marvelous details! I was madly in love with Nacho Bergman. I was 28 years old and had the most gorgeous fiancé in the world. We had set the wedding date, sent out invitations, everything was perfect until my brother Javier fell in love with Nacho. He seduced him, and two weeks before the wedding, Mom and Dad found them in bed together.

Simon In our wedding bed!

Mariana I'd gone to visit a girlfriend, Mami and Papi had gone out, but they came back early and, well, Papi threw them both out.

Simon I told him that this was no longer his home, and that I was no longer his father!

Mariana They went to India on what was supposed to be my honeymoon! They shaved their heads and sent me pictures of them dressed in orange, standing beside the Maharishi. They wrote on the pictures "Loving you while we make love." Do you want to see them? I still have them. They were divine! It was unforgettable! I almost committed suicide, it was so great! *(She pauses and regains control.)* But, it's all a part of the past. Papi, he's your son, my brother. He's a millionaire. He can help the family.

Simon Help? Call "that" to help me? *(Pause)* This is a plot. But why would you want to kill a bankrupt man? You should have killed me earlier. This is surreal.

Luna What's surreal?

Gregorio What's real is Simon Goldberg who lived here, an honorable man who never cheated anyone. A man worthy of being called a man. Or is there no reality left?

Mariana What's real is that you have a son who can help.

Simon I want you to know something. These symptoms are real. *(Simon doubles over with stomach cramps. He spins around the stage and falls.)*

Luna That's not how you have a heart attack, Simon. That's how clowns walk around in the circus. You don't even know how to have a heart attack!

Simon *(From the floor)* I don't have a son! Isn't that true, Luna? *(He stands up.)*

Luna You have a son, and I don't know him, so I'd say this is a good time to get to know him!

Simon I do not have a son! I only have a miserable atmosphere. *(He doubles over in pain.)* I think I'm going to disintegrate in the bathroom! Luna, all you have to do is flush the toilet to get rid of what's left of me!

Mariana *(Confronts her father harshly.)* I'm letting you know that I'm going to call him!

Gregorio He won't come!

Mariana *(Determined)* I'm going to make him come. He can't deny us help.

Gregorio He can deny us anything that he wants.

Mariana I'm going to bring him here.

Simon *(Defiantly)* You're not going to mock me any more.

Mariana Papi, stop being so stubborn!

Simon Now you're being disrespectful! Luna! Say something to her!
Luna *(Sarcastically)* Daughter!
Simon *(Pointing to Luna)* She doesn't respect me either. My wife would have respected me under these circumstances.
Luna Unfortunately, I am your wife under these circumstances.
Simon I'm referring to the mother of my children.
Mariana You see, you have a son.
Simon Stop confusing me. This must be a bad dream. Could it be a post-infarction dream?
Mariana You're not having a heart attack, Papi. You're just broke.
Simon *(Leaning on Luna)* Beg them, if they ever had any respect for me, not to call Javier.
Luna Javier is YOUR son. I want to meet him.
Simon To meet him? That never concerned you before.
Luna I never lived with a philosopher of misery before. I never needed anything by your side before, but now I need everything.
Simon And what does this have to do with my son?
Luna Mariana says that we can ask him to help us out of this miserable atmosphere. And the idea makes him adorable to me. I love him already, even though I don't know him.
Simon You love him? Now you love him?
Luna He has money. And I don't have your sexual prejudices.
Simon I'm not sexually prejudiced. I'm ashamed.
Luna You're old Simon. Old, broke, and living with a false sense of macho pride.
Simon Yes, macho! Do you have any doubts about that?
Luna Lately, let's just say you're not necessarily "King of the Jungle!"
Simon *(He falls on his knees.)* Have mercy on me! A little mercy for Simon Goldberg, in his last moments!
Gregorio Enough already! *(He falls on his knees at Simon's side and kisses his hands.)* I love you, Simon. I am your real son. The other one is a nincompoop.
Luna A nincompoop with millions!
Simon His millions don't interest me!
Luna You refuse to ask for help from the only member of your family who can help us. *(She begins to cry and Simon hands her a hankie.)*
Simon *(Crying)* I can't stand to see you cry.
Luna Then call your son.
Simon I'd rather see you cry. *(Luna cries ostentatiously. Mariana hugs her and cries. Gregorio begins to cry, and finally they all cry. Simon*

distributes hankies among them.) You all have me. I must say that it bothers me to think that my only asset was my money. *(They all stop crying.)*

Luna It was an attractive asset, Simon.

Simon *(Simon clutches his chest.)* You always said that money was the least attractive!

Luna That's what I thought.

Simon I think that if you can convince me that you married me for my money, I'll get the heart attack I so much want! Shall we begin?

Luna I also married you for your money, Simon.

Simon So, my toilet factory was the source of my animal attraction?

Luna I said that the money was one of your strong points.

Simon Say it: I married old Simon Goldberg for his money! Come on, we are getting closer to my heart attack. Say, "he was a dirty old man, but he had a lot of dough!" Come on! We're almost there!

Mariana Enough! Papa, you're falling apart. Come on, lean on me.

Simon On you, who wants to see me on my knees in front of that pervert? I can feel my large intestine in my ears. Is that normal? And my small intestine is dancing between my eyebrows. Bury me in the Jewish cemetery, near Dorita. Call Rabbi Steinberg; he knows I'm a good man.

Luna *(Concerned)* What do you feel?

Simon I feel very loved. I am a loved man. *(He collapses.)*

Luna *(Exasperated)* Heart attacks are not like that, Simon.

Simon Put me in a comfortable coffin. With air conditioning. I don't like the idea of being confined underground, nor do I like being hot.

Mariana *(To Simon)* Enough with the drama! I'm telling you, I've made up my mind and you won't change it!

Simon *(Standing up)* Luna, would you come with me? I know it isn't very sexy, but...

Luna The bathroom again?

Simon It's the only place where I feel that I'm doing something positive. *(They exit.)*

Mariana *(To Gregorio)* I'm going to call him now.

Gregorio *(Moving toward the front door.)* I'm not going to help you with this.

Mariana Go out and get us something to eat. We're all starving.

(Gregorio exits. Mariana looks through her phone book. She picks up the portable phone and dials nervously. She changes her mind and hangs up. She dials again.) Good afternoon. I would like to speak to Mr.

Goldberg.   Yes,   yes,   Goldberg.   *(Surprised)*   Dolly   Goldberg?
(Uncomfortable) No, excuse me. I must have dialed the wrong number.
(Composed)   Is this 0897... *(Listening)* Yes, but Dolly Goldberg?
(Pause) Look, perhaps there is a Dolly Goldberg that I don't know. It's
been a long time since I've seen my brother. Maybe he got married.
(The person on the line confirms it.) Ahhh, he's married! How long?
Six years!!!   Well! What a surprise!!! I'm so happy for him! This is
quite a change! Look, I'm Javier Goldberg's sister and we haven't been
in contact for years. I didn't know he got married. Well, I'm married
too, and he doesn't know it. *(Pause)* Excuse me, to whom am I speaking?
Ahhh! You're Dolly's secretary! Well, I want to leave a message for
my brother. Can you take it? Yes, thank you very much! *(Waiting)* He
got married! He got married! Javier got married! *(The secretary returns
to the phone.)* Ah, yes. *(Getting emotional)* Tell him his sister called.
(She begins to cry.) I'm sorry, but I've called to ask him to come home
quickly because Papi, Papi... *(Cries inconsolably.)* Papi is...Tell him
that... *(She goes in for the kill sobbing loudly with hiccups.)* He needs
to come now because there's no time left. He's in his last... He's not
dead. *(Cries louder.)* I hate to give him the news over the phone, but he
only has two children. Thank you. You're very kind. *(She hangs up.
Her demeanor changes abruptly.)*   Well, that should be convincing
enough.
(Gregorio enters carrying a pizza.)
Gregorio What's convincing? *(He opens the pizza box and offers
Mariana a slice.)*
Mariana My message. He simply has to come. Papi is dying.
Gregorio *(Dryly)* Well, you sure are all upset. I don't even recognize
your voice. You must be planning some amazing story to get that faggot
here!
Mariana I will not let you talk about my brother that way! I'll just have
you know that my brother is married to a woman named Dolly! He's a
married man! His gay period is over!
Gregorio *(He pauses.)* He...he told you that he got married?
Mariana Yes! I spoke to his wife's secretary! See? People do change!
Gregorio So Javier got married! Well, that's news! He's straightened
up! All man! This will make things easier for Simon. I'm going to go
tell him!
Mariana We'll take care of that later. We must proceed now!
Gregorio Proceed?
Mariana I said that Papi *(She begins to eat her pizza.)* is in his last

moments, or perhaps already dead. *(She eats anxiously.)* I was vague, but tough. *(Crying)* Daddy, I love you, *(Crying)* but I had to kill you. There was no other way!

Gregorio You're not making any sense. As soon as he arrives he'll find your Dad is alive.

Mariana *(Logically)* We have to kill him.

Gregorio *(Shocked)* What are you saying? *(He and Mariana continue to eat pizza.)*

Mariana Javier and his wife Dolly will arrive at any moment to mourn our beloved dead father, and we don't have a dead father! We have to kill him.

Gregorio You're mad! You're mouth is foaming!

Mariana A gentle death; a temporary death.

Gregorio Are you saying that we need to bring him to a pre-attack stage?

Mariana *(Furious with him)* Did I say that? That would make me a murderer of my own father!

Gregorio Mariana. Stop! You have time to stop this!

Mariana Don't give me any of this, "Mariana, stop!" You've never provided me with moral or economic support. You've never had problems living off of my father!

Gregorio I admit that I was a jerk when I married you. And I let Simon give me a job. We had everything. But I've learned to love him like a son. Now that he's broke we're screwed.

Mariana Screwed?

Gregorio Broke.

Mariana But our savings? Our account in New York?

Gregorio I gave everything to your father to try to save the business.

Mariana Why didn't you tell me? That money belonged to the two of us.

Gregorio Would you have told me not to help your father?

Mariana Of course not!

Gregorio Well, that's why I didn't say anything to you.

Mariana And how about us?

Gregorio Completely bankrupt. *(They embrace.)*

Mariana Well, my brother has the means to save the whole family.

Gregorio What reasons would he have to save this family?

Mariana *(Lowering her voice)* Well, with Papi in critical condition, at death's door.

Gregorio The only thing your father has is diarrhea. No one dies of that.

Mariana *(Suggestive)* How about chloroform?

Gregorio Darling, I've never staged a death.

Mariana *(Caressing him to persuade him)* Well, sometimes people do something they've never done before. And now, destiny has decided that today is our day! Chloroform. Chloroform and courage, my love!

Gregorio I'm not going to be your accomplice!

Mariana *(Kissing him)* I can't do it alone, and Luna won't go along with it.

Gregorio *(They plot.)* What do you want me to do?

Mariana Go to the pharmacy and come back with something that will kill him, without killing him. Something that'll put him out for a good while.

Gregorio Sleeping pills?

Mariana No. *(Secretive)* I think chloroform will do.

Gregorio Mariana, there's a glitter in your eye.

Mariana It's the glitter of salvation.

Gregorio It's pure libido glittering, it's making me hot! *(They kiss passionately.)* We need something that will put him under on contact.

Mariana Something like you. You've always put me under on contact.

Gregorio *(Caressing her breasts)* And if it gets out of hand and we really kill him?

Mariana Your hands feel good. *(They kiss.)* Go, go. We've got to move fast before Javier and Dolly get here.

Gregorio This is crazy. This frightens me.

Mariana Me too. I've never killed my father before.

Gregorio All this for your brother!

Mariana We need him to save us. We have to fix it so that he won't turn us down. We have to make a big impact. My brother always liked being the hero. Let's give him what he wants, now that he's a man!

Gregorio Give me another kiss and I'll go. *(They kiss passionately.)*

Mariana Your eyes are also glittering like burning coals in an endless night! *(Pause)* There might be some new products.

Gregorio I love you. *(He lets her go and leaves. Mariana is left alone. Luna enters. She sits near Mariana. She is disheveled.)*

Mariana Would you like some pizza?

Luna I'm not hungry, thank you. Did you call your brother?

Mariana Yes, of course. And I have some news! He isn't gay anymore! He got married!

Luna But, is he still a millionaire?

Mariana Multimillionaire, darling.

Luna He won't come.

Mariana I would think that a son would want to see his father at a time like this.

Luna You think so?

Mariana *(Taking Luna's hand)* Where's Papi?

Luna On the maid's bed. Is the only thing they left us. Just to leave us something to sleep on.

Mariana Luna, I don't want to be a pessimist, but Papi is very sick. The.prognosis is uncertain. I know him. I know him very well.

Luna He wants to die. He doesn't understand how everything got so bad, and I don't know how to help him. I think that at this moment he'd rather have your mother by his side than me. *(She pauses. Mariana caresses her.)* I've been happy with Simon, but without money, he's a different man.

Mariana Luna, Papi is really sick.

Luna Ruined.

Mariana There's more. I don't think he'll survive.

Luna What are you saying?

Mariana You haven't talked to a doctor, have you?

(Gregorio returns with a small bag in his hand.)

Gregorio Where's Simon?

Mariana *(Complicitous)* He's resting in the maid's room. Can you go check on him while we finish our private conversation?

Gregorio Sure. You two enjoy your talk. *(He exits.)*

Mariana *(Continuing the conversation)* I understand that you haven't called the doctor, you don't want to frighten him.

Luna What Simon needs is rest. And now on top of everything else, he's going to see the son he hasn't seen in ten years.

Mariana It'll help that, as Papi would say, "Javier has returned to normal."

Luna Honestly, this will be the first good news that poor Simon has had all day. *(Gregorio returns, pale and upset.)* Gregorio, what's wrong with you?

Gregorio *(Hugs Luna and begins to cry.)* He was more than a father to me. And now, suddenly...

Mariana Papa... *(She hugs Luna.)* Papa...

(Luna jumps up convinced that Simon is dead.)

Luna What's wrong with Simon?

Gregorio *(Not letting Luna move)* Calm yourself, Luna, there's no need to rush now.

Luna What do you mean there's no need to rush? *(Gregorio holds her and she struggles to free herself to go to her husband.)*

Mariana *(Crying loudly)* Papa! Papa!

Luna Let go of me! I want to see him! I have to see him! *(She hits Gregorio.)* I have to see my husband!

(They struggle. Gregorio takes out chloroform soaked cotton from his pocket and puts it over Luna's face. She faints and collapses.)

Mariana Her too?

Gregorio She was getting out of control. *(He lifts her up and sits her on a chair.)* I'm going to bring your father in here, bed and all. Give me a hand.

Mariana *(Framing the "scene")* We'll sit Luna next to Papi, and we'll throw a black mantilla on her. *(They go out. Gregorio returns carrying the unconscious Simon in his arms. Mariana rolls in the bed that has wheels. They lay Simon on the bed and prop Luna slumped over, leaning upon him. Mariana covers her with a black mantilla.)* Look what you've created, Gregorio.

Gregorio *(Proud of himself)* Not bad.

Mariana And to think, two hours ago we were good people.

Gregorio You're still a good person. I'm the executioner.

Mariana I can't tell you how thankful I am that you killed Daddy.

Gregorio Don't put it like that. I didn't kill him.

Mariana Well, as far as I'm concerned, you killed him. Congratulations. *(Stands back to take in the scene.)* Impeccable work. *(She puts the finishing touches on the tableau.)* Look at them: livid, motionless, rigid. A gem of a scene. Don't you feel powerful?

Gregorio Yes. *(Looking at them. Puffs out his chest.)* I feel quite...quite powerful.

Mariana *(Proud of her husband)* What you did with Luna was a stroke of genius! That was pure inspiration. You know occasionally you have sparks of brilliance.

Gregorio This is the first time I've ever felt that you were proud of me.

Mariana This is the first time I've ever been proud of you. *(A long kiss. The doorbell rings.)* That must be my brother! *(She throws on something black and puts on a sad face, about to cry. She places herself at the side of the bed with her head drooping as if she were overcome by grief. She carefully considers the image that she is creating. Gregorio opens the door and Dolly Goldberg enters. Dolly is a spectacular woman with a stunning body she uses in a way that provokes men, and she knows it. She wears a low-cut dress and very high heels. Very hip* *and modern.)*

Dolly *(Enchanting, fragile, moved)* Good evening. I'm Dolly Goldberg.

Gregorio *(To the supposed wife of Javier)* Ah yes. Dolly! I'm Gregorio Murray. Mariana's husband. *(Gregorio is overwhelmed by Dolly's beauty.)*

Dolly Well, we're like... in-laws. *(The two of them are not sure whether to shake hands or kiss. Gregorio decides.)*

Gregorio Yes! We can kiss. *(They kiss. Gregorio prolongs it.)*

Dolly And, the others? *(Gregorio gestures toward the funerary couple of Simon and Luna in their deep sleep and Mariana crying. Dolly looks at them and the empty apartment.)* But, what happened? Was it sudden, or...?

Gregorio Well it was caused by an economic catastrophe. Simon went bankrupt. He's completely broke. Today they emptied the house and closed the factory. The impact is practically killing him.

Dolly Ah, I arrived just in time! I knew that I'd find him with some life left in him yet!

Gregorio Did you come alone?

Dolly I came with my husband. He's parking the car.

Gregorio Mariana is dying to see him.

Dolly *(Surprised, she doesn't understand.)* My husband?

Gregorio Of course!

Dolly And me?

Gregorio And you too. She's curious.

Dolly Curious?

Gregorio Well, it's only logical.

(The bell rings. Gregorio opens the door and sees Dolly's husband. Gregorio assumes that this is Javier. He is very sexy and dressed impeccably. He is tall, dark, and muscularly athletic. He looks around the empty apartment.)

Paco Excuse me, I couldn't find a place to park. *(To Gregorio)* And you are...?

Dolly *(Introducing Gregorio to her husband)* Mariana's husband.

Gregorio *(Emotional. Hugs Paco.)* You don't know how much it means to us to have you here, brother! *(He slaps Paco's back effusively.)* Thanks for coming in spite of everything. *(Paco looks around again at the empty space. He looks at Dolly with a questioning look.)* We can't thank you enough for your generosity.

Paco *(Surprised and confused)* I came for Dolly's sake.

Gregorio Did she help you overcome your resentment?

Paco No, this time it was I who helped her! Right, sweetheart? It wasn't easy for her to come.

(Paco looks toward Simon, Luna, and Mariana. He smells the chloroform. He's suspicious. Gregorio looks at Paco. In order to ease the awkward situation, Gregorio goes over to Mariana and speaks to her in a low voice. Mariana goes right over to Paco wiping away her tears. She ignores Dolly.)

Mariana *(Perplexed)* No, no... You, but what have you done Javier? You used to be more...less...you used to be blond. You...you aren't my brother!

Paco Javier? I'm not Javier. My name is Paco Frias. Dolly's husband.

Mariana *(Looking Dolly over from head to toe)* And my brother didn't want to come?

Dolly I'm your brother.

Gregorio and Mariana Whaaaaaaaaaaaaaat? *(There is a stony silence.)*

Mariana You're Javier Goldberg?

Dolly I was Javier Goldberg. Fortunately, I've been Dolly Goldberg for seven years now, my esteemed sister!

Mariana You made yourself...you...you changed...to a woman? *(Beside herself)* You had an operation?

Dolly Yes, of course. I had the operation in London, by the best surgeon. I am woman from head to toe. I got my papers in Chile and it says: "sex": female.

Mariana Let me see them.

Gregorio What for?

Mariana *(Extremely upset)* What for? What do you mean, "what for?" Gregorio?

(Dolly takes out papers from her purse.)

Mariana ID number: 5-223-669. Date of birth, April 12 1964. Dolores Goldberg. Sex: female. *(Astounded)*

Dolly Didn't I turn out divine?

Paco Divine!

Gregorio *(Involuntarily)* Divine! *(To Mariana)* Well, spectacular! No one would even know. When she came in I saw this "babe" and I was convinced that this was Javier's wife!

Mariana But did they operate on everything? I mean, private parts and all?

Paco Dolly has everything she needs. *(He takes the identification card from Mariana and puts it away.)* Everything.

(Paco walks away from the group and begins to look over the place.)
Dolly It was a well thought out decision. I went through a lot of therapy until my decision was finally clear.
Mariana Psychoanalyzed and operated on. Who was your shrink?
(Paco from the door leading to other rooms in the apartment.)
Paco I was.
Gregorio You're a psychiatrist?
Dolly Of course! I wouldn't go to a vet for psychoanalysis! I went to a first-rate post-Lacanian, Paco Frias. And after he cured me, he confessed his love for me!
Mariana In other words, you didn't have sex with him while he was your therapist.
(Paco looking at the deathbed scene staged by Gregorio and Mariana. He's figured out that the entire scene is an act they put on.)
Paco I have my standards. *(He approaches Mariana.)* Let's not change the subject. We're talking death and money here.
Gregorio This is getting interesting.
Paco *(Smiling at Dolly)* Dolly. So innocent. *(He kisses her.)* So brave. *(They stand embraced.)*
Dolly It was the most courageous act of my life. From then on everything changed. I'm happy. *(She looks at Paco lovingly.)*
Mariana Happy? To top it all off, you're happy! And you say it so calmly! *(Threateningly)* Don't you think that anyone can say "I'm happy" so easily. *(Pause)* Take me, for example, it's been centuries since I've been happy! *(Pause. To Gregorio)* How about that? On top of everything else, you're going to throw your happiness in our faces!
Dolly I'm very happy!
Mariana You turned out just like Mami! Just like Mami!
Dolly *(Lets Paco go.)* Mariana, give me a hug. I'm a transsexual, not a leper. *(She tries to kiss Mariana, who shouts out, frightened.)* Listen, I'm not contagious. Give me a kiss!
Mariana *(Furious)* A kiss? Oh no you don't, Javier! Stop testing me like this! You took Nacho away from me just before our wedding, and now you've turned yourself into a woman when I was the only daughter in this family! And to top it all off, a knockout of a woman!
(Paco laughs at Mariana's reaction, and he slowly approaches the scene of Simon and Luna. He looks at them. He touches them.)
Dolly Why are you reacting this way?
Mariana How would you react if you suddenly saw me with a moustache, a beard, and a pair of... between my legs?

Dolly If that's what makes you happy. I'd say, it's great that you had the balls to do it!

Mariana What really surprises me is that you even dared to come here!

(Paco finds the chloroform soaked cotton under the bed. He sniffs it and puts it in his pocket.)

Dolly I got the phone call from you! "Papi is dying!"

Paco   *(From the bed area, suspiciously)* Is there a diagnosis? Have you called a doctor?

(Gregorio looks at Mariana, alarmed.)

Mariana There wasn't time. I mean...

(Paco signals to Dolly to come over to him.)

Dolly I want to see him.

Mariana *(Stands in Dolly's way.)* In your dreams.

Gregorio *(Trying to avoid a confrontation. To Mariana.)* "It" came to see "its" father, whether or not it is Dolly or Javier, "its" father is on his deathbed!

Dolly Sis, I didn't turn myself into a woman to spite you!

Mariana Don't you call me sis!

(This response bothers Dolly.)

Dolly What do you want me to call you? We are sisters, Mariana!

Gregorio *(To Mariana. He leads her away from Dolly.)* Get a hold of yourself, darling!

Mariana Why did I even call you? I should have expected this. I should have known that you'd upstage me.

Dolly I'm not upstaging you Mariana!

Gregorio *(Interceding. To Dolly)* She needs time. She expected to see Javier. She called Javier.

Dolly She has all the time in the world. I'm leaving.

Paco *(Approaching the group again)* No, Dolly. You have to stay here. You have to go over to your father.

Dolly My father! My beloved father who never showed me a moment's affection my entire life.

Paco You know you love him, Dolly. You've told me a thousand times how much you love him.

Dolly Of course I love him! It's just too bad that he doesn't love me back. On the other hand, if my sister is so upset, just imagine my father's reaction! I can't add more pain to the pain he's already feeling. Javier called to give him a final hug! Let's go, Paco! I made a mistake coming here. You all tell him that his son Javier called to send him a great big final hug'

Paco Dolly, it's not a good idea for you to leave.

Dolly Can't you see, Paco? My sister can't handle the fact that I'm a woman. Why would I want to kill my father with the novel idea that he has another daughter? Let him die of something else. Let him die because he's a coward, because he's a failure, because he doesn't have the guts to live!

Paco You're the only one who can help him, my love. Leaving won't solve anything. Simon needs you, although he doesn't know it yet.

Dolly I've needed him too. It's been ten years since I've seen Papa.

(Mariana is about to speak and Gregorio silences her with a look.)

Paco Don't go away like this. At least say good-bye to him. He's unconscious. He won't see you. I'll walk over to the bed with you. Come, come closer!

Mariana *(Standing in her way)* She can't go over there. I have to defend my father! I called Javier, and Dolly showed up.

Dolly He's my father too!

Mariana And if he opens his eyes? What are you going to tell him? How happy you are?

Dolly Why not?

Mariana I'm going to kill you!!! *(She rushes at Dolly. Dolly gives her a punch that sends her reeling. Paco picks Mariana up.)*

Paco She has a lot of physical and spiritual strength. Come on, you can't keep her from going over to her father. This is not the time to get all worked up. Come on.

(Paco moves Mariana away. She resists him with force, and he takes out the chloroform soaked cotton and covers her face with it. Frightened, not knowing what to do. He realizes that Paco knows the whole set up.)

Gregorio We're ruined!

(Mariana faints in Paco's arms.)

Paco *(Theatrically placing Mariana in Gregorio's arms.)* "When night balances day, the storms of the equinox gather. When false light balances the violence of the sun, it unleashes the violence of the game. When two women are balanced in our minds, pleasure's equinox begins." Have you ever read Baudrillard?

Gregorio How did you figure it out?

(Dolly looks at Paco. Confused, she tries to understand what's going on.)

Paco Your sister's in shock.

Dolly Is everyone here in shock?

Paco Everyone except Gregorio. But Gregorio is going to behave himself. Right?

Gregorio *(Frightened and very respectful toward Paco.)* Absolutely! I think that Dolly should go over to her father now.

Paco Agreed. We agree on something.

Dolly Don't think it's easy for me. *(Dolly doesn't dare, Paco takes her hand. He holds her. He leads her over to the "tableau." She gets on her knees by her father at the head of the bed. She touches his forehead, his nose. She takes his hand and kisses it.)* Papa, Papa... *(She makes a face of disgust and looks at Paco.)* What an odor! Papa, Papa... *(Holding her nose)* But who can stand that smell! *(Luna begins to snore.)* And who's this?

Gregorio *(Follows with Mariana in his arms, paralyzed with fright.)* His wife. Her name is Luna. She's in a deep sleep.

Dolly She's snoring! How disgusting! A suspicious odor, people snoring. This "scene" requires silence. It requires sensitivity. *(Dolly moves Luna's head so that she'll stop snoring. The snoring stops. Dolly takes out a spray bottle of perfume and sprays Luna and Simon.)* Well at least now they smell like Kenzo! *(Dolly extends her hand to Paco who helps her stand up and move away from the "scene." Simon and Luna continue sleeping. She plays along with Paco.)* I needed to see him, to touch him. *(To Gregorio)* To smell him. After all this time.

(Frightened, Gregorio tries to wake Mariana.)

Paco *(To Dolly)* So you've figured it out.

Dolly Yes, I could tell when I got close to them, the way they were breathing so heavily. *(Pause)* I realized...

Paco You realized that he really does need you.

(Mariana wakes up in Gregorio's arms. She looks at him, then at Dolly.)

Dolly Would the two of you like to tell me what's going on?

Mariana I didn't know any other way to get you to come.

Dolly To come. And I came to...

Gregorio *(He lets go of Mariana and stands up.)* So, you're going?

Dolly On the contrary! I'm staying!

Paco *(Triumphant)* She's staying! She's staying! She's staying in spite of you. She's staying with her father! Kids, your plans went awry!

Mariana *(Gregorio helps her up from the floor.)* When Papi opens his eyes and sees that you're a woman, he'll close them again for good!

Dolly That depends.

Mariana On what?

Dolly On me.

Mariana And him.

Dolly Paco, I need you to leave.

Gregorio Do you always make such quick decisions?

Paco Always. She "SEES." She has an uncanny understanding of business, life, money, parents. When she needs to, she changes her course, her direction, her attitude...

Mariana ...her sex.

Paco That's beside the point. She always gets it right. That's how she's made millions.

Dolly Oh go on, Paco.

Paco Are you sure about what you just decided?

Dolly Completely. I want to help him and I want him to love me.

Mariana To love you? You want Simon Goldberg to love you?

Dolly He's going to adore Dolly!

Mariana I give up. Do whatever you want.

Gregorio Do you believe in miracles?

Dolly I believe in love.

Mariana *(Ironically)* "Loving you while we make love." *(She laughs.)* Do you remember the pictures you sent me from India when you were with Nacho? "Loving you while we make love." Poor old man. This is going to be the last straw!

Paco I'm leaving now. *(He looks at Mariana and Gregorio.)* You were expecting a check, but you got Dolly instead! Dolly is much more than a check. Dolly is Dolly! *(Dolly accompanies her husband to the door. They say good-bye. Before leaving)* Dolly knows what she's doing.

Mariana *(Mocking Paco)* "Dolly knows what she's doing."
(Dolly approaches, determined, to the bed, Gregorio and Mariana follow her. Dolly holds her father's hand. They speak in low tones so that they don't wake either Simon or Luna. Mariana's tone turns sarcastic.) So you have three daughters? *(Dolly nods her head, takes out a photo from her wallet and shows it to Mariana.)* But you gave birth... normally?

Dolly *(Irked. Looking at the photo)* What do you call normal? We used a surrogate.

Mariana *(Passing the photo to Gregorio)* I didn't mean to upset you, Javier.

Dolly *(Correcting her)* The name is Dolly.

Gregorio *(Looking at the photo)* They look like normal children.

Mariana Yes, yes. They look like a happy family.

Dolly *(Looking at her directly)* I waited a long time for you to call me, Mariana.

Mariana And why didn't you call me, Javier?

Dolly *(Taking the photo from Gregorio)* Dolly.

Mariana I'm sorry. It's not easy to get used to it. Please have a little patience!

Dolly I have to get used to things too. *(Looking at Simon)* How I wish Dad would open his eyes.

(Luna opens her eyes. She's befuddled and disoriented. The chloroform has side effects.)

Luna Is the party over? Or should we keep drinking champagne? *(To Simon)* Hey old man, shouldn't we go home? I don't like this house. It's got a miserable ambience!

Gregorio *(Slapping Luna)* Luna, come on. Wake up!

Luna *(Looking at Dolly)* And who's this woman?

Dolly Hi. I'm Javier Goldberg's wife. *(Gregorio and Mariana look at each other, embarrassed.)* I'm Dolly Goldberg.

Luna *(Looking Dolly up and down)* I imagined that his wife would be more...less...well, I don't know...not so...

Dolly Do you know Javier?

Luna Did he come? I'm dying to meet him!

Dolly No. He told me to come in his place.

Luna Are you a millionaire too?

Dolly Yes. If it makes you feel better?

Luna It depends. Because if the son doesn't want to come, the wife has no reason to give us a dime.

Gregorio *(Furious with Luna)* Luna, don't you have anything to do around here? Get some air. Throw yourself out the window.

Dolly *(Laughing, amused)* But she's the only honest one.

Luna I am the only honest person around here. D'you hear that, Gregorio? And that's a millionaire talking.

Dolly It appears that you like millions.

Luna They make me crazy. They're a turn-on. Aren't they like aphrodisiacs? And to think that I married a millionaire who looks like a bag of potatoes.

Dolly Yes, it's a good thing that Javier can't see him like this.

Luna On the contrary! I think that if Javier came here in person to tell Simon that he has returned to the great brotherhood of men, he would forgive everything!

Dolly The one who would not forgive Simon everything is Javier.

Luna Then he won't give us a dime.

Gregorio *(Enraged)* Luna, since when does Javier Goldberg's money interest you?

Luna Why? What interests you? His hands, his voice, his absence? *(To Dolly.)* This is going to make my husband very happy. *(Shaking Simon)* Simon, surprise! Simon, your son isn't gay anymore. And he has a divine wife!

Dolly *(Calmly and firmly stopping Luna's shaking)* He'll decide when to come out of it. *(She kisses Simon. She looks at everyone.)* Now we're all going to concentrate and kiss him with love!

Mariana *(Flustered)* What are we going to do, Dolly Goldberg?

Luna *(To Mariana in a low voice)* All millionaires are eccentric. They believe in positive energy and all that. *(To Dolly)* I'll do anything you ask.

Dolly Kisses! Let's go then! Everyone together!

Mariana *(Adamantly)* This is ridiculous.

Gregorio *(Aside to Mariana)* Just play along with her.

Dolly Luna is sincere and dumb, but Gregorio knows how to negotiate.

Luna I don't like you calling me dumb.

Dolly And I don't like the fact that the only thing that you like about me is my money.

Luna I like your ring too. What is it? An emerald?

Gregorio *(Putting his hand over Luna's mouth)* She's out of it. I've never seen her like this!

Dolly Well, with all the drugs you gave her! *(Gregorio turns pale.)* Come on now. Let's kiss Papi! One...two...three! *(On Dolly's signal, they all, except Mariana, cover Simon with kisses.)*

Mariana *(Desperate)* Dolly Goldberg has us in the palm of her hands!

Dolly Dolly Goldberg does not want Simon in the palm of your hands! *(Simon begins to move his head and murmur confused words in his sleep. Everyone watches him closely.)*

Luna He's responding. *(She lifts his head.)* Simon.

Simon *(Looking at everyone. He stops at Dolly.)* Dorita. How young you look. *(To everyone else)* My wife! *(To Dolly)* You finally came back, Dorita!

Dolly *(She turns his head toward Luna. Firmly)* That's your wife.

Simon *(To Luna)* Dorita is my wife!

Dolly Gregorio. Luna woke up dumbfounded, but Simon is trapped in the past! Fix it, Gregorio, because if you don't I'll see you in jail!

Simon *(To Dolly)* Will you marry me? We'll have a big wedding.

Luna *(Furious)* Dorita is dead!

Dolly I'm...I'm married to your son, Javier.

Simon *(To everyone)* The things she says. *(To Dolly)* Javier turned out strange. He likes men, Dorita. You're so pretty! I can just see you in a bridal gown, Dorita.

Dolly Gregorio Murray, all this confusion is very difficult for him and for me. Fix this!

Gregorio Simon, cut-it-out!!! We're in the present!!!

Mariana *(Taking her father's head in her hands)* She's not Mami. Her name is Dolly.

Simon *(Caressing Dolly who responds by removing his hands)* Do...Do...Dorita! I've been waiting for you for so long. You are my one true love!

Luna It hurts, it offends, it kills me that you still call out for Dorita!!!

Dolly *(To Simon)* This is your wife now. Dorita is dead. Come on Luna, kiss Simon.

Luna Let Dorita kiss him! *(She goes inside slamming the door.)*

Dolly Gregorio Murray! This is going to cost you a lot!

Gregorio Simon, come on old buddy, say hello to your daughter-in-law.

Simon I always loved you, Dorita.

Dolly *(Fed up)* I am Dolly, not Dorita!!!

Simon Come here. Get in bed with me. Let's make love, not war.

(Simon tries to get Dolly into the bed. He tries to disrobe her. Dolly defends herself, but she begins to panic. Mariana intervenes in order to help Dolly. Simon tries to get her out of the way so he can get into bed with Dolly. Out of control) Come here, Mamacita. Don't worry about the children. Come to your papi. *(He manages to get on top of her.)*

Dolly *(To Gregorio)* Do something!

Gregorio ENOUGH!

(Gregorio pulls Simon from the bed and puts him on his feet. Mariana helps Dolly get up from the bed. Dolly smoothes out her clothing. Luna returns with a bucket of water in her hands.)

Luna So, you want to go to bed with your daughter-in-law? You bastard! I could kill you! *(She throws the water on Simon, who falls to the floor. Red with fury she shouts.)* I'm your real wife! *(Dolly helps Simon up. Simon looks at Dolly.)*

Simon Gregorio, bring me a bucket of water. *(Gregorio brings it.)* Throw it on me. Don't be afraid. *(Gregorio doesn't dare. Dolly takes it from him and throws it on Simon. He is soaked)* No one can kill me! No one! Understand? I was dreaming about Dorita, that's all. Luna, give me a towel. I'm cold.

Luna They took the towels, Simon.

(Dolly dries him off with the sheet from the bed.)

Simon *(Looking at her strangely.)* Thanks. *(He looks at Luna, Greg, and Mariana.)* Did they take away your tongues too?

Luna No, dear.

Simon Then, can you explain to me who this...ma...this woman is and what she's doing at my funeral?

Gregorio Of course! She's...

Mariana *(Cutting her husband off)* Papi, we called Javier.

Simon You all double-crossed me. You called him, Mariana?

Mariana Yeeees!!! I caaaalled him!!!

Simon I heard you. You called him. And you asked him for help. I'm warning you that I won't accept his help or see him! I may be poor but I still have my dignity.

Mariana You can't talk to him?

Gregorio Simon. People do change.

Luna Your son is no longer gay.

Simon What?

Mariana He's married. Javier got married.

Simon Yes, yes! While I was sleeping.   So now you are going to tell me he's married. I have to get out of this absurd dream, I have to go to work, I'll go crazy if I don't work. I like to work, I pulled myself up from nothing. I have to go to the factory. The things I have to put up with, please. Give me my tie and start the car. Let's go to work, Gregorio.

Gregorio We don't have any place to go, Simon. We're broke.

Simon Broke and delirious. Now it turns out that my son is married.

Mariana I'd like to introduce you to Dolly Goldberg. Javier's wife.

Simon Quit pulling my leg! Now you're going to tell me that my son married this specimen of...of a woman?

Dolly We've been married for seven years.

Simon I'd like to hear that from Javier!

Dolly Javier doesn't want to see you.

Simon Why not?

Dolly What do you mean, why not?

Simon What did I do to him?

Dolly You threw him out of the house ten years ago and you told him that he was no longer your son!

Simon *(Pauses.)* Well, of course. But as you see, it seems that it did him good to be thrown out!

Dolly *(Her eyes fill with tears.)* Throwing him out! Simon Goldberg, what are you saying? Throwing him out hurt him badly!

Simon And how would you know?

Dolly *(Furious)* I just know! I know that it took years for him to recover from what you did to him. And I also know that he never wants to see you again!

Simon I don't want to argue about it, but perhaps we can talk about it, man to man.

Dolly *(Cutting)* He does not want to see you.

(Simon is silent. There is a general silence.)

Simon So Javier...?

Dolly We have three girls.

Simon I'm a grandfather?

Dolly Yes, Simon.

Simon Good. I thank you. At least you...

Dolly Yes, I came. I'm at your disposal.

Luna She's leaving out the other half.

Simon What other half?

Luna My darling, the main half. She came to bring us money.

Dolly Money? Who said that? I came to bring you love.

Blackout

ACT TWO

Scene 1

Some months later.

(As the lights come on, the space that had been empty in the first act is now furnished in a modern and daring style. It all looks very chic, fresh, and reflects a creative spirit. Gregorio is dressed in a gray suit and a tie, a symbol of resistance to all the contemporary chic of the furnishings and the other characters. He is loaded down with rolls of toilet paper in a variety of bright colors: blue, red, purple, green, etc.. Luna checks her make-up.)

Gregorio Luna, Luna, I need to talk to you.

Luna *(She gives him a kiss, while looking at the rolls of toilet paper.)* They're done already?

Gregorio *(Indignant)* My dear Luna: I present to you our new line of Goldberg toilet paper! Launched under the slogan: "Butts in Bliss." They're divine!

Luna *(Enchanted, she unrolls some and wraps it around her like cloth.)*
Gregorio They're useless, Luna! We've made a huge investment in a product that will never sell!
Luna Why are you so pessimistic, Gregorio?
Gregorio Because I know people. We live in a respectable society. The Argentines have always cleaned themselves with pastels. White being the preferred color. And the more daring ones choose pale yellow, baby pink, or light blue! That's the reality of our private lines.
Luna But we do have a sense of humor! You'll see how popular this new line will be.
Gregorio Imagine, if you will, a senator. Or a general. Or the CEO of the Kito Bank! Think of a metallurgist. Think of them in the inexorable, routine, inevitable moment of cleaning their asses.
Luna *(Closing her eyes and imagining)* I see them now. They all have their pants down. They're at the point of tearing off the paper.
Gregorio All right. Do you think this piece of paper should be lettuce green, bright red, or electric blue?
Luna *(Closing her eyes again)* I can see them. I see them wiping back and forth with the piece of paper. *(Celebrating)* These colors look wonderful, in contrast to their asses!
Gregorio Wonderful?
Luna Fun! Considering the fact that we all have to wipe our asses, it's a lot more fun in Technicolor!
Gregorio This is going to make some sectors of our society very uncomfortable! This goes against the fundamentals of family values!
Luna Gregorio, up to this point, the change in design has turned out very well.
Gregorio Up to now! But everything has its limits!
Luna And the limit is bright colors?
Gregorio It is not very Argentine to wipe your butt with bright colors.
Luna I don't understand what the ass and bright colors have to do with Argentine culture.
Gregorio If you don't understand it, you don't understand the basic nature of the people who live in this country. You could write a dissertation on it. The relationship is more than obvious!
(Mariana arrives and sees the toilet paper.)
Mariana The paper has come off the lines already? They look wonderful!
Gregorio You too?
Mariana You don't like them?

Gregorio My dear, you know I've been against this idea from the very beginning!

Mariana You've been against every idea from the very beginning.

Luna And all the new designs have been selling like hot cakes!

Gregorio This used to be the most respectable sanitary business in the country!

Mariana And away it went, with all its respectability!

Gregorio Is there some subtle accusation in what you're saying?

Luna Subtle? I think that Mariana is suggesting quite frankly that Simon's partner has considerable lack of imagination.

Mariana You're the one who's saying that, Luna!

Luna Alright. Then, you tell him what you think.

Mariana Gregorio, dear.

Luna I need to give some instructions to the cook. He knows that Simon's on a diet. *(She exits.)*

Gregorio *(Ironically)* We all know that Gregorio is a new man! He used to like pasta with pesto, and now he loves lettuce with lemon a la Dolly! *(Gregorio is worked up.)*

Mariana I think all this toilet paper has you a bit unraveled.

Gregorio Listen to me, Mariana. You wouldn't dare give me "fire red" toilet paper in the bathroom because...

Mariana Because you're a serious man.

Gregorio I'm a man. That's all.

Mariana I think you're obsessed by this "I'm a man and that's all" business.

Gregorio Luckily for this family there is someone who is not into the "I was a man and that's all," business.

Mariana Gregorio. I think you're angry, and unfairly so.

Gregorio And who treats me fairly? I was at Simon's side during the worst moments, and now Dolly's got him all tied up in this humiliating situation. That psychopath has us all dancing to her tune. Simon most of all! How come she doesn't tie me up in her perverted games, or in her colored paper. I can tell right from wrong. I have all of my genitalia in its proper place! And no transsexual is going to distract me with little tricks!

Mariana And if it had been your brother or sister, Gregorio?

Gregorio In MY family we're all normal. Nor-mal! The men are men, we like being men and we like women. But in YOUR family, dear, everything is turned upside down and back to front. And an abnormal has taken over, manipulating us and telling us that life can be fun! And comes up with some genius ideas that dammit, always succeed! But there are times, like now, that I see clearly that this investment in colored toilet paper is not going to work. But no one will pay any attention to me!

Mariana *(Trying to calm him)* Gregorio, in a very short time; less than a year, in fact, Dolly has managed to design ultramodern sanitary items that have proven to be successful. This tells me that she knows what Argentinean consumers need. She might be a transsexual, but that doesn't take away her talent for marketing, her ability to take risks, her successful visions.

Gregorio *(Cutting her short)* I'm not going to discuss her successful visions because the numbers speak for themselves.

Mariana My love, Dolly brought us back from the dead, she paid our debts. *(She puts her arms around his neck, trying to calm him.)* And only on the condition that we support the changes she made in the business.

Gregorio I'm sick of so much change!

Mariana Are you sick of our new car? Sick of our house? *(She kisses him seductively, unknotting his tie.)* Money looks good on you, Greg! Italian silk ties that fall from your neck to your crotch are so seductive. *(She opens the buttons of his shirt.)* Even the way you kiss me has a new style, slow, with no economic angst! Kissing without money worries changes a couple's life. People with money problems have tense kisses. They can't concentrate. On the other hand, these kisses are rich, opulent! Compare these to the other ones. Come on, think! *(They kiss each other, and she pulls him to her.)*

Gregorio I'm just a zero in this business.

Mariana But our bank account has lots of zeros. *(Kissing him)* Didn't we want that when we brought her? Didn't we want to get our zeros back. It didn't turn out too bad!!!

Gregorio What do you mean, it didn't turn out too bad? She's settled in. She's taken over the entire business!

Mariana But did you believe that you would get back all that money without giving up something in return? Do you still believe in "Santa Claus?" Get real!

Gregorio I can't be happy with this, but the vote is always the same: two to one! Simon never agrees with me! What the hell did "it" do to him? He's hypnotized!

Mariana Hypnotize him yourself, then. Gregorio, you have what it takes to do it.

Gregorio *(Kissing her)* Of course. You're right. I have what it takes! *(Fondling each other. They fall together on an armchair. Gregorio is turned on.)* I'm not going to be beaten down! I swear it!
(They entangle passionately. Dolly comes in and sees them. She is overloaded with rolls of colored toilet paper. They don't see her. Dolly watches them and then screams out at them.)
Dolly Am I interrupting, kids?! Did I interrupt something important? Don't let me stop you. I love uncomfortable sex, point blank, in public.
Mariana *(Harshly)* Interrupting? You? You've always shown me so much respect!
Gregorio We were just talking about you.
Dolly I can imagine. Is there anything hotter than me?
Mariana Me!!!
Gregorio *(Standing up)* Ladies, ladies. Don't fight over me! There's enough for everyone!
Mariana *(Standing up)* What? What do you mean everyone?
Dolly I only fight over the toilet paper colors! Look at what just came out of the factory! Imperial gold! Florescent blue! Van Gogh yellow! *(Looking for Simon)* Is my partner here?
Gregorio And what am I? Your errand boy?
Dolly I'm referring to my father. I mean, my father-in-law.
Gregorio Mariana. I want to speak alone with this woman. I mean with your brother. I mean, with your brother's wife.
Dolly *(Flirting)* Alone? With me?
Gregorio Yes, my treasure. Yes, my little piece of heaven. Yes, precious. Alone, with you.
Mariana Don't play with fire, you might get burned.
Dolly How insecure! What's wrong? Afraid your husband turns me on?
Gregorio I'm not unattractive, am I?
Dolly What do you want, my love? You want to tell everyone that we're lovers?
Mariana I'm leaving, because if I stay, I'll kill the two of you!
(Mariana goes out slamming the door. Gregorio changes his tone, becoming serious.)
Gregorio Dolly, I...
Dolly I know. You think they're horrible.
Gregorio Hideous!
Dolly They're already out.
Gregorio And you love them!

Dolly Well, it flies in the face of convention, considering that everyone takes the act so seriously. And if it's a success...

Gregorio *(Cutting her short)* It's going to be a huge failure.

Dolly You won't bet on the possibility that attitudes change? *(Pause)*

Gregorio Dolly. I don't want you to take this the wrong way, but I don't feel right about producing all this brightly colored paper. I can't go along with it. So therefore...

Dolly Yes?

Gregorio I don't mean to hurt you, and while I appreciate your talent and hard work. I...I would like to participate in some of the business's investments, but not in all of them. *(He pauses.)* Is that possible in our business?

Dolly Of course. But don't do this foolish thing now.

Gregorio I want you to give me back my part of this venture. I want out of this investment.

Dolly Don't be stupid! This is going to be a tremendous success! You have to believe in people!

Gregorio It's because I believe in people, and in myself, that I want to withdraw my investment from "Butts in Bliss."

Dolly All right, we'll give you back your portion of the investment.

Gregorio Yes. I want officially out of this venture.

Dolly Do you want to wait for Simon to tell him first or should I give you a check for your part of the investment?

Gregorio I'll wait. But I've made up my mind.

Dolly You're making a big mistake.

Gregorio You're the one who's made the big mistake.

Dolly Well, your decision appears to be based on principle.

Gregorio It is a question of principle.

Dolly You should become a politician and run under the slogan "Boring Butts, Unite."

Gregorio I hate your sarcasm couched in morality.

Dolly And I detest your morality couched in sarcasm.

Gregorio Dolly, let me make this absolutely clear. I refuse to be a part of this investment.

Dolly Dignity is not negotiable!

Gregorio Exactly!

(Mariana and Luna enter.)

Mariana Well, my husband is in a good mood!

Gregorio Your husband is very satisfied with himself!

Dolly *(Ironically)* Your husband is a man. Very much a man.

(Simon comes in radiant. The new Simon should contrast dramatically with the Simon of Act One. He is very content, dynamic, happy. He is wearing a hip new purple suit and a fun tie in good taste.)

Simon Dolly, Gregorio, my family. We've done it!

Mariana What have we done?

Simon I have big news!

Dolly What happened?

Simon Four supermarket chains have bought our entire supply of colored toilet paper, and we have to triple the production because everyone has bought the paper without even seeing it first. It's an enormous financial triumph! That's what happened!

Dolly I told you, Simon!

Luna I told you, Simon!

Simon *(To Dolly)* What you told me is nothing compared to your accomplishments. You're a design genius! You have impressive talent! You're one of a kind! *(Scrutinizing Gregorio.)* Gregorio! You're speechless.

(A pause. Gregorio looks straight ahead with stony stare. Mariana looks implacably at her husband. Luna laughs.)

Simon Gregorio, aren't you going to give me a hug?

Gregorio A hug? Sure. Of course.

Mariana And?

Simon *(Grabbing Gregorio and hugging him)* We have to enjoy this success in order to appreciate it all the more.

Gregorio Yes.

Mariana It's just that Gregorio can't believe it.

Gregorio No.

Simon Are you overcome by emotion, as am I.

Dolly *(Facing Gregorio)* Is that what you're really feeling?

Luna He feels happy.

Dolly *(Rebuking him)* Do you feel happy?

Gregorio Yes, I am because...I feel...it's marvelous! I'm too happy for words! *(He blows up. He grabs the rolls of colored paper and throws them in the air like party favors.)* I'm delighted to be a part of this business! I'm delighted with the success! I'm elated to be associated with people like Dolly Goldberg!

Mariana Gregorio, you don't need to make a spectacle of yourself.

Luna If I were you, Gregorio, I'd keep my mouth shut and put the profits in my pocket.

Gregorio Mariana! Luna! I told you that this was what the country needed to feel like part of the first world.

Dolly *(Harsh)* Gregorio, what you said was that you wanted to get out of this particular venture.

Gregorio Well, I'm the impulsive type!

Dolly You said that as soon as Simon arrived you were going to ask him for your investment back.

Gregorio Me?

Mariana Gregorio, did you really say that?

Gregorio Well, it doesn't really matter what I said, what matters is that this is a complete success!

Luna You're absolutely right! Let's party! *(She exits.)*

Dolly Gregorio, I presume that you're going to do the right thing and announce your retirement. Unless you've lowered your standards of the national butts for a few "bucks."

Simon You must have misunderstood, Dolly.

Dolly *(Taking charge of Gregorio)* Gregorio! After all, you're all man.

Gregorio Of course I am.

Dolly A man of his word.

Gregorio A man of only one word!

Dolly Then, make yourself clear!

Mariana Dolly. Please.

Dolly Please, what?

Mariana You said that you came to this house to bring us love.

Dolly Love yes, but to sanction lies, no.

Gregorio *(He jumps up. Challenging)* Oh really? You didn't come here to sanction lies? You're always transparent and sincere? Are you sure? Are you sure that Dolly Goldberg is telling the whole truth and nothing but the truth? Or would you like me to be more explicit? In other words, would you like me to tell it like it is? Do you want us to let the whole truth unfold, Dolly dear? So I'm a hypocrite! Would you like to compare our respective abilities to lie?

Mariana That's enough, Gregorio!!!

(Dolly is very hurt.)

Gregorio The sincere, untouchable, impeccable, perfect Dolly!

(Pause)

Dolly Are you threatening me?

Gregorio You're accusing me of lying! It's possible that I...at times...am not completely truthful. At times...well...they're not big lies, at least they're not serious. They're not questions of integrity like yours! *(Luna enters looking questioningly at Simon.)*

Simon I don't understand anything that's going on. Everything is going well, we've succeeded in a way that we could never have imagined, and they're fighting.

Gregorio *(On the attack again)* Are your sure you're not hiding anything?

Mariana Gregorio! Knock it off!

Simon Dolly, what are you hiding?

Dolly *(Serious)* Undoubtedly, Gregorio is referring to your son, Javier.

Gregorio You bet I am! It's Simon's favorite topic!

Simon Ay! Why? Why, Luna?

Luna Petty things don't concern me at all. I'm not interested in people who can't enjoy life. Now, I'm going to open this great big bottle of champagne! Let's explode with happiness! *(She kisses Simon.)* You promised me an emerald, Simon, and now you have no excuses not to buy me one. *(Luna rings for the servants.)*

Simon But, why?

Gregorio Why what? Why doesn't he come to see you now that he's become all man?

Mariana *(Trying to make Gregorio stop talking)* Gregorio.

Simon Gregorio is right! I'm ready to patch things up. If I can wear this purple suit, I can reconcile with my son. And today's the day! This is his triumph too!

Luna Today? Today of all days? I want to enjoy this. Why do you insist on ruining our fun? Let's enjoy our newfound wealth! I've never been so rich! Who could have dreamed that a few rolls of toilet paper were the key to paradise? *(Two servants enter with champagne for all.)* I always wanted to have a bunch of male servants. French champagne for everyone!

(As the two servants open the bottles the corks burst out with a great deal of noise.)

Gregorio *(Ironic)* Long live brightly colored toilet paper!

(The champagne is served. Luna hands out the champagne.)

Luna Now we're living the way we should. We're people of the world!

Dolly Of what world, Luna?

Luna The world of the well-to-do.

Gregorio Cheers!

(Everyone toasts.)

Simon We're all reunited! Call him, Dolly, tell him that I forgive him!

Mariana *(Drinking)* But he didn't ask for your forgiveness.

Luna Drink up, Simon, stop complicating things…
(Luna serves everyone more champagne.)
Simon *(Taking a sip)* You can't deny me the pleasure of seeing my son!
Dolly *(Approaching Simon)* Simon Goldberg!!! I don't know if you're deaf, blind, or both, but I have told you a thousand times that Javier does not want to see you!
Gregorio *(Provoking)* But you can see her. Do you see her, Simon?
Simon Yes, I see her.
Gregorio *(Drinking his champagne)* And what do you see?
(Simon falls to the floor.)
Luna Again with the heart attacks!
(Dolly and Mariana help Simon up.)
Mariana *(To Gregorio)* You shouldn't keep upsetting someone of Daddy's age.
Simon Please, someone get me a doctor. *(He sits on a chair. He closes his eyes.)* Air. Air.
Luna *(Fanning her husband with one hand and drinking champagne with the other)* Before you have your heart attack you are definitely going to buy me an emerald ring, and a ruby choker and a bracelet just like the one the queen of England wears! Do you hear me, sweetheart?
Gregorio Open your eyes and tell me what you see. What do you see, Simon?
Simon I see that we're rich. And that I have the runs.
Luna Does everything give you the runs, Simon?
Simon Everything.
Dolly Well, look on the bright side. We've got plenty of toilet paper, Simon. So you can have the runs as much as you want.
Gregorio But before he does, he's going to tell me what he sees when he looks at you.
Mariana *(Nervous)* Gregorio, what's wrong with you?
Luna *(Trying to change the mood)* He needs a drink. He's worked very hard to make us happy. Champagne for Gregorio!
(Luna serves Gregorio more Champagne, which he drinks.)
Gregorio Why don't you smell her, Simon. Doesn't she smell familiar?
(Simon sits up and smells her.)
Simon You changed perfumes, Dolly? I can't stand it. It's making me dizzy. Luna, hold me up.
Mariana *(Takes Gregorio to the side.)* He's an old man!!! He can't handle these kinds of tests.
(Simon faints. Luna throws some champagne to wake him up.)

Luna Don't make him faint.

(Simon gets up without any help.)

Simon Feeling bad feels so good! I don't know what I see, but I see everything double. Luna I promise as soon as Javier comes over you'll get your emeralds and rubies.

Luna We have to get him over here. It's...

Simon If you get him over here, I will die of happiness!!!

(Luna opens another bottle of champagne and serves everyone.)

Luna Don't you dare die now. *(Everyone toasts. She says with biting irony)* Health, money, and love.

Dolly *(The same)* Money, money, and money!!!

Mariana *(The same)* Love, love, and love!!!

Gregorio *(The same)* Health, health, and health!!! *(They clink their glasses together with such force that they spill champagne all over. They're all a bit tipsy. The telephone rings and Gregorio answers it.)* Hello? Yes Leonor, it's me, Gregorio. Congress has ordered 10,000 rolls of Imperial Gold? Great!!! Of course we'll take the order! I'll be right there! *(He hangs up.)*

Mariana Ten thousand rolls!

Luna Do the senators have the runs too?

Dolly Gregorio, this business isn't big enough for the two of us. Either you go, or I go.

Simon *(Breaking in)* You're both staying!

Dolly But...

Simon You're both staying because I said so!

Luna What??? This is the Simon that I love!

Simon Me too! This is the Simon Goldberg that I love! *(He is very drunk.)* The one that has the powerful voice and indisputable authority! *(Drinks some champagne.)* The one that's going to get his son to come see him! Because my family comes first! I want to see my family united! Enough of these stupid fights!

Dolly Stupid?

Simon *(Ordering)* Kiss Gregorio, Dolly!

Luna *(To Dolly)* That's an order!

Dolly Me? Kiss him yourself!

Luna *(To Simon)* That's an order!

Simon It wouldn't bother me at all to kiss him! *(Simon goes over to Gregorio and gives him a theatrical kiss.)* See, that doesn't affect my masculinity! Am I any less masculine because of an insignificant little kiss? On the contrary, my masculinity is irrefutable! *(He gives Gregorio* *another theatrical kiss.)*

Gregorio That's enough! Another kiss and I'll throw up!

Simon I had hoped for a more romantic response, Gregorio! Now kiss Dolly. I won't allow any quarreling during the moment of my greatest success!

Gregorio Why did I ever marry into this family? I'm just a regular guy! A normal Argentine! But you're all driving me crazy! Crazy! *(To Simon)* You want me to kiss Dolly?

Simon Of course I do!

Dolly and Mariana Nooooo!

Luna Yeeeees!

(Gregorio goes to Dolly and kisses her on the mouth. Dolly slaps him. Mariana slaps Dolly.)

Gregorio That's it. I've had it with family quarrels! I'm going to the office! I have to work! Someone has to make sure this business is running!

(Gregorio goes out slamming the door. Dolly and Mariana remain facing each other. Simon begins to cry.)

Luna You're happy! I've never seen you happier!

Simon *(Crying)* I have to go to the bathroom. I think I'll try the Fucia Pink paper.

Luna *(Picking up some rolls and takes them in to Simon)* Excuse me. I have the runs too. I think I'll try Tropical Amethyst!

(They go out leaving Mariana and Dolly alone.)

Dolly What's wrong with you?

Mariana Well you've managed to make Gregorio crazy about you. We're all crazy about you. What else do you want?

Dolly To leave.

Mariana Oh no, Dolly Goldberg! I won't let you. You can't do that and you can't steal my husband!

Dolly Listen to me...

Mariana Have you two already slept together? Tell me the truth! Are you two pretending to fight so you can hide the truth? *(Dolly laughs and kisses Mariana who is overcome with jealousy.)* That kiss he gave you didn't look like the first one. You have always liked my men! Always!

Dolly I know, darling. You haven't talked to me for ten years!

Mariana We were just about to get married and you...!

Dolly *(Upset)* Listen, are you going to keep opening old wounds?

Mariana No, I'm opening new ones!

Dolly If you didn't open new ones...

Mariana *(Unable to contain herself.)* Do you make love in motels?

Dolly I've never stepped into a motel in my entire life! And I own four of them! One for gay men. One for lesbians. Another for soldiers who sleep with transvestites. And another for old folks.

Mariana You're going off on a tangent! Look me in the eyes and tell me the truth! Are you my husband's lover?

Dolly Me? Dolly Goldberg? Do you really think so?

Mariana And to think that I'm the one who called you! I just handed my husband over to you! Don't take him away, Dolly. I love him!!! I'm not going to humiliate myself. I'll let Gregorio choose. *(She pauses.)* I had to call you. Papi was suffering!

Dolly What? You called me to save all your asses! That's why you called me! And I came, and I fulfilled your request my dear sister! Or didn't I? Perhaps I haven't completely paid off my debt.

Mariana *(Interrupts.)* How long have you two been cheating on me? Tell me. Don't look at me with an innocent face. I'd rather know the truth.

Dolly The truth! The truth is that you all are using me! Do you have another accusation to make? So I'm sleeping with your husband? If you're having problems with your husband...

Mariana Problems? We've never had problems. And you're not about to become one!

Dolly For the moment, I'm your solution! I'm yours, your husband's, Luna's and Simon Goldberg's solution! You asked me for help and I brought it! Now, if you want to throw a bucket of shit on me, throw it in peace! There's more than enough diarrhea here, and toilet paper galore! But I do not like Gregorio! I DON'T LIKE HIM! I don't like him!

(Simon and Luna enter, ready to go out.)

Simon You don't have to like him, you just have to love him, dear!

Dolly I have to love my husband! I have the best husband in the world! He's a great guy, brilliant. He loves me, and he puts up with everything I do!

Simon Javier…Bring him to me, Dolly!

Dolly He can't come.

Luna He has to come.

Simon I want him to come!

Luna And I want my jewelry!

Mariana And I want you all out of here!

Simon Exactly what we were doing. And I have plenty of toilet paper in case of emergency!

Luna If you also have your checkbook in case of emergency, you'll make me the happiest woman in the world!

(Luna drags Simon out the door. Dolly looks at Mariana sternly.)

Dolly You were accusing me. Don't stop now. Go on, my dearest sister, I want to know how much resentment you have piled up. Go on. Go on! What else?

Mariana Dolly...

Dolly It was senseless for me to stay. I don't fit in here!

Mariana Dolly, forgive me. I'm imagining things.

Dolly *(Shrugging her shoulders)* We'll let it go at that.

Mariana Dolly, I want you to know that I, in spite of the fact that at times I don't show it. And that other times I have to make an effort not to show it... and other times, when it shows, I try to make it look like the opposite... I want you to know that I love you.

Dolly What? *(Mariana kisses her.)* Girl, enough with the absurd sentiments. You just accused me of the worst and now...

Mariana I just asked you to forgive me! Or didn't you hear me?

(They look at each other and laugh.)

Dolly I didn't hear you. Ask me louder!

Mariana *(Shouting as loud as she can)* Go to hell, Dolly Goldberg!

Dolly *(Shouting)* Now I heard you.

(They laugh. They're still drunk. They hug each other.)

Mariana Don't you have to go home?

Dolly Paco and I had a fight.

Mariana Again?

Dolly Again.

Mariana What's wrong with him?

Dolly He's jealous. He feels left out of the family!

Mariana Of course! He has a right to be angry. You haven't even introduced him to Dad!

Dolly Everyone here has a right to be angry about something. Gregorio, because ever since I showed up he's had to take second place. Paco, because I hardly see him since I entered this house. Daddy, because he desperately wants to see Javier, his legitimate son. He doesn't want to see me because I'm his illegitimate daughter-in-law! And you're angry because, because...

Mariana *(Laughing uncontrollably)* Why, Dolly?

Dolly Because you lost a brother, and you want to be the only daughter, and...

Mariana And why are you upset?

Dolly Because I've lost my mind! Among such reasonable people, what shred of reason could I have left?

Mariana The reason for being Dolly.

Dolly That isn't a reason, that's a person! Don't confuse me, Mariana!

Mariana I'm the confused one!

Dolly You? And what confuses you?

Mariana I look at you and I miss Javier.

Dolly Well, the same thing happens to me. I look at you and I miss Javier.

Mariana Oh no, not that! You were Javier! And I miss him! The one who misses Javier is me! Especially when I look at you.

Dolly Mariana, you're not going to doubt that I could actually miss myself!!!

Mariana Maybe you miss being Javier. But I miss being with Javier!

Dolly I miss being with you, being Javier. What fun we had!

Mariana *(They embrace.)* Yes, what fun. What fun... we had together.

Dolly I remember when we lived in Flores. We used to go to the park to coax money out of people? In costumes.   We were the hit of the neighborhood. THE GOLDBERG BROTHERS! Our first job. Our first step into the world! What a wonderful time it was.

Mariana *(Moved)* You really think so? *(Incredulous)* Dolly, do you really miss Javier?

Dolly Very much. Not only do I miss Javier. I miss the way we were then. I miss the Goldberg Brothers!

Mariana You don't know how happy it makes me to know that you haven't denied...that you haven't denied our childhood.

Dolly How could you think that I would? I absolutely remember all of the details. We even had a portable dressing room in the attic. You'd put on my makeup and I'd put on yours. *(She pauses.)* We were very daring.

Mariana I... *(She pauses, confessing something very secret.)* Do you know in all these years since we've seen each other how often I've slipped into the basement and taken out our costumes?

Dolly Don't tell me that we still have some of our life...it's...don't tell me there's still something left from those days!

Mariana One day, when I was looking for a fan in the basement, I discovered a box. I opened it and found that Mami had preserved our costumes in mothballs.

Dolly Mami! Thank you! You're an angel!

Mariana Do you want to see them?

Dolly I'm dying to see them! Yes! The Goldberg Brothers! How young, how beautiful and how crazy.

Mariana Help me.

(Dolly and Mariana exit and return with a giant box and two pairs of stilts. The box holds costumes: tuxes with tails, top hats, and long pants to cover the stilts. There are juggling items, bowling pins to throw in the air, magic games, and a small box with a crank. Crazed by discovering reminders of their youth, the two put on costumes and climb on the stilts. Mariana begins to juggle. As Dolly begins to turn the crank on the box, it plays various tangos in the tinny sound of the organ grinder.)

Dolly Ladies and Gentlemen of Flores. For all of you who recognize the tremendous talent in front of you. For you who see our promising and prosperous future! We are here, The Goldberg Brothers!

Mariana We were born to entertain, and that's good. There's nothing better than helping people forget their frightening real lives for a moment. For a moment we'll let them fly like this dove *(She takes out top hat, and inside is a stuffed dove.)* So it's stuffed; but it's a real dove from our town, specially stuffed by our very own artist, Celedonio Marturano; and when I let it out my brother begins his magnificent act!

Dolly What act?

Mariana You used to breathe fire, Javier!

Dolly Me? Breathe fire? How did I do it?

Mariana You'd put kerosene on your teeth, you lit a match and put it near your mouth and flashhhhhhhh! Everyone applauded. They would throw money at us. A lot of money. It was our first big enterprise!

Dolly I'm not in the mood. It's easier to make colored toilet paper! If I burn my tongue, what will I use to kiss Paco when I try to make up with him tonight?

Mariana You see? That's the Javier that I miss! The one who used to burn his tongue!

Dolly But our other acts were as popular as the fire act. We had our song and a dance.

Mariana Yes, after the fabulous fire number, we sang and danced. Remember our theme song?

Dolly The whole town would sing it, we could've became famous.

(They prepare themselves and recall the song from the past. They dance and sing together.)

Dolly and Mariana

> Today my love, since it's not raining
> Let's open the umbrella of our light dreams

Days filled with blue skies, sweet and brief
Gusts of love that chase us both.
Don't let yourself come down from this beautiful place
Today my love, since it's not raining
climb the stairs towards heaven
absurd afternoons that ride on trains
crazy passions that always remain.
Don't let yourself come down from this beautiful place
Today my love, since it's not raining
put on a dress light and gay.
Magical kisses sublime.
We are as we'll be all through time.
Don't let yourself come down from this beautiful place
Today my love, since it's not raining
come fly with me and together we may
sketch time with its tenuous hold,
It's worth it to touch its face.
Don't let yourself come down from this beautiful place
(They embrace and fall on the floor exhausted.)
Mariana Sometimes I think there are three of us, Mariana, Javier, and Dolly!
Dolly There are three of us.
(They take off the costumes and put them back in the box.)
Dolly and Mariana *(To the box)* We love you, Javier! *(To Dorita's picture)* We love you, Mami!
(They embrace, happy.)
Dolly Can I put on "Casta Diva" in tribute to Mami?
Mariana Of course.
(Dolly puts on the CD of Maria Callas singing "Casta Diva." The two lie down, exhausted. They listen to the aria. The lights dim until they go out. "Casta Diva" keeps playing at full volume. As the music ends, the lights slowly go back on.)

Scene 2

(It is another day and Dolly is alone typing at the computer. She is wearing glasses and has a pile of papers on the desk. She is like any executive working at a frantic pace. She is drinking a shake. The phone rings and she answers.)

Dolly Yes, Oh Gimenez! We were waiting for your call! What? We agreed on the imports. Well, half national and half imported, then. Yes, buy, buy Gimenez. We're behind on the deliveries. But those are mere details! The important thing is to buy now. Buy! *(The doorbell rings.)* I have to go, but keep in touch. Ciao, yes…yes, all right. Ciao. *(She hangs up. She opens the door with a folder in her hand, submerged in her work without expecting to see her husband. When she sees him she drops the file. Takes off her glasses. She can't believe it.)* What are you doing here?

Paco Can I come in?

Dolly *(Hesitating. She lets him in, aware that there is no one there.)* Come in, come in. But…

Paco I shouldn't have come. *(He looks around the room, interested.)* I like what you've done with the place. Very amusing! *(He walks around taking in the surroundings. Dolly is very nervous. She watches him.)* You don't seem pleased with my surprise visit.

Dolly Paco, you didn't come here just to please me.

Paco There's always a glimmer of optimism for a soul in love. I thought: "If Dolly sees me, she'll like the idea, even if it's out of pity."

Dolly Do you want to show me something?

Paco I want to warn you.

Dolly *(Cutting him short)* I don't like your tone.

Paco Well I don't like the tone, the melody, the words, or the place where I fit in all this.

Dolly I'm very sorry sweetheart.

Paco "I'm very sorry sweetheart" means that "I'm not going to change anything in this chapter, sweetheart"

Dolly I…

Paco *(Cutting her short)* I! III! IIIIII! Everything is happening for you. What about me? I didn't marry Javier's wife. I married you. And because I married you and love you…

Dolly I love you too. But I'm very much involved in fixing my own biography, if you can call it that.

Paco Dolly, this can't go on.

Dolly Paco, I need your help.

Paco You had it, but I'm tired of being alone. I miss you.

Dolly And I miss you too. But I have to admit that I have this need, this crazy desire for…*(It's difficult for her to say it.)* For vengeance. I need my father to need me out of vengeance. To make everyone around here need me is very satisfying. Very, very satisfying.

Paco All right, Dolly, it's done. Mission accomplished. You pulled them from the brink of ruin, you gave them back their reputation, you brought in innovative ideas, you gave them back the will to live. I think that if you wanted tribute and recognition, you got it. Now we want you at home.

Dolly Paco, give me time.

Paco No.

Dolly I have to find a way to introduce you as my husband.

Paco I am your husband. Your father is my father-in-law. Let's get together on this, Dolly. Either I come into this house through the front door, or I withdraw all my support.

Dolly *(Furious)* You can't do this to me!

Paco And you can erase me off the map so easily? So you're allowed to turn me into a nobody, to decide that I don't exist? It's all right for you to do that?

Dolly Don't be idiotic, Paco.

Paco Idiotic? This "vanity fair" that you've created makes me tired. Vanity is coming out your ears, it's encrusted around your waist and is orbiting around your head. I'm fed up with your vanity. How long do you think I'm going to put up with it, darling? How many pounds of vanity do you need to be satisfied?

(Dolly slaps him. Paco does not return in kind. A tense pause.)

Dolly Forgive me. It's just that you've never spoken to me like that before.

Paco I was never a clandestine part of your life before. You've never had to worry about someone coming in and finding us. You've never made us suffer, so that you could fix I-don't-know-what-kind-of-irreparable-shit, irr-e-pa-ra-ble!

Dolly I feel like a fool!

Paco You are ridiculous. And you're ruining our relationship. I want you at least to realize this, that you're ruining our relationship.

Dolly I thought I could count on your support.

Paco You didn't think anything! You decided! You decided that the least I could do was to disappear in silence, without protesting, to take care of OUR house, OUR family while you gave yourself the luxury of rubbing it in to YOUR family, the family that kicked you out on your ass ten years ago!

(Dolly looks toward the front door.)

Dolly Just be a little more patient.

Paco I'm finished.

Dolly You're forcing me.

Paco *(Cutting her short)* You forced me. Don't turn everything around. I don't want to have anything else to do with this place. I'm handing it over to you in a package with a bow. *(Fed up)* Why do you keep looking at the door?

Dolly My father could come in at any minute.

Paco And?

Dolly Do you really want to destroy everything that I've worked so hard to build during this time?

Paco I'm dying to.

Dolly You want to crush me.

Paco I want... I want my Dolly back. That's what I want.

Dolly Get her back or kill her?

Paco Get her back or kill her. *(Pause)* I want to be part of your family, I want to be received as your legitimate husband. I want them to know that I had the guts to marry you.

Dolly Do you expect my father to give you a medal for marrying me?

Paco He *should* give me one!

Dolly I didn't know that you were so special. I thought I was the star of this movie.

Paco Yin and yang, the cooked and the raw, the possible and the impossible. Our relationship has been a delicate balance. Now that you've turned yourself into the daughter that you never were, our marriage is slipping through our fingers. And when something begins to fall apart, someone has to have the foresight and the courage to prevent disaster before it happens.

Dolly I can't give him the truth in one blow.

Paco *(Provoking)* And just how are you going to tell him?

Dolly You came here to cause an uproar!

Paco Of course, because if I don't do it, you'll come back home and you won't find me there.

Dolly *(Crying)* On top of everything, now you threaten me like the classic macho, and in my father's house.

Paco At the moment it's your father-in-law's house, and your husband's name is Javier Goldberg and I don't exist.

Dolly Don't do this to me.

Paco I want to begin to exist, Dolly. I want to exist again for you.

Dolly I also want to exist, as that man's daughter and not his daughter-in-law. I want to be Paco Frias's wife and not my own.

Paco *(Hard)* Well, you're the one who invented all this. So disinvent it, baby!

Dolly I can't. *(Pause)* Help me!

Paco Well, that's why I came. I came to help the two of us. This is absolutely crazy. You're living a lie. And if you keep playing this deceitful game, just so your father will owe you his life, you'll have to play alone, Dolly. I'm leaving.

(Dolly is completely upset. Mariana arrives loaded down with packages. She expects to find her sister alone, but she is surprised to see Paco.)

Mariana Huh? You?

Paco Me. Yes, your brother-in-law, the ghost. But don't fool yourself into thinking that I'm really here. I'm an apparition. You've all managed to make me disappear so that my wife can exist!

Mariana What? Don't blame us. I was informed and not consulted in making Papi think that she was my sister-in-law.

Paco Mariana, do you think that this can be fixed?

Mariana Ask your husband, I mean my brother, in other words, your wife.

(Paco looks at the two of them. He begins to move toward the door as if to leave.)

Paco She is your ex-brother and my soon to be ex-wife!

(Furious, he leaves slamming the door.)

Dolly I suppose you think that I'm a control freak, a puppeteer controlling everyone.

Mariana No, not exactly, but I think you're running out of string. Watch out, sister-in-law, one day the puppets leave the stage.

Dolly *(Furious)* Don't you call me sister-in-law!

Mariana But for now we are sisters-in-law. Now, if someone were to wonder why my sister-in-law is so generous, and soooooo affectionate and caring, people could come to any kind of conclusion.

Dolly And what conclusion have you come to?

Mariana *(Shrugging her shoulders)* I'm up to my neck in this, so I can't use you and criticize my life at the same time.

Dolly Paco's right! Paco's right! *(Dolly grabs her purse.)* Paco's right! *(She goes to the front door.)* Tell Papi that Javier will be here in a few minutes! *(Dolly goes running after Paco.)*

Mariana *(Addressing the packages)* Oh sure! Paco is completely right! *(She begins to pick up the packages from the floor. She puts them on a chair and looks at the things that she has bought. Luna and Simon come in.)*

Simon Good morning, Mariana. Where's Dolly?

Luna *(Looking at what Mariana has in her hand)* Wow! How pretty!

Mariana Papi, Javier's coming over today.

Simon Whaaaaat?

Luna Hooooow?

Simon When?

Mariana In a little while.

Simon Are you sure that this isn't a joke?

Mariana Dolly doesn't play these kinds of tricks. Luna, let's leave them alone. I'm going to take these things to the car, in two minutes I'm coming back to get you.

(Mariana leaves with the packages.)

Simon Well, how about that!

Luna Isn't this what you wanted?

Simon Yes.

Luna You've wanted to see Javier for months.

Simon Yes, yes.

Luna Good! You got your way, Simon Goldberg!

Simon But why did he decide so suddenly? If he has refused for so long?

Luna Simon, before you wondered why he wouldn't come see you, and now you're wondering why he's coming.

Simon No. After so many years, I think it's good that Javier and I have a talk. Face to face.

(Mariana comes in the door.)

Mariana Come on, Luna. He should be here any minute.

Simon Wait until he gets here. Don't leave me alone.

Luna Simon. You're the one who started all this. It was you who pressured Dolly day after day.

Mariana It's the best thing that could happen. We all need this. I don't understand why I'm so nervous. *(To her father)* Papi, I hope you're calm.

(Luna touches up her makeup before she leaves.)

Simon Calm? *(Trembling)* It's cold? Where are you going? I need you with me.

Mariana Be strong, Papi. Your children demand you to be strong. You drove us crazy insisting that you couldn't live without seeing my brother. Now stop trembling. Javier is on his way. Do you understand?

Simon What will I say to him?

Mariana Well, you're the one who called him. Now you want me to tell you what to say?

Simon I know very well what to say to my son.

Mariana He's also thought of lots of things to say during these ten years. *(Pauses.)* Papi, wasn't this what you wanted?

Simon Yes, yes. But just when it seemed I'd never see him again, he changed his mind. *(Pause)* I'm afraid of putting my foot in my mouth, of not knowing what to say.

Luna Tell him you're sorry, whatever comes to mind. Come on, he's your son.

Simon Yes, of course.

(Simon looks at her seriously.)

Mariana Smile. *(He forces a smile.)* If he sees that face he'll run away.

Simon OK. Is this a more fatherly smile? *(He tries to relax. He smiles.)*

Mariana More what?

Simon Fatherly.

Mariana And what kind of fatherhood are you trying to sell to Javier? *(Simon looks serious.)*

Luna Just smile, that's it!

(Gregorio enters.)

Gregorio Why are you still up here? I've got the car running, and Dolly is about to arrive. I mean Javier.

Simon Is he coming with Dolly?

Gregorio *(Giving Simon a slap on the back)* A historic encounter is about to take place, Simon. Are you ready?

Simon No.

Gregorio Now don't tell me you're afraid of that pansy? He's a pussycat. Be tough with him. Don't get weak on me.

Mariana Gregorio. You're turning into a sarcastic, bitter man, and bitter people are unattractive. Their skin turns gray, their eyes become fixed, their mouths twist to the southeast, their ears dry up and fall off, and their hair curls up and they begin to emit a foul odor that makes everyone around them hold their nose. *(She holds her nose.)*

Gregorio Are you in love with me?

Mariana Madly.

(They leave. Simon remains alone waiting for Javier. He paces around the room. He looks at himself in the mirror. He doesn't like his tie, so he changes it. He puts on cologne. He combs his hair. He is very impatient. The doorbell rings, he opens it and sees Javier there. The actor who plays the part of Dolly enters dressed as a man. His clothing

is ultramodern, in very good taste and subdued. Simon forces a smile.
He is not sure whether to greet Javier with a kiss or a handshake. He
doesn't do either. Javier looks intensely at his father.)
Simon Well. Finally.
Javier Yes, finally.
Simon Come in. Make yourself comfortable. After all, you are at
home. *(Simon studies Javier. Javier looks at him seriously.)*
Javier I'll try to make myself comfortable.
Simon Yes, and I'll try to make myself comfortable too.
(They are tense and timid. There is a mutual lack of confidence.)
Javier You have a very interesting house.
Simon Dolly decorated it.
Javier Ah yes, yes, Dolly, of course. You can see her touch.
Simon Dolly turned my life around.
(Simon smiles. Javier does not.)
Javier Let's talk about each other, Simon.
Simon Sure, that's why I came here.
Javier I'm the one who came here.
Simon Yes, of course. I meant to say, that's why you came.
Javier Well, you insisted so much on seeing me.
Simon Yes, I wanted to see you, well, I wanted to see Javier again.
Javier OK, now that you see me, what do you see?
Simon I see that you're very tense. Are you OK?
Javier Yes, thanks. *(Pause)* Are you going to keep me standing?
Simon Sit down. Please, sit down. *(Javier sits down. Simon remains*
standing. Javier stands up. Simon sits down. Javier sits down. Simon
stands up.) Can I get you a whiskey?
Javier I don't drink, Simon.
Simon Are you going to call me Simon?
Javier Isn't that your name?
Simon I'm your Father.
Javier You want me to call you Papa?
Simon I would like that.
Javier I'll have to practice it.
Simon *(Anguished)* Well, I'm going to have a whiskey, Javier. Dolly
gave me a bottle of very good scotch.
Javier I don't want you to talk any more about Dolly. You and I
haven't seen each other in ten years, and it seems that we should talk
about us.
Simon *(Simon pours himself a drink and drinks it.)* It's that she's, she's

...unique. Dolly is marvelous, she's sweet, she's a good person, she's creative, really intelligent, an unusual personality, she's all a woman should be and more. She has something that shines from within. She truly has changed my life. She is irreplaceable, and she knows it. She knows it, she knows that she has a permanent place in my heart because she's no fool, she is very bright, very talented, she gave me back the will to live. She...

Javier *(Cutting him off)* Enough already! Please don't mention her name again! *(Simon is quiet.)* Dolly, Dolly, Dolly! You insisted on meeting with me to talk about her? What am I doing here? I feel ridiculous talking about Dolly. You're making things very difficult. And they're already difficult enough. Or perhaps you think it's easy for me to come to your place! I'm a busy person, I thought you made this appointment for a reason! What do you want to see me for? Speak up!

Simon It's not easy to get to the point. And Dolly is the link between you and me. That's why I mentioned her, as a connection.

Javier All right. Now that we've identified the connection, you can fill me in on whatever made you want to see me.

Simon *(Uncomfortable. Not knowing what to say)* Yes, of course.

Javier You're sure? Why are your legs shaking?

Simon *(Simon controls his shaking.)* I never thought Dolly would affect you so much.

Javier I know Dolly's virtues.

Simon She really is a treasure.

Javier *(Javier would like to kill Simon.)* Again?

Simon *(Uncomfortable)* How are you, Javier? So much time! A lot of years have gone by since you left.

Javier *(Interrupts.)* I didn't leave, you kicked me out.

Simon On your ass. I kicked you out on your ass. I found you in... *(He interrupts himself.)* And to top it all off, he was Mariana's. On your ass! *(An uncomfortable pause)*

Javier Yes, on my ass.

Simon *(Standing up)* Throwing you out hurt me too, you're my only son.

Javier *(Standing up)* And you're my only father. Unfortunately.

Simon I'm not a monster.

Javier Neither am I.

Simon I want to tell you that in spite of the horrifying image you have of me, I'm a good guy.

Javier I also want to tell you that in spite of the horrifying image you have of me, I'm a good guy.

Simon Are you going to repeat everything I say?

Javier Up to now you haven't said a thing, Papi.

Simon I liked the sound of that "Papi." You said it very naturally.

Javier Dolly told me you want to ask my forgiveness. Papi...

Simon Sit down. It makes me nervous when you're standing. *(Javier sits down. He shifts his legs and body as if he cannot find a comfortable position. He walks around the room.)* Dolly picked out those chairs. They're trendy, but it's hard to get comfortable.

Javier *(Standing up)* Dolly lied to me! You don't have the least intention of asking my forgiveness!

Simon *(He pushes Javier into one of the chairs.)* Dolly is incapable of deceiving anyone!

Javier Dolly? Incapable? Don't you believe it!

Simon If there is anyone truly sincere, even her slightest gestures are transparent, if there is anyone truly honest, it's Dolly. So if she told you I wanted to ask your forgiveness, she was telling the truth. The truth, I tell you. She's as clear as glass. I'm not saying that she doesn't lie from time to time, but they're such little white lies. They're lies that bring out the truth. *(Javier covers his ears. He doesn't want to hear another word about Dolly. Simon stops talking.)* Javier! Always so melodramatic! *(He uncovers Javier's ears.)* I wasn't talking about Dolly, I was talking about the truth. *(Mechanically)* And the truth is that I want to reestablish a cordial and affectionate relationship between father and son based upon mutual tolerance and the extraordinary respect that we've always held for each other.

Javier *(Perplexed)* Did you memorize that?

Simon How did you know?

Javier *(Smiling)* In order to talk to me you had to memorize a speech?

Simon I was afraid to embarrass myself.

Javier Give me a whiskey.

Simon But you don't drink.

Javier I didn't until a minute ago. *(Simon serves him.)* From now on I'm going to spend the rest of my life sipping whiskey so that I can forget this nightmare called "The Reunion with Old Simon Goldberg After Ten Years." Cheers!

Simon Cheers!

(They both drink.)

Javier Give me that speech again. I don't want to miss a word of it.

Simon "And the truth is that I want to reestablish a cordial and affectionate relationship between father and son based upon mutual tolerance and the extraordinary respect that we've always held for each other."

Javier That's just marvelous! A real literary masterpiece! To your health! To Dolly!

Simon Now you're the one who mentioned her! *(Pause)* It wasn't easy for me your "strange" period.

Javier Is that why you called me, old man?

Simon No, I thought I'd gotten over it, but I don't want to lie to you, I've only recently learned to forgive you.

Javier You've learned what?

Simon To forgive your past.

Javier But you're the one who's supposed to ask for my forgiveness! I'm not asking you to forgive me! I don't need forgiveness! I love my past. I'm happy to be who I am. Happy!

Simon Look me in the eyes!

Javier *(Fixing his eyes on Simon who approaches him)* Why the hell did you call me, Simon Goldberg? I'm leaving! Our time is up. We've run out of time. Make believe you never saw your son, that I never agreed to come, and that you're dreaming and that when you wake up I'll no longer be a part of your life.

Simon Wait. Don't be so stubborn. *(Javier grabs him by the lapels and pulls him around the room.)* Let me go!

Javier Take a good look at me, for the last time!

Simon Let me go! Let me go you shitty queer!

Javier *(He lets go of his father. His eyes fill with tears.)* There's the truth. That's what you wanted to say to me. *(Javier laughs. He puts on music and begins to behave in a very effeminate way, aggressively provocative.)* Shall we dance, love. What lovely eyes you have, too bad your teeth are a little crooked.

Simon Forgive me, you made me say what I didn't want to say and don't really think.

Javier *(Walking provocatively)* You think so?

Simon Everything came out wrong.

Javier *(Takes out high heels and puts them on.)* Do you like these heels, Papi? Or do you prefer the spike heels?

Simon Seriously, Javier, I didn't mean to offend you.

Javier No? What was that marvelous speech? *(A pause. Simon does not answer.)* You don't know anything about me. I never mattered to you. I never understood you either, and I still don't.

Simon *(Interrupting)* I love you, Javier.

Javier "I love you if you're like I want you to be." But your children are not cardboard cutouts. You just don't have the son you wanted to have.

Simon That's true.

Javier And I don't have the father I wanted either!

Simon That's true. But, in spite of everything...

Javier In spite of everything what?

Simon ˙I love you, son. *(He wants to hug Javier but his son stops him cold. The two look at each other.)*

Javier But that isn't going to be enough. *(Pause)* Do you remember when you took me to the soccer game? Boca was playing.

Simon Are you still a fan?

Javier Go Boca! Go Boca! Go Boca! Go Boca! You thought that would make me a man, but instead of watching the game, I spent the evening looking at the players' legs. And what legs, what shoulders. What bulges! Mama mía!

Simon *(Simon gives him a swat. Angry. Provoking)* With all those pretty girls around. You know, I managed to marry a pretty young thing.

Javier *(Takes Simon's face in his hands.)* Did you hear me, old man? Seriously, are you stupid or just pretending to be?

Simon *(Pause)* I'm pretending to be.

Javier *(Pause. Javier is moved.)* Ahhhh haaaaaah! So you know?

Simon Well, you're the spitting image of your mother.

(A long pause. They're both very moved.)

Javier Was... was that what you wanted to tell Javier?

Simon Yes.

Javier And how long have you known?

Simon I realized little by little.

Javier Aaaaah!

Simon But this has to be a secret between you and me. I... in front of everyone... no. I don't know anything.

Javier Just between us men.

Simon Yes.

(Simon extends his hand. Javier puts out his. They look at each other.)

Javier Well, I don't think we have anything else to say to each other, old man.

Simon I wish I could find the words, so I could speak to my son.

Javier *(Transition)* Now I'm the one who has the runs. May I use your bathroom?

(Simon hands him a roll of the colored toilet paper.)
Simon We'll be a family of shits, right?
(Javier laughs and kisses his father on the cheek.)
Javier You're the shit.
(He goes inside, leaving Simon alone on the stage. A long pause.)
Simon *(Speaking to his son.)* Javier. If you were to return to, I mean, there's no way to go back and... *(Pause)* I'm not criticizing when I say... *(Pause)* Javier, thank you for coming. I know I forced you into it, but we both needed this. *(Pause)* Do you hear me, or am talking like a fool?
Javier *(Off stage)* The Black Tulip is like velvet!
Simon The black what? *(Pause)* Javier, something just occurred to me. We could pretend you've gone on a long trip. *(Pause)* Don't pay attention to me, I don't know what I'm saying.
Javier *(Laughing hard)* Something occurred to me too.
Simon Something else?
Javier *(In a conspiratory tone)* Javier and Dolly split up some time ago, and today you just found out, and she's bringing her real husband to the house.
Simon Not today, Javier! I beg you to let us end this day in peace.
Javier Exactly.
Simon I know that I won't like this guy.
Javier The important thing is that Dolly likes him.
Simon I don't need to meet anyone else. He'll get between her and me, and he'll have an opinion about everything.
Javier Are you jealous?
Simon Terribly.
(Dolly comes out of the bathroom, splendidly dressed.)
Dolly How's it going, Simon?
Simon *(Profoundly affected)* Dolly...
Dolly Do you feel all right, Simon?
Simon I never felt better.
(Simon falls to the floor. Dolly walks over to him and looks at him. She smiles.)
Dolly Papi, are you dead?
Simon *(Standing up suddenly)* Don't call me Papi! That's going too far!
Dolly Perhaps I've gotten too close.
Simon Dolly... I... *(He stops himself.)*
Dolly What, Simon?
Simon Don't call me Simon!

Dolly Yes, Papa.

Simon Papa? Me? *(Pause)* Call me Simon! And with respect!

Dolly Yes, Simon.

Simon The irony is that I love you.

Dolly Well, Simon, ya' win some, ya' lose some.

Simon We have to call 'em as we see 'em. Call me whatever you think you should.

Dolly Yes, Dad.

Simon Dolly, I'm not in any condition to be...

(Simon collapses on the floor and Dolly looks at him. A pause)

Dolly Well, old man, we tried. At least we tried. *(She looks at him waiting for him to get up. Simon does not get up. Dolly grabs her purse and touches up her makeup.)* I'm warning you, if you're really dead I'm not going to feel guilty about it; and if you've only fainted, get up! *(Simon does not get up. Dolly takes him in her arms and puts him on a chair. She takes his pulse and with the other hand picks up the cordless phone and dials a number.)* Hello? Is Mariana there? Well, when she arrives tell her that Dolly called. She needs to come home immediately. Tell her that her father, her father, *(Crying)* her father is, tell her that...*(She lets loose and cries desperately.)* Tell her to come...because we don't have time, he's in his last...if he's not already dead. *(Cries loudly.)* I'm sorry to give her this kind of message over the phone. Thank you. You're very kind. *(She hangs up the phone. She changes her tone.)* Well that should be convincing enough. *(Dolly kisses her father's hand. She moves away from him.)* It was nice knowing you, Papa.

(Dolly looks at him. She looks around the room and gestures good-bye with her hand. Simon is alone on stage.)

Simon *(Suddenly standing up)* Mister Simon Goldberg!

The End

ACTOS DESAFIANTES

LAS OBRAS

DIANA RAZNOVIG

COMBATIENDO EL FUEGO CON FRIVOLIDAD:
Los actos desafiantes de Diana Raznovich

Diana Taylor
Traducido por Daniel Beke

Desde su inicio en Buenos Aires cuando en 1967 ganó un concurso de teatro, la trayectoria de Diana Raznovich como dramaturga ha sido caracterizada por su sentido de humor, su inteligencia, y su inquebrantable reto a la delimitación de los sistemas sociales: Bien sean dictaduras militares autoritarias, sistemas económicos coercitivos, o los más tenues pero no menos restrictivos sistemas de género y constitución sexual. A lo largo de su trabajo, ella indica cómo estos sistemas se interconectan para crear y manipular el deseo mientras definen, posicionan, y controlan los cuerpos deseosos. A través de la presión constante de socialización, las identidades se conforman y los cuerpos se moldean. Las obras de Raznovich representan no solo una cultura *de* reproducción (parecida al fetichismo de los artículos de consumo de Marx) sino también una cultura *como* representación, como una máquina deseosa de generar series de repeticiones y pronunciamientos sin original (un poco parecidos al concepto de lo "hiper-real" de Baudrillaurd).[1] Como dramaturga y dibujante de tira cómica, Raznovich utiliza sus sistemas artísticos para criticar y transgredir las restricciones impuestas por su sociedad, las cuales han sido bastantes por no decir muchas, considerando que es una mujer a la Oscar Wilde, judía y bisexual que alcanza la mayoría de edad durante la Guerra Sucia (1976–83).

A partir de *Plaza hay una sola*, su segunda producción—una *performance* que comprende ocho escenas simultáneas, en un parque público, las cuales el público recorre encontrando una serie de circunstancias (una persona a punto de suicidarse, otra persona dando un discurso sobre una caja de jabón, etc.)—Raznovich ha desafiado las normas tradicionales del teatro, rechazando el ponderado estilo realista tan popular entre sus colegas dramaturgos. Su sentido de humor, su amor por la discontinuidad, la inversión, y lo inesperado, han marcado su trabajo tanto en el teatro como en las tiras cómicas. Pero su carrera como dramaturga fue varada cuando víctima de numerosas amenazas de muerte por parte de las Fuerzas Armadas, tuvo que exilarse en 1975, poco después del golpe de estado que dio inicio el *Proceso de Reorganición Nacional.* Vivió y trabajó en España enseñando dramaturgia en una escuela independiente de teatro, hasta que en 1981 volvió a Argentina para tomar parte en el Teatro Abierto.

El Teatro Abierto reunió a dramaturgos, directores, actores y técnicos, nerviosos porque sus nombres ya aparecían en la lista negra, para producir un ciclo de obras de un acto, y así demostrar que los artistas argentinos no habían sucumbido a los artificios silenciadores de la dictadura. ¿Cómo resistirse a un acto de desafío colectivo tan importante? Aún así, incluso este acto de solidaridad de la oposición pretendía controlar el límite de desafío "aceptable". A varios de los demás dramaturgos les pareció la contribución de Raznovich (*El desconcierto,* una obra interpretada sólo por una actriz) al ciclo "abierto" y contestatario, inapropiado. ¿A quién le pudiera interesar una obra sobre una pianista que no puede hacer que su piano suene en el contexto de la censura y silenciamiento general del *Proceso*? Mientras que las intenciones de Raznovich siempre eran (y son) el reto y la transgresión de los límites represivos, no siempre han sido reconocidas como tal por sus colegas más abiertamente "políticos". Si bien, se le pidió que retirara su obra y sometiera a consideración otra, ella se rehusó.[2] Los militares reaccionaron más violentamente, no sólo hacia su obra sino hacia el proyecto entero, quemando el Teatro Picadero la noche que se puso en escena *El desconcierto.*[3] El Teatro Abierto tuvo que mudarse a otro local, y continuó presentando las producciones entre la creciente oposición gubernamental, y el creciente apoyo popular. No obstante, algunos de los otros artistas "comenzaron a decir que yo era frívola. Lo tomé como un cumplido. No había permiso para mi postura o estilo, y yo lo encontré estupendamente transgresivo".[4] Lejos de ser frívolo, *El desconcierto,* retrata una sociedad atrapada en la producción activa de ficciones nacionales, ficciones que a la postre convierten a toda la población en cómplices silenciosos.

La pianista, Irene della Porta, es contratada por su representante para tocar la *Patética* de Beethoven en un piano que no suena. El público compra boletos para ver a Irene arrancarle sonidos a la nada: "Es como si la mujer y el público, a pesar de que saben que la Sonata de

Beethoven no puede oírse, son misteriosamente capaces de componer 'este otro concierto inexistente'", dicen las direcciones escénicas. Pero después de tantos conciertos silenciosos, Irene della Porta ya no sabe cómo tocar música "real". Los dedos desensibilizados producen notas ásperas y discordantes. Conmocionada y derrotada por su fracaso supremo como artista, della Porta se regocija cuando el piano vuelve a ser mudo.

En el nivel más obvio, *El desconcierto* es una crítica a ambos artistas y público argentino que estuvieron dispuestos a aprobar la censura impuesta por una dictadura militar, convencidos de que estaban involucrados en una comunicación significativa. Lo que atrae a los miembros del público al teatro noche tras noche es, en parte, compartir una complicidad colectiva que pueden interpretar como una "resistencia". Aunque no producen ningún sonido, el razonamiento parece ser que sólo por su presencia los miembros del público desafían a aquellos que imponen la censura y la autocensura.[5] La idea de que la presencia del público en un evento teatral funciona como un acto de resistencia, en parte subyace todo el proyecto del Teatro Abierto. El hecho de que miles de personas se alinearan para ver obras "bajo vigilancia"[6] fue interpretado por los líderes militares y la población en general como un movimiento de la oposición.

Sin embargo, *El desconcierto* parece estar dirigido a aquellos argentinos que fueron cómplices de la dictadura, y cuya pasividad frente a la brutalidad gubernamental hizo posible un nuevo orden social, la cultura del terror. El "espectáculo", lejos de ser oposiciónal, es producido por los agentes del poder. La mera presencia y voluntad de ser parte de la representación, hace que los espectadores contribuyan a la construcción de una nueva comunidad basada en ficciones. Pero los espectadores no se reconocen a sí mismos en el escenario –cegados por su situación, creen que el drama (que les elude al igual que el sonido elude a Irene) está ocurriendo en otro lugar. No obstante, el silenciamiento y el desplazamiento son precisamente lo que caracterizó el *Proceso*.

El proceso *performativo* de atar/cegar comunal retratado por Raznovich, apunta a dos formas de violencia de género. En un nivel, la feminidad es una representación que Irene implementa día a día. Ataviada en un ajustado traje rojo de gran escote, y empapada de joyas, ella se convierte en la Otra por la cual el público paga por ver. Incluso se refiere a sí misma en tercera persona, como Irene della Porta, como un producto que ha aceptado su objetivación y degradación porque a cambio recibe beneficios tangibles: "Un sin fin de años de comodidad por aceptar ser Irene della Porta tocando silenciosamente." Raznovich presenta el género como algo *performativo*, bastante parecido a lo que Judith Butler ha desarrollado: "el género es un acto que se ha ensayado, parecido al guión que sobrevive a los determinados actores que lo usan, pero que requiere de actores individuales para ser actualizado y reproducido como una realidad otra vez."[7] Pocos papeles disponibles a la mujer en el patriarcado ofrecen alguna visibilidad—la "estrella" es uno de ellos. Pero la "estrella" como advierte explícitamente Irene, encarna los deseos del espectador masculino. Es la "Mujer" como proyección de las fantasías patriarcales la que actúa en el escenario. Ya no se reconoce a sí misma en el espejo, no hay "ego" que reconocer.

En otro nivel, el proyecto de construcción comunitaria emprendido por la junta es genérico también. Desde el principio la junta hizo explícito que la formación del estado era inextricable de la formación de género. En su primer pronunciamiento, publicado por *La Nación* el 24 de marzo de 1976 día del golpe militar, la junta se declaró como "órgano supremo de la nación" lista para "llenar el vacío de poder" encarnado por la viuda de Perón, Isabelita, la presidenta constitucional de Argentina. En su esfuerzo por transformar las "enfermas" e inertes masas argentinas en un auténtico "ser nacional", la junta se encargó de eliminar los elementos tóxicos (o *subversivos*) del "cuerpo" social. La guerra se llevaba a cabo en los intersticios de la Madre Patria, en sus entrañas sangrantes; de esa manera era transgresiva, oculta, "sucia". La imagen materna de la Patria era la justificación y el lugar físico de las políticas violentas. El término "Patria", que tiene la misma raíz etimológica que "padre", refleja una imagen feminina de la nación mediada a través de un sistema patriacal—un trasvestismo político e ideológico. Detrás de la imagen materna apelada por los militares, no hay una mujer. A pesar de eso, la imagen femenina (Patria, Irene della Porta) sirve una función real en la construcción comunitaria, al unir a todos aquellos que se imaginan a sí mismos atados o fieles a ella. Sin embargo, lo "femenino" es útil para los agentes del poder mientras su imagen se mantenga sin ninguna agencia real. Tal como es, ella le da identidad a los espectadores. Así como las Fuerzas Armadas definen a los "verdaderos" argentinos, los admiradores de Irene della Porta forman un grupo (una "comunidad imaginada" como diría Benedict Anderson[8]) por su relación con ella: "¿Quién soy? ¿Quién eres?". La naturaleza de esta construcción comunitaria es circular, la imagen femenina es la creación de un orden patriarcal, pero "ella", en cambio, da origen a la imagen de sí misma de la nación. De esta manera Irene della Porta admite cándidamente que ella misma es la creación de sus admiradores: "[Ellos] me han hecho lo que soy hoy. ¿Pero quién soy?". Y con todo, su tenue y ensayada identidad une a la audiencia.

Mientras la mujer desaparece en la imagen de la *Patria*, Raznovich no le permite a su público pasar por alto la violencia misógina de este discurso creador de comunidad. Su personaje deja claro que lo que atrae al público al teatro es también la "presentación" de humillación pública que Irene della Porta entrega noche tras noche. Los temas de complicidad colectiva, silenciamiento, e inhabilitación, son representados en el cuerpo expuesto y humillado de la "Mujer": "¿Qué quieres de mí? (*De pronto se abre el vestido, y comienza a desvestirse*). ¿Quieres desenredar verdades escondidas? ¿Quieres verme sin disfraces? (*Se desviste, y queda en ropa interior*) ¿Ahora que me ves desnuda hasta los dientes, me conoces mejor? ¿Acaso mi desnudez trae el éxito? ¿Qué es una mujer desnuda? ¿Un esqueleto a la intemperie cubierto por una membrana vital?". Como feminista, Diana Raznovich entendió el aspecto de producción cultural de la comunidad y el silenciamiento que otros dramaturgos recrearon sin reconocer que el pacto social entre los agentes del poder y el público cómplice se está negociando (en el discurso militar y el arte) en el cuerpo de la "Mujer". El público explora su identidad en sus intersticios corporales, busca la verdad en su piel desnuda. Su cuerpo funciona como un texto en el cual el destino de la comunidad está grabado.

Paradójicamente, *El desconcierto* señala el fracaso y el poder del arte en el contexto del *Proceso*. La presentación del cuerpo de Irene della Porta como expuesto en vez de desnudo, y los sonidos grotescos que emite el piano, desafían la *estetificación* de la violencia y la articulación de la cultura mientras se retrata. Raznovich denuncia el fetichismo mientras Irene della Porta sucumbe en él. Como dijo Theodor Adorno a finales de los años sesenta, "Una obra de arte que está comprometida despoja de magia a aquella obra que se contenta con ser un fetiche, un pasatiempo ocioso para aquellos que les gusta dormirse mientras el diluvio que les amenaza pasa, en un apoliticismo que de hecho es profundamente político".[9] Raznovich deja bien claro que el arte no comprometido y evasivo, durante períodos de catástrofe social ayuda a constituir y fijar una cultura de terror, en la cual finalmente el pueblo pierde su capacidad de entender realmente. Aún si las restricciones se levantaran súbitamente, y el piano recobrara mágicamente su sonido, aquellos que están involucrados en la producción de ficción no podrían reestablecer una comunicación real.

La oposición de Diana Raznovich a los límites impuestos por la misma "izquierda" de la oposición fue más allá de los asuntos de su estilo dramático personal. Como feminista la protesta de lo que ella ve como la naturaleza masculina del Teatro Abierto, se hace evidente no sólo en el contenido de las obras escritas y producidas casi en su totalidad por hombres, sino también por la decisión de llevar el Teatro Abierto al Teatro Tabarís, después de la quema del Picadero. El Teatro Abierto comenzaba, al igual que antes, a las seis y media de la tarde. En la noche Tabarís seguía su programación regular de Cabaret, animada por chistes misóginos y presentando *Show Girls* poco vestidas. Cuando las mujeres del Teatro Abierto se quejaron por utilizar ese lugar para presentar su teatro políticamente progresivo y de oposición, fueron denegadas. En vez de subvertir el espacio de degradación femenina, el Teatro Abierto, decidió explotarlo para asegurar su continuidad y supervivencia. Los hombres militares que frecuentaban el Cabaret durante las horas regulares, difícilmente destruirían un espacio que asociaban con su propio placer. Esta estrategia de proteger el contenido político detrás o dentro de un contexto de explotación sexual femenina no fue algo nuevo en la época.[10] Pero la consecuencia de esto fue, claro está, que la desigualdad de género y la explotación femenina no pudiera ser el tema a analizar, debido a que la transmisión del mensaje político era vista como dependiente de que esa explotación continuara. Así, el Teatro Abierto estableció una circunstancia en la cual el público, preparado para encontrar una crítica de su sociedad represiva, tendría que pasar los afiches de mujeres semidesnudas para entrar al teatro. La yuxtaposición del evento político y el cuerpo femenino semidesnudo reproducía las estrategias visuales utilizadas por revistas pro-militares (tales como *Gente*) que superponían titulares de eventos atroces de la Guerra Sucia en los cuerpos femeninos en bikini que agraciaban la mitad de sus portadas. Una vez más, lo femenino se reducía al puro cuerpo de fondo, como el lugar de la violencia y el conflicto político. El sujeto femenino no podía reclamar participación política o una representación no explotadora, ya que ella sirve de escenario en el cual la lucha entre los hombres (agentes políticos) puede ocurrir.

La lucha para una dramaturga feminista en Argentina durante el *Proceso* era más complicada que tomar una posición antimilitar, a pesar de lo peligroso y heroico que esto es. Significaba no sólo enfrentarse al régimen sino también al imaginario argentino, que imaginaba un sentido de comunidad que definía "lo argentino" como una lucha entre hombres

–lidiada sobre y a través de "lo femenino" (ya sea el cuerpo simbólico de la Madre Patria, Irene della Porta, o el cuerpo físico de una mujer). Y esto a su vez significó enfrentarse a los autores "progresivos" de la oposición quienes retrataban la construcción de la identidad nacional predicada en la destrucción femenina (como en el trabajo de Ricardo Monti, o el de Eduardo Pavlovsky). Esta crítica izquierdista del ejército seguía tomando parte en la misoginia militar. En la lucha por definir y reclamar la identidad nacional "auténtica", ambos militares y hombres progresivos peleaban por ocupar la posición "masculina" mientras se emasculaba, feminizaba y marginaba al "otro". Incluso aquellas obras que pretendían ser una crítica al hombre macho militar por un hombre intelectual (*La cortina de abalorios* de Monti) todavía necesitaban el cuerpo femenino desnudo para expresar sus objeciones e involucrar al público.

En uno de esos ejemplos de inversiones irónicas que tanto adora Diana Raznovich, la Guerra Sucia terminó, los militares fueron más o menos castigados, cambiaron los gobernantes, y aun así ella todavía tenía mucho por lo cual ser desafiante. A diferencia de varios dramaturgos importantes de Argentina, que podían identificarse y dirigirse a los males de la dictadura militar pero que no entendieron que el sistema coercitivo (no sólo los líderes) debía cambiar, Raznovich había recién comenzado a escribir sobre cuestiones de género y sexualidad que habían eludido por completo a la mayoría de sus colegas. Sus luminosas obras, *Jardín de otoño, Casa Matriz, De atrás para adelante*, siguen explorando la premisa feminista de que el deseo es creado a través de sistemas económicos y de alcance-ámbito-esfera especular que presuntamente sólo lo representan (la televisión en el *Jardín de otoño*), que el género y la sexualidad son *performativos*, y que la subjetividad es construida socialmente. Las mujeres no nacen mujeres, como Simone de Beauvoir observó décadas atrás, se convierten en mujeres a través del proceso de socialización. Así como Irene della Porta era un producto de un sistema patriarcal que se beneficia política y económicamente de su habilidad para convertir en espectáculo su humillación, los otros papeles y alternativas sexuales disponibles fueron similarmente generados.

En *Jardín de otoño*, Raznovich cambia su análisis de estos forzados sistemas de género y formación sexual hacia la telenovela, un género tan popular en Latinoamérca. Las telenovelas también están, por supuesto, en el negocio de producir ficciones. Como el concierto silencioso puesto en escena por el representante de Irene della Porta, la telenovela está controlada por un agente de poder que se ubica detrás del telón: En este caso, el detestable Gaspar Méndez Paz. Los consumidores de estas ficciones, como el público en *El Desconcierto*, viven la fantasía de que al participar en alguna batalla romántica en contra del *status quo* se oponen a las autoridades, incluso mientras se entregan sumisamente a la diminuta pantalla. Los dos personajes principales—Griselda y Rosalía, dos mujeres de mediana edad que han vivido juntas por veinte años—se pasan todas las tardes frente al televisor involucradas apasionadamente en los altibajos de Marcelo el mecánico, su héroe adorado. Aunque es de humilde cuna, grosero, y vestido con un grasiento overol, Marcelo desafía las barreras sociales que lo separan de la mujer de sus sueños: Valeria, una encantadora chica de clase alta que está comprometida con otro. Y las mujeres viven consumidas en una intensa pasión el drama con él. ¿Será capaz el padre de Valeria de mandar a Marcelo a la cárcel? ¿Acaso morirá allí? Como una de las mujeres comenta, ésta es una telenovela "moderna", que significa que los finales felices no están garantizados. La telenovela, como el concierto mudo, provee a estos espectadores de la ficción de que están participando en una vida (erótica) que en realidad las elude.

En un nivel, aunque quizá no el principal, la obra da espacio a los debates sobre la dimensión política de la cultura popular. ¿Acaso las telenovelas, uno de los mejores ejemplos de cultura popular en el ámbito de producción y consumo masivo, inculcan una ideología anti-popular en sus espectadores que hace que deseen valores y visiones del mundo que reflejan los intereses de la industria en vez de los propios? Si bien las telenovelas no intentan abiertamente controlar al público (a diferencia de *El desconcierto*), el producto, sin duda, lleva la estampa ideológica de los productores. Como dice John Fiske, "cada artículo reproduce la ideología del sistema que lo produce: Un artículo es la ideología hecha materia."[11] La sencilla trama de David versus Goliat de la telenovela aparentemente enfrenta el prejuicio social (específicamente el conflicto de clases). Mientras las mujeres vitorean a su ídolo a la victoria, y esperan que las barreras sociales simplemente se evaporen, desde luego no piensan *hacer* nada al respecto. Quizá no estén conscientes de los conflictos de clase como problema social, especialmente cuando lo personalizan y concluyen que el padre de la ricachona es "un viejo podrido" y que el rudo productor "odia a los televidentes". Lo único que les queda es llamar al productor, y como televidentes leales exigir que aquellos que están a cargo formulen un final satisfactorio. Así, según el argumento anti-telenovela, estos programas estimulan a las clases trabajadoras (quienes constituyen la mayoría de los televidentes de estos programas) a soñar con el triunfo en una estructura social que, de hecho, está predicada en su exclusión.

El jardín de otoño, no se suscribe a esta posición "anti-popular" categóricamente. Hay un elemento de retozo en la manera en que las mujeres participan en el drama, que apoya la contención de Carlos Monsivais (compartida por otros analistas de la cultura popular como Fiske, Rowe y Schelling) que dice que los públicos populares encuentran una manera de resemantizar los materiales culturales proveídos desde arriba. Monsivais sostiene que "las clases subalternas aceptan, porque no les queda otra alternativa, una industria vulgar y pedestre, y la transforman indiscutiblemente en indulgencia propia y degradación, pero también en una identidad jubilosa y combativa."[12]

La aseveración de Monsivais, que los espectadores subalternos pueden involucrarse "emocionalmente" sin "cambiar ideológicamente" es el punto crucial de la cuestión—y es el que la obra desmantela más lúcidamente. Pero para desarrollar este punto necesito proveer más información sobre la trama. Griselda y Rosalía desean, anhelan, aman y sienten intensamente sin tener un desembocadero adecuado para este amor. Griselda escribe poesía y habla con sus plantas, Rosalía va a un psíquico, anhelando que un hombre buen mozo aparezca en su futuro. Mientras tanto, se pasan las tardes deseosas de Marcelo el mecánico, besando la pantalla y deseando ser la adorada mujer en la televisión. Un buen día, deciden secuestrar a Marcelo y vivir sus fantasías, incluso si después tengan que morir. Lo hacen, y la obra muestra su creciente frustración con la decepcionante estrella. Él, por supuesto, no es el hombre sencillo, honesto y trabajador que tanto han amado durante la novela. Es encantador y bueno, pero mucho más complicado que lo que habían anticipado. No les puede hacer el amor apasionado que ellas tanto habían soñado, aunque no pueden entender por qué. Quizá es impotente, se preguntan, quizá es gay. Bueno, quizá no sea gay sino homosexual. Cuál es la diferencia, se preguntan, aunque sienten que probablemente haya alguna. Y así siguen, hasta que descubren que se aclara el pelo, se hace la permanente y se maquilla. El hombre "real" es más artificial que el Marcelo "real" de la televisión. Entonces deciden poner la telenovela, y dejar que el actor se vaya. Lo "real" es un pobre sustituto de la fantasía. Se ven tan cómodas volviendo a la seguridad, predecibilidad, y honestidad de un mundo que provee una ilusión "real". Así, pareciera que se ilustra el punto de Monsivais: los espectadores pueden conectarse sentimentalmente y desconectarse ideológicamente.

Sin embargo, *El jardín de otoño*, a mi parecer, está

específicamente preocupado con las restricciones impuestas sobre las expresiones emocionales y sexuales por los sistemas dominantes de representación, que no sólo reproducen escenas de deseo (Marcelo y Valeria) sino también demarcan sus límites. Estos sistemas de significación (las telenovelas no son sólo productos si no también sistemas) no ofrecen tanto espacio para la resemantización como pareciera. La "verdadera" historia de amor aquí no es entre Marcelo y Valeria, sino entre Griselda y Rosalía. Viven juntas, comparten una cómica y tumultuosa relación doméstica; no pueden imaginar la vida sin la otra. A pesar de eso, nunca se han permitido imaginar su relación más allá de las etiquetas banales que tienen disponibles: "mi amiga, mi compañera de habitación-digamos mi inquilina." La estrella masculina idealizada de la telenovela sirve para canalizar y contener el amor y el deseo entre ellas. Sus deseos circulan a través de él. Cuando Griselda ve el "mejor episodio del año" en el cual Marcelo besa a Valeria y le confiesa que "está mal por ella", la sensación más aguda es la decepción de que Rosalía no está allí para verlo con ella. Este amor en la pantalla es para ser compartido por ambas, a pesar de momentos de irritación en los que cada una declaran suyo a Marcelo. Así, las telenovelas como sistemas de significación confirman ciertas formas de amor y a la vez hace que otras sean impensables. Las barreras sociales pueden ser el tema de la telenovela, pero no se puede (aún) cuestionar las barreras que hacen del amor heterosexual la norma. Griselda y Rosalía, no sorpresivamente, están tan ciegas hacia la naturaleza de sus deseos, como la sociedad que los crea. Pueden decirse que se quieren, pueden mirarse fijamente, abrazarse, y admitir que no pueden vivir separadas, pero sólo la fantasía de la pasión heterosexual puede permitirles hacerlo sin asumir el peso y la vergüenza tantas veces atribuidos a la homosexualidad. Las mujeres sencillamente desplazan su pasión hacia la bella estrella de la televisión. La historia de sus vidas no les pertenece—ocurre en la televisión; el amor que siente la una por la otra (al cual aluden muchas veces) no es suyo—ocurre entre Marcelo el mecánico, y Valeria la ricachona. Las mujeres pueden adueñarse de su intensa pasión cada tarde, precisamente porque no tienen que reconocerla como *suya*. Al final del primer acto, en uno de los momentos más tristes de la obra, las mujeres rezan por el perdón de la vida que no han vivido:

> "Perdóname por lo que no he hecho.
> Perdóname por lo que no he tenido.
> Perdóname por lo que no he tomado.
> Perdóname por lo que no he sentido.

Perdóname por no haberme reído suficiente.

Perdóname por no haber gastado mis lágrimas."

La trama que sugiero de *El Jardín de otoño*, demuestra que ideológica y emocionalmente los sujetos sociales son producidos y delimitados por los mismos sistemas que en teoría están allí para incitar el deseo. Pero la obra también invierte el paradigma que posiciona a lo "femenino" como el objeto del deseo que sirve para estabilizar la comunidad dominada por lo "masculino" que Raznovich mostró en *El Desconcierto*. En aquella obra, los espectadores se transforman en una comunidad al aplaudir a Irene della Porta. Sin embargo, en *El jardín de otoño* hay una dimensión sexual más explícita en la mediación, que he contendido, es esencial en el imaginario social argentino. De nuevo vemos el caso de la triangulación del deseo—canalizando la intensidad erótica a través de un símbolo seguro de sexualidad, sea masculina o femenina, que permite la proximidad sin incurrir en el estigma social de una sociedad tan homofóbica como la argentina. Y bien, esa triangulación es cardinal tanto para las vidas de estas solteronas, como para el imaginario nacional. Como sometí a consideración en *Disappearing Acts: Spectacles of Gender and Nationalism in Argentina's 'Dirty War'*, "La nación femenina, o Patria, media el autoeroticismo de la *performance* militar. Las Fuerzas Armadas evocaban obsesivamente a la mujer smbólica para evitar que su sociedad homosocial se convirtiera en una homosexual. Los hombres militares se reunieron el lenguaje heterosexual del 'amor' a la patria" (68–69).[13] Bien sea la Patria, Irene della Porta, o Marcelo el mecánico, el discurso de la pasión circula a través de una economía de amor heterosexual rígidamente custodiada.

En su siguiente obra, Diana Raznovich extiende la exploración del "sustituto" y de lo supuestamente "real" (¿Acaso Marcelo es menos "real" para estas mujeres que el actor que lo interpreta?) a los pronunciamientos sociales de roles en general. Viniendo de una sociedad que valora a la madre, casi a cuestas de la exclusión del resto de las mujeres, pareciera inevitable que escogiera ese rol. *Casa Matriz*, una obra de un acto, muestra a Bárbara, una hija de 30 años de edad, que contrata a una "madre" en una agencia que se especializa en ese servicio. Ambas mujeres ensayan una serie de papeles, que van desde la madre en pena tan popular en la literatura latinoamericana, hasta la madre profesional que vuela alrededor del mundo; desde la madre fría y rechazadora, hasta la transgresora que compite con su hija por la amante lesbiana. Cada madre, por supuesto, produce una "hija" diferente, y

Bárbara experimenta una serie de transformaciones, mientras frunce los labios, exige compensación, llora, suplica amor, y le pide a la madre substituta que le devuelva el dinero.

La maternidad, tantas veces *esencializada*, como la condición natural que por sí sola justifica la existencia de las mujeres en Latinoamérica, queda expuesta no sólo como una construcción patriarcal, sino también como una construcción comercial. Cuando a la madre "substituta" se le pide que sea la "madre en pena" por ejemplo, ella declara que ése es el papel más cotizado: "Todos, absolutamente todos, necesitan verme en el estado más lacayo de servidumbre". La presentación de la sumisión femenina, tal como en *El desconcierto*, sigue siendo un "best-seller". Sin embargo, la lucidez de la obra está en la distancia *performativa* que Raznovich establece entre la representación y ese referente ausente que uno supone "real". Pero, incluso lo "real" está desestabilizado a través de la naturaleza sumamente teatral de las iteraciones. Mientras la "madre substituta" hace un espectáculo de llanto que produce lágrimas "reales", le pide a su "hija" que las toque: "No podrías pedir un efecto más trágico. Soy la madre en pena por excelencia. Vestida de negro, limpiando, llorando ¡Mira estas lágrimas enormes!" Así, la idea de "lo real" sólo le da peso a la representación, y no al revés. El espectáculo no "representa" lo real—como en la lógica Aristotélica. Más bien, lo real es producto de estas representaciones constantes. Así también, la "madre substituta" señala la cualidad construida de la madre "real", aquella mujer que reclama su identidad y visibilidad dependiendo de su capacidad de ser una artista de cambio súbito—ser material disponible para todas las personas. El papel de maternidad tan claramente *deconstruida* por Raznovich, es de gran importancia porque ha limitado y a la vez, proveído visibilidad a mujeres argentinas tan diferentes como Evita (la "madre" de la patria argentina), y las Madres de la Plaza de Mayo. Como *mujeres* no podían reclamar poder o desagravio, pero como *madres*, simbólica o políticamente, activaron los movimientos políticos encabezados por mujeres, más visibles de sus tiempos. Pero la realidad radica en el acto mismo—Evita nunca tuvo hijos; las Madres, aceptando la muerte de sus hijos en privado, aseguraban ser las madres de todos los desaparecidos. La maternidad entonces, pasa del dominio biológico al socio-político. La eficacia del papel no está en su esencia "natural" sino en su actuación. En la muy pública reclusión de la agencia de alquiler, Bárbara le paga a la "substituta" para que produzca lágrimas y angustias reales.

La economía del "substituto" usualmente sirve para reforzar "lo real", ¿qué podría significar "substituto", qué función podría tener, sino fuera reemplazar, llenar el lugar o de alguna manera reemplazar lo "real"? No obstante la noción de lo "real", tan privilegiada por el despliegue del "substituto" es precisamente lo que se estremece en este pronunciamiento. Más bien lo "real" se produce a través del sistema de mercado capitalista que comercia los deseos y las emociones. En vez de permitirnos adquirir participación en la aparente experiencia natural entre madre e hija, idealizarla o analizarla psicológicamente, Raznovich deja las cuerdas *performativas* al descubierto.

En ningún lugar queda más clara la interconexión entre lo "actuado" y lo "real", entre lo *performativo* y lo así llamado "natural", que en *De atrás para adelante*. Esta comedia, estructurada más convencionalmente en tres actos, gira alrededor de Simón Goldberg, un rico hombre de negocios judío, que cae en tiempos difíciles cuando su industria de baño y plomería queda en bancarrota. Todos, su joven esposa, su hija y yerno, están en un pronunciado estado de nerviosidad mientras la fortuna y los negocios parecen desaparecer literalmente por el canal de desagüe. Simón, quien no soporta fuertes dosis de realidad, se encoge en un desmayo. Mariana, la hija, insiste en contactar a su rico hermano Javier, quien diez años antes había sido echado a la calle por Simón, cuando este lo encontró en la cama con el prometido de Mariana. La ayuda llega, pero como siempre en las obras de Raznovich, no de una manera reconocible o anticipada. La encantadora Dolly, también conocida como Javier, quien es ahora una primorosa y cariñosa mujer casada y con tres hijas, entra en escena. Dolly salva el negocio convenciendo a los argentinos que ellos adoran el papel higiénico de color (que sus traseros no merecen menos), pero le es mucho más problemático, convencer a su padre homo fóbico que él merece su apoyo y amor como Javier, su hijo(a) transexual—No como Dolly, a quien Simón está dispuesto a adorar, siempre y cuando ella pretenda ser la *esposa* de Javier.

Evidentemente las cuestiones planteadas aquí, van mucho más allá de las ideas de género como algo *performativo* presentadas en *El desconcierto* y *Casa Matriz*. El género por supuesto sigue siendo *performativo*, un acto que el cuerpo aprende a representar con el pasar del tiempo, y a través del riguroso transcurso de la socialización. Sin embargo, la figura transexual cuestiona la noción de que el sexo (masculino-femenino) es alguna vez una marca estable. ¿A qué sexo pertenece Javier-Dolly? ¿Cómo empezar a pensar, mucho menos definir, la diferencia sexual? ¿Acaso la diferencia está en los órganos reproductores (de tal manera que Javier "muere" mientras Dolly nace)? ¿O en el ADN o las hormonas? ¿Cómo pensar la diferencia de género en un sistema que niega la subjetividad de la mujer? ¿No son las mujeres (como en la Guerra Sucia) más que el "enemigo" o el *otro* "peligroso" en un sistema binario basado en la vertiente sexual, parte de la *dialéctica* entre masculino y femenino como sugieren pensadoras como Simone de Beauvoir? O, como implica la figura de Irene della Porta, las mujeres son simples proyecciones de las fantasías masculinas y las prohibiciones de un sistema cerrado cuyo único referente es lo masculino, un sistema *monológico* o un orden fálico singular que niega incluso la existencia del *otro*. Siendo ese el caso, el sujeto femenino queda para siempre lingüísticamente ausente e irrepresentable. ¿Acaso esta ausencia indica los límites de las formaciones discursivas y sugiere, quizás, la posibilidad de una existencia negociada entre los discursos, en los márgenes y las fracturas? ¿O, más bien, pone en duda la existencia material de seres históricos reales, situados en formaciones discursivas que los borran? Si la subjetividad es generada por la entrada dentro de la cultura, como han argumentado teóricos como Beauvoir, Foucault, de Lauretis y Butler,[14] entonces es genérico, y más específicamente genérico desde la posición masculina *monológica* en un sistema cerrado de auto referencia. Hay muchas ausencias aquí: La ausencia discursiva de lo "femenino" en un imaginario masculino, la ausencia de mujeres históricas y "reales" en papeles protagonistas en Argentina, la ausencia de los cuerpos materiales de mujeres que fueron permanentemente "desaparecidas" del panorama político.

La desaparición de Javier invierte el sistema que borra a la mujer como sujeto lingüístico y protagonista. Dolly se vuelve visible, y a su vez, la aparente imposibilidad cultural de que un hombre socializado en una sociedad masculina como la argentina pueda elegir ser "mujer". El sexo no es una determinación estática. Javier siempre será una parte de Dolly, así como Dolly siempre será una parte de Javier. La identidad sexual no es simplemente marcar cualquiera de los dos, o M o F. Como dice Mariana después de que ella y Dolly revisan el viejo baúl de disfraces y realizan algunas de las escenas que actuaban de pequeños, "Creo que somos tres, Mariana, Javier, y Dolly." Más que un "real" inmutable que engendra una serie de actos, hay una serie de actos que construyen lo "real". Estas representaciones incluyen aquellas a las que J.L. Austin se refiere, cuando escribe sobre acciones de hablar que efectúan cambios.[15] Los sistemas sociales sólo permiten que se vean dos representaciones de género aceptables, y éstas están marcadas como dominante (masculino) y subordinado (femenino) en un sinfín de maneras. El lenguaje (el español en este caso) también le da a los sustantivos un género, y a la vez incorpora al subordinado dentro del dominante. El dúo de Mariana y Javier es denominado "Los hermanos Goldberg", borrando las distinciones entre los dos. Entonces, Javier masculino desaparece detrás de Dolly femenino, borrando así cualquier inicio visual de su presencia en ella, tal como "Los hermanos Goldberg" borra la presencia de Mariana. De esta manera las identidades desaparecen y reaparecen (más o menos violentamente) a través de toda una serie de sistemas—sean desapariciones políticas y lingüísticas o a través de sistemas que dictan los pronunciamientos apropiados de género y sexualidad.

Apropiados. Quizá la palabra misma resume el código *normalizante* de comportamiento admisible que tanto exaspera a Diana Raznovich. La junta militar impuso e implementó reglas que regían el comportamiento apropiado; la oposición dictó los términos de resistencia apropiada. La sociedad exige que los ciudadanos actúen su género y sexo apropiadamente. Los sistemas económicos—la televisión, la publicidad, etc.—nos dicen qué se vende y qué no se vende, qué productos culturales pueden adentrarse en el mercado y qué productos quedan excluidos (aquí no hay censura, nos dicen, simplemente no son "comerciables"). La manera en que lo apropiado se convierte en lo normal se vincula al deseo. Uno de los retos que enfrenta un gobierno autoritario es enseñarle a la población a desear un nebuloso bien "más elevado" (por ejemplo, la unidad nacional, o la defensa apasionada de la Madre Patria), de esta manera el pueblo acepta las restricciones civiles (esto es, la pérdida de las libertades personales—el derecho al sufragio, a organizar, a ponerse en huelga, a protestar, etc.). Aquellos que se rehúsen a desear lo que se les ha pedido, figurativa o literalmente "desaparecen" como ciudadanos. Los sistemas económicos capitalistas no sólo crean el deseo y lo cumplen a cabalidad al proveer el artículo deseado, sino también, como sostenía Marx, borran la mano de obra requerida para la producción. El obrero desaparece, dejando sólo los objetos cuyo valor de intercambio, y no, valor de producción, valen la pena. El género y las identidades sexuales se conciben y reproducen en economías similares. El hombre ocupa la posición de productor y consumidor, mientras lo meritorio de la mujer reside en su valor de intercambio—como una estrella, ella encarna la fantasía masculina de mutuo beneficio entre el productor y consumidor. Como madre ideal, ella representa el acto de vasallaje—un acto que, como observa

Raznovich, está en demanda. La eficacia de estas encarnaciones, depende, claro está, de su naturalización—en la voluntad del pueblo de verlas como normativas y deseables a la vez. Aquellos que no participan en esa deseabilidad de este deseo socialmente construido, desaparecen dentro de alguna categoría reservada para los "desviados" y *dobladores de género*. Diana Raznovich parece preguntarnos en sus obras, ¿qué es más violento, la violencia auto impuesta de aquellos que intentan ajustarse a las normas apropiadas, o aquella otra violencia (desde la desaparición al ostracismo) que se impone en aquellos que no obedecen? Hay muchos tipos de violencia, y muchos tipos de represión. Una dramaturga como Diana Raznovich, que ve la interconexión entre los diferentes tipos de violencia sistémica tiene bastantes obstáculos que lidiar—desafiante, transgresiva, y nunca del todo apropiada.

Notas

1. Ver Karl Marx, Capital, vol. 1 (Moscow: Foreign Languages Publishing House, 1961) y Jean Baudrillard, Simulations (New York: Semiotexte, 1983).
2. Entrevista Raznovich-Taylor, Dartmouth College, septiembre 1994.
3. Juana A. Arancibia y Zulema Mirkin, "Introducción" al Teatro Argentino durante el proceso (Buenos Aires: Instituto Literario y Cultural Hispánico, 1992), 21.
4. Entrevista Raznovich-Taylor, Buenos Aires, 1994.
5. Es interesante notar que el mutismo y el silencio público fueron interpretados como un acto de complicidad y de resistencia a la vez, durante la Guerra Sucia. Por un lado aquellos que no hablaron en contra de la brutalidad gubernamental permitieron que las prácticas criminales del secuestro, la desaparición y la tortura continuaran. Sin embargo, el no hablar fue también visto como un desafío heroico a un sistema que pedía conformidad, tal como era visto el desafío en contra del torturador que pedía información durante la tortura.
6. Este es el término que Miguel Ángel Giella al describir el Teatro Abierto en su estudio-antología: Teatro Abierto, 1981: Teatro Argentino Bajo Vigilancia (Buenos Aires: Corregidor, 1991).
7. Judith Butler, "Performative Acts and Gender Construction" en Performing Feminisms: Feminist Critical Theory and Theatre , editado de Sue-Ellen Case (Baltimore: Johns Hopkins University Press, 1990), 277. Ver también Gender Trouble (New York: Routledge, 1990) y Bodies That Matter (New York: Routledge, 1993) de Butler.
8. Benedict Anderson, Imagined Communities (London: Verso, 1983).
9. Theodor Adorno, "Commitment" en Aesthetics and Politics (London: Verso, 1977), 177.
10. El eminente cineasta Adolfo Aristarain, que dirigió Time for Revenge in 1981, hizo lo mismo. Incluyó largas e innecesarias escenas sexuales, explicó en una entrevista con Annette Insdorf, "Para que los censores pasaran cinco días cuestionando, en vez de política e ideología, sexo. Sólo tuve que cortar unos cuantos encuadres al final de algunas escenas, como la de un striptease. No afecta a las escenas, especialmente si uno las hace más largas de lo que deberían ser," dijo mientras sonreía pícaramente". (Annette Insdorf, "Time for Revenge: A Discussion with Adolfo Aristarain," Cineaste (1983): 16–17, 17.
11. John Fiske, Understanding Popular Culture (London, New York: Routledge 1989).
12. Citado en William Rowe y Vivian Schelling, Memory and Modernity: Popular Culture in Latin America (London: Verso, 1991).
13. Diana Taylor, Disappearing Acts: Spectacles of Gender and Nationalism in Argentina's "Dirty War" (Durham: Duke University Press, 1997).
14. Ver Michel Foucault, The History of Sexuality, vol. 1 (New York: Vintage, 1980) y Discipline and Punish (New York: Vintage, 1979) y Simone de Beauvoir, The Second Sex (Harmondsworth: Penguin, 1984).
15. J. L. Austin, How To Do Things With Words (Cambridge: Harvard University Press, 1962).

EL DESCONCIERTO

Diana Raznovich

EL DESCONCIERTO

Personajes
Pianista Irene della Porta

Escenario

(*En la escena vacía un piano. Después de una pausa, una mujer vestida de largo con un traje rojo muy entallado y enmarcado en joyas, saluda al público y se dispone a tocar. Arremete con furiosa vehemencia. El piano no suena. El silencio embarga la sala. Es el silencio del no sonido. El inesperado silencio de un piano vehementemente pulsado por ella. Silencio que, por unos instantes, parece querer derrotar o disimular o encubrir con su vehemente ejecución. Como si ella y el público, aún sabiendo que Beethoven no suena, fueran capaces de construir "ese otro concierto" misteriosamente pactado, inexistente. Después de la pausa creada por la pianista tocando en silencio, ella se levanta inesperadamente del teclado y, visiblemente disgustada, se dirige al público.*)

Pianista Señoras y señores: un nuevo episodio de sabotaje en la larga fila de episodios de sabotaje que me asedian desde que ustedes y yo intentamos de alguna manera dar este concierto. Ustedes siguiéndome fielmente y yo tocando para ustedes a pesar de todo. ¡No, de todo no! A pesar de un empresario que se ensaña en demostrarnos que este concierto...¡ningún concierto mío es ya posible! (*Vuelve al piano y nuevamente el piano no suena. Vuelve al público.*) El mundo de mis admiradores- yo lo sé fatalmente- está muy dividido. A todos, a los de antes y a los de hoy quiero agradecerles su apoyo. Sin ese apoyo no sabría vivir. Sin ese apoyo Irene della Porta no sabría quién es. Los de ayer porque me piden que vuelva a tocar. Los de hoy porque me piden que siga dando estos conciertos silenciosos que tanto éxito han tenido. Unos y otros tienen razón. Unos y otros, con su conmovedora presencia, han hecho de mí lo que soy. Pero ¿quién soy? ¿Eh? ¿Mi empresario sabe quién soy?¿Yo misma sé quién soy? ¿Soy yo o es otra la que no toca? Y la que toca ¿dónde quedó? (*Se ríe.*) "Menos preguntas"- me dice mi empresario. "El éxito nos corona, el público aplaude, la sala se llena y tu personalidad irradia un magnetismo desbordante que no necesita ningún sonido para brillar". Tal vez tenga razón. Tal vez todos tengamos razón. Tal vez ustedes, al asistir a este acto humillante, sientan que la verdad los asiste. (*Pausa. Vuelve al piano. Intenta nuevamente concentrarse y tocar pero el piano no suena.*) ¡Ah! ¿Cuándo sonará ese piano? ¡cuándo caerán las notas como agua bendita desde mis dedos hasta el centro del mundo? ¿Cuándo volveré a tocar? ¿Cuándo me dejarán otra vez libre de este compromiso de llenarles la curiosidad con inútiles relatos sobre mi vida? ¿Qué más quieren saber? ¿Qué esperan que les revele? ¿Por qué asisten a todas las funciones colmando esta sala y esperando que yo confiese todo? ¿Pero qué tengo que confesar? ¿Qué tengo que decirles de mí que los periódicos no hayan dicho? Pero si ustedes lo saben todo, pero si ustedes han seguido hasta los últimos desesperados detalles mi pacto con la mediocridad. (*Pausa. Vuelve al piano. Repentinamente se levanta.*) ¡Y bien! He pactado. La mediocridad me ofrecía su cálida protección. Años interminables de confort por aceptar ser Irene della Porta tocando silencio. "Pianistas que tocan como vos hay muchas- me decía el empresario-. Pero Irene della Porta no tocando va a haber una sola". (*Pausa*) En todas las vidas hay un instante que marca la diferencia, un instante secreto que destruye todo lo transitado, todas las verdades propias. Un instante en que se acepta perder creyendo que se va a ganar. ¿Cuál era mi ceguera? ¿Quién me cegó? ¿Estaba realmente ciega? ¿Cuándo comencé a aceptar? ¿Mucho antes de decir que sí yo todavía me sigo negando? (*Pausa. Se ríe.*) ¿Qué importancia tienen las razones cuando estoy atada ante ustedes y ustedes lo festejan con su concurrencia? Esto es un éxito. Irene della Porta gana mucho dinero con todo esto. Mi empresario festeja el triunfo noche tras noche. Ustedes, la misma historia, los mismos hábitos, los mismos rasgos reproducidos en el espejo: ustedes vienen entonces corriendo al teatro y pagan para que yo arranque de esa oscuridad inobjetable esta maravillosa escala inexistente, inexistente: re do sol fa la mi re si do: y todo cae de un marasmo espejado, y esta parcela fantástica del universo horada en nuestros oídos memorias de caricias interminables, largas lenguas oceánicas, perfiles de otras vidas que no nos pertenecen, amores desconocidos a los que nunca rozaremos ni siquiera la mano, grandes pasiones que todos llevamos guardadas dentro para entregarle a alguien que nos ignora lejos, alguien que también nos busca: do re sol mi la fa do sisisi faremidosol. El destino, esa pompa inútil de agua bendita, esa ficción es sólo un pacto idiota con un Dios que emerge en este momento en un misoldorefa mi redododo que aunque no exista es interminable. (*Se levanta conmovida. Abre místicamente los dedos.*) ¿Qué quieren de mí? (*Se abre repentinamente el vestido y comienza a desnudarse.*) ¿Quieren desentrañar verdades ocultas? ¿Quieren verme sin más disfraces? (*Se quita la ropa hasta quedar en ropa interior.*) ¿Saben más de esta Irene della Porta antes que ahora? Ahora que me ven así, despojada hasta de mi aliento, ¿saben más de mí que antes? ¿Qué es una persona? ¿Quién soy yo? ¿Qué es el éxito? ¿Mi desnudo trae éxito? ¿Qué es una mujer desnuda? ¿Un esqueleto al aire, con su frágil membrana vital? ¿Qué es un piano si no suena? (*Vuelve así desnuda al piano que no suena y lo toca ardientemente.*) Ustedes me consagran esta noche. Llueven rosas sobre mi cabeza. En mi camarín me aguarda una botella de champagne helado. El aire atravesado de murmullos dice mi nombre. (*Al público*) ¿Son ustedes los mismos que venían a verme a mis conciertos? ¿O son otros? (*A un espectador*) Usted señor. Usted que me seguía en todos mis conciertos. Usted que ahora también me sigue. Usted que tiene esa mirada profunda y secreta. Usted que antes me mandaba rosas y que ahora también me manda rosas ¿por qué viene? ¿Le causa gracia mi derrota? ¿este show armado para reemplazar mis conciertos? Y comentan, "qué pena, una pianista de su categoría". "Con lo bien que tocaba". Comentan mientras comen y yo los veo comentar y reírse y los veo comprar entradas y colmar estas salas y y asisto a mi suicidio, que también es un crimen. Ustedes me están matando. Ustedes ya me mataron. Soy un cadáver que deambula por una escena muerta representando cada vez, siempre lo mismo, su propia muerte, su momificación y su derrota. (*Se ríe.*) Voy a volver al piano. Voy a abrirlo y voy a extraer un revólver (*Se ríe y cumple con lo que dijo antes.*) Ustedes ya conocen esta parte del show. ¿Es la que más les atrae? Yo hablo de mi momificación y mi derrota y extraigo el revólver y los apunto. (*Apunta a un espectador.*) Todos saben que este revólver está cargado pero no tienen miedo. Ya me han visto apuntarlos sin consecuencias. (*Se ríe.*) También han esperado que yo enfilara hacia mi propia cabeza la puntería (*Lo hace.*) y han visto cómo a pesar del suspenso (*Crea suspenso.*) termino bajando el arma y guardándola. Tampoco esta noche me verán caer, tampoco esta noche llorarán por mí cubriendo de flores el cuerpo inerte de que alguna vez fuera Irene della Porta (*Se ríe. Guarda el arma. Se sienta nuevamente al piano. Silencio ejecutorio. Adopta un tono confesional, alucinante.*) Feliz, me siento feliz de no poder darles este concierto. Feliz de ejecutar esta no sonata de

Beethoven para ustedes. Gracias por estar aquí esta noche. Gracias a ustedes he comprendido algo sobre el arte. El arte no está en los sonidos. La música no está en los acordes. Ahora ustedes deberían dejar que una corriente de aguas estremecedoras les cavara en el pecho hoquedades secretas, que algo distraídamente, un bemol o tal vez este frío, los levantara del confín de ese estar alojados allí en las butacas y los arrastrara hacia este fa sostenido que resplandece como una piedra preciosa invocando lo mejor de nosotros: algo que no es un acorde en re mayor, los hace olvidar que están allí sentados en el silencio de esta sala, pidiéndome que los despegue de ese fragmento patético de la realidad que consiste en ser el mismo todos los días, despertarse y tener la misma madre. ¿Por qué vienen todos? (*Se viste.*) Mi contrato termina pronto. Y yo voy a volver a tocar. Yo tengo que volver a ser Irene della Porta. ¿Vendrán? ¿Vendrán conmigo o me dejarán sola tocando la Patética de Beethoven en una enorme sala vacía? (*Se emociona.*) Esto tiene que terminar...Estas han sido unas hermosas vacaciones en una isla desierta. Este ha sido un paréntesis gracioso. Un viento blanco que arrasó conmigo. Una tormenta que me arrancó de cuajo de mi taburete. Y ahora ¿dónde estoy parada? Estoy en la cúspide del éxito. La sala está colmada. Hemos ganado mucho dinero. ¡Qué bello desierto!...a veces dan ganas de quedarse, de no volver.   A veces dan ganas de que el tiempo confortablemente pase. A veces dan ganas de quedarse aquí dentro, con ustedes (*Llora desconsoladamente.*) Alguna vez, frente a un espejo opaco, mi propio rostro desdibujado por el tiempo me preguntará ¿por qué? Me preguntará ¿cómo? Y yo le daré explicaciones inútiles sobre las tentaciones originales, explicaciones sobre la jugosa manzana de la felicidad (*Se ríe.*) Qué fácil es dar explicaciones a un espejo. (*Se ríe*) Espejito, espejito ¿Quién es la más hermosa de todas las mujeres? ¿Y la más talentosa? ¿Y la más inteligente? ¿Y la más atractiva? (*Se ríe.*) Espejito, espejito ¿Cuál es la más exitosa de todas las mujeres? (*Se ríe. Vuelve alegremente al piano y toca en silencio. Como si fuera una fiesta su propio tocar se ríe alegremente y toca.*) Tienen razón, yo también vendría, yo también pagaría por ver el espectáculo que ofrezco cada noche. Colmaría esta sala todas las noches y gritaría "bravo". Y al terminar tiraría rosas que cayeran al azar sobre esta fiesta (*Saca un ramo de rosas y lo tira sobre la platea.*) Rosas, rosas para festejar el éxito de la insólita función que aquí se ofrece. Rosas cayendo sobre un mar de aplausos, rosas soñando con otras rosas en un inmenso prado abierto a la luz de la memoria. Rosas para no olvidar, rosas para aspirar la noche que encierra cada pétalo (*Termina de repartir las rosas. Explota totalmente poseída por un sentimiento muy profundo.*) Ay, ahora mismo ¡cómo me gustaría tocar la Patética! Ludwig Van Beethoven, ¡cómo me gustaría encontrarme con los tormentos de tu generosa alma!¡Cómo me gustaría alimentarme de tu fértil y generosa vertiente, hundirme en esas aguas que conservo todavía adentro mío!...Basta mirar hacia adentro y verte, Beethoven, haciendo sonar tu Patética constantemente en mí, muero y resurrezco cada día dentro de tus aguas, Beethoven, amigo mío, me paseo secretamente de tu mano sintiendo tu corazón en mi mano como una piedra preciosa. ¡Ay, si yo pudiera tocar!¡Si yo pudiera sacarte de adentro mío para que dejes de ser este paisaje ahogado! ¿Soy un alma penando o un cuerpo errante? Ay ¡cómo me gustaría romper estos días circulares y vacíos, y asomarme a lo verdaderamente vivo! (*Vuelve al piano con este estado de exaltación. Repentinamente el piano suena. Ella se queda paralizada. No puede creerlo. Toca nuevamente, prueba con distintos sonidos y el piano suena. Mira al público alelada y vuelve a demostrarles que suena.*) ¿Qué es esto? Nosotros no habíamos quedado en esto (*Pausa*) Yo no firmé un contrato para esto (*Prueba y el piano suena. Pega un alarido.*) ¡Suena! Ahora resulta que suena (*Prueba.*) Ahora suena...(*Se ríe.*) Señores, ustedes no han pagado para...(*Se ríe. Llora y prueba los sonidos del piano.*) Hace tanto...hace siglos de vida no vivida que no escuchaba estos sonidos...hace un milenio dentro de otros milenios que no sonaba la inocente nota saliendo de mi dedo (*Juega y se ríe.*) Las leyes físicas de la caída quedan destruídas por un hermoso fa...(*Se ríe. Se dirige al público.*) Señoras y señores, esta noche inesperada, ¿existirá en el calendario? ¿Será cierto que yo tengo de nuevo la oportunidad de tocar ante ustedes la sonata Patética de Ludwig Van Beethoven? ¿Serán ustedes mis primeros testigos, mis últimos jueces o mis condenados? (*Se ríe. Vuelve al piano.*) Beethoven, hola Beethoven.

(*Con profunda emoción arremete. Se ha olvidado completamente todo. Intenta tocar la Patética y sus dedos, oxidados por el tiempo de inactividad, no le responden. Intenta desesperadamente recuperar su posibilidad de tocar como antes, como entonces, pero cuanto más se empecina, más fracasa y de sus dedos salen horrendos sonidos que evocan malamente la sonata, deformados sonidos cuya torpeza hiere los oídos. Golpea las teclas con los puños. Se enardece de furia y de impotencia, golpea su cabeza contra el teclado como intentando arrancar de las entrañas del piano aquella música que tiene dentro. Después el sonido se interrumpe. Hay una larga pausa en la que ella trata de reponerse. Comprueba que el piano ya no suena. Vuelve al*) *público, hace una pequeña y digna reverencia, y, con el mismo patético silencio, vuelve a sentarse en el taburete y toca con dignidad el piano silencioso. Las luces la dejan ahí, tocando nada, mientras disminuyen hasta el apagón final.)*

Jardín de otoño

DIANA RAZNOVICH

JARDÍN DE OTOÑO

A la memoria de mi padre, Marcos Raznovich.

Personajes
Rosalía *Una mujer madura, soltera. Dueña de la casa.*
Griselda *Mujer de la misma edad y estado civil que Rosalía. Inquilina y compañera desde hace veinte años.*
Mariano Rivas *Estrella de la telenovela "Marcelo el mecánico"; es* **Marcelo**

Personajes en "Marcelo el mecánico"
Valeria *Novia de Marcelo*
Padre *Padre de Valeria*
Tachuela *Asistente a Marcelo en el taller*

Escenografía
La obra transcurre en la sala de estar de la casa de Rosalía. Esta sala de estar es parte de un antiguo caserón de un barrio de clase media, que Rosalía heredó de su familia. Por las características de la casa, esta habitación de techos altos tiene numerosas puertas que dan al resto de la casa. Rosalía vive de alquilarle una habitación a Griselda, su inquilina desde hace veinte años. Ambas han desarrollado aquí su vida en común.
La sala tiene anexado un jardín vidriado lleno de plantas, ubicado al fondo del escenario. Esta cristalera da transparencia y profundidad al espacio escénico. A través de este jardín se filtra la luz de la luna, se ve el golpeteo del agua cuando llueve y se perciben los virajes violáceos del crepúsculo. Estos ventanales vidriados redimensionan el lugar, permitiendo una iluminación a veces fantasmal, en otras a contraluz que acompaña la irrealidad de sus vidas.
La sala tiene muebles antiguos, macizos y pesados: mesa de comedor con cuatro sillas y una serie de sillones desgastados por la vida. Puede haber fotografías sepias en las paredes (de los padres y abuelos de

Rosalía) o huellas despintadas de cuadros que ya no están colgados; un arcón donde Griselda guarda sus capelinas, quizás una antigua máquina de coser donde todavía la misma Griselda cose. Una pátina cenicienta cubre el ambiente que Rosalía nunca ha renovado porque no le alcanza el dinero, ni el entusiasmo. En medio de esta sala, mirando hacia el público hay un televisor de pantalla gigante, única nota de color en medio de tanta vetustez. Este desproporcionado televisor es el centro de la vida de ambas. Los sillones lo rodean, siempre listos para que ellas se enfrasquen en la pantalla. El televisor está rodeado de mística y es una especie de altar que tanto Rosalía como Griselda alimentan constantemente, llenándolo de jarrones con flores frescas, retratos de Mariano Rivas, su ídolo televisivo y una cantidad de santos y velas que le dan un carácter semireligioso. Es el corazón de la sala, un santuario alrededor del cual consumen sus vidas, siguiendo los teleteatros en los que actúa su galán amado. El tamaño de la pantalla permite que los espectadores sigan los distintos episodios, que la obra incluye, del teleteatro que tiene a ambas tan atrapadas. Por lo tanto se constituye en un personaje más, con el que ellas se relacionan permanentemente y que nos permite conocer a Marcelo el mecánico (Mariano Rivas) durante el primer acto, a quien veremos en vivo en el segundo.

En el segundo acto la casa cambia: ellas la ponen de fiesta. Debe notarse este cambio en todos los detalles. Han puesto todo su empeño en embellecer el ambiente, limpiarlo, preparar la mesa con la vajilla inglesa heredada por Rosalía, cambiar los muebles de lugar, preparar la casa para la llegada del hombre que aman.

PRIMER ACTO

Primera Escena

(Sobresaltada por sus propios sueños Rosalía pega un grito. Se levanta intempestivamente y apaga el televisor. Se reubica. Ve a Griselda dormida.)

Rosalía   ¿No habíamos quedado en algo para esta noche vos y yo? *(Griselda duerme profundamente. Trata de serenarse. Se sienta. Pausa. Se levanta y abre la ventana.)* Mirá que luna. Toda para nosotras. Pero ¿vos qué sabés de la luna? Vos no tenés fuerza necesaria para quedarte despierta conmigo. Yo ya lo sabía. Y además estoy tan acostumbrada...

Si yo pudiera dormir así...con el cuerpo relajado y las manos tan caídas. (*Le acaricia la cabeza.*) como una criatura cansada de jugar que cae rendida después de comer el flan de dulce de leche. Ni buenas noches me decís...ni buenas noches. Yo tampoco te diría buenas noches. (*Se acerca a la ventana y mira la luna en silencio.*) La luna está muerta de risa hoy. Se ríe de vos que ibas a pasar la noche despierta. ¿Vos no te quedabas despierta toda la noche en Carnaval?

Griselda ¿Hoy es Carnaval?

Rosalía ¡No ves cuántas cosas te perdés!

Griselda ¿Qué hora es?

Rosalía Si te digo la una, si te digo las dos, si te digo las tres, si te digo las cuatro...

Griselda ¡Son las cuatro! (*Va a sentarse alarmada por la hora.*)

Rosalía Son todas las horas que vos no conocés.

Griselda Por que yo no tengo insomnio.

Rosalía Insomnio. Qué palabra. Como moño. Moño. Insomnio. Somnio. Yo no tengo insomnio. Vos tenés insomnio.

Griselda Exactamente. Yo tengo somnio. ¿No podemos apagar un poquito la radio? Son la cuatro de la mañana m'hijita.

Rosalía No son las cuatro. Son las doce y media de la noche.

Griselda ¿Y es Carnaval?

Rosalía El jueves 22 de septiembre. Y yo hace un mes había invitado a una amiga, a la señorita que vive conmigo, a mi inquilina, digamos, a pasar toda la noche despierta conmigo.

Griselda Tenés razón. Perdóname. Me quede dormida. Decime qué tengo que hacer. ¿Qué tomas vos en tus noches de insomnio?

Rosalía Leche.

Griselda ¿Leche?

Rosalía Whisky.

Griselda ¿Importado?

Rosalía Conformate con uno nacional.

Griselda ¡Importado! (*Rosalía sale. Griselda vuelve a dormirse.*)

Rosalía (*Volviendo la ve dormida. Le sirve y la despierta.*) Tengo hora en lo de Félix.

Griselda ¡Siempre tenés hora en lo de Félix!

Rosalía Una hora distinta.

Griselda ¿Qué hora?

Rosalía Las tres y media de la tarde.

Griselda Te vas a perder el teleteatro.

Rosalía Voy a llegar. Ya vas a ver. Tengo que verlo a Felix. Jupiter estaba mal sobre mi luna pero esta semana me libera. He decidido ser otra.

Griselda Yo también. Dame más whisky. (*Rosalía le sirve. Griselda se queda dormida instantáneamente.*)

Rosalía Contame algo. Algo personal.

Griselda (*Despertándose medio atontada*) Sí. Sí. ¿Nunca te hablé de Daniel?

Rosalía ¿Quién es Daniel?

Griselda Un novio que yo tuve. Era estudiante de literatura y a mamá no le gustaba nada. Me decía dónde vas a llegar con la literatura. A la poesía, mamá. A la poesía. (*Pausa*) Gira todo. Y todo gira. Los planetas giran. La luna.

Rosalía Sí. Tenés que venir conmigo a lo de Félix.

Griselda ¡No. Rosalía, no! Yo tengo unos principios. Y unas creencias. Y he vivido en tu casa 20 años tolerando pero no asistiendo. ¿Querés que te cocine algo?

Rosalía ¡No!

Griselda Te canto

Rosalía Sí. Algo español. (*Griselda se pone a cantar algo flamenco.*) ¿Y qué pasó con Daniel?

Griselda Me mintió. El conocía poetas difíciles. Que yo no conocía. Y un día me trajo un poema de un poeta difícil, y me dijo que era de él. Y yo me lo creí. Y me enamoré más de él pensando que era de él.

> "En nuestras aguas oscuras
> brilla fijo un resplandor:
> el anillo de una novia
> o el ojo alerta de Dios".

Rosalía Ese se quería casar con vos, es evidente.

Griselda Pero el poema era de otro. Gabriel Celaya. (*Se duerme.*)

Rosalía Yo tampoco te diría buenas noches si pudiera dormir. Me dormiría así, como vos. De repente. De un instante para otro. En mitad de un gesto. (*Prueba.*)

Rosalía El anillo de una novia o el ojo abierto de Dios. (*Hace como que se duerme, abre un ojo.*) El ojo alerta de Dios. Ese es un insomnio. El ojo alerta de Dios. ¿Qué me importa que el poema no haya sido de él? ¡El ojo alerta de Dios, Griselda! Yo le hubiera perdonado ¿Sabés?

Griselda El anillo de una novia o el ojo alerta de Dios. (*De pronto llora.*) Yo también hoy lo perdonaría.

Segunda Escena

(*En la oscuridad total se ve el diálogo del televisor encendido: es un diálogo entre los protagonistas del teleteatro. Marcelo y Valeria. Marcelo es mecánico de autos y tiene lenguaje de un muchacho de barrio. Valeria es una jovencita de clase media alta. La luz del televisor ilumina el rostro de Griselda, que tiene un vestido azul con flores y una enorme lata de galletitas sobre la falda que devora vorazmente mientras mira televisión.*)

Marcelo ¿Le quedó bien el auto a su novio?
Valeria Si, usted se lo arregló muy bien. Gracias.
Marcelo Dígale a su novio que cuando quiera pase, que siempre es bueno darle una revisadita. Y también dígale que... (*Se interrumpe.*) Casi meto la gamba.
Valeria ¿Por qué?
Marcelo Porque le iba a mandar a su novio un mensaje que le hubiera caído como un bulón en medio del puchero.
(*Valeria se ríe.*)
Griselda Sos divino. Te comería todo. ¡Hay Rosalía lo que te estás perdiendo! ¿Justo hoy se te ocurrió pedir hora en lo de Félix? ¡Qué lástima!
Valeria ¿Y qué mensaje le iba a mandar a mi novio?
Marcelo ¡Uy no! Eso no se lo puedo decir.
Griselda ¡Para mí que se lo dice! Ay, por ese maldito Félix mirá lo que te perdés Rosalía. El mejor capítulo del año.
Valeria ¿Algo sobre la mecánica del auto?
Marcelo Algo sobre usted. (*Música de suspenso*)
Valeria (*Nerviosa*) Bueno, me tengo que ir.
Marcelo Le queda muy bien
Valeria ¿Qué cosa?
Marcelo Cuando se pone nerviosa y se le suben los colores a la cara...
Griselda ¡Qué dulce! Yo me muero.
Valeria Usted es un pirata.
Marcelo Le hubiera mandado el siguiente mensaje: flaco tenés una novia que tiene una boquita chiquitita como una frutillita.
Griselda ¡Se armó! ¡Para mí que se armó!
Valeria Marcelo.
Marcelo Y sabés una cosa flaco, yo me pegué un metejón de novela con tu novia.
Griselda (*Pega un salto en la silla.*) Besala, besala. ¡Ahora o nunca! ¡Besala con todo pichón!

Valeria Marcelo, yo, yo... (*Casi llorando*) Yo también me pegué un mete, un metejón. (*Caen uno en brazos del otro. Música de fondo*) Un hermoso metejón como dice, como decía... vos... (*Se besan.*)

Griselda ¡Rosalía te perdiste el mejor capítulo del año! ¡Qué bien besas mi amor, qué bien besas mi vida!

Marcelo Yo sé que usted piensa que soy una rata, que ando siempre con la mano llena de grasa con este mameluco que camina solo, en serio, camina solo. El otro día fui al zoológico con la nena de Juan y me empilché de verdad, y cuando llegamos a la jaula del hipopótamo nos dimos cuenta que el mameluco nos venía siguiendo desde hacía más de media hora. No se ría, yo creo que nací con el mameluco puesto y el día que me case con usted me voy a casar con el mameluco puesto y que me voy a morir con el mameluco puesto. Y el día que me case con usted me voy a casar con el mameluco para que usted no se olvide que se está casando con un laburante de esos que los pitucos de su familia desprecian porque es mersa o porque como manzanas y las hace crujir. (*Saca una manzana del bolsillo.*) El día que usted pruebe esta manzana pierde para siempre. (*Se la come.*) Por eso no la quiere morder, porque usted sabe que esta manzana es más peligrosa para usted que todos esos caviares y esos langostinos que le sirven de desayuno todos los días ese mayordomo con cara de paraguas que le inaugura el día.

¿Sabe como le voy a inaugurar yo los días a usted?

Valeria ¿Cómo me los va a inaugurar?

Marcelo Así se los voy a inaugurar. (*La besa apasionadamente.*) Así se los voy a inaugurar.

Griselda ¡Otro beso más. Ay, como me gustaría que me besaras así! (*Besa la pantalla. Cortina final con "leit-motiv" del teleteatro*) Terminó. Terminó y te lo perdiste todo. Terminó. (*Apaga el televisor.*) En el fondo me gusta que hoy haya sido todo mío. Creo que era mi destino. Creo que ciertas cosas suceden cuando no las esperas. Como este beso repentino. (*Besa la planta.*) ¡ Qué beso amor, qué beso! (*Besa las hojas.*) (*Agarra su planta predilecta.*) No tiene cabeza esta mujer.

¿No te parece, Begonia? No tiene cabeza (*La arregla, la riega.*) Vení que te voy a poner un poquito de agua, que en esta casa si yo no me ocupo de ustedes no se ocupa nadie. (*Le pone agua. Habla con ternura*) ¿Te gusta, Begonia, el agüita fresca, eh? (*Prueba un poquito.*) Está muy rica. Mirá el capítulo que se viene a perder... ¿Qué le va a decir ese vidente que ella no sepa? (*Agarra otra planta.*) ¿Qué le va a decir mi querida Violetita de los Alpes, qué le puede decir de nuevo? Vos también tenés sed. Son estas estufas a gas. Vos me entedés, ¿no Violetita? Cuando yo trabajaba en

Madame Rifau, tenía mi propia oficina de diseño, y en esa oficina la ventana estaba siempre abierta, invierno, verano, siempre porque el aire no tiene estación. Si el aire le cierran el paso, el aire te abandona, te deja de lado. Se ocupa de otros. Las plantas que tenía en esa ventana crecían como matas tropicales. Y yo no tenía asma. (*Pausa*) Bueno...por lo menos no tenía este asma producto de la estufa. ¡Qué feliz hubieras sido en esa ventana mi querida Violetita de los Alpes! ¡Qué feliz! Feliz como Valeria en los brazos de Marcelo. Feliz... (*Después de regar a la violetita de los Alpes agarra un helecho.*)
Y usted mi señor Don helecho. ¡Mire que caiducho que se me ha puesto! ¡Venga para acá, no se haga el mimoso! (*Le echa agua.*) Con esa melena toda verde...toda desparramada como un galán de televisión. (*Arregla el helecho. Lo abraza como si fuera Marcelo.*) ¿Qué te pasa? Vamos a ver. Cuénteme. ¿Estás asfixiado? Algún día yo me voy a ir de esta casa, y me voy a llevar todas mis plantas. Estoy esperando que se resuelva el problema de los abogados de la herencia de mi tío y me los llevo a todos bien lejos, a un lugar sin estufas. ¡Finalmente estoy dejando mi vida por pagarle esta habitación a ella! Me los llevo a todos a una casa en el mar. Me encantaría vivir en el mar como Alfonsina Storni.
(*Caminando místicamente con el helecho en la mano.*)
> "Quisiera una tarde divina de octubre
> pasear por la orilla lejana del mar"
> Siempre quise ser Alfonsina Storni.
> Tengo todas las condiciones para serlo.
> Que la arena de oro y las aguas de verano
> y los cielos puros me vieran pasar"

Pero yo no fui Alfonsina Storni, estoy acá encerrada cosiendo para la gorda de al lado.
> "Ser alta, perfecta, soberbia quisiera
> como una romana para concordar"

Yo he trabajado para Madame Rifau, yo que he diseñado sus mejores modelos, mi querido Don helecho.
> "con las grandes olas y las rocas muertas
> y las anchas playas que ciñen el mar"

(*Sobre esta situación llega Rosalía agitada de la calle, ha corrido para llegar a tiempo para no perderse el capítulo de hoy.*)
Rosalía ¿Ya terminó?   (*Griselda no le contesta todavía con el helecho en la mano.*) ¿Se vieron?
Griselda (*Por los paquetes*) ¿Qué trajiste?
Rosalía ¿No se vieron?

Griselda (*Griselda abre un paquete.*) ¡Qué hermoso! Compraste una lámpara igual a la del teleteatro. ¿Dónde la conseguiste?

Rosalía Me volvió loca ese hombre. Tuve que comprarme algo. Cuando salí de su casa estaba con un ataque. No me paraba nadie. Me fue bárbaro. No sabes las cosas que me dijo. (*Pausa. Retoma lo del vidente.*) Este año viene con todo. Hay un hombre en mi camino. ¿Podés creerlo? Me senté, me miró a los ojos. Qué ojos que tiene, son casi amarillos. Nunca vi un color tan horrible de ojos. Pero te penetran, te traspasan la cabeza. Sentía los ojos de él en el centro de mi cuerpo "Hay un hombre" me dijo. Inevitable. Te lo juro que me dijo eso. "Un hombre joven". Después recién tiró las cartas. Salían triunfos por todas partes. "Y amor, amor". Felix usted me está macaneando, le dije. No me contestó pero tiene una seriedad que mata. No le gustó nada. (*Pausa*) Me debo haber perdido un capítulo bárbaro. Yo quería llegar, pero vi la lámpara y me perdí. ¿Viste? Es igualita a la del escritorio del Padre de Valeria. (*Retoma.*) No le gustó nada, y entonces me dijo, "Hágame preguntas Usted". "No se enoje Félix", le dije, "Lo que pasa es que viene todo tan bien, que no lo puedo creer". "Hágame preguntas", me contestó. "Con eso me mató. ¿Qué hombre"?, le pregunté. "El hombre que usted quiera", me contestó. Con eso me mató. El hombre que yo más quiera. "Pero yo estoy enamorada de un galán de televisión", le dije. No me contestó nada, pero tiró dos cartas y salió triunfo. Creer o reventar. Dos cartas seguidas, "Hágame otra pregunta", me dijo. Entonces le pregunte por vos. Tiró dos cartas y lo mismo.

(*Griselda que mientras tanto ha encontrado un lugar para la lámpara le ha colocado una bombita y la ha encendido.*)

Griselda ¿Cómo lo mismo?

Rosalía ¿Se vieron o no se vieron? Hice lo imposible por llegar, te lo juro.

Griselda ¿Cómo lo mismo?

Rosalía ¡Un hombre!

Griselda ¿Qué hombre?

Rosalía Triunfo. Tres triunfos seguido tuviste.

Griselda ¿Yo?

Rosalía El hombre que vos quieras. "Ella también está enamorada de un galán de televisión", le dije.

Griselda ¿Y?

Rosalía Ojos amarillos: nada. "El mismo que yo", le dije.

Griselda ¿Y?

Rosalía Ojos amarillos: nada. "Esto no es perjudicial para nuestra íntima amistad?", le dije.

Griselda ¿Y?

Rosalía Tiró cartas de nuevo.

Griselda ¿Y?

Rosalía Triunfos. Triunfos por todas partes. Le pagué y me fui. Cuando salí a la calle no sabía que hacer conmigo. Es la primera vez que me dice algo bueno. Algo tan rotundo. A veces me ha dado aliento. Me ha dado optimismo, no sé...pero hoy... ¿Se vieron o no se vieron Valeria y Marcelo?

Griselda Sí.

Rosalía ¿Qué pasó?

Griselda ¿Sirvo el té?

Rosalía ¿Él le dijo algo?

Griselda Le dijo todo.

Rosalía ¿Todo? ¿Qué todo?

Griselda Estuvo genio, para comérselo. Con esa cancha que tiene para hablar...tan zafado... (*Se ríe mientras Rosalía la mira seria.*)

Rosalía ¿Qué le dijo?

Griselda Le dijo todo, y después la besó.

Rosalía No me digas que la besó. (*Se angustia.*) Hace tres meses que venimos esperando que la bese. ¿Cómo la besó?

Griselda En la boca.

Rosalía (*Malhumorada*) ¿Qué le dijo? Contáme como fue.

Griselda Te estoy contando Rosalía.

Rosalía Eso no es contar. Eso es todo en general, una porquería que no entiendo nada. No te puedo creer que la besó.

Griselda No me acuerdo todo, palabra por palabra. Te cuento lo que me acuerdo.

Rosalía La besó. Jurámelo. Me lo decís a propósito para hacerme sufrir. Lo que pasa es que a vos no te gusta que yo vaya a verlo a Félix. No la besó nada. Me estás cargando. (*Griselda se va para la cocina.*) ¿A dónde te vas?

Griselda Tengo el té preparado.

(*Rosalía se sienta sola después de sacarse el saco.*)

Rosalía No pasó nada. La conozco muy bien. Me lo hace totalmente a propósito.

Griselda (*Entrando con la bandeja del té*) No te lo hago a propósito.

Rosalía Entonces me perdí el mejor capítulo.

Griselda El mejor.

Rosalía ¿Y cómo la besaba?

Griselda La agarró con las dos manos de la cara, y le dio un beso largo, largo, largo.

Rosalía ¿Cuánto de largo?

Griselda Bien largo.

Rosalía ¿Cuántos minutos?

Griselda No sé…no le tomé el tiempo…pero bastante…

Rosalía ¿Y después?

Griselda Después le dijo que la quería.

Rosalía ¿Y el novio?

Griselda ¡No pasa nada con el novio querida! Le dijo que la quería y le encajó otro beso.

Rosalía ¿Largo?

Griselda Más largo que el anterior. (*Pausa*) Qué bien besa, si vieras. ¡Con ese overoll! Todo manchado de grasa y esas manos enormes todas mugrientas. Le agarró la cara y ella temblaba. Viste como ese ella, tan frágil, parece que se fuera a deshacer.

Rosalía ¡Que le va a deshacer esa! Tiene cuerda para rato.

Griselda Y él la hablaba en su idioma.

Rosalía ¿Qué idioma?

Griselda Ese idioma medio bruto que a mí me encanta, le hablaba y la miraba, y ella se iba aflojando, hasta que la tuvo bien cerca y le decía "Estoy chiflado por vos. Este es un metejón de novela". Y algo de los bulones de un puchero.

Rosalía ¿De qué puchero?

Griselda No me acuerdo. Parece que tenía hambre sabés. Algo de los bulones de un puchero. Y de que había metido la gamba.

Rosalía ¿Dónde había metido la gamba?

Griselda No me acuerdo. Y después la besó.

Rosalía No ves que me contás todo mal.

Griselda Es que yo estaba mirando todo el tiempo como la besaba, y lo miraba a él, y ese mechón que se le cae sobre la frente, y es tan hermoso, tan bruto, y no me podía concentrar en otra cosa, es tan lindo con esa nariz tan fuerte, no sé, me viene como una alegría de verlo, y me pierdo en la voz, qué voz que tiene, ¿de dónde la saca?, es tan dulce además, y al mismo tiempo tan hombre, me tiene loca.

Rosalía ¿Cómo habrá hecho la madre para tener un hijo tan lindo?

Griselda Y…a lo mejor ella era muy linda.

Rosalía O el padre.

Griselda O los dos. ¿Te imaginás? El padre, la madre, y los tres hermanos todos lindos.

Rosalía No pueden ser nunca tan lindos como él, si no serían todos famosos.

Griselda ¡Qué mechón! Cuando se le cae sobre la frente, y se lo levanta así, con esa mano mugrienta…

Rosalía Grasienta, no mugrienta.

Griselda Mugrienta de grasa.

Rosalía La grasa no es mugre. Es trabajo.

Griselda Y ese mechón…

Rosalía Ya dijiste lo del mechón.

Griselda Me gusta decirlo. No es un mechón igual a los de los otros hombres.

Rosalía ¿Qué otros hombres?

Griselda Otros

Rosalía Tu novio el veterinario era pelado.

Griselda ¡Qué vas a comparar! El otro era flaco, con anteojos, tartamudo y medio chueco. ¿Ese es un hombre? En cambio éste es alto, de mirada despejada, ojos que te atraviesan, no sé, y esa cosa de muchachón tan tierno, me vuelvo loca. ¡Ay! Me vinieron ganas de decir el poema que le escribí. Unas ganas así, de repente, no se... (*Emocionada*) Me siento inspirada.

Rosalía Te escucho. ¿Qué otro remedio me queda de escucharte?

Griselda
> "Si supieras amor,
> si tú supieras,
> desde donde me nace esta pasión,
> viene del fondo mismo de mi pecho,
> desde mi corazón hasta tu corazón".

(*Camina totalmente poseída por el recitado.*)
> "Cuánto más cerca estoy,
> más inasible,
> más lejano de toda mi ilusión
> te quisiera conmigo, y sin embargo,
> vives dentro de un televisor".

(*Levanta el televisor en brazos.*)
> "¡Oh! Terrible aparato que interpone abismos
> elevándole un puñal a mi dolor,
> y sin embargo al mismo tiempo amigo
> de mi desconsolado corazón.
> ¡Al suelo te echaría en mil pedazos"!

Rosalía (*Grita.*) ¡No!

Griselda
      "Pero una voz desde adentro grita ¡"No"!
      Porque entonces, amor, que quedaría
      de tantas largas tardes de ilusión".
(Desde la última estrofa las luces han ido disminuyendo hasta apagón!)

Tercera Escena

(Al encender las luces Griselda está rodeada de sus plantas, vestidas con una bata blanca de corte oriental haciendo una gimnasia respiratoria muy lenta, concentrada y armónica, mientras Rosalía barre frenéticamente.)

Griselda Elevamos los brazos hacia el cielo. Mantenemos la columna erguida y el centro de la energía cae ahora en la espalda, la espalda es el sostén del cuerpo. Y en esta posición rotamos hacia el Este para saludar al sol. Y en esta posición rotamos hacia el Oeste para saludar a la luna. *(Se interrumpe.)* ¿No podés hacer otra cosa? Planchar por ejemplo. O cocinar. *(Rosalía sigue barriendo. Griselda trata de volver a concentrarse.)* Aspiramos con los pulmones abiertos al aire que nos envuelve. *(Aspira y tose.)*
Rosalía Hay plazas. Hay jardines públicos. Hay centro de rehabilitación del asmático. Hay grandes espacios abiertos.
Griselda Y hay personas malas. Hay de todo.
Rosalía Y hay personas inoportunas. Hay de todo.
(Rosalía sigue barriendo, Griselda retoma sus ejercicio.)
Griselda Estiramos los brazos hacia lo alto tratando de tocar el sol.
(Rosalia se ríe a carcajadas. A Griselda se le llenan los ojos de lágrimas de la ira. Rosalía reprime la risa y sigue barriendo.) Tratando de tocar el sol, y mantenemos la posición en puntas de pié para que nuestro cuerpo se estire completamente al máximo de sus posibilidades *(Se pone en esa posición. Rosalía barre muy cerca. Griselda se interrumpe muy violentada.)*. Esta es la última perrada que me hacés. A fin de mes me voy.
Rosalía Yo te alquilo una habitación no un gimnasio.
Griselda Y yo soy una persona. ¿Entendiste? Una persona.
Rosalía Una persona enferma. Estoy harta de enfermedades. Quiero un poco de salud.
Griselda Por eso hago gimnasia. Para curarme.
Rosalía *(Se ríe.)* ¡Gimnasia! ¿No te das cuenta que Samatra no es

hindú? ¿No te das cuenta que esa no es ninguna gimnasia? ¿No te das cuenta que te saca el dinero como a una pobre idiota? ¿No te das cuenta de nada en esta vida?

(*Sigue barriendo. Griselda agarra otra escoba y barre en dirección contraria. Arman una especie de batalla de escobas barriendo enérgicamente.*)

Griselda ¿Querés limpieza? Aquí tenés limpieza.

Rosalía Me arruinás lo que ya barrí.

Griselda Y vos me arruinás la vida.

Rosalía ¡Ay, si te viera tu querido Mariano Rivas! ¡Si te viera ahora.!

Griselda Creo que sería mucho más grave que te viera a vos. No podría resistirlo.

Rosalía (*Le arranca la escoba.*) Vas a dejar de barrer.

Griselda Esa escoba es mía y me la vas a dar.

(*Pelean por la escoba.*)

Rosalía La escoba es tuya pero el piso es mío.

(*Griselda se sube a un sillón con la escoba en mano.*)

Griselda Entonces barro este sillón que es mío. Mío. Mi sillón. Mi escoba. Mi Mariano Rivas. Mío. Mío. Lo mío es mío. Mi gimnasia. Mi asma. (*Barre frenéticamente el sillón.*)

Rosalía ¿Tengo que esperar a fin de mes para que te vayas? ¿No podemos adelantar un poco la fecha?

Griselda Sí que podemos. Me voy ahora mismo. ¡Estoy harta de tus maldades! Estoy harta de verte esa cara.

Rosalía (*La retiene.*) ¿Mi cara? ¿Qué tenés contra mi cara?

Griselda Tu cara. Tu pelo. Tus manos. Tu manera de caminar. Tus modales y tu envidia.

Rosalía (*Se ríe.*) ¡Yo te envidio! Pero ¿Cómo creés que tenés algo digno de ser envidiado? ¿Qué puedo envidiar de una esmirriada que saluda con los brazos hacia el este? ¿Qué envidia puede despertar una asmática sin pasado ni futuro que no tiene donde caerse muerta? ¿O vos te crees que aunque sea un segundo Mariano Rivas podría siquiera fijarse en vos? ¿Vos creés que te miraría?

Griselda No metas a Mariano Rivas en todo esto. El no tiene nada que ver. No lo metas ¿entendiste?

Rosalía Yo meto a Mariano Rivas en lo que se me antoja, porque Mariano Rivas es mío. (*Pausa*) O por lo menos yo tengo derecho a sentir que es mío. (*La suelta.*)

(*Griselda la mira en silencio.*)

Griselda (*Levanta los brazos.*) Saludamos a Rosalía por el Norte y nos vamos después de veinte años de tontería a buscar el sol en otra parte. (*Hace lo que acaba de decir.*) Saludamos a la casa por el Sur y la dejamos con su dueña para que ella disfrute de todos sus alegres beneficios...(*Lo hace. Se va para adentro. Rosalía se queda barriendo. Griselda sale con una valija dispuesta a irse.*) Voy a mandar a mi primo con el camioncito para que me recoja las plantas y lo demás te lo dejo. (*Le paga el alquiler.*) Te pago el mes entero total falta poco y a vos el dinero te viene bien. (*Rosalia rompe el dinero. Después le arranca la valija la abre y tira todo su contenido. Caen algunas ropas y muchos poemas. Hay un silencio espeso. Después Rosalía misma comienza a recoger las cosas de Griselda.*)

Rosalía Quedate.

Griselda No puedo. Me tengo que ir.

Rosalía ¿Adónde te vas a ir?

Griselda No sé. Ya voy a encontrar un lugar con patio. Yo soy una persona asmática, necesito un patio.

Rosalía Y yo soy una persona sola. Te necesito a vos.

Griselda No. A mí no. Lo necesitas a Mariano Rivas. A mí no. Yo te molesto.

Rosalía Quedate. Te puedo dar otra habitación más. La del fondo para que te instales un gimnasio allí.

Griselda No te la puedo pagar.

Rosalía Te la regalo...no puedo imaginarme esta casa sin vos. Te estaría buscando todo el tiempo...

Griselda ¿No te das cuenta que no puedo quedarme?

Rosalía ¿No te das cuenta que no podés irte? (*Pausa. Finalmente se abrazan.*) Perdoname, perdoname, te pido que me perdones Griselda. Sos la mejor persona que conozco. Sos la única persona que me quiere de verdad. Sos mi amiga.

Griselda Vos también perdoname. Perdoname mi asma. Perdoname.

Rosalía (*Se ríe.*) Tenés un asma maravilloso. (*Se ríen.*) A Mariano Rivas le deben gustar las mujeres asmáticas. Dan ganas de protegerlas. Uno se siente necesario.

Griselda A Mariano Rivas le deben encantar las mujeres enérgicas como vos. Decididas a todo.

Rosalía Yo creo que nos necesita a las dos.

Griselda Ay, si lo supiera. Si él supiera como nos necesita a las dos.

Rosalía Algún día va a saberlo.

Griselda Algún día, algún día, algún día, algún día...

Rosalía Sí Griselda, algún día seremos felices, algún día seremos jóvenes, algún día Mariano Rivas se enamorará de nosotras, vestido de Marcelo el mecánico, lleno de esa grasa que le queda tan bien, nos besará en la boca, y nos dirá, chiquitas mías, algún día, algún día... algún día...

Apagón.

Cuarta Escena

(*Al encenderse las luces se ve a Griselda y a Rosalía recostadas cada una en un sillón. Rosalía tiene la cara recubierta de rodajas de naranjas y Griselda de rodajas de tomate. Están abocadas a un tratamiento de rejuvenecimiento facial. Rosalía se ríe a carcajadas. Griselda quieta, casi estática, muda.*)

Rosalía ¡Qué gracioso! (*Se ríe.*) ¡Qué gracioso! (*Se ríe.*)
Griselda (*Finalmente le pregunta.*) ¿De qué te reís?
Rosalía (*Seria*) Estaba pensando en la muerte.
(*Pausa muy seria de las dos. Después Griselda empieza a reírse sola. Rosalía se contagia, y finalmente se ríen las dos. Hay mucha ansiedad y miedo en esta risa que sin embargo no deja de ser alegre.*)
Rosalía ¿Vos como te la imaginás?
Griselda ¡Ay! ¿ Quién puede imaginarse La Muerte?
Rosalía (*En medio de otro ataque de risa*) Yo puedo.
Griselda (*Se ríe.*) Yo también. Me la imagino siempre.
(*Se ríen juntas.*)
Rosalía Para mí La Muerte tiene zapatos brillantes. No es ni blanca ni negra, de un color que no existe. (*Se ríe.*) Me mira y me dice (*Se ríe.*) Vamos, piba.
Griselda (*Se ríe.*) ¿Habla así de La Muerte?
Rosalía Vamos piba, se te cortó la piola.
(*Silencio*)
Rosalía ¿No te viene el asma?
Griselda ¡No! Al contrario me divierto mucho.
Griselda ¡Pero La Muerte es un tango!
Rosalía La Muerte habla como Marcelo en el teleteatro. Es gordísima y tiene el pelo fosforescente y una lengua de trapo.
Griselda (*Se ríe.*) Sí, sí.
Rosalía Una lengua de trapo para envolverme.
(*Griselda se saca ceremoniosamente los tomates. Los coloca ordenadamente sobre una mesa.*)

Griselda Ya pasó el tiempo ahora viene la máscara facial vegetativa.
(*Rosalía se saca las naranjas, Griselda agarra un plato donde hay preparadas tiras de distintos vegetales verdes y los coloca ordenadamente sobre la cara de Rosalía.*)
Rosalía ¿Y a vos qué te toca?
Griselda Circulación de la sangre. Llegó la hora de las cachetadas. (*Griselda se da cachetadas sola.*) Para mí la muerte es un hombre muy alto que me hace preguntas. (*A cada pregunta se da una cachetada más fuerte.*) ¿Cuál fue tu comida preferida? ¿Qué número de zapatos calzas? ¿Cuántas veces te acostaste con un hombre? ¿Cuál es el río más ancho del mundo? ¿Qué países del mundo conociste? ¿Le tenías miedo a las tormentas con relámpagos? ¿Cuánto dejaste de creer en la cigüeña? ¿Te jugaste por algo alguna vez? ¿Vos también creíste que la Argentina ganaba la Guerra de las Malvinas? ¿Fuiste feliz durante más de media hora? ¿Te hubiera gustado tener tres hijos? ¿Te hubiera gustado publicar un libro de poesía?
(*Se ha pegado muy fuerte y le saltan las lágrimas. Se acerca a Rosalía y le saca las verduras, se miran intensamente en silencio, sin decirse nada, después Griselda, tratando de repararse. Rosalía enciende el televisor.*)
Teleteatro
Valeria (*Feliz*) Papá papito papitín (*Lo llena de besos. Se sienta en las rodillas del Padre.*)
Padre Te tengo miedo... (*Se ríe.*) Estás por pedirme algo...
Valeria (*Se ríe.*) Nada que ver. (*Lo besa.*) Estoy feliz...eso es todo.
Padre (*La abraza.*) Entonces yo estoy feliz también.
Valeria (*Más seria*) Te necesito.
Padre Me tenés.
Valeria Estoy enamorada. Yo nunca había estado enamorada. ¿Vos estuviste alguna vez perdidamente enamorada?
Padre Algunas veces... (*Se ríe.*) Algunas veces sí. (*Pausa. La besa.*) Javier Ugarte es un muchacho muy serio. Es difícil para mí no sentir celos, pero tengo confianza en Javier. Me gusta su entereza, me gusta su manera de ser joven. Un joven con los pies sobre la tierra, que fuerte. Lleno de vida, lleno de posibilidades. (*La besa.*) Que seas muy feliz hijita, muy feliz... (*Emocionado*). Tan feliz como yo te lo deseo...fuerte. Lleno de vida, lleno de posibilidades. (*La besa.*) Que seas muy
Valeria No estoy enamorada de Javier Ugarte. (*El Padre la mira absolutamente sorprendido.*)
Padre ¿Qué?
Valeria Yo sé que vos me vas a entender. El amor es así. Uno no se

propone nada. Le pasa. (*Pausa*) ¿Me vas a ayudar, papá?

Padre (*Muy desconfiado*) ¿Ayudarte a qué? ¿Ayudarte a qué?

Valeria Papito...yo estoy enamorada de otra persona. Una persona maravillosa, una persona con un corazón enorme y con las manos fuertes de trabajar.

Padre Pero si ya está todo en marcha para tu casamiento con Javier Ugarte...¿cómo podés ahora no ser fiel a tu palabra? ¿Cómo puede mi hija hacer una cosa así? (*Pausa*) Y ¿de quién estás enamorada? ¿Quién es el loco que te sedujo?

Valeria No hables así papá.

Padre Yo hablo como quiero. ¿De quién estás enamorada?

Valeria De...de Marcelo...de Marcelo el mecánico...

(*El Padre le da una cachetada. Ella llora. Sobre esta plano corte.*)

Griselda ¡Que viejo jodido!

Rosalía Mirá, si él se lo propone, te juro que lo revienta a Marcelo. (*En el teleteatro corte a Marcelo que está en su taller. Canta y trabaja.*) ¡Miralo, qué divino!

Griselda ¡Cómo querés que lo mire si me tapás todo!

Rosalía Oíme, yo también quiero verlo o es tuyo sola. (*Forcejean y se acomodan.*) Qué naricita tan perfecta tiene...

Griselda Mirá ese pelo. Hoy lo tiene más lindo que nunca...

Rosalía Felix me lo dijo. Hay un hombre en mi vida. Lo veo venir.

(*Besa el televisor.*)

Griselda ¡Sacá la cabeza!

(*Teleteatro*)

Marcelo Pasame la bisagra. Tachuela, querés.

Tachuela ¿Qué bisagra, Marcelo?

Marcelo La de la ventanilla, flaco.

Griselda Mirá como se pone los tornillos en la boca, qué bien le queda.

Rosalía Es que tiene los dientes de caníbal. Viste cómo mastica. Me encanta verlo comer, sobre todo cuando se traga a mordiscones una manzana.

Griselda Callate la boca que no se escucha.

Rosalía Yo lo haría comer manzana todo el tiempo. Así debe besar a mordiscones.

(*En el teleteatro timbre*)

Marcelo Atendé Tachuela, ¿querés?

Voz de Policía Buenas tardes. Soy el oficial Ramírez. Tengo orden de detención del señor Marcelo Bragante. ¿Se encuentra en la casa? (*Música de suspenso y "leit-motif" del teleteatro. Rosalía apaga el televisor.*)

Griselda ¿Cómo sabés que se terminó?

Rosalía ¿No viste los cartones? Terminó.

Griselda Terminó que se lo llevan preso.

Rosalía Lógico, el padre de ella le mandó la policía. Es un tipo muy influyente, yo te dije que lo iba a aplastar como una mosca.

Griselda ¡Pobrecito! ¿Y ahora qué hacemos?

Rosalía Imaginate que si le pasa algo grave a Marcelo, se acaba el teleteatro. Así que no puede ser.

Griselda Son teleteatros modernos. Algunos terminan mal. Acordate el año pasado con esa tira "Simpático adolescente", terminaba que ella se moría. Sí, para mí que es moderno y va a terminar mal. Marcelo ahora va preso, y después el padre va a contratar a alguien que lo mate. Un accidente casual, y mucho dinero encima para tapar la cosa.

Rosalía También puede terminar bien. Marcelo se casa con Valeria y Javier reconoce sus errores y se va del país.

Griselda Y el padre dónde lo metés en todo esto. No querida. Hay un padre que es un personaje muy importante, y que está decidido a todo. No ves que ahora le ha mandado un policía a la casa. Por de pronto ahora va preso, y son un montón de capítulos de sufrimientos en los que van a estar separados.

Rosalía ¿Pero cómo va a ir preso si él no hizo nada?

Griselda ¿Y eso que tiene que ver? ¿O solamente van presos los que han hecho algo?

Rosalía No nos podemos quedar así, de brazos cruzados. Hace cuatro años que venimos siguiendo los teleteatros donde trabaja Mariano Rivas. Acordate el año pasado con "Muchacho terrible". Que sufrimiento, corría carreras de auto como un desafortunado. Nunca sabíamos si iba a vivir o no.

Griselda Pero "Marcleo el Mecánico" es mucho más moderna. ¿No te das cuenta? Va a morir en la cárcel. Es una novela con final trágico. Acordate lo que te digo.

Rosalía Alcanzame el teléfono. (*Griselda se lo alcanza sumisamente.*) ¿Cuál es el número del Canal?

Griselda ¿A quién llamás? (*Griselda le alcanza una agenda donde figura. Rosalía marca.*)

Rosalía El número del Canal. Al autor del teleteatro, por supuesto. (*La atiende.*) Hola, buenas tardes. Comuníqueme por favor con el Señor Gaspar Méndez Paz. (*Pausa*) De parte de Lolita Torres. (*Pausa*) Hola, sí, no, no soy Lolita Torres pero dije que era Lolita Torres porque si no usted no iba a querer atenderme. Yo soy Rosalía Echage una constante, una apasionada espectadora de sus tiras y lo llamaba para preguntarle si el teleteatro va a terminar mal, y para pedirle por favor que no lo meta preso a Marcelo, ya que ha sufrido bastante para conseguir el amor de Valeria, y ahora que lo tiene, justo se lo va a arruinar. (*Pausa*) Me cortó. (*Vuelve a llamar.*) Con en el señor Gaspar Méndez Paz. De parte de Susana Giménez. (*Pausa*) Hola, soy Rosalía Echague otra vez. (*Pausa cortada*) ¡Dios mío! (*Cuelga.*)

Griselda ¿Qué te dijo?

Rosalía Una mala palabra. Es un guarango este hombre. Y pensar que la vida de Marcelo el mecánico depende de gente como este señor. Está cantado: lo va a reventar a Marcelo. Aunque sea para llevarme la contra. Le tendría que haber pedido que lo meta preso. Así lo dejaba en libertad. Ese hombre me odia.

Griselda Ese hombre no te conoce.

Rosalía Ese hombre odia a los espectadores, y yo soy una espectadora.

Griselda Entonces también me odia a mí.

Rosalía Sí. Pero a mí me odia más, porque yo me atreví a enfrentarlo. Le hablé por teléfono. (*Pausa*) Pobre Marcelo, ahora por mi culpa todo el sufrimiento que le espera.

Griselda ¡No digas disparates! ¿Qué tiene que ver?

Rosalía (*Le agarra un ataque.*) Tiene mucho que ver, sabés. Felix me lo dijo. Mi vida pega un salto en este momento. Mi vida cambia pero no cambia sola. Vos también tenés que cambiar conmigo. Hay un hombre. Tenemos que hacer algo.

Griselda ¿Qué?

Rosalía No sé. Algo definitivo. Algo donde le demostremos a Mariano Rivas lo que sentimos por él. ¿Entendés?

Griselda Sí, pero ¿qué?

Rosalía El tiene que saber que existimos. El tiene que meterse en nuestra vida. Me lo dijo Félix. Es cuestión de atreverse.

Griselda Sí, pero ¿A qué?

Rosalía A algo que nos arroje a la vida verdadera. Algo que nos sacuda de raíz y nos dé vuelta. Algo sin regreso. ¿Entendés? (*Como una alucinada.*) Presiento grandes cambios Griselda. Estoy harta de cosas pequeñas. Harta de ponerte tomates en la cara para detener el tiempo. El tiempo pasa igual Griselda. Nos hemos cuidado demasiado. Pero ¿para quién nos hemos cuidado? Para Dios.

Griselda (*Con mucho miedo*) Dios. Mi Dios.

Rosalía Dios creó la vida para ser vivida. Dios nos va a perdonar. Arrodillate Griselda. Pidámosle perdón a Dios.

Griselda ¿Perdón? Si nunca hemos pecado.
Rosalía (*Reza en voz alta.*)
>   Perdón por lo que no hice.
>   Perdón por lo que no tuve.
>   Perdón por lo que no tomé.
>   Perdón por lo que no sentí
>   Perdón por no haberme reído.
>   Perdón por no haber usado mis lágrimas.

(*Griselda se ríe repentinamente. Rosalía la mira muy seria.*)
Griselda Perdón.
Rosalía A mí no. A Dios. A Dios.

Apagón

Quinta Escena

(*Es de noche. Una luz violácea cruzada por el brillo de los relámpagos cruza la escena vacía. Afuera llueve intensamente, y durante unos instantes las ventanas abiertas golpetean ininterrumpidamente, la jaula de los loros oscila movida por el viento, después la pausa, Rosalía, furiosa y desencajada entra a escena. Tiene el pelo muy revuelto, y la cara cubierta con una crema muy blanca. Descalza, y con un ancho camisón sin gracia. Parece un fantasma de sí misma.*)

Rosalía ¡Otra vez las ventanas abiertas! ¡Pero vos qué tenés en la cabeza? ¡Se nos viene abajo la casa, y vos seguís durmiendo tranquilamente! ¡Nos vas a matar a todos! (*Cierra furiosamente las ventanas que se le resisten por el viento.*) ¡Hace veinte años que abrís las ventanas que yo cierro! (*Un odio casi descontrolado ocupa su cuerpo, da vuelta por el escenario como buscando una presa para matar. Finalmente agarra un helecho.*) Hace veinte años que vivo entre las verduras. Veinte años escuchándote hablarle a la Begonia para que nos quite el mal de ojo, y a la violetita de los Alpes para curar el catarro, y a mi Don Helecho macho para conseguir novio. (*Levanta en alto el helecho como una ofrenda ante un altar.*)
>   "Don helecho dame amor
>   que yo te voy a cuidar
>   dame felicidad
>   quitame la soledad"

(*Baja el helecho y lenta y destructoramente le arranca las hojas.*)

¡Mirá como te quito la soledad! ¿No te sentís mejor ahora? Yo no espero más Griselda. ¿No te das cuenta? Yo no puedo más. Ni begonias, ni hortensias, ni malvones, clavelinas del aire...en esta casa hace falta un hombre! ¡Un hombre, no verduras! (*Deja el helecho, saca violentamente a los loros de la jaula. Y los arroja por la ventana. Después, dificultosamente, vuelve a cerrar el ventanal.*) ¡A volar, muchachos, a volar! ¡En esta casa nadie los necesita! ¡Quitame la soledad! (*Después de cerrar el ventanal vuelve a rondar por el jardín de invierno como buscando algo.*) Yo voy a traer un hombre a esta casa. Y vos me vas a ayudar. Vos Griselda. Despertate. (*Se trepa a una escalera y busca sobre un armario o una alacena una caja de hierro oculta. Todavía ahí arriba la abre y saca un revólver. Lo mira asustada y casi embelesada.*) ¡Quitame la soledad! ¡Quitame la soledad!

(*En ese momento entra Griselda. También despeinada. En camisón y con la cara llena de crema. A manera de máscara. Rosalía la mira desde arriba de la silla y le apunta con el revólver.*)

Griselda Rosalía... (*Trémula*)

Rosalía Ves que no soy sonámbula. Estoy despierta. Tengo los ojos abiertos. Mucho más abiertos que vos.

(*Griselda respira con fatiga.*)

Rosalía Una vez vos quisiste usar este revólver para dejar de sufrir. ¿Te acordás? (*Griselda no le contesta.*) Habías dejado una carta y todo. ¿Te acordás? (*Pausa*) ¿Te acordás?

Griselda Sí.

Rosalía El veterinario se fue con la veterinaria y Griselda se quedó con el Don Helecho macho ¿Te acordás?

Griselda Sí.

Rosalía Vos le cantabas todas las noches al Don Helecho macho. ¿Te acordás?

Griselda Sí.

Rosalía Pero el Don Helecho macho no te quitó la soledad.

Griselda No.

Rosalía Repetí: el Don Helecho macho no me quitó la soledad.

Griselda No.

Rosalía Repetí: el Don Helecho macho no me quitó la soledad.

Griselda No.

Rosalía Repetí que te mato. (*Apunta con el revólver.*)

Griselda El Don Helecho macho no...no...no...no me quitó la soledad.

Rosalía Yo te la voy a quitar. ¿Entendés?

Griselda Sí.

Rosalía Te la voy a quitar yo, con esto. (*Por el revólver*)

Griselda (*Temblando porque cree que la va a matar.*) Sí...

Rosalía Vamos a traer a Mariano Rivas a casa. Con esto, vos y yo.

Griselda (*Aliviada*) ¿Sí?

Rosalía Solito para nosotras dos. (*Se ríe. Griselda sonríe.*)

Griselda Sí. (*Le saltan las lagrimas.*)

Rosalía Repetilo.

Griselda Solito para nosotras dos.

Rosalía Aunque sea por unas horas

Griselda Solito para nosotras dos. (*Se ríe.*)

Rosalía Lo vamos a hacer feliz.

Griselda (*A las carcajadas*) Solito para nosotras dos.

Rosalía Marcelo el mecánico va a venir a casa. (*Se ríen.*)

Griselda Me voy a atrever Rosalía. ¡Me voy a atrever! ¡Siento que me voy a atrever!

(*Pausa. Rosalía baja de la escalera. Sin dejar el revolver.*)

Rosalía Al principio no va a querer venir.

Griselda Pero lo traemos igual.

Rosalía Y después no se va a querer ir. (*Se ríen.*)

Griselda Vamos a prepararlo todo. Detalle por detalle. Total por unas horas, nadie se va a dar cuenta.

Rosalía ¡Marcelo el mecánico en casa!

(*Cae una en brazos de la otra.*)

Rosalía Te quiero tanto, tanto.

Griselda Yo también.

Rosalía Sos lo único que tengo en este mundo.

Griselda Vos también sos lo único que tengo en este mundo.

(*Se besan con mucho afecto.*)

Rosalía Vamos a ser felices aunque sea por una hora.

Griselda Como la Cenicienta...

Rosalía ¡Basta de novelas! ¡Ahora Marcelo el mecánico se representa en casa!

Griselda ¡Si, si basta de novelas! ¡Ahora la novela somos nosotras!

Rosalía ¡La mejor de las novelas! ¡Nuestra novela!

Griselda ¡La gran novela de nuestra vida!

(*Rosalía abre el arcón y se mete adentro.*)

Rosalía ¡Yo sabía...yo sabía que a nosotras nos esperaban grandes momentos. Yo te dije Griselda que algún día...

Griselda (*Se ríe.*) ¡Hoy es ese día Rosalía! ¡Hoy es nuestro día! ¡Ahora nos toca vivir a nosotras! ¡Ahora por fin nos toca vivir a nosotras nuestro gran amor...! ¡Ahora!

Rosalía Ahora, sí ahora! Ahora, ahora, ahora, ahora y acá. Traerlo... traerlo...saborearlo...

Griselda Mirarlo...sentirlo...cuidarlo...

Rosalía Mariano Rivas con nosotras, acá...

Griselda Nuestro Marcelo el mecánico nos va a arreglar todos los coches que queramos.

Rosalía Quiero ahora quiero...¡te quiero!

Griselda Vamos a morder la manzana. ¡La gran manzana de la felicidad!

SEGUNDO ACTO

Primera Escena

(*El espacio es el mismo pero ha sido cuidadosamente ordenado como para recibir a Mariano Rivas. Presenta una apariencia festiva. Sobre una mesa hay un balde de metal con una botella de champagne dentro y tres copas. El arcón ha sido puesto en un lugar de privilegio. Lo mismo que el espejo. Todo ha sido lustrado y brilla. El orden creado es alterado desde el comienzo del acto por las corridas que se producen. Sin embargo ellas tratan de volver a rearmarlo. Tratan de no perder su propio montaje escenográfico. Al comenzar la escena se percibe un violento movimiento dentro de este lugar. Mariano se resiste como un caballo encabritado. Ellas tratan desesperadamente de reducirlo. Pelean con violencia pero sin hacerse daño. Por momentos parece que él puede lograr escaparse. Pero entre las dos... y sacando afuera una fiereza inusitada... Logran finalmente cercarlo. Sin embargo el sigue ofreciendo de una resistencia muy fuerte. Hasta que finalmente Rosalía recurre al revólver y lo encañona. Ahí Mariano se paraliza. Ya no lucha. Da unos pasos. Cercado. Y finalmente muy enojado y con mucha furia se sienta de brazos cruzados en un banco alto que tienen en el lugar. Hay una pausa tensa. Rosalía mantiene el revólver en alto.*)

Mariano Estoy quieto. ¿No ve que estoy quieto?

Rosalía En cualquier momento puede volver a saltar.

Mariano No. No voy a saltar. (*Con ira contenida*) Ya no. (*Pausa*) ¿Puede por favor apuntar para otro lado? (*La señala a Griselda.*) ¿Por qué no la mata a ella?

Rosalía Yo no pienso matar a nadie.

Mariano ¿Y ese arma para qué es?

Griselda Pero Mariano…¿usted nos ve cara de asesinas?

Mariano Uy, pero eso está muy pasado de moda. Ahora los asesinos vienen con cara de ángeles. Y de los ángeles. Y de los ángeles hay que cuidarse las espaldas. Ya no es como cuando era chico que el malo tenía cara de malo, y al bueno se lo reconocía hasta por la manera de caminar. ¿Quién diría por ejemplo que ustedes dos me van a matar?

Griselda No somos asesinas.

Mariano Todavía no, pero dentro de breves instantes pueden serlo.

Griselda (*Desesperada a Rosalía*) Mirá lo que logramos con todo esto. Mirá lo que opina de nosotras, Rosalía.

Rosalía Este revólver no es para matarlo.

Mariano ¿Ah, no? ¿Y qué vamos a hacer con él? ¿Nos lo vamos a comer? ¿Para qué sirve un revólver? ¿Eh? ¿Para qué sirve? ¡Contésteme!

Rosalía Para matar.

Griselda Pero el revólver, sinceramente no tiene ninguna importancia. Usted le da más importancia de la que tiene. Lo importante es que usted esté aquí adentro con nosotras.

Mariano Mire yo estoy aquí gracias a ese revólver. Y como la vida…al menos para mí tiene importancia…¿ de qué quiere que le hable? De lo estúpido que fui cuando dejé el coche abierto para que ustedes se metieran? Ya es tarde para hablar de eso. Ahora me tienen aquí. Y habló del revólver porque yo estaría aquí si no fuera por ese revólver.

Rosalía (*Le da un acceso de risa histérica.*) ¿Usted sabe qué significa para nosotras tenerlo hoy aquí? ¿Nunca leyó nada sobre los espejismos en el desierto? Mirarlo todos los días por esa pantalla es un espejismo y esta casa era un desierto hasta que entró usted. (*Se ríe.*) Se despiertan hasta las plantas. No, no tiene idea de nada. Por eso piensa que lo vamos a matar, querido mío. ¿Usted se cree que yo voy a apretar este gatillo contra lo que más quiero en la vida? (*Se ríe.*) Es un instante…no tiene idea de lo que despierta.

Mariano (*Cortante*) Bueno, si no me van a matar me voy. (*Se pone de pié dispuesto a irse.*) Fue un placer conocerlas.

Rosalía Quedate donde estás. (*Lo apunta implacablemente.*)

Mariano Ah, nos empezamos a tutear. El arma trae confianza, eh…(*Se ríe.*) así que no me iban a matar…(*Se ríe.*)

Rosalía ¿De qué se ríe?

Mariano De mí, por supuesto. Ustedes no me hacen ninguna gracia como se imaginarán.

Griselda Ríase todo lo que quiera. La risa es un buen punto de partida. Ríase, y haga de cuenta que usted quiso venir a visitarnos. Se va sentir completamente diferente. Hágame caso, haga la prueba. Juguemos a que vino porque nos quería ver, porque nos extrañaba. Usted es un gran actor, si se lo propone va a lograr creerlo. ¿Acaso no logra que nosotras nos creamos todas las tardes que es Marcelo el mecánico? Si se concentra puede olvidar los malos momentos que tuvimos que pasar. No perdamos el tiempo en tonterías. No perdamos también hoy el tiempo, querido. (*Esto último se lo dice muy emocionada.*) ¿No se ríe más? ¡Vamos ríase! ¿No quiere reírse conmigo? (*Se ríe para que él se ría.*)

Mariano (*Cortante*) ¿Cuánto quieren?

Rosalía (*Desconsolada*) ¿Qué?

Mariano Soy un actor exitoso y con trabajo pero eso no quiere decir que sea millonario así que no estoy dispuesto a pagar sumas delirantes para que me dejen tranquilo. Eso se los aviso de antemano. ¿Cuánto quieren?

Rosalía ¡Cállese la boca, por favor! Aquí nadie le va a sacar dinero. No nos siga humillando de esa manera. No sabe con que personas está tratando. Está completamente equivocado. Ni lo vamos a matar. Ni le vamos a sacar su dinero. Pero ¿con quién se cree que está?

Mariano Llamemos a las cosas por su nombre, ¿eh? Las personas que privan a otro de su libertad y se lo llevan, se llaman secuestradores. Y las personas que amenazan a otro con un arma son asesinas aunque todavía no hayan matado a nadie. Llamemos a las cosas por su nombre. (*Pausa*) (*Están muy impactadas por lo que él acaba de decir.*)

Griselda (*Se planta delante de él en un arranque desesperado.*) Míreme a los ojos. ¿Qué ve?

Mariano ¿Qué veo?

Griselda ¿Ve a alguien que lo va a matar?

Mariano No.

Griselda ¿Ve a alguien que le va a sacar dinero?

Mariano No.

Rosalía Me encanta verlo mirar. (*Enternecida*) Por fin se está pareciendo a Marcelo el mecánico. (*Rosalía atrae la atención de a Mariano para que le siga mirando a ella.*)

Griselda ¿Qué hay en el fondo de mis ojos? ¿Atrás, atrás, atrás? Usted sabe ver muy atrás. Me está taladrando.

(*El la mira como si la estuviera hipnotizando.*)

Griselda ¿Qué ve? ¿Humo? ¿Miedo? ¿Una tormenta?

Mariano No.

Griselda ¿Ve deseo?

Mariano Sí.

Griselda ¿No lo tranquiliza mirarme?

Mariano Sí.

Griselda ¿Por qué?

Mariano No lo sé.

Griselda Sí que lo sabe. Siempre lo supo, desde que entró por esa puerta. ¿Sabe cuando me enamoré de usted? Hace casi tres años, un jueves. Usted hizo un gesto de rascarse la cabeza, un gesto sin importancia un gesto cualquiera. Era un día muy frío, y yo estaba tomando chocolate porque era mi cumpleaños. Rosalía se había ido a La Plata. Y usted se rascó la cabeza de aquel modo tan inocente. De aquel modo tan de niño travieso. ¿No podría volver a rascarse la cabeza así, ahora? ¿No me haría ese regalo otra vez?

Mariano Me quiero ir.

Rosalía ¿Ves? ¿Ves lo que conseguís? Ahora se quiere ir. No le haga caso. Ella necesita hablar constantemente. Hace veinte años que la escucho. Lo mejor es no hacerle caso. Míreme a mí. (*Le agarra la cabeza.*)

Mariano Me quiero ir.

Griselda Mírela, sí. Mírela a ella también. ¿No hay toda una mujer allí dentro? ¿Le parece que esa mujer puede lastimarlo?

Mariano ¡Me quiero ir! ¡Lo único que quiero es irme! (*Se larga a llorar para lograr su objetivo.*) Me están esperando. Me tengo que ir. Es tarde. ¿No se dan cuenta?

Rosalía Ya no fue. Si lo estaban esperando ya no llegó.

Mariano ¿Qué quieren de mí?

Rosalía ¿Quién lo estaba esperando?

Mariano ¡Y a usted que le importa!

Rosalía Me importa, me importa. ¿Sabe una cosa? ¡Me importa muchísimo!

Mariano ¿Qué quieren de mí?

Griselda (*Lo huele.*) Olerlo, nada más que olerlo. (*El se pone a llorar.*) ¿Por qué llora querido? ¿Por qué llora?

Mariano ¿Por qué me huele?

(*Llora tratando de contenerse.*)

Rosalía ¿No te das cuenta que no quiere que lo hueles? ¿No te das cuenta que lo estás molestando? ¿No te das cuenta que se nos está poniendo cada vez más triste? Nada de nosotras le interesa. Quiere irse. Lo único que quiere es irse. Y nosotras no se lo vamos a impedir. Si él no es feliz aquí adentro lo vamos a dejar ir. (*El no puede parar de llorar.*)

Lo vamos a dejar ir para que vuelva a su vida. No podemos seguir entreteniéndolo con tonterías. El es un caballo de caza. Necesita libertad. ¿No es cierto mi amor? No llores más que te vamos a dejar ir. (*Lo protege. Lo acaricia.*)

Griselda ¡No! Yo te aseguro que de aquí no se va de esta manera. No hicimos todo esto para dejarlo ir así. No. Rosalía, no. Lo hubieras pensado antes porque ahora es tarde. (*Agarra ella es revólver.*) Ahora se queda hasta el final. (*El la mira desconsoladamente.*) Ahora se queda hasta el final. ¿Entendiste Rosalía? Ahora se queda hasta el final.

Apagón

Segunda Escena

(*Al encenderse la luz hay completamente otro clima. Los tres están sentados a la mesa comiendo la cena fría que prepararon para recibirlo. Se los ve entretenidos, relajados y conectados.*)

Mariano Y entonces el productor se hacía el exquisito y amenazaba sutilmente con reemplazarme por Julián Iraola si no bajara mi cachét. Pero yo me puse firme, y le dije a mi representante que no nos íbamos a dejar mover el piso. ¡Hay que agarrarse de las paredes!

Rosalía ¡Eso! ¡Hay que agarrarse de las paredes cuando el piso tiembla!

Griselda Yo estuve en el terremoto de San Juan.

Mariano ¡Y yo estuve en el maremoto del Canal! (*Se ríen.*) Los maté con la indiferencia. Agarradito a las paredes. Sin moverme. (*Estira los brazos y cierra los ojos.*) Porque lo que el productor no sabía es que yo sabía que el productor me iba a tener que venir a buscar a mi casa para pedirme por favor que hiciera la tira. (*Disfruta del recuerdo.*) Y me iban a tener que pagar todo lo que yo pedía peso sobre peso. Porque yo sabía que Julián Iraola había ya firmado contrato en otro canal (*Se ríe.*) Ese dato me lo había batido el propio Julián que es mi amigo y no de ellos, como ellos se creían. No solamente el productor, sino todo el equipo… Julián es mi amigo…así que me tuvieron que venir a buscar con la cola entre las patas.

Rosalía ¿Y le pagaron todo lo que pedía?

Mariano Todo, todo. Todo lo que pedía.

Rosalía Y gracias a eso esta noche hay una luna llena. (*Se ríen.*) Y con ese dinero yo pude cocinar mi famoso paté trufado.

Mariano ¿Me puede dar un poquito más?

Rosalía Todo. Le doy todo. (*Le da todo.*) Si lo hice para usted.

Mariano Es el mejor paté trufado que me dieron en todos mis secuestros. En los otros me trataban a pan y agua. Pero ustedes: paté trufado y champagne.

(*Se ríen.*)

Griselda ¡Si nunca lo habían secuestrado antes! No sea mentiroso. Se nota que usted es virgen en secuestros.

Mariano Sí, en secuestros sí. Creo que es el único rubro que me quedaba.

Rosalía A nosotras en cambio nos quedan muchos rubros.

Mariano Y por eso yo estoy aquí

Griselda Bueno, no nos vamos a poner tan exigente.

Mariano Ah, yo en cambio sí. La próxima vez que me secuestren, me preparan pato a la naranja. Y la tercera vez jabalí macerado en cognac y flambeado con azúcar. Me encanta el jabalí. Voy a hacer correr la bola en el ambiente. "Si querés un buen restaurant, por Griselda y Rosalía hacete secuestrar".

Griselda Se está burlando de nosotras.

Mariano Soy un muchacho cruel. (*Pausa*) Y eso las vuelve locas. ¿No? Cuanto más cruel, más locas. ¡Mire que cosa! Los días en que me pongo buenito las chicas cambian de canal. (*Agarra la cara de Griselda con fuerza.*) Te gusta que tenga cortita no, a vos también te gusta. Confesá, total no te escucha nadie.

Griselda Yo soy…(*Muy nerviosa*) yo soy así.

Mariano Te gusta que haga sufrir, que te arrincone, que te apriete un poco. Te cambió el brillo de la mirada, eh. Pareces una gata. Te gusta que te haga marcar el paso, al compás del miedo. (*Se ríe a Rosalía.*) Vení, vení, vos también (*Le agarra también a ella.*) No te asustes, no te va a pasar nada.

Rosalía No tengo miedo.

Mariano Miren, miren, como tiemblan. Así las tengo todas las tardes. Así tengo un millón de mujeres todas las tardes. Así, como están ustedes en este momento.

Griselda ¿Un millón?

Mariano Altas, gordas, bajas, feas, amas de casa, sirvientas, mamás, empleadas. Todas tiemblan por mí durante media hora todos los días.

Rosalía ¿Qué se siente?

Mariano (*Las tiene.*) Se siente esto, esto que yo siento ahora. (*Se ríe.*) Y esto es el éxito. Cuando sentís esto quiere decir que triunfaste (*Se ríe.*)

Rosalía ¿Le da risa el éxito?

Mariano Me da risa mi vida (*Las suelta.*) Cuando era chico construía torres. Mi papá era carpintero y me dejaba las maderitas que sobraban y yo me armaba torres que llegaban hasta el techo. Y depués intentaba subirme hasta la punta. Pero las maderitas no aguantaban. Se quebraban y yo me caía al suelo y me golpeaba la espalda. Pero no me desesperaba. Empezaba de nuevo a construir otra torre más fuerte. Le metía remaches por todas partes. La apuntaba con travesaños especiales. Clavaba clavos como loco por todas partes. Y depués volvía a probar. Pero por algún lado la torre fallaba y me volvía a probar. Pero por algún lado la torre fallaba y me volvía a caer. Hasta que un día...un día de febrero...un 7 de febrero...me acuerdo porque era mi cumpleaños...cumplía 11 años ese día. Hice la torre más fuerte de mi vida. Y me dije que yo voy a festejar mi cumpleaños allá arriba. Y me vestí de cumpleaños con un pantaloncito blanco y una camisa escocesa que me había regalado Inés y subí, Subí. Subí. (*Se ríe.*) Subí. Subí. Y esa vez la torre no se quebró. Pasé todo el día allí arriba. Y decidí vivir para siempre allí. (*Pausa*) Y allí estoy todavía. Todavía estoy allí. Soplando las velitas. (*Se para en una silla.*) Tengo miedo de bajar. Porque no conozco nada de lo que pasa allá abajo.

Rosalía Abajo pasan cosas tristes y feas. Mejor que se quede allí arriba. Cumpliendo años todo el tiempo pero sin envejecer nunca. Alguien tiene que estar allí arriba.

Mariano Aquí arriba también pasan cosas tristes y feas.

Griselda No se nota. Desde aquí abajo no se nota.

Mariano Pasan cosas más tristes y más feas que las que pasan allí abajo porque además no se notan. (*Se ríe.*) Ay si ustedes supieran las cosas que hay que hacer para mantenerse aquí arriba. Sí ustedes supieran, ay queridas ay, (*Se ríen.*) Si supieran las cosas que he tenido que hacer para no caerme de la torre. Si supieran qué se siente desde este cuerpo y desde esta jeta. Si supieran lo que es tener una cara como ésta... (*Se palmea.*) ¡Ay si yo les contara como se ve el mundo desde una torre podrida! ¡Una torre podrida en un mundo podrido! ¡Y aquí arriba, en la punta una estrella podrida! (*Pausa*) Pero nadie me va a mover de aquí. Nadie, se dice la estrella. Nadie y un día pum. (*Se tira al suelo desde arriba.*) Cae. Cae con todo. (*Se incorpora y las mira.*) ¿Quién lo tiró? No se sabe. No quiere saberlo. No puede perder tiempo. Pide una manzana. (*Grita.*) ¡Una manzana, necesito una manzana! (*Rosalía le trae corriendo una hermosa manzana roja.*) Los dientes. Tengo que mostrar los dientes. Una buena dentadura está llena de promesas. (*Vuelve a subir al banco.*) Y así empecé a morder la manzana. Fue la clave del éxito. (*Se *ríe.*) El pecado capital. Firmé contrato para comerme una manzana por capítulo.

Griselda   ¡Con lo sanas que son las manzanas! Es un gesto extraordinario. Es la mejor campaña contra la drogadicción que conozco.

(*Mariano pega un salto y les ofrece, ellas lo miran extasiadas.*)

Mariano   Es otro tipo de drogadicción.

Rosalía   Mordela, vamos, mordela.

Griselda   Nos hemos pasado años mirándote morder manzanas por televisión.

Rosalía   Acá no comemos otra fruta.

Mariano   (*Se ríe.*) Yo en cambio los jodo a todos. Porque aunque tengo prohibido por contrato comer ninguna otra fruta, mi vieja me compra mandarinas secretas que como antes de dormir debajo de la cama.

Rosalía   (*Se tapa los oídos.*) No quiero enterarme de esas cosas.

Griselda   No lo trajimos aquí para eso.

Mariano   ¿Me trajeron aquí para que les coma personalmente una manzana? ¿No es cierto? Eso es lo que están buscando. ¿No es cierto?

Griselda   He buscado eso toda mi vida. No hice más que buscarlo. (*Se le llenan los ojos de lágrimas.*) No hice más que buscarlo.

(*Tira la manzana al aire. Hace malabarismo como un mago de circo. Amenaza con morderla y no la muerde. Les ofrece la manzana a ellas y se las quita justo cuando van a morderla.*)

Mariano   Así empezó la ruina de la humanidad. Por una manzanita. Si Adán no la hubiera mordido seríamos inmortales. Pero Adán no podía dejar de morderla, no podía, no podía…no podía.

Rosalía   No. No podía. No podía.

(*La vuelve a tirar al aire. Juega con el deseo de ellas.*)

Mariano   Aunque fuera pecado.

Griselda   Aunque fuera pecado.

Mariano   (*Divertido*) No podía. Y entonces…entonces acercó la manzana a la boca y (*La muerde con mucha sensualidad. Ellas lo miran locas de deseo. El siente que las tiene con él. Mastica vorazmente. Y pega otro mordisco. Ellas gritan excitadas. El les ofrece la manzana.*) No podía. No podía decir no. (*Las provoca con la manzana. Ellas lo siguen. El levanta la manzana.*) No podía decir no. Pobre Adán. ¿Cómo iba a decir no, si no podía? (*Finalmente les deja morder la manzana, y ahí repentinamente les da un golpe para reducirlas. Por un instante las reduce.*) Y esa fue su perdición. La perdición de la humanidad. Porque si se hubiera podido decir no, se salvaba y nos salvaba a todos. (*Las tiene agarradas a las dos. Rosalía está con la manzana en la boca. Tratan* *desesperadamente de zafar. El las arrastra por la habitación hacia la puerta. Ellas se resisten, le pegan. Hay un forcejeo muy violento. Griselda lo muerde.)* ¡A mí no, a la manzana! (*Griselda lo muerde más y esto lo obliga a soltarla. Griselda cae, e inmediatamente agarra el revólver. El entonces la toma a Rosalía de rehén y se resguarda detrás de ella. Hay una pausa tensa. Rosalía estalla en pánico. Griselda apunta con firmeza y dolor.)*

Griselda Tengo que hacerlo, tengo que hacerlo.

Rosalía ¿Cómo llegamos tan lejos?

Griselda Tengo un arma en la mano. Mirá las cosas que me preguntás. (*Griselda le apunta casi haciendo puntería.*)

Rosalía Yo te quiero Griselda.

Griselda ¿Y eso qué importancia tiene? Cuando uno atraviesa ciertos límites ya no puede volver.

Rosalía Es la primera vez que te veo de verdad.

Griselda Es que yo antes era otra cosa.

Rosalía Yo traté de ayudarte, pero salió todo mal. Mirá que mal salió. Mirá que mal.

Mariano ¿Vas a disparar o no vas a disparar?

Griselda Sí. (*Dispara al aire. Rosalía cae. Se da vuelta y golpea a Mariano. Mucha ira contra él.*)

Rosalía ¿Por qué nos traicionaste?

Griselda Dejalo. Dejalo. (*Rosalía lo deja.*) Dejalo en paz al muchacho. (*Mariano asustado se pone en pié. Pausa.*)

Mariano Ustedes dijeron que no me iban a matar.

Rosalía Pero vos no nos creíste.

Griselda (*Se ríe.*) Pude disparar. ¿Viste Rosalía? Pude disparar.

Mariano Sí. Les creí. Les creí. Todavía les creo. (*Se le llenan los ojos de lágrimas pero se ríe.*) Todavía les creo. ¿Ven?

Rosalía Hacés bien en creernos. Pero no sé si tan bien como antes.

Griselda (*Todavía apuntándolo*) ¡Agarrá la manzana! (*El agarra una manzana.*) Agarrala bien. Como antes. Bien. Vos sabés agarrarla bien. (*El la agarra con más energía dibujando los gestos de antes.*) Mordela.

Rosalía Con ganas, como cuando te pagan. Con ganas. (*Mariano la muerde con ganas.*) Con más ganas. Clavá los dientes. (*El clava los dientes.*)

Griselda Ahora dale a morder a Rosalía. (*El duda.*) Dale de morder a Rosalía. (*El le da de morder, la manzana a Rosalía. Rosalía la muerde y se ríe. Muerde más y se ríe.*)

Rosalía Es la manzana más rica de mi vida. En realidad es la única manzana de mi vida. (*Muerde más.*) Las otras no eran manzanas. Eran mandarinas.

Griselda Subite a tu torre. (*El lo hace.*) Sacate los zapatos. (*El lo hace, subido en el arcón que fue su torre.*) La remera. (*El se saca la remera. Ella la toma, la huele. Luego lo rodea como quien rodea una estatua.*) El pantalón. (*El se saca el pantalón.*)

Rosalía (*Llora. Balbucea.*) Es la primera vez que veo un hombre desnudo. A mí papá nunca lo vi…mí papá era tan severo…tan severo.

Griselda Sacate todo.

Apagón

Tercera Escena

(*Al volver a encender las luces no ha pasado tiempo. Mariano va a representar el teleteatro para ellas dos y se dispone a hacerlo. Hay un silencio tenso. Mariano esta fuertemente iluminado por focos como si se tratara de un estudio de televisión. Mariano está solo en medio del escenario. Las dos se quedan mudas mirándolo. Mariano va poniéndose la ropa de Marcelo el mecánico. Es un mameluco que se pone con el cierre bastante abierto. Crea el tipo de muchacho de barrio. Mecánico, bonachón, dentro del arcón hay herramienta, las distribuye en los bolsillos.*)

Rosalía Espere un momento. Espere un momento. (*Saca una máquina de flash.*) Sacame Griselda, sacame con él. Levantame en tus brazos mi querido mecánico. (*El la levanta. Ella sonríe. Griselda la fotografía.*) Voy a hacer doscientas mil copias y las voy a distribuir por todos los subtes de Buenos Aires.

Mariano Va a ser un buen dato para que la policía la ubique.

Rosalía ¿Y qué me va a hacer la policía por haber sido feliz? ¿Es que alguien puede ir preso por ser feliz? (*Se ríe. El la baja. Ella repentinamente le da un beso en la boca.*) Ahora que me lleven presa por el resto de mi vida! (*Se ríe.*) Ahora que me encierren en un calabozo hasta el fin de mis días. Ya tengo recuerdos…ya tengo recuerdos… (*Se le llenan los ojos de lágrimas.*)

(*Griselda la saca de un tirón.*)

Rosalía ¡Me besó! ¿Viste como me besó? Está loco por mí.

Griselda (*A Mariano*) Si pudieras concentrarte y comenzar… sería tan bueno… (*Se vaporiza porque tiene un comienzo de acceso de asma..*) Antes de que ella o yo nos descontrolemos o no podamos siquiera antes de que ella o yo nos descontrolemos o no podamos siquiera responder de nosotras mismas... si pudieras calmarnos con tu ternura, como nos calmás desde hace tres años... todas las santas tardes de esta perra vida... (*Se vaporiza.*) Ni a ellas ni a mí nos va a importar morir después de hoy. ¿Sabés? (*Pausa*) Ella nunca le había pasado nada en toda su vida. Y a mí tampoco. Y de repente en un instante pasa todo. (*Se abraza a Rosalía.*) Y ya no hay miedos. Ni fantasmas. Estamos usted y nosotras en algún lugar perdido de este planeta...

(*Mariano comienza a actuar el teleteatro. Ellas lo miran extasiadas.*)

Marcelo Yo sé que usted piensa que soy una rata, que ando siempre con la mano llena de grasa y con este mameluco que camina solo...en serio...camina solo...el otro día fui al zoológico con la nena de Juan y me empilché de verdad...y cuando llegamos a la jaula del hipopótamo nos dimos cuenta que le mameluco nos venía siguiendo desde hacía más de media hora. No se ría...yo creo que nací con el mameluco puesto y que me voy a morir con el mameluco puesto...y el día que me case con usted me voy a casar con el mameluco para que usted no se olvide que se está casando con un laburante. Un laburante de esos que los pitucos de su familia desprecian porque es mersa o porque come manzanas y las hace crujir. (*Saca una manzana del bolsillo.*) El día que usted pruebe esta manzana pierde para siempre. (*Se la come.*) Por eso no la quiere morder...porque usted sabe que esta manzana es más peligrosa para usted que todos esos caviares y esos langostinos que le sirven de desayuno todos los días ese mayordomo con cara de paraguas que le inaugura el día. ¿Sabe cómo le voy a inaugurar yo los días a usted?

Griselda (*En el personaje de Valeria.*) ¿Cómo me los va a inaugurar?

Mariano Así se los voy a inaugurar. (*La besa apasionadamente.*) Así se los voy a inaugurar.

Griselda (*A Rosalía*) Viste esta es justa la parte que te perdiste. ¿Viste cómo la besó? ¿Viste que era verdad que la había besado? Besame otra vez.

Mariano No.

Rosalía Otra vez. Toda la última parte otra vez.

Mariano No.

Griselda Nada más que la parte de la inauguración del día. Nada más que ese cachito.

Mariano (*Accede pero lo hace mal.*) Porque usted sabe que esta manzana es más peligrosa que todos esos caviares y esos langostinos que le sirven de desayuno todos los días ese mayordomo con cara de paraguas que le inaugura el día. ¿Sabe cómo le voy a inaugurar yo los días a usted?

Rosalía (*La empuja a Griselda.*) ¿Cómo me los va a inaugurar?

Mariano Así se los voy a inaugurar. (*Le da una cachetada.*) Así se los voy a inaugurar. (*Le da otra cachetada.*) Así se los voy a inaugurar. (*Le da otra cachetada más.*)

Rosalía (*Enceguecida*) Igual me gustás. Igual me gustás. Aunque me pegues. (*Se recompone.*) Yo nunca quise tanto a nadie.   ¿Sabés? Te quiero más que a mi misma. Te quiero más que a mi hermano que vive en Luján. Y aunque te rebeles, aunque me dés vuelta la cara de una cachetada porque te da bronca sentir atracción por mí... te da bronca que esta mujer te pierda. ¿No es cierto? Vas a volver a hacer la escena. ¿Sabés? Vas a volver a hacer la escena. (*Pausa*)

Mariano Porque usted sabe que esta manzana es más peligrosa para Usted que todos esos caviares y esos langostinos que...(*Se le llenan los ojos de lágrima.*) que todos esos caviares y esos langostinos que le sirven de desayuno. (*La angustia y la desesperación lo sobrepasan.*) ¿Mamá como llegué aquí? (*Trata de sobreponerse.*) esos caviares y esos langostinos que le sirven de desayuno todos los días. (*Tratando de no llorar.*) Yo solamente quería vivir en una torre...(*Sigue con el personaje.*) de desayuno todos los días todos los días todos los días mamá en la torre todos los días ese mayordomo...yo nunca tuve mayordomo mamá... nadie tiene mayordomo mamá...ese mayordomo con cara de paraguas que le inaugura el día. ¿Sabé cómo le voy a inaugurar yo los días a usted? (*Llorando, increpándola a los gritos.*) ¿Sabe cómo le voy a inaugurar yo los días a usted? ¿Sabe cómo le voy a inaugurar yo lo días a usted? (*Cae de rodillas. Sobre esta imagen que las deja perplejas y desoladas.*)

Apagón

Cuarta Escena

(*Al volver a encenderse la luz la atmósfera se ha tranquilizado. Mariano duerme en un sillón, agotado, rendido por las emociones que ha vivido. Una luz azulina tiñe el ambiente. Rosalía se ha instalado frente a él y lo mira dormir con inmensa ternura. Griselda revuelve el arcón y encuentra una antigua capelina. Se la pone y también se pone un chal. Y después revuelve sus poemas guardados en una caja enorme.*)

Rosalía ¿Con qué estará soñando?

Griselda Conmigo por supuesto. Conmigo. No va a soñar con vos.

Rosalía Tal vez no sueñe con ninguna de las dos. (*Pausa.*) Mueve las aletas de la nariz. A lo mejor sueña con un perfume en el cuello de una mujer muy hermosa. Parece que sonriera al dormir. Tal vez haya llegado por fin a su torre. Y allá arriba hay una luna llena y la noche es tibia y alguien lo está esperando.

Griselda Yo lo estoy esperando. ¿No te das cuenta? (*Se envuelve en el chal.*)

Rosalía ¿Por qué te pusiste eso?

Griselda Nunca me lo debí sacar. Yo he nacido para caminar envuelta en una bruma. Mi error fue entrar en la rutina de todos los días. Yo pertenezco a otras situaciones. No estoy regida por las leyes de la conveniencia, o por el código del mercado de aquí a la esquina. (*Pausa*) Siempre me mandás a mí al mercado. Por eso me tengo que sacar la capelina. Por eso.

Rosalía Podés hacer la prueba de ir así.

Griselda Ya he sufrido un largo calvario de humillaciones por intentar adaptarme a este mundo agobiante. Pero él me desata el espíritu. Y ya no me importa nada. Ahora estoy tomada pro certezas oscuras. ¿No me ves la mirada cambiada? ¿No me ves las manos pálidas?

(*Le muestra las manos.*)

Rosalía Lo vas a despertar…¿no te das cuenta que necesita descansar? ¿No te das cuenta que necesita soñar?

Griselda Esta soñando conmigo. Yo me paseo por un cuarto azul y agito irreflexiblemente mi fajo de poemas.

(*Recita hacia él.*)

> "Aunque no me comprendas amor mío
> mi soledad sin fin, ni mi tristeza
> tengo melancolía del verano
> que no pasamos juntos ni nos vimos.
> Melancolía, amor, melancolía"

(*Se pasea con su melancolía a cuestas tomada por un recitativo apasionado.*)

> "Melancolía, amor, melancolía
> de lo que hubiera sido
> y es tan honda y tan triste mi tristeza
> que a pesar del verano, dulce mío,
> que a pesar del verano
> tengo frío".

(*Pausa. Hacia el final del poema Mariano ha abierto los ojos y la mira como a una aparición.*)

(*A Mariano*) Es un sueño…estás soñando. (*Se ríe.*) Es un maravilloso sueño.

Griselda Me he pasado estos últimos años escribiéndote poemas. Todo lo que siento por vos está entre estas páginas. ¿Acaso te importa? ¿Acaso te conmueve? ¿Acaso algo de todo esto te roza siquiera el corazón?

"Mariano mi doliente amor
mi realidad ficticia
mi incierto sueño
mi mecánico de barrio, mi Marcelo"

(*Mariano no atina a reaccionar.*)

Rosalía Así son los sueños Mariano. Todo aquí es posible. Somos libres de desatar los nudos que nos atan. Somos mucho más verdaderos mi amor.

Mariano (*Entra en pánico.*) ¿Qué me van a hacer?

Rosalía ¿Cómo qué te vamos a hacer? ¿Qué nos vas a hacer vos a nosotras?

Griselda (*Busca entre los papeles.*)

"Haz de mí lo quieras
quiero ser la escultura que tus manos trabajen
quiero ser la madera
donde tallas tu idea.
De todos modos los caprichos
quiero ser prisionera…"

Mariano Yo creo…yo creo que he llegado la hora de irme. (*Se abre le mameluco.*)

Rosalía Se quiere desnudar. (*Le abre repentinamente el mameluco.*) Yo te voy a ayudar a desnudarte.

Griselda (*Continuando*)

"No me importa la carne, quiero el alma
más si la carne llega y nos devora
sabrá el alma cederle su lugar efímero
porque es el alma lo que queda
mientras la carne se evapora"

Rosalía Ayudame que no voy a poder sacarle esto yo sola. (*Lo agarra por detrás para sostenerlo. El se defiende y patalea.*)

Griselda (*Mientras trata de quitarle el mameluco.*) Es turbulento.

Rosalía Es un hombre.

Mariano (*En pánico*) Por favor, ahora suéltenme, no se metan conmigo, déjenme por favor, qué me hacés? Salí, salí, dejame ahora por favor, les doy lo que quieran por favor. (*Lo tiran al suelo y lo montan.*)

Rosalía Entregado, entregado como un buzo a las profundidades del mar. Entregado como un marinero a navegar. Entregado, amor entregado.

Mariano Lo que quieran. Yo les juro que nadie se va a enterar de que me secuestraron. Yo les prometo que esto no se va a saber. Yo les prometo que no va a salir de mí. Por favor, no, qué me hace, ay, no, no, no. No me toque por favor.

Rosalía ¿Y…dale. O no sabés hacer el amor?

Griselda ¿Cómo no voy a saber? Lo que pasa es que él no ayuda nada. Y a mi siempre me dijeron que el hombre lleva la parte activa…

Rosalía No vas a venir con prejuicios justamente ahora.

Griselda No son prejuicios, son principios.

Mariano Suéltenme, suéltenme por favor…les juro que hago todo lo que me pidan les juro que las vengo a visitar todos los días…por favor…

Griselda Pero no te va a pasar nada…es cuestión de poner un poquito de buena voluntad…no se te pide más que eso, querido.

Mariano No puedo. No se da cuenta que no puedo.

Griselda ¿No podés nunca?

Mariano No puedo ahora.

Griselda Un hombre siempre puede.

Mariano No. No es cierto.

Griselda ¿Estás enfermo?

Mariano No. No estoy enfermo.

Griselda Entonces somos dos ángeles en el cielo. (*Se le tira encima. Lo llena de besos. El la rechaza como puede. Rosalía lo sostiene.*)

Rosalía Para mí que es maricón…

Mariano No soy maricón. No soy maricón. (*Trata de zafarse sin lograrlo.*)

Rosalía Un poco maricón debe ser porque con dos mujeres como nosotras que lo rodeamos de amor…algo debería haber pasado en todo este tiempo. No digo que no vayas a dejar embarazada a las dos…pero algo…yo no sé si me entiende…algo un poco más fuerte. (*Lo besa apasionadamente. El la rechaza. La muerde. Ella le pega. Y vuelve a besarlo.*)

Griselda A lo mejor es impotente.

Rosalía Entonces sos las dos cosas juntas: maricón por un lado e impotente por el otro.

Mariano No. No. Les aseguro que no. Les aseguro que no.

Griselda Aquí no es cuestión de asegurar querido, aquí, como verás es cuestión de empezar hacer algo.

Mariano Si ustedes…si ustedes me ayudaran, a lo mejor… (*Pausa. Lo miran.*)

Rosalía Pedinos lo que quieras. Lo que necesites.

Mariano Necesito un poco de distancia.

Griselda ¡Qué pedido tan raro! Siempre creí que la proximidad de los cuerpos estimulaba el aspecto todo el aspecto erótico. Pero claro yo soy de otra época…no tan lejana, pero otra…ahora les gusta la distancia.

(*Las dos se separan de él. Pausa*)

Rosalía ¿Y?

Griselda Empezá con la que quieras. Ya nos hemos puesto de acuerdo. No somos celosas.

(*El las mira. Intenta desearlas.*)

Mariano (*Se ríe a carcajadas.*) ¡Qué ridículo, por Dios! ¡Qué ridículo! (*Se ríe casi con desesperación.*)

Rosalía No es maricón pero es probable que sea homosexual.

Griselda ¿Qué diferencia hay?

Rosalía Después te explico.

(*El las mira casi con piedad.*)

Griselda Nos va a tener así toda la noche.

Mariano Griselda. (*Se ríe.*) Yo tenía una maestra que se llamaba Griselda…y era muy linda…muy morena…con el pelo largo sobre el delantal blanco y…era mi maestra de sexto grado…y tenía unos enormes pechos, unos pechos que se le movían debajo del delantal. Claro a los doce años a mí esas tetas me parecían un mundo Griselda…y tus pechos ahora.

Griselda Los míos…los míos no son así.

Mariano Pero el nombre…

Griselda Ah, sí el nombre sí…

Mariano Vení. (*Le toca los pechos.*) No, no. No puedo. Por favor volvete a alejar. Me estaba viniendo algo…volvete a alejar. (*Griselda se vuelve a alejar.*)

Rosalía ¿Y Rosalía no tenías alguna tía, o alguna amiga de tu mamá?

Mariano No… (*Se ríe.*) No…pero tenía una potranca, una potranquita azul.

Rosalía Azul…

Mariano Azul… (*Le atrae hacia sí.*) Y me gustaba galoparla y galoparla y saltar los cercos y galoparla y galoparla y pegarle hasta lastimarla. (*Le da una palmada en el culo.*) No puedo…no se trata de querer sino de poder! ¡No puedo! ¿Entienden bien? ¡No puedo!

Griselda ¿Tiene problemas…? Digo…problemas de tipo…

Mariano No tengo ningún problema con las minas, tengo las minas que quiero. Las mujeres me gustan mucho. (*Se ríe.*)

Griselda (*También se ríe.*) ¿Y entonces?

Rosalía (*Se acerca. Lo acaricia.*) Necesitás entrar en clima, dejame que te ayude a salir del pozo, dejate llevar, cerrá los ojitos y pensá en un mar inmenso y mi cuerpo son las olas y vos te entregás a nadar.

Griselda Y viene un tiburón (*Le muerde una oreja. El grita.*) Los tiburones muerden. Pero vos seguís nadando. Te sumergís.

Rosalía Mirá que mar generoso. Todo para vos.

(*El se siente ahogado por las dos. Se las saca de encima con rechazo y desesperación. Ellas quedan insatisfechas: frustradas mirándolo con rencor.*)

Griselda Hemos hecho todo lo posible por ayudarte…hemos sido comprensivas con tu problema pero si vos nos indicaras por donde…tal vez llegaríamos más rápido al bosque y seríamos más felices.

Rosalía Tal vez te hemos abrumado… (*Le acaricia la cabeza.*) Yo con acariciarte la cabeza ya toco el cielo con las manos

Mariano Sí…

Rosalía ¿Me dejás que te acaricie?

Mariano Sí. (*Le entrega la cabeza.*)

Rosalía Griselda mirá… (*Griselda se acerca.*)

Griselda (*Se ríe de angustia.*) Permanente. Estoy segura. Se hace la permanente

Rosalía No son rulos naturales.

Griselda ¿Desde cuándo se hace la permanente?

Mariano Cuando empecé la carrera de actor me aconsejaron aclararme un poco el pelo y hacerme la permanente…y gusta mucho. ¿No es cierto?

Griselda ¿Y la nariz es tuya?

Mariano Sí, la nariz sí…(*Se ríe.*) es mi nariz.

Rosalía Tiene maquillaje. (*Le pasa el dedo por la cara.*)

Griselda ¿Siempre se pinta la cara? ¿Siempre se pasa colorete? ¿Y rimel en las pestañas? ¿Y rouge en la boquita? (*Le besa la boca.*) Hum humm tiene rouge del que uso yo. (*Se ríe.*)

Mariano Ustedes me agarraron a la salida del Canal. Todos los actores nos maquillamos para salir en televisión.

Rosalía No quiero saber. No quiero saber nada más. Me da pena. Mucha pena de haberme equivocado tanto…pena por Griselda. Pena por mí. Pena. (*Llena de dolor*)

Griselda (*Explotando*) Mi pelo, mi querido pelo…el pelo con el que me acuesto, el pelo enmarañado que me hace escribir. Yo lo único que tenía en la vida era el deseo de hundir mi mano en ese pelo…como quien mete la mano en la tierra para conocer sus propias raíces así su pelo me llamaba, y cuando lo veía tirarse al suelo entre las ruedas de su auto yo sufría porque pensaba que se le iba a ensuciar…y me imaginaba el momento en que se duchaba y se llenaba la cabeza de jabón…ese pelo rubio y brillante y crespo. ¿Cómo me pudo hacer eso?

Rosalía Conteste. Diga algo. Defiéndase. Algo que demuestre que usted vale la pena. Algo más que estar ahí parado con esa cabeza de mentira y ese maquillaje pastoso que le tapa los pozos de la cara.

Mariano Pero ustedes están confundidas…todo el mundo.

Rosalía El mundo…guárdese el mundo en el bolsillo…no quiero saber nada del mundo. Me alcanza con todo lo que usted me enseñó. (*Se angustia mucho.*) Sabe, nunca llegué tan lejos por nadie. Y nunca me caí de tan arriba. Me siento como parada en un abismo. Y ya no me importa nada. (*Pausa*) Pero hay algo que me alegra. Usted no existe. Pero nosotras sí…nosotras estamos vivas. (*Griselda abre puertas y ventanas. El mira todo abierto.*)

Griselda ¿Qué espera? Ya debería estar corriendo, su auto esta estacionado aquí a la vuelta y su vida lo espera allí afuera y nosotras ya no lo retenemos… (*Le viene una ráfaga de desesperación.*) Permanente y tintura y maquillaje y maricón. ¿No te falta nada, eh?

Mariano Pero, ¿Qué disparate es éste? Ustedes están muy equivocadas.

Griselda Nosotras estabamos muy equivocadas. (*Se enfurece.*) Muy equivocadas, demasiado, demasiado equivocadas. ¿Pero quién nos hizo equivocar?

Mariano Yo creo que es lógico que yo no haya podido, pero creo que ahora voy a poder…lo siento, lo siento de verdad… (*Agarra a Griselda.*) Creo que sos más linda que mi maestra de sexto grado y además yo ya no tengo doce años y puedo demostrarte.

(*Griselda lo empuja violentamente.*)

Griselda Sáquenme a este muñeco de encima. (*A Rosalía*) ¿Por qué dejás que me toque?

Rosalía Váyase. Nosotras…no vamos a contarle a nadie lo que vimos de usted…a nadie. No se preocupe. Nos alcanza con saberlo nosotras.

Mariano Yo soy un hombre. Yo soy un tipo macanudo. Todo el mundo me quiere mucho. Las mujeres.

Rosalía Vaya vaya con las mujeres que lo están esperando para pedirle autógrafos…vaya.

Mariano Yo me quiero quedar. ¿No se dan cuenta de que me quiero quedar? Ustedes me tienen que dejar quedarme…yo necesito que dejen…

Griselda Mire: no se puede quedar. No se puede quedar. (*Le tira la ropa de él encima.*) No se puede quedar. No lo queremos.

(*El se queda arrodillado, destrozado.*)

Rosalía Además es la hora del teletexto. Y yo no me voy a perder un capítulo por usted…

Griselda (*Enciende el televisor.*) Lo único que faltaba… (*Se ríe.*) Encima perdernos un capítulo.

(*Con él destrozado se ve la imagen del teletexto. El sale de la cárcel y se encuentra con Valeria que lo abraza.*)

Valeria Mi amor…saliste…te dejaron en libertad.

Mariano Es que no tenían ninguna prueba contra mí. Yo soy un tipo honrado, que vive de su trabajo. ¿De qué me pueden acusar?

Valeria Te pueden acusar de tener el pelo crespo y rubio. (*Le hunde la mano en el pelo.*) Y de tener la sonrisa más transparente del mundo. (*El sonríe y la abraza. La levanta en brazos y la hace girar.*) Te pueden acusar de ser feliz.

Mariano Te quiero. (*Se besan largamente.*)

Valeria Mirá lo que te traje. (*Le da una manzana. El brinda como si se tratara de una copa de champagne.*)

Mariano Hum que rica que está. Es la manzana más rica de todas las que me comí en la vida… Porque es la manzana de la felicidad…

(*Se ríen y él come la manzana. Sobre esta imagen con los tres mirando el teleteatro. El recoge lentamente sus cosas y se va. Ellas ni lo miran entretenidas con verlo en la pantalla.*)

Marcelo (*Ha seguido tratando de que lo escuchen diciendo por ejemplo:*) Yo soy un hombre, voy a demostrarles que soy un hombre. (*Hasta llegar al final a un único texto.*) Yo soy ese, yo soy ese, ese soy yo. Soy yo. ¡Soy yo! (*Que es el último texto de la obra, mientras ellas siguen agarradas al televisor hasta apagón final*).

Apagón

CASA MATRIZ

Obra en un acto

Personajes
Bárbara: *30 años. Muy atractiva, sensual y complaciente. Sin embargo de repente entra en zonas sombrías y se torna irascible. Estas contradicciones personales, permitirán que se adapte en velocidad a las diversas hijas que deberá componer.*

Madre Sustituta: *Mujer bella, de edad indeterminada, alrededor de los 40 años. No es imprescindible una marcada diferencia de edad entre ambas, ya que es una Madre Sustituta de su cliente y no real. Tiene rasgos finos, delineados y hermosos. Es extremadamente histriónica, expansiva y obviamente, tiene dotes de actriz consumada. Es una empleada de Casa Matriz, entrenada profesiónalmente para actuar todos los roles de madre que contraten sus clientes.*

Escenografía
La obra transcurre en uno de los estudios de Casa Matriz Inc. Agency. Se ha creado una habitación de soltera, estratégicamente decorada para que los elementos que contiene puedan mutarse rápidamente o transformarse en otros. Al igual que los personajes, la escenografia sufrirá fuertes cambios estilísticos, según la escena que se esté viviendo adentro. Por eso deberá resolverse con elementos sencillos y mutables. Hay dos puertas, una de ingreso a la supuesta casa de Bárbara y otra que da al interior. Hay un perchero con ropa colgada preparado para las distintas madres e hijas que durante la obra representaran ambas. Puede haber, según lo estime el escenógrafo, un bar con bebidas. Unas sillas y una mesa. Puede ser interesante que las luces permitan demarcar dos zonas afectivas de la obra: una que tiene que ver con la relación cliente-Madre Sustituta, más bien fría, azulina. La otra más emocional, impregnada de las pasiones que se desataran según las escenas. La Madre Sustituta traerá además una maleta personal con

complementos de la ropa que hay en el escenario. Vestida de seda color salmón. Se oye el Magnificat de Bach. Bárbara se para encima de un banco con una batuta y de espaldas al publico "dirige" la orquesta. Suena el timbre. Ella parece no oírlo, absorta en la música que invade la habitación. El timbre suena con mas insistencia. Bárbara en un ataque repentino de furia, rompe la batuta; mágicamente la música cesa.)

Bárbara Era un momento privado, de gran envergadura. Yo había logrado un encuentro decisivo con lo que algún día, sin duda, llamaría "mi felicidad". *(Abre con paciencia la puerta.)* y usted lógicamente no tolera la diferencia enajenada del goce.
(Al abrirse la puerta comienza a sonar música hindú. Vestida con ropa india la Madre Sustituta ingresa hablando ostentosamente.)
Madre Sustituta ¡Nunca debí creerle! ¡Él era demasiado fuerte, demasiado hermoso, demasiado moreno! Hacíamos el amor seis veces al día. Siempre sobre elefantes blancos, bajo un arcoiris de música sacra! Le encantaba verme sonreír. Querida hija: ¿Alguna vez tuviste un orgasmo solar? ¿O tus orgasmos sólo han sido lunares? Yo sé que las madres no debemos hablar de estas cosas con las hijas. Pero nuestra relación siempre ha sido tan intensa... Si me suicido me gustaría hacerlo en casa de mi hija. Y ella lo comprendería como un acto de amor. Yo he comprendido muy tarde la diferencia entre amor y pasión. India es un buen lugar para perderse para siempre. Yo lo he amado. Creo que no voy a poder vivir sin él. ¡Es demasiado!!! ¿Por qué no me consolás hijita? Sos lo único que tengo. Soy una sombra de mi misma en las arenas de la nada. Me dejó sin decirme una palabra. Y al día siguiente lo vi pasar en elefante blanco con otra mujer. Voy a morirme de tristeza. Hacé algo por tu mamá querida. ¡Ayudame a morir con dignidad!
Bárbara Te queda fantástico es traje mamá. *(La besa fríamente.)* ¿Cocó Chanel? ¿Qué tal el viaje? Disculpame que no te fui a buscar al aeropuerto, pero...
(Madre Sustituta cortando el clima anterior, en su carácter de empleadade casa Matriz. Algo perdida porque no recuerda los detalles de la madre que debe interpretar.)
Bárbara A París. Tenés una casa en París, mamá. Y pasás mucho tiempo ahí. Estás lo más lejos posible de tus hijos. Hace un año que no nos vemos. Y tengo que aceptar el hecho de ser una hija no querida. *(Bebe angustiada.)* ¡Pensar que me pasé todo el año esperando una miserable tarjeta postal de mi madre! *(Bebe whisky.)* ¿Pero no le

informaron de todo esto en Casa Matriz?

Madre Sustituta ¿París? ¿Y nunca una postal? ¿Pero no acabo de llegar de la India? ¿Usted es la que necesitaba comenzar con una madre adicta a pasear en elefante, vestida de blanco y con un amante negro?

Bárbara (*Indignada por la ineficiencia de un servicio tan caro.*) Yo jamás contraté ese servicio. ¡No me hace ningún efecto! (*Alterada*) Yo no pienso perder mi tiempo y mi dinero con una madre destruida porque su amante la dejó. ¡Yo pagué por una madre fría y desconsiderada que me hiciera sentir una!

Madre Sustituta ¡Así tratan mis grandes entradas operísticas!! ¡En vez de aplaudirme me humilla! Yo tendría que triunfar en Broadway. Ese es mi lugar. ¡Ser una estrella de Broadway!.

Bárbara Yo aprecio su esfuerzo shakespereano señora, ¡pero póngase en mi lugar! Imagínese que pagó para atravesar la barrera del sonido con sus emociones y no sucede nada de eso.

Madre Sustituta (*Molesta por su gaffe profesiónal.*) Tiene razón. Me confundí. Le sucede a los mejores actores. Le podría contar grandes errores de Madona o de Meryl Streep sin ir más lejos.

Bárbara ¿Se equivocó? ¿Y lo dice así, tan ligeramente? Yo aquí esperando a una gélida madre de París que me destrozara el corazón y aparece una mujer de la India con el corazón destrozado ¿a la que tengo para colmo, tengo que contener?

Madre Sustituta (*Perturbada por su error se pone un par de anteojos para leer y extrae unos papeles de Casa Matriz. Examina los papeles y se ríe de sí misma.*) Oh, sí ¡aquí está! "Llego desahuciada de la India dispuesta a suicidarme en casa de mi hijo y él me salva". La confundí con un cliente adicto al sufrimiento que tengo que visitar mañana Aquí está el error ¿quiere leer? (*Le muestra a Bárbara sus papeles.*) Le pido disculpas. Estoy excedida de trabajo. Soy una de las Madres Sustitutas más requeridas y a veces me confundo...

Bárbara ¿Pero usted se iba a suicidar en mi presencia?

Madre Sustituta Aquí dice que usted me iba a salvar.

Bárbara ¡Pero que comienzo de función, un suicidio en mis narices y para colmo, un suicidio equivocado!

Madre Sustituta Paramos todo a tiempo, no hubo grandes daños. Usted sintió alguna emoción y nosotras trabajamos para producir emociones, aunque sean equivocadas. Perdone pero quisiera estar segura: ¿usted eligió el plan "Be In" o el plan "Hello My Little Princess?"

Bárbara (*Desbordada va y viene por la habitación.*) ¡Oh no! Esto es inhumano. Hace la entrada de la madre que le tiene que hacer mañana a otro cliente y ¿después me pregunta qué plan contraté? Yo ahorré un año para llegar a este momento. Junté dólar por dólar para tenerla aquí conmigo. Venir a Casa Matriz no es fácil para alguien como yo. Y si he llegado a esto es por...

Madre Sustituta (*La interrumpe abruptamente.*) ¡No se le ocurra decirme por qué contrató este servicio! No forma parte de mi trabajo escuchar eso. ¡Imagínese si tuviera que escuchar las confesiones de cada uno de mis clientes! Vaya a un psicoanalista o a un rabino o a un sacerdote. Yo estoy aquí para hacer bien mi trabajo. Vamos a concentrarnos en eso.

Bárbara ¿Me está dando órdenes?

Madre Sustituta Quiero estar segura de que usted conoce las reglas de juego.

Bárbara Yo soy quién tiene que dar las órdenes. Usted me pertenece y no lo digo en sentido figurado.

Madre Sustituta ¿Y en qué sentido lo dice entonces?

Bárbara Lo digo literalmente. Lo digo sobre bases sólidas.

Madre Sustituta (*Se ríe de un modo hiriente.*) Me parece que la idea que usted tiene de la solidez es bastante precaria.

Bárbara ¿De qué se ríe?

Madre Sustituta Quiero aclararle para que usted se ubique que yo le pertenezco a usted tanto como a otros.

Bárbara Yo he pagado por esa pertenencia. No quiero ser vulgar, pero digamos que la he adquirido.

Madre Sustituta No quiero decepcionarla pero digamos que hoy me han adquirido ocho.

Bárbara ¡Ocho!

Madre Sustituta Mire, puede comprobarlo usted misma (*Le ofrece la agenda. Bárbara no quiere mirarla.*) Corrobore la fecha de hoy. Son ocho.

Bárbara ¿Quiere decir que hoy me visita a mí entre otros siete?

Madre Sustituta Un día de trabajo normal. Ocho clientes.

Bárbara (*Reacciona.*) ¿Y quién le ha pedido ese dato? ¿No le parece promiscuo decirme qué cantidad de hijos pagan hoy para que usted sea su madre? ¿Quién le ha pedido ese tipo de detalles?

Madre Sustituta Nadie me los ha pedido. Simplemente creí que...

Bárbara (*Furiosa con ella*) ¿En qué parte de nuestro contrato, en qué cláusula, en qué versículo está escrito que yo quería saber cuántos clientes tiene que visitar hoy?

Madre Sustituta En ninguna parte. No se lo dije por atenerme al contrato, sino porque usted alardeaba de ser mi cliente exclusiva. ¡Y para colmo mi dueña! Dijo que yo le pertenecía.

Bárbara ¡Pues bien, lo reafirmo! Usted durante este lapso de tiempo es mía! Mía. Le guste o no le guste. Mía. Usted es *mí Madre Sustituta*. ¿Ha entendido bien?

Madre Sustituta Si está segura de esa pertenencia, ¿por qué le duelen tanto los otros siete que tengo que visitar hoy?

Bárbara No me duelen. Simplemente no me interesan, eso es todo.

Madre Sustituta ¿Está segura de que *eso es todo*?

Bárbara Indiferencia total. Para mí no existen.

Madre Sustituta Bueno... para mí si existen. Y no sólo ellos, sino otro ocho clientes mañana y otros ocho pasado mañana y así sucesivamente. Multiplique ocho por treinta: doscientos cuarenta clientes al mes. ¿Usted se imagina satisfacer las demandas de doscientos cuarenta hijos al mes? ¿Sabe que paciencia tengo que tener? ¿Se imagina por ejemplo la cantidad de madres diferentes que tengo que interpretar? ¿Se imagina la cantidad de exigencias y demandas delirantes que tengo que satisfacer?

Bárbara Mire, por el momento no puedo imaginarme nada, porque ni siquiera ha satisfecho mis más mínimas demandas. Y para colmo pretende que me apiade de que usted sea una...una...*(Esta a punto de decir "prostituta.")* una...una...

Madre Sustituta ¿Una qué?

Bárbara Una *Madre Sustituta*, bueno...tan...tan...tan repartida. *(Se le quiebra la voz.)* ¿Quiere saber la verdad? ¡Claro que me importan los otros. ! Los detesto. Me encantaría ser la única. Comprarle las doscientos cuarenta horas del mes. Si tuviera dinero ahora mismo la contrataba por un mes seguido.

Madre Sustituta Esta voracidad no es sólo suya. Tengo comprometido todo el resto del año. Hay una viciosa como usted que va a llevarme de vacaciones con ella, para que le actúe miles de madres sustitutas en el Caribe. Hay una famosa actriz de cine que gasta todo lo que gana para lograr que yo le asegure que es mi hija favorita. Hay un senador que paga el triple todos los jueves por mi dedicación exclusiva. Hay una mujer obesa que me paga solamente para que le cocine sus ravioles predilectos y... *(Interrumpe el recuento.)* ¿Pero por qué le estoy contando todo esto? ¿A usted qué le importa? Usted eligió mi foto entre otras miles. Hoy no estoy teniendo un buen día, evidentemente. Por que le estoy hablando de mí, cuando usted contrató una Madre Sustituta? Ninguno de mis clientes quieren saber nada acerca de mi persona.

Bárbara ¡No me compare con todos esos pervertidos! Soy diferente.

Madre Sustituta ¿Diferente en qué? ¿Usted como todos no me querría los trescientos sesenta y cinco días del año, si tuviera con qué pagarme? ¿O entendí mal?

Bárbara Me entendió muy bien señora. Debo admitir que logró despertar en mí intensos sentimientos de celos y exclusión. Usted es una mujer fascinante. Elegí muy bien. Usted es encantadora aunque haya que tolerar que se equivoque y que hable de otros.

Madre Sustituta ¡Ultimamente he despertado grandes pasiones en mis clientes! ¿Quiere que le describa alguna? Hay un músico de jazz, muy joven, gay, maravilloso, que mientras bailamos me…

Bárbara ¡No! No me describa ninguna pasión. No me hable de los otros clientes. ¡No quiero saber ni siquiera sus nombres! ¡Imagínese si llego a conocer a alguno!

Madre Sustituta Por supuesto que conoce a alguno. El viernes tengo que visitar a un amigo suyo llamado Manuel. Creo que él es su ex-marido, ¿verdad?

(Bárbara se abalanza sobre ella y le tapa la boca. Forcejean. Caen al piso. Bárbara se coloca sobre la madre sustituta y le aprieta violentamente el cuello.)

Madre Sustituta ¡Suélteme! Me va a ahorcar. Mire que si me lesiona va a tener que pagar mucho dinero por mí a Casa Matriz.

(Esta frase asusta a Bárbara. La Madre Sustituta se defiende y domina la situación. Esta entrenada para la autodefensa. Es evidente que maneja artes marciales. Hace volar a Bárbara por el aire y en una sorprendente toma de yudo la inhabilita para defenderse. Bárbara queda inmovilizada por esta toma.)

Madre Sustituta *(Controlando físicamente la situación)* ¿Pasó la crisis querida?

Bárbara ¡Parece bien entrenada!

Madre Sustituta Es parte de nuestra formación. Recibimos entrenamiento en defensa personal, además de formarnos para actuar, bailar y cantar. Tenemos que estar dispuestas a todo. No podemos descuidar ningún detalle.

(Bárbara trata de ingresar en una zona de calma y autocontrol.)

Bárbara No vuelva a mencionarme a mi ex-marido.

Madre Sustituta De acuerdo. ¿Pero usted no había solicitado sentir celos? ¡La combinación entre una entrada equivocada y la mención de otros clientes da siempre excelentes resultados para desatar celos! ¿No logré realmente sacarla de sí?

Bárbara ¿Usted intenta hacerme creer que su error fue intencional?

Madre Sustituta ¡No me diga que usted piensa que realmente me equivoqué! Bueno…bien…si le gusta así…me equivoqué…

Bárbara ¿Y la mención a los otros clientes?

Madre Sustituta Usted me acaba de hacer jurar que no volvería a hablar de ellos.

Bárbara Bueno. Me arrepiento de ese pedido. Ahora dígame si realmente mi ex marido la contrató o si fue una estrategia suya para hacerme enloquecer de celos.

Madre Sustituta Imagine lo que quiera. La imaginación es un buen ejercicio cuando se ha perdido el sentido de la realidad. (*Bárbara le da una bofetada. Madre Sustituta le devuelve otra.*) ¡Usted adelantó el momento de la bofetada! Esto venía después.

Bárbara Y usted me hizo la entrada pagada por otro. ¿Qué le va a hacer al otro mañana? ¿La entrada que pagué yo?

Madre Sustituta ¡Oh no! Le voy a repetir la misma entrada. Ese tipo de personajes me atraen enormemente. ¡Madre con amantes negros que llega de la India... me piden tan pocas veces! En cambio la entrada que usted contrató es un cliché.

Bárbara Yo alquilé una madre gélida para la entrada, que me hiciera esperar mucho. Pedí tener tiempo para que se agudicen en mí los sentimientos fantasmagóricos del desasosiego. No me dejó tiempo para dudar. ¡Yo necesitaba dudar! ¡Pagué por la incertidumbre de saber si mi madre vendría o no vendría! Pero usted redujo todo. *(Pausa fugaz)* ¿Tiene más trabajo después?

Madre Sustituta No se preocupe por mí. Estoy llena de trabajo. *(Preocupada)* ¿Pero usted no llegó a temblar por mí?

Bárbara Un poco. Si hubiera demorado cinco minutos más y no se hubiera equivocado de cliente su entrada hubiera sido exitosa.

Madre Sustituta ¿Exitosa? ¡Mi entrada fue inolvidable! ¡Fue un alarde de virtuosismo técnico! ¡La combinación entre esa madre y esa hija fue un verdadero volcán en erupción! Pero usted tiene derecho al reclamo. ¿Quiere que le haga la entrada por la cual pagó?

Bárbara ¡Por supuesto que quiero la entrada que pagué! Exijo lo contratado en vuestras oficinas centrales.

Madre Sustituta Bien. Pero le ruego que previamente aclaremos qué quiere. (*Toma un block y se dispone a tomar nota puntual de lo que Bárbara le dicta.*)

Bárbara *(Buscando exactamente las palabras)* Quiero una madre hierática, que me haga estremecer de desasosiego. Una madre helada como el hielo.

Madre Sustituta (*Anotando*) ¡Las cosas que nos piden que hagamos!

Bárbara Distante, imprevisible, fantasmática, mala. Demoníaca.

Madre Sustituta ¡Un carácter delicioso!

Bárbara Yo pagué por esperar. Yo pagué por padecer. ¡Hace tanto tiempo que deseaba esperar a mi madre! Yo pagué por una madre que me hiciera sufrir por sus continuas inasistencias a nuestras citas.

Madre Sustituta (*Relee y memoriza.*) Muy bien. Serán satisfechas todas sus demandas. Hagamos de cuenta que todavía no he llegado. Adiós Bárbara.

Bárbara Adiós señora.

(*Madre Sustituta sale. Las luces descienden. El espacio queda en penumbras. En esas tinieblas Bárbara intenta recuperar la atmósfera del comienzo. Vuelve a poner "El Magníficat" de Bach, toma la batuta. Intenta dirigir la supuesta orquesta. Se da cuenta de qué puede volver al comienzo como si nada hubiera sucedido. Interrumpe la música.*)

Bárbara Hemos cometido un error al querer empezar de cero. Yo ya la conozco. Ya me he decepcionado. Este simulacro de entrada no sirve. Vuelva de una vez y sigamos con la madre siguiente. (Camina ansiosa por el set.) ¿Se habrá hartado de mí? Esto es inaceptable. Ella no puede hacerme esperar así. Estamos perdiendo un tiempo precioso. (*Abre la puerta de entrada esperando encontrarla allí. No está.*) Estamos perdiendo un tiempo precioso. Admito que no la traté bien. Fue todo culpa mía. Ella tiene sus límites y yo fui muy dura con ella. La humillé y ahora se fue. Ella es realmente muy buena actriz. La entrada equivocada fue maravillosa. Es realmente única. ¿Por qué no fui capaz de decírselo? (*La madre entra con un talleur muy elegante. Tiene un sombrerito y un par de guantes que no se quitara en toda la escena.*)

Bárbara ¡Mamá! ¡Todo un año sin vernos! (*La abraza.*)

Madre Sustituta (*Fría. Distante. Empuja a Bárbara para alejarla de sí.*) Ahorrame las efusiones por favor. Veo que todavía recibís a las personas con besos.

Bárbara Disculpame mamá. Es que hace tanto tiempo! Pasá por favor…tengo tantas ganas de que veas mi casa.

(*La Madre Sustituta no mira la casa, se sienta muy tensa en el borde de una silla. Saca un espejito de la cartera para chequear su maquillaje.*)

Madre Sustituta (*Trata de quitarse el efecto del beso en su cara.*) ¿Me corriste el maquillaje de las mejillas?

Bárbara Estás preciosa Mamy. ¿Que tal tu París? ¿Por qué nunca me escribiste? ¿Me extrañaste en algún momento? ¿Pensaste en mí en algún momento? ¿Por qué no me llamaste para Navidad o para Año

Nuevo?

Madre Sustituta No puedo contestar todas esas preguntas al mismo tiempo, María. Ni siquiera entiendo qué me estás preguntando.

Bárbara Yo no soy María mamá. Soy Bárbara.

Madre Sustituta *(Saca el regalo de su cartera.)* Te traje tu perfume predilecto. Eau Savage para hombre. *(Se lo da.)*

Bárbara Este es el perfume predilecto de mi hermano Guillermo. El mío es Samsara de Guerlein.

Madre Sustituta Qué hija desagradecida. Crucé el Océano Atlántico únicamente para traerte tu perfume favorito y ahora tratás de confundirme con tus hermanos, María.

Bárbara *(Angustiada)* Mamá…mirame a los ojos. Soy tu hija Bárbara. Te quiero mama, te quiero mucho. Estoy muy feliz de que me hayas venido a visitar. Esperé mucho tiempo para tener el privilegio de estar a solas con vos. *(La toma de las manos afectuosamente. La madre se irrita por el contacto.)*

Madre Sustituta Todo este manoseo me pone muy nerviosa. ¿Podrías evitarlo? ¿Así que querías estar a solas conmigo? ¿Para qué?

Bárbara *(Bárbara vuelve a tomar las manos enguantadas de su madre, que se las deja tiesas.)* Quería decirte que te amo. Para mí era importarte poder decirte eso. Te amo mamá.

Madre Sustituta *(Le retira las manos.)* Bien. Ahora sé que me amás, María. *(Se aleja físicamente de su hija.)*

Bárbara ¡No vuelvas a llamarme María! María es mi hermana. Yo soy Bárbara.

Madre Sustituta Ya lo sé. No tengo ninguna duda de que no sos María. María nunca me hubiera tenido quieta en una silla para decirme todas esas tonterías. "¡Te amo mamita y para mi es muy importante *(Cruel y sarcástica)* que lo sepas, etcétera…"¡ María nunca me hubiera apretado las manos. Nunca. Ella sabe que todo ese tipo de manifestaciones no me parecen higiénicas. *(Se pone de pie.)* María nunca me hubiera besado de esa manera. ¿Hay algo menos elegante que apoyar tus labios en las mejillas de la persona que tienes más a mano y oprimirla, produciendo ese desagradable sonido? *(Imita un sonido de beso muy desagradable.)* Devolveme el perfume. Se lo voy a dar a Guillermo. Prometo no equivocarme el próximo año cuando te visite nuevamente. *(Bárbara le devuelve el perfume.)*

Bárbara ¡Esta es la primera vez que te acordás de traerme un regalo para mí cumpleaños mamá, y me trajiste un regalo equivocado! Siempre hacés lo mismo mamá. Siempre me das a mí los regalos para

Guillermo y a Guillermo los regalos para María y a María los regalos para Genoveva.

Madre Sustituta *(Divertida)* ¿Hago eso? Qué encantador. Esa distracción que tengo me parece simpátiquisima.

Bárbara Cambié todos los colores de mi casa especialmente para vos. Mirá por lo menos mi casa si no podés mirarme a mí.

Madre Sustituta *(Sin mirar)* Quedó preciosa tu casa, María.

Bárbara Bárbara.

Madre Sustituta Quedó bárbara tu casa, María.

Bárbara No, no. *(Saliendo del personaje y reclamando como clienta)* Le dije veinte veces que mi nombre es Bárbara. No quiero ser dura con usted, pero ya casi más que gélida, parece amnésica, señora.

Madre Sustituta Tengo amnesia emocional. No sé a quién amo.

Bárbara *(Vuelve al personaje.)* ¿Entonces no sabés si me querés?

Madre Sustituta ¿Yo? Quererte... ¿Yo te quiero?

Bárbara *(Como cliente)* Excelente. Lo ha logrado...nunca me sentí peor.

Madre Sustituta ¿Y no era eso lo que quería?

Bárbara Sí, sí. Muchas gracias. Nunca me sentí tan bien de sentirme tan mal.

Madre Sustituta ¿Se sintió la hija de una mujer de hielo?

Bárbara Sí. La sentí mala, cruel, helada.

Madre Sustituta Puedo ser mucho más terrible. Se necesita grandeza para el mal y yo la tengo *(Se saca el cinturón a modo de látigo.)* Me encanta encarnar madres demoníacas.

Bárbara Para mí ha sido suficiente. No quisiera más crueldad.

(Madre Sustituta guarda su cinturón.)

Madre Sustituta Es una pena que no quiera profundizar en el mal. Amo las madres sádicas.

Bárbara Suficiente.

Madre Sustituta ¿Hemos alcanzado el punto de desesperación que contrató?

Bárbara Sí. Ahora usted debería reprocharme por no haber sido suficientemente bárbara.

Madre Sustituta Eso se lo dejo a la próxima madre.

(La Madre Sustituta sale de escena. Se escucha una canzonetta napolitana. Entra al escenario ropa colgada de sogas para que parezca más humilde. Exterior. Terraza. Barrio de inmigrantes italianos. Bárbara se adecua poniéndose debajo de su falda un almohadón que simula un embarazo. Cambia su estilo por el de una humilde muchacha

de barrio embarazada y con una "mamma" que la llena de reproches.
Entra la madre sustituta con ropa mojada para colgar en los broches.
Bárbara la ayuda.)

Madre Sustituta *(Con un dejo de acento siciliano)* Mabelita te tendrías
que haber llamado. Mabelita como quería tu padre. Pero se me ocurrió
ponerte Bárbara. Y ese nombre te trajo mala suerte. Nadie en este barrio
se llama Bárbara. Bárbara es un nombre de persona fina, exitosa. ¡Mirá
que exitosa resultaste! ¡Y sobre todo qué fina! ¡Maldigo el día en que
se me ocurrió ponerte Bárbara!

Bárbara *(Sosteniéndose la cintura porque le pesa el embarazo)* Yo
también lo maldigo. Me obligaste con el nombre a fracasar.

Madre Sustituta ¡Te hubieras casado con el diplomático ése que
conociste en casa de esa amiga sofisticada que tenías! Hoy sí que
estarías gloria. ¡Pero te casaste con *El Poroto*! Te llenó de hijos, no
trabaja, y todos viven pidiéndome dinero a mí. ¿Qué le viste al *Poroto*
nena?

Bárbara El fue el único en la vida que me dijo, "¡Qué gloria que sos,
Bárbara"! Estábamos nadando y le vi esas piernas musculosas que tiene.
¡Dios mío, qué bien estaba! Y cuando se secaba despacito con la toalla.
Mamma yo me sentí suya para siempre.

Madre Sustituta ¡Ay nena! Ahora estás llena de chicos, él ni te mira y
vive protestando porque no le doy bastante dinero para las carreras.

Bárbara Cada vez que te pido dinero me tirás mis fracasos en la cara.

Madre Sustituta *(Le da dinero que saca del corpiño.)* Aquí tenés otros
500 dólares. Pero no se te ocurra dárselos a él. Son para mis nietos.

Bárbara *(Guarda el dinero en su corpiño.)* Gracias mamma... No puedo
salir a trabajar hasta que no tenga mi bebé. Me siento tan sola.

Madre Sustituta ¡Pero seguís teniendo hijos con *El Poroto*!

Bárbara Es que todavía me sigue diciendo, "Qué bárbara que sos
Bárbara". Y estoy perdida. ¿Cómo puede un hombre volverte tan loca?

Madre Sustituta ¿Un hombre? ¿Volverme loca?¿ A mí? *(Hace la señal
de la cruz.)* ¡Todo el mundo sabe que tu padre *nunca* me vio desnuda!
Siempre me dejaba el camisón cuando hacíamos "*la porquería*". Y lo
hacíamos por él. No porque a mí me gustara como a vos. ¡Dios!
¡Perderte un diplomático por *El Poroto*!

Bárbara *(Demanda como cliente.)* ¡Usted me está tratando cómo una
idiota!

Madre Sustituta Usted pidió en su plan una madre decalificadora,
jodida, que hace reproches. Y ahora que la tiene ¿se queja?

Bárbara La madre que está haciendo es perfecta. Lo que no concuerda es el aspecto sociológico de su planteo. ¿Dónde pude yo haber conocido un diplomático? El barrio limita mucho. ¿Qué diplomático viene a un barrio de inmigrantes sicilianos a buscar novia?

Madre Sustituta ¡Dije que lo habías conocido en casa de una amiga sofisticada!

Bárbara Quiero que insista en el punto en que se arrepiente de haberme puesto el nombre Bárbara.

Madre Sustituta *(Retomando la mamma italiana)* Maledetta la hora en que te llamé Bárbara! Te encantaba escribir y te dedicás a vender caramelos. Te atraía un Diplomático y te casate con El Poroto. Querías ser hermosa y me saliste bizca y con las piernas torcidas!

Bárbara Vos tenés las piernas torcidas. ¡Mirá como caminás arrastrando esas pantuflas!

Madre Sustituta Las piernas torcidas las heredaste de mí. Pero esos ojos con forma de huevo los heredaste de tu padre. Te quedaste con lo peor de los dos.

Bárbara Hoy es mi cumpleaños mamá. ¿Cómo podés tratarme así?

Madre Sustituta *(Interrumpe la escena. Vuelve a ser la empleada de Casa Matriz.)* Usted pagó para que esta madre la tratara así.

Bárbara Le hablaba a mi madre señora. No estoy cuestionando su profesionalismo.

Madre Sustituta Bien, continuemos... *(Recupera el personaje.)* Concentración...

Bárbara Estaba sumergida en la escena ¿Por qué la interrumpió?

Madre Sustituta Tu cumpleaños. ¡El día que naciste fue uno de los más negros de mi vida!

Bárbara *(Interrumpe la escena.)* Yo no pagué para que me dijera eso. Revise el contrato. Hoy es realmente mi cumpleaños señora. Y me estoy regalando un service de Casa Matriz. Usted es un regalo que me hice para mi cumpleaños.

Madre Sustituta Un regalo...yo...un regalo. *(Le desagrada la idea de ser un objeto de regalo.)* Pasemos a otra madre...a ésta le duele la cintura.

(La Madre se va con la palangana de ropa mojada. La ropa colgada sale de escena. Bárbara se quita el almohadon de embarazada. Se pone un impermeable empapado y abre un paraguas. Se moja la cara para simular lluvia. Recoge libros y se pone anteojos para tener un aspecto de intelectual. Su personalidad se adapta al cambio. La luz da una sensación de estación de tren. En off se escucha la voz de la madre. Tiene un dejo de acento ruso. Es una "idische mame" una típica madre

judía. Bárbara está sola, leyendo una carta. Ella busca sentarse en un rincón de la supuesta estación de tren. En off se escucha la voz de la madre. Bárbara no verá entrar a la Madre Sustituta.)

Bárbara Hijita mía: tanto tiempo sin recibir noticias tuyas! Pero ahora ya no puedo postergar mi necesidad de verte. Esta es la última carta que te escribo antes de que nos veamos. Pues, mañana llegaré a la ciudad. Te ruego que vengas a buscarme a la estación de tren. Sé que esto te presupone una molestia pero tengo algo muy importante que decirte y prefiero decírtelo personalmente. Llegaré en el tren de las nueve de la noche. Te adora y siempre te adorará. Tu madre.

(Se escucha el ruido de un tren que llega. Bajan los pasajeros y se van. Por detrás de Bárbara entra la madre en silla de ruedas, toda enyesada de pies a cabeza, excepto el rostro que asoma por debajo del yeso de la cabeza. Bárbara al verla se queda totalmente shockeada. Tira al suelo los libros y la carta y se abraza a las piernas de la madre.)

Bárbara Mamita, mamá...qué te ha sucedido? Oh mamá!

Madre Sustituta *(Acerca la cara a Bárbara para que pueda darle un beso en la porción de rostro que asoma en el vendaje.)* Nada importante querida. ¿Tus estudios como marchan?

Bárbara *(Muy angustiada de verla así.)* Por qué nadie me avisó?

Madre Sustituta Levantate. Levantate *meidele*. No puedo verte si estás agachada. Te traje unos bagels. *(Le acerca como puede el paquete de comida.)* Esta vez no los hice yo, los hizo tu tía Sarah. No son tan ricos como los míos, pero no están mal. *(Bárbara abre el paquete y se los come con ansiedad.)* Ves, ves. Estás con hambre. ¡Hasta los bagels de Sarah te resultan deliciosos con hambre!

Bárbara Están riquísimos. ¿Tuviste un accidente?

Madre Sustituta No hablemos de mí. Fue un golpecito sin importancia. Hablemos de cosas interesantes. Hablemos de tu pasión por la Ontología.

Bárbara ¡Un golpecito sin importancia! ¡Te rompiste todos los huesos, Mamá! ¡Quiero saber cómo te hiciste todo este desastre!

Madre Sustituta Trabajando.

Bárbara ¿Trabajando en la bombonería?

Madre Sustituta Ese lugar cerró. Y tuve que buscar otro trabajo para poder enviarte dinero.

Bárbara ¿Qué clase de trabajo mamá?

Madre Sustituta Limpio cristales en los altos rascacielos. Nadie quiere hacer ese tipo de tarea. Pero a mí me encanta estar ahí, colgada en el andamio, al aire libre, tocando el cielo con las manos. Tenía la maravillosa impresión de estar volando. Y me caí del tercer piso. No tiene ninguna importancia. Lo hice por la Ontología, por vos. Limpiaba y pensaba que mi hija Bárbara gracias a mi trabajo pronto sería Doctora en Ontología. ¡Eso me daba fuerzas! ¡Mi Barbarita, Doctora en Ontología!

Bárbara Están riquísimos. ¿Tuviste un accidente?

Madre Sustituta ¿A quien le puede interesar, finalmente, lo que puede pasarme a mí?

Bárbara ¡A mí, por supuesto!

Madre Sustituta No hablemos de mí. Fue una golpecito sin importancia. Hablemos de cosas interesantes. Hablemos de tu pasión por la Ontología.

Bárbara Un golpecito sin importancia: ¡te rompiste todos los huesos mamá! ¡Quiero saber como te hiciste todo este desastre!

Bárbara ¿Desde cuándo limpiás cristales en las ventanas de los rascacielos?

Madre Sustituta ¡Sabía que te ibas a enojar, por eso no te lo quería decir!

Bárbara ¿Desde cuándo arriesgás tu vida así?

Madre Sustituta Desde hace cinco años que te miento. Lo hice todo por tus estudios. Yo no tengo ninguna importancia.

Bárbara ¿Limpiando cristales en los edificios para que yo estudie? Yo no quiero que hagas esas cosas por mí. No quiero que me envíes un solo centavo más mamá. Sos demasiado buena. Mucho más buena que yo.

Madre Sustituta Oh, dejame ayudarte. Bárbara. Puedo pegar sellos postales en la Oficina de Correos. No me he roto la lengua. *(Saca la lengua.)* Pagan poco por poner la lengua, pero es mejor que nada. *(Saca una bolsita con dinero.)* Mirá ahorré un poco de dinero para vos, Barbarita. No es mucho, pero la sola idea de que te pueda servir, me alcanza. No lo desprecies. Una madre enyesada que trabaja con la lengua, merece tu compasión.

(Bárbara toma el dinero emocionada. Se arrodilla y besa las manos enyesadas de su madre. Apoya la cabeza sobre el regazo de la mamá. La madre canta una bella canción de cuna en idisch, muy popular y conocida. Bárbara tararea con ella.)

Bárbara Mamá. me siento tan culpable....Es horrible, siento como si yo te hubiera empujado al abismo.

Madre Sustituta Lo hago con gusto, no te preocupes.

Bárbara ¿Cómo no voy a preocuparme? *(La contempla con mucha culpa.)* Mira como estás por culpa mía. Me siento culpable, culpable de haber nacido. Culpable de estar viva.

(Comienza a mover la silla de ruedas de su madre. La Madre Sustituta da por terminada la escena. Pega un salto de la silla. Camina con los yesos por el escenario.)

Madre Sustituta Bien. Me ha salido muy bien, como siempre. La idishe mame es uno de mis grandes éxitos. Surte efecto. Cada vez que solicitan culpa yo la actúo con gran suceso. Surte efecto. ¡Mire como la dejé! ¿O me va a decir que no sintió una terrible culpa?

Bárbara *(Asiente.)* ¡Sentí una culpa tremenda!

Madre Sustituta *(Se quita los yesos con energía.)* ¿Me ayuda a desenyesarme la cabeza?

Bárbara *(La ayuda.)* Sentí una culpa sin salida.

Madre Sustituta Oh no "la culpa sin salida" viene ahora. ¿Usted encargó la muerte de la madre verdad?

Bárbara *(Asustada)* La puedo liberar de hacer ese rol si no lo desea.

Madre Sustituta Oh no me libere de nada! Me encanta el rol de muerta.

(Se pone una larga camisa fúnebre. Se maquilla de blanco la cara. Bárbara se pone ropa negra de luto. Llora.) ¿Me morí de muerte súbita?

Bárbara Completamente súbita. Necesito sentir ese impacto.

(La madre ha preparado la cama fúnebre. Muere de golpe sobre el lecho. Tiene flores entre sus manos. Un crucifijo aparece sobre la cama. Las luces cambian hacia tonalidades más blanquecinas. Suena música fúnebre. Bárbara se queda a solas con su madre muerta.)

Bárbara Qué hermosa estás mamá. Cuánto te ha embellecido la muerte. Siempre he tratado de ser la más madura de las dos, la más serena de las dos. Mamá, cómo me gustaba caminar contigo del brazo bajo la lluvia. Cómo disfrutaba de tu compañía en el campo, cuando andábamos juntas a caballo. Aunque siempre terminábamos peleándonos. No eran peleas profundas. ¿Verdad mamá? Mamá…yo nunca te dije claramente…yo nunca te dije yo nunca te dije que…te amaba. *(Se acerca a su madre.)* Nunca me permití besarte. *(La besa.)* Nunca pude estar cerca tuyo, ni dejé que te acercaras a mí. *(La besa más.)* Nunca, nunca. ¿Cómo pude hacerte eso, mamá? *(Llora desconsoladamente.)* ¡Contestame mamá! Decime que a pesar de todo me quisiste. Quiero volver a oír tu voz. Decime algo reconfortante mamá. Abrí los ojos, por Dios. *(Agita a la madre enérgicamente como si en vez de muerta estuviera desmayada.)* Decime que todavía estamos a tiempo. Regresá mamá y dame una oportunidad de ser diferente con vos. *(La toma de la cabeza y la sacude sin dar crédito a su muerte.)* Decime que sí, que todavía tenemos tiempo. Sólo te pido un poco de tiempo mamá. Tiempo nada más.

Tiempo. ¡Dame un poco de tiempo mamá!

Madre Sustituta *(Abre los ojos. Se sienta en la cama.)* ¿Tiempo para qué?

Bárbara *(La suelta bruscamente.)* ¡Los muertos no hablan, señora!

Madre Sustituta Pero usted me está atosigando de preguntas querida.

Bárbara Los muertos no responden preguntas señora! *(Acusándola)* ¡Rompió el misterio! Profanó lo más sagrado. ¡Arruinó la muerte de la madre! ¡Y con lo bien que venía todo! ¡Con lo mucho que estaba sintiendo yo! Me estaba cayendo en un abismo. ¡Estaba indagando mi propia dimensión trágica, señora mía! ¡Usted no tiene ningún respeto por mis emociones profundas! Usted frivoliza todo.

Madre Sustituta Mire. Ya le hemos dado bastante tiempo a la madre muerta.. Hay otras madres esperando, mucho más divertidas.

Bárbara Aquí la que se tiene que divertir soy yo. Y como esta diversión tan particular cuesta mucho dinero, usted debe cumplir con su responsabilidad. Vuélvase a morir si es tan amable.

(La madre de mala gana vuelve a acostarse. Se sienta.)

Madre Sustituta Yo me vuelvo a morir, pero usted no me bombardee con preguntas.

Bárbara Pero son preguntas sin respuesta. Justamente las preguntas sin respuesta nos permiten cruzar al otro lado. Conocer un tipo de soledad casi absoluta. Yo no le estoy formulando preguntas que esperan ser respondidas. *(La madre vuelve a morirse.)* Bárbara *(Vuelve a llorar.)* Mamá. Mamá necesito decirte que, que…que *(Se interrumpe.)* No se me ocurre nada para decir. ¡La interrupción fue terrible!

Madre Sustituta ¡Por fin! *(Se quita la ropa fúnebre.)* ¡Por fin! Atravesamos la muerte, ahora nos toca festejar la vida. ¡Feliz Cumpleaños Bárbara!

(La madre sale de escena con una mesa de cumpleaños, llena de masas, tortas, bombones. Hay una torta con 30 velitas. Por encima de la mesa cuelgan globos y un cartel donde dice ¡Happy birthday Bárbara! Clima festivo que contrasta con el anterior. Bárbara se viste con un vestido precioso, muy festivo. La Madre toca el timbre por la puerta de entrada. Bárbara le abre con una enorme sonrisa. La Madre llega con un vestido con lunares, muy llamativo y una preciosa caja con moño rojo conteniendo el regalo de cumpleaños para Bárbara.

Madre Sustituta *(Canta.)* ¡Qué cumplas feliz! ¡Qué los cumplas feliz! Mi preciosa Barbarita. ¡Qué los cumplas feliz!

(Bárbara también canta a duo con ella. Abre el regalo que le trajemadre. Es un vestido idéntico al que la madre tiene puesto.)

Bárbara Mamá, es divino. (*Se lo pone encima del que tiene puesto.*) ¡Parecemos mellizas! (*Festejan con un abrazo. Bárbara trae un teclado y tocan el piano a cuatro manos. Cantan juntas una canción de amor. Mirando cantar a su madre*) Mamá, me hace tan feliz escucharte cantar!

Madre Sustituta Me imagino. (*Encantada de sí misma.*)

Bárbara (*Interrumpe el juego.*) No señora. ¡Yo no pagué para que usted se vanagloriara de sí misma!

Madre Sustituta ¡Es que me imagino que a usted yo le encanto!

Bárbara Pero de paso, se publicitaba a usted misma. ¡Nunca debió decir "*me imagino*" cuando le dije que escucharla cantar me hacía feliz!

Madre Sustituta (*Soluciona el problema.*) Cambio la respuesta.. Dígalo de nuevo.

Bárbara Mamá, ¡me hace tan feliz escucharte cantar!

Madre Sustituta Bárbara, ¡lo mejor que te pasó fue tenerte a ti!

Bárbara ¡Eso ya me lo dijo antes y mucho mejor formulado!

Madre Sustituta (*Intenta no impacientarse.*) Bárbara, ¿sabés que tu nacimiento le dio sentido a mi existencia?

Bárbara Me imagino.

Madre Sustituta (*Corta.*) Usted tampoco puede decir "*me imagino*". Todas las hijas piensan que le arruinaron la vida a su madre.

Bárbara ¡No con una madre así! Yo a esa madre la contraté para darle sentido a su vida. Es un pequeño lujo que me quiero dar.

Madre Sustitua (*Retomando la parte de madre encantadora*) Bárbara, ¡luz de mi vida! Darte la vida le dio sentido a mi efímera existencia.

Bárbara Su tono es distante, sarcástico, con un dejo algo profesiónal. Se supone que usted tiene que hacerme olvidar que lo está haciendo por dinero, sino no tiene gracia. Construya mejor las frases. Explicite.

Madre Sustituta (*Bien dispuesta*) Mi hija Bárbara es absolutamente insustituible.

Bárbara (*Feliz*) ¿Verdad que soy insustituible, mamá?

Madre Sustituta Sí. (*Angustiada por su profesión de Madre Sustituta*) insustituible. ¡No como yo que soy una Madre Sustituta! Absolutamente sustituible. (*Una pausa extraña. La Madre Sustituta se recupera. Abraza a Bárbara.*) Perdón... (*Retoma.*) Sí mi amor, sos insustituible, singular hasta en la forma de ser común, original hasta en tus obviedades, y sobre todo, sos una gran persona.

Bárbara Repita esas palabras. Costaron muchos dólares.

Madre Sustituta Sos la mejor persona que he conocido en mi vida.

Bárbara Basta. Ya ni yo lo creo. (*Se aleja de ella.*) Usted hace todo un poco excesivo hasta volverlo asfixiante.

Madre Sustituta Estamos instruidas para eso. Nuestra formación exige un cierto plus. Si no nadie contrataría una Madre Sustituta. El cliente se quedaría con su madre naturalista real. No podemos, no debemos caer en el realismo de las madres que nuestros clientes ya tienen.

Bárbara Entonces quizás todavía no hemos dado en la tecla de mis necesidades.

Madre Sustituta Quizás el programa de madres que usted eligió no sea el adecuado. O quizás yo no sea la empleada adecuada para salir al encuentro de sus necesidades.

Bárbara (*Repentinamente*) No perdamos el tiempo. Comience a ordenar esta habitación. Esmérese en poner orden en toda la casa. ¡Poblemos de atraso y sometimiento esta relación!

— **Madre Sustituta** (*Resistente, furiosa, consulta el plan.*) Todos, pero absolutamente todos, necesitan verme en la más triste de las servidumbres¡ ¡Nunca me salvo de limpiarles la casa! ¡Este trabajo de Madre Sustituta tiene aspectos francamente denigrantes. Esto ya lo hemos discutido en las reuniones de nuestro Sindicato.

(*Bárbara se cruza de brazos, despótica, implacable. La Madre Sustituta se coloca una peluca desgreñada sujeta a la cabeza con un pañuelo a lunares. Un vestido negro abotonado, medias negras y zapatillas. Saca de una maleta plumero, escoba, franela y todo tipo de elementos de limpieza. Suena un tango. Madre Sustituta ordena la habitación en silencio mientras Bárbara frente al espejo se cepilla el cabello.*)

Madre Sustituta ¿Vas a salir otra vez con ese sinvergüenza?

Bárbara No te metas en mis asuntos mamá.

Madre Sustituta (*Barre.*) ¡Pero si vos sos lo único que me queda! Mi hijo mayor fugado por estafas; Beatriz, ¡tu hermana se enamoró de un guerrillero en plena dictadura militar! Ni una foto de ella me dejaron para llorarla…y vos hijita…(*Madre Sustituta suspira y trabaja.*)

Bárbara ¿ Me planchaste el vestido fucsia? (*La madre le trae solícitamente el vestido planchadísimo.*) ¡Te dije que le pusieras apresto!

Madre Sustituta (*Asustada*) ¡Es que queda mucho más elegante!

Bárbara (*Le grita.*) Yo quiero estar sexy, no elegante mamá...(*Arruga el traje.*). Me tenés harta mamá! (*Deshace la cama. La madre vuelve a hacerla de inmediato.*) ¿Para qué hacés la cama? A Marcelo le gusta coger con la cama revuelta. (*Desordena una cajonera. Tira toda la ropa. La Madre Sustituta vuelve a poner orden a una velocidad inusitada en camara ligera.*)

Madre Sustituta Hijita mía…¿estás comiendo bien? ¿Qué te pasa? (*Lamentando*) ¡Si tu padre no se hubiera escapado por la puerta de atrás!

Bárbara (*Feróz*) ¡Se escapó con tu hermana, mamá!

Madre Sustituta Y bueno...mi hermana siempre fue más atractiva que yo...(*Bárbara se calza un pantalón ajustado y una musculosa muy provocativa*) Vos no podés salir así a la calle.

Bárbara Yo salgo a la calle como quiero. ¿O querés que me vista de portera como vos?

(*La Madre Sustituta vuelve a hacer la cama. Bárbara toma whisky.*)

Madre Sustituta (*Con un hilo de voz*) ¿Estás tomando otra vez? ¡Me dijiste que habías dejado!

Bárbara (*La enfrenta.*) Te mentí. ¡Me divierte mentirte, vieja! Es lindo ver como te crees todo. (*Pausa*) Estoy embarazada, mamá.

Madre Sustituta (*Llorando*) Hijita mía, sentate. ¿Y de cuántos meses estás?

Bárbara De tres.

Madre Sustituta Pero ese hombre es casado. ¿Cómo pudo hacerte eso?.

Bárbara No sé si me lo hizo él. No sé de quién es ese hijo.

Madre Sustituta (*Temblando*) Entonces te acostás con más de uno.

Bárbara (*Rompe el juego.*) Es obvio señora, que si le digo que no sé de quién es ese hijo, es porque me acuesto con más de uno. ¡Además usted prometió sufrir!

Madre Sustituta (*Profesiónal*)   Estoy padeciendo enormemente. ¿Quiere que exteriorice?

Bárbara Por supuesto señora, es mi cumpleaños. ¿Qué mejor regalo que una madre sumisa que exteriorice su sufrimiento?

(*Madre Sustituta vuelve al personaje y llora estrepitosamente. Bárbara pone a sonar un rock para tapar el llanto.*)

Bárbara No soporto tu llanto mamá. ¿Por qué llorás? Si la que está jodida soy yo. ¿Por qué no me ayudás a buscar soluciones en vez de derramar lágrimas sobre mis sábanas? Vos me hiciste así. Ahora bancate a esta nena de treinta años que no quiere largar la adolescencia y sigue atada a la falda de su mamá.

Madre Sustituta (*Madre Sustituta llora copiosamente con verdaderas lágrimas. Después interrumpe. En tono profesiónal, altamente competente*). Venga, acérquese señorita. (*Bárbara se acerca.*) Son lágrimas de verdad. Toque. (*Bárbara toca y comprueba.*) No puede reclamar un efecto más trágico. Soy la Mater Sufriente por excelencia. Vestida de negro, limpiando, llorando, con una hija alcohólica y embarazada. Soy La Gran Madre Sufriente. Soy la madre consagrada por el Tango. La literatura se ha ocupado vastamente de mí. Soy una madre bíblica: "Parirás con dolor". Soy la Santa Madrecita. Mire qué lagrimones.

Bárbara Se ve que conoce muy bien este tipo de madres.

Madre Sustituta Es muy requerida por la clientela de Casa Matriz. ¡Todos quieren ser hijos rebeldes! Y rebelarse contra tanta sumisión es muy sencillo. (*Corta este personaje haciendo un desafío personal.*)Yo la desafío a rebelarse contra una madre emancipada. O contra una intelectual de gran prestigio. O simplemente, contra una diva internacional. (*Revuelve su maleta.*) Tengo todos los atuendos intactos. ¡Estas madres las piden poco! Todos buscan la cosa facilona, denigrable. Les gusta verme llorar, porque se sienten libres, rebeldes, jóvenes. Pero — no les gusta verme reír. ¿Quién paga por verme gozar? ¡Nadie contrata una madre que la pasa bien! ¡Yo la desafío a rebelarse contra una madre que se divierta, señorita mía!

(*El lugar en el estudio de una escritora de teatro: libros, cuadros, computadora, papeles revueltos. Cuando se van entra con llave propia la Madre Sustituta. Madre Sustituta se cambia. Se quita la ropa negra. Se transforma diametralmente. Se convierte en una mujer internacional, viajada, exitosa, divina. Lleva una capelina esplendida, un zorro al cuello, camina como una modelo, imprime ritmo. Velocidad a todo. Tiene hermosas alhajas de buen gusto. Clase. Bárbara se deja el mismo pantalon ajustado con la musculosa del personaje anterior.*)

Madre Sustituta (*Irrumpe.*) Te queda espléndido ese look zafado. ¿Abortaste o vas a tener el chico?

Bárbara (*Se adapta rapidamente.*) Lo perdí. No vas a ser abuela. Quedate tranquila, ¡Te acabás de hacer un lifting y yo iba a darte un nieto!

Madre Sustituta Reconocé que era una mala jugada. Además, estoy saliendo con un tipo tan joven…y vos y yo odiamos la norma general.

Bárbara No decidas mis odios, mamá.

Madre Sustituta ¿Tenés whisky en este antro rosado? (*Bárbara le da.*) Es el cuarto que tomo en la mañana de hoy. Demos el día por perdido. ¿No vas a emborracharte conmigo mi vida? Hace tanto que no nos vemos. (*Bárbara se sirve. Beben.*) ¿Terminaste tu obra de teatro?

Bárbara ¿Cuál?

Madre Sustituta Esa que me tiene a mí de protagonista. ¡Qué bien me retrataste! Las escenas que me mandaste por correo a mi oficina de New York me resultaron desopilantes. Me tenés calada. Despótica, maléfica, fascinadora, divina. Hasta me ponías esta capelina y este zorro. Desde que lo leí en tu obra no me los saco ni para viajar en avión. Los encuentro tan teatrales. Me dan otro andar. (*Camina de aquí para allá.*) En la obra vos dudabas de que yo fuera realmente tu madre? ¿Han logrado confundirte vida mía?

Bárbara Si, la terminé. Ya la están ensayando.

Madre Sustituta ¡Te la arrebataron de la mano! También, con ese personaje central. ¿Y quién hace de mí?

Bárbara Glenn Close.

Madre Sustituta Espléndida actriz. Pero no da el tipo. Quiero decir, con todo respeto por Glenn Close, yo podría enseñarle algunos trucos para parecerse más a mí. No quiero sugerirle que tome el modelo real. Eso es inalcanzable. Es mejor que me reinvente. Pero hay ciertas claves de mi personalidad.

Bárbara Te imaginás que entre el señor director y ella sabrán cómo encarar el personaje.

Madre Sustituta Pero el personaje sabe cómo puede ser encarnado. (*Rompe el clima.*) Le falta rebeldía señorita. ¿No quedamos en que se iba a rebelar? Esa era mi exigencia. Ese es mi desafío ¡Vamos!

Bárbara (*Harta*) Soy yo la que exijo. Usted es mía. La alquilé muy caro. Pagué muy bien todo este esplendor que despliega. Pero usted puede más.

Madre Sustituta La tengo fascinada querida.

Bárbara (*Vuelve al rol de hija escritora de teatro.*) Nunca me dijiste lo de la adopción.

Madre Sustituta (*Revoleando el zorro*) Es un delirio de tu padre. Decile a mi ex marido que deje tranquila a las niñitas de quince años con las que circula por mis lugares preferidos de New York y que admita con cuánto amor te concebimos, Bárbara. Hoy es tu cumpleaños ¿no, mi vida?

Bárbara Cumplo treinta años mamá.

Madre Sustituta Cuánto tiempo. Qué vieja me estás poniendo. ¿Se me notan tus treinta años? Yo ya no sé qué estirarme. ¿Y vos te estiraste algo?

Bárbara ¿Te parece que necesito? ¿Me ves arrugada?

Madre Sustituta Esta es la edad de comenzar. Una edad peligrosa. Además, una estupenda escritora de teatro, que sale todo el tiempo en las revistas al lado de las actrices.

Bárbara ¿Te parece ? (*Se mira al espejo.*)

Madre Sustituta (*Rompe el juego.*) ¿Y la rebelión? Pero si está a punto de aceptar hacerse una cirugía estética cuando tiene el cutis perfecto.

Bárbara No puedo rebelarme contra vos, mamá. No puedo más que mirarte ir y venir, como una idiota! ¿Será por eso que me gustan las mujeres?

Madre Sustituta ¿Cómo que te gustan las mujeres?

Bárbara Me acuesto con hombres, pero me enamoro de mujeres.

Madre Sustituta En cualquier momento vas a tener curiosidad de saber qué es acariciar un cuerpo femenino. Te veo tentada.

Bárbara Estoy viviendo una gran pasión mamá. Ya di ese salto.

Madre Sustituta Espléndido. Me parece fantástico que te asumas. Basta de mundos hipócritas. ¿Y con quién estás viviendo esta gran pasión?

Bárbara Con tu amiga Lourdes.

Madre Sustituta ¡Lourdes! Me muero. ¿Cómo Lourdes que es tan moralista pudo hacernos esto?

Bárbara Las dos necesitábamos rebelarnos contra vos mamá. *(Se ríe a carcajadas. Corta el juego.)* ¿Vio como me rebelé? ¿Vió como la maté señora?

Madre Sustituta Admito que fue ingenioso lo de la pasión con la tal Lourdes.

Bárbara *(En hija)* ¿Te sirvo whisky mamá?

Madre Sustituta Es que tenés siempre un whisky tan malo.

Bárbara Me lo regala Lourdes.

Madre Sustituta Se repite hasta en eso.

Bárbara ¿A vos también te regalaba el mismo whisky?

Madre Sustituta El mismo whisky y en las mismas circunstancias. Fue la primer mujer de mi vida. Lourdes es hipnotizante. O por lo menos sabe donde golpearnos a vos y a mí.

Bárbara *(Corta el juego.)* Se está pasando de límite. Yo no pagué para que usted también tuviera una historia con Lourdes.

Madre Sustituta ¡Rebélese! No soy una madrecita incondicional que le ordena los cajones. Yo no sufro querida. ¿Cómo se rebela uno con una madre que no sufre?

Bárbara Usted vino aquí a darme los gustos.

Madre Sustituta Esta madre que le propuse da de este modo los gustos. No me va a dejar como una perdedora, acostándose con mi mejor amiga!

Bárbara Y usted no me va a revelar el día de mi cumpleaños, que el gran amor de mi vida fue también su amante. Me parece excesivo.

Madre Sustituta Ya le dije que estamos formadas para ser excesivas.

Bárbara Voy a matar a Lourdes, mamá. *(Pone el "Magnificat" de Bach.)*

Madre Sustituta O no. Escribí. Vos elaborás muchas cosas escribiendo. Además tenés mucho material. Una pasión triangular, todo servido. Si la matás en la ficción te va a aliviar la furia. Una pregunta ¿Esa camiseta te la regaló Lourdes?

Bárbara   La camiseta, los pantalones, el color de este cuarto y el Magnificat de Bach.

Madre Sustituta ¿También el Magnificat? Sacalo.

Bárbara (*Bárbara lo pone mas fuerte.   Toma una batuta y dirige la orquesta imaginaria.*) Celos ya tenemos. Y ahora sos vos la que está celosa, mamá. (*Se rie. La Madre Sustituta le arranca la batutta y la rompe. El Magnificat cesa.*)

Madre Sustituta Para eso pagó tan caro a Casa Matriz. Para salir ganadora en algunos juegos. No la dejé con culpa. Se pudo vengar. En fin...estas son alguna de las satisfacciones que Casa Matriz ofrece a su clientela.

Bárbara ¿Me va a dar la teta?

Madre Sustituta ¡No con esta ropa! (*Se quita la capelina. Se pone una combinación blanca, una enorme teta redonda. Se sienta. Bárbara se pone alegremente en sus brazos. Madre Sustituta saca el pecho lleno de crema.   Bárbara se prende al pezón. Suena una hermosa nana bellamente cantada.*)

Bárbara Hummmm Hummmmm Hummmmm...

(*Madre Sustituta aprieta la teta y empieza a salir una especie de espuma blanca como crema de afeitar con la que baña totalmente a Bárbara que asi, llena de esa crema, se le aferra al cuello.*)

Bárbara Es un final operístico. La voy a contratar la semana que viene.

(*Madre Sustituta se pone de pie. Se quita la teta y la guarda. Se viste con la ropa con la que vino. Bárbara sigue con su dedo llevandose crema a la boca. La madre sustituta hace las maletas. Guarda todos sus equipos.*)

Bárbara   No me dé detalles. Detesto los detalles cuando me abandonan...abandóneme con todo.   Déjeme destruída. Puede hacer la madre que debía hacer al comienzo.

Madre Sustituta ¿La que la llamaba María?

Bárbara (*Se acerca implorante.*) ¿No vas a darme un beso mamá?

Madre Sustituta Estás llena de...estás toda manchada...yo tengo un traje de Christian Dior (*La mira asquerada.*)

Bárbara Creía que era Coco Chanel.

Madre Sustituta Me estoy aburriendo de tus errores.

Bárbara (*Se limpia la crema.*) ¿Qué más?

Madre Sustituta Y también de tus aciertos.

Bárbara ¿A qué viniste mamá?

Madre Sustituta A que me devolviera los mil dólares.

Bárbara (*Corta el juego.*) Yo le debo setescientos dólares. Fíjese la factura de la Casa Matriz, señora.

Madre Sustituta El servicio de dar de mamar se cobra aparte. Y la limpieza de la habitación, también. Fíjese. Están en el contrato. (*Le muestra el contrato. Bárbara lo mira. Saca mil dólares del cajón y se los da.*)

Bárbara Ya no nos debemos nada mamá.

Madre Sustituta Preferiría no verte por un tiempo. Sos una hija muy.. ¿demandante? ¿Esa es la palabra?

Bárbara (*Rompe el juego.*) Si yo la elijo la semana que viene y pago, va a tener que volver.

Madre Sustituta ¿Con qué dinero?

Bárbara Voy a pedir prestado. Hay una serie de madres que me interesa que usted me haga.

Madre Sustituta La semana que viene comienzan mis vacaciones. Va a venir otra señora. Le recomiendo que pida por Anita Zavala. Es muy dúctil y además es gorda. Eso le agrega atractivos insólitos.

Bárbara Yo…la quiero a usted…es decir, no la quiero.

Madre Sustituta Yo tampoco la quiero. Aquí los sentimientos los dejamos de lado. Para eso tiene a su madre verdadera ¿Tiene madre verdad?

Bárbara Sí, claro.

Madre Sustituta ¿Y a cuál de todas se parece?

Bárbara ¿Y a usted qué le importa?

Madre Sustituta Me dio una ráfaga de celos verdaderos. Eso no debe sucederme. Adiós Bárbara. (*Le extiende la mano.*)

Bárbara ¿Y usted tiene hijos?

Madre Sustituta Las madres sustitutas nunca contestamos preguntas realistas. La imaginación se ve limitada. Recurra a Casa Matriz cada vez que lo necesite.

Bárbara (*Saca dinero. Le da cien dólares más.*) Merece una propina señora.

Madre Sustituta Los honorarios reales querida. No aceptamos propina. (*Tira el dinero, recoge su maleta y se va. Bárbara se queda sola en el escenario.*)

Bárbara (*Grita.*) ¡Mamá!

Apagón

de atras para adelante

DE ATRÁS PARA ADELANTE

Personajes
Simón Goldberg, 57 años. Industrial. Fabricante de elementos para baños (bañeras, inodoros, bidés,
etc.) Viudo hace diez años y casado hace ocho con una mujer que hoy tiene 35.
Luna Mantovani, 35 años, segunda esposa de Simón, ex-actriz.
Mariana Goldberg, 35 años, hija de Simón, íntima amiga de Luna.
Gregorio Murray, 37 años, esposo de Mariana hace seis años. Desde que se casó con Mariana ha trabajado con su suegro en la empresa.
Dolly Goldberg, 30 años, hija de Simón. Empresaria multimillonaria. Transexual. Antes se llamaba **Javier Goldberg.**
Paco Frías, 35 años, psicoanalista. Pareja estable de Dolly, con quien ha tenido tres hijas.
Operarios y Utileros

Escenario
(*Cerca de fin de año, mes de diciembre, época actual, día de calor tórrido en Buenos Aires. Living comedor del piso de Simón y Luna. Dos operarios en ropa de trabajo terminan de vaciar el piso por embargo de bienes. Se llevan cuadros, muebles, electrodomésticos, etc. Deben ser objetos caros y ostentosos. Uno se lleva un precioso candelabro de plata de siete brazos, símbolo religioso judío.*)

PRIMER ACTO

Simón   El candelabro de mi abuela Rebeca, ¡no! ¡A mi abuela no me la embarga nadie! (*Pelea por el candelabro. Finalmente el tipo se lo deja. Simón queda abrazando el candelabro.*)
Luna   Simón, ¡se llevaron cosas mucho más valiosas!
Simón   ¡Depende de lo que llames valioso! ¡El candelabro de mi abuela

no se lo van a llevar! ¡Tiene el valor de los afectos!

Luna (*Ríe angustiada viendo la reacción de Simón mientras se llevan todo.*)

Simón (*Mientras se llevan unas copas tipo trofeo de golf.*) Señor, ¡esas copas me las gané jugando al golf! ¡No creo que tengan valor de embargo!

Luna (*Se larga a llorar, perdida entre el infantilismo de Simón y el despojo general.*) Esto debe ser una pesadilla...yo tengo que despertarme. ¡Dios mío! ¡Esto no nos está pasando de verdad!

(*El hombre, indiferente, se la lleva igual. Finalmente queda el departamento vacío. Sólo con las sillas donde están sentados ellos. Los embargadores les hacen firmar un papel y se van. Luna y Simón quedan en las sillas, él con su candelabro.*)

Luna ¡Todo! ¡Se llevaron todo! (*Deambula por el espacio vacío, anonadada.*) ¿Cómo permitiste que las cosas llegaran a este extremo? ¿Cómo yo no me di cuenta? ¿Có-mo?

(*Ambos van y vienen como tratando de darse cuenta de la pérdida de todo.*)

Simón (*Camina abrazando al candelabro.*) Algo que no comprendo falló...Algo debo haber hecho mal...Quizás estoy viejo... Quizás ya no sirva...Nunca fui pobre, Luna... y ahora no tengo nada. Nada... Ahora veo las cosas del otro lado. Con este candelabro de plata llegó mi abuela a la Argentina... Y he llegado al mismo punto...Perdí todo.

Luna (*También camina.*) Yo sí fui pobre, Simón...y te aseguro que el otro lado es francamente inhóspito.

Simón (*La mira con gesto filosófico.*) Inhóspito...sí...inhóspito es un adjetivo adecuado. Pero no sólo es inhóspito, también es...desolador. Mirá este piso vacío... ¿No tiene una atmósfera...(*Busca las palabras.*) desasosegante?

Luna Bueno, desasosegante es una palabra sofisticada. ¡Para mí, tiene una atmósfera de mierda! ¡Si es que a esto lo podemos llamar atmósfera!

Simón ¡Atmósfera, claro! ¡Porque la atmósfera no se embarga! (*Desafiante*) ¡La atmósfera no se las puede llevar mis acreedores! ¡Al contrario, querida, cuantas más cosas se llevan los acreedores, más atmósfera te dejan!

Luna (*Cortando el lirismo*) ¡Yo me casé con el dueño de una gran fábrica de sanitarios, no con el poseedor de la atmósfera más desasosegante del planeta!

Simón Bueno, frente las experiencias límite, la gente cambia. ¡Quién antes fabricaba sanitarios, hoy es un filósofo del desasosiego que descubre que es dueño de una magnífica atmósfera! Si me viera mi mujer no lo podría creer, ella siempre vivió en la abundancia. Viajes, joyas, pieles, chofer... No le faltó nada a mi mujer.

Luna (*Harta*) ¡Tu mujer soy yo!

Simón (*Disculpándose*) Me refiero a Dorita, que en paz descanse. Ella vivió siempre como una reina. Y vos también, desde que te casaste conmigo... ¿O acaso te podías imaginar vernos algún día... así?

Luna ¡No, no me le podía imaginar! Es más, cuando me decías que no se vendía nada y que todo andaba mal, me parecía que te quejabas porque sí. No lo decías muy convencido.

Simón No quería asustarte, Luna...creí que entre Gregorio y yo íbamos a parar el desastre...pero...se precipitaron las cosas. Y ahora sólo nos queda transitar nuestra nada.

Luna ¡Querés decir que para vos es una experiencia existencial atractiva esto de haberte fundido?

Simón (*Calmo*) Quiero decir que me está por agarrar un infarto.

Luna (*Furiosa*) ¿Un infarto? Reventaste la fábrica, perdiste todo lo que teníamos y ahora para colmo ¿te vas a infartar?

Simón Me parece que sí, querida. (*Detectando síntomas*) Decime, ¿los infartos comienzan con cosquilleos en la lengua?

Luna No, así empiezan los flemones.

Simón Los infartos ¿no dan una cierta rigidez en las mandíbulas?

Luna Oíme, Simón: vos ¿dónde tenés el corazón? ¿En el paladar?

Simón (*Tocándose el paladar*) Es posible...es bastante posible...que tenga el corazón en el paladar. (*Cae redondo al suelo.*)

Luna Oíme, ¡vos no te podés borrar así!...Simón...dale, ¡esto no es un infarto...despertá! (*Se acerca. Lo ayuda. Simón se incorpora.*)

Simón (*Con nostalgia*) ¿Qué hay que hacer para infartarse, Luna?

Luna Me imagino que lo que nos ha pasado puede justificar un infarto. ¡Sólo que tu corazón parece estar bastante fuerte!

Simón (*Se pone de pie.*) Bueno, si no me voy a morir, ¡hay que vivir! Me fundí, pero te tengo a vos. ¡Nos tenemos el uno al otro! ¡Y eso es lo importante! (*Tratando de darle ánimos a su esposa*) ¡Luna te amo! Tenemos toda la vida por delante...¡empecemos de cero! (*La toma de la mano y la pasea por el espacio vacío.*)

Luna ¿Empecemos de cero? ¡Empecemos de bajo cero, porque sólo tenemos deudas! ¡No tengo fuerzas ni ganas! ¡Yo me casé con un hombre poderoso!

Simón (*Se agarra el estómago.*) Tengo miedo. El inodoro no se lo llevaron los embargadores, ¿verdad? (*Va corriendo al baño. Ella queda* *sola en escena. Pasea por el espacio vacío.)*

Luna ¿Por qué no me habrán llevado a mí también, junto con todas las cosas?

(Suena el timbre. Va a abrir. Son Mariana y Gregorio.)

Luna ¡Adelante, adelante! ¡Pónganse cómodos!

(Quedan petrificados ante la casa totalmente vacía. Hay un instante de estupefacción. No atinan a pronunciar palabra.)

Gregorio Es...insoportable...nunca creí que realmente fueran capaces.

Luna Fueron capaces. *(Luna y Mariana se abrazan.)*

Mariana ¿No hubo modo de impedirlo?

Luna ¡Todo lo contrario! ¡Cuanto más les rogaba que no se llevaran un cuadro que me gustaba, o mi colección de compact-disc, más placer sentían en arrasar con todo!

Gregorio ¡Qué manga de vampiros! ¡Se llevaron todo! ¡Nunca vi nada igual!

Mariana ¿Y el piano? ¿Mi piano?

Luna ¡Ah, les encantó! Un piano de cola...tan elegante...con tan buen sonido...¡debe dar gusto embargarlo!

Gregorio *(Se acerca a Luna y la abraza.)* Luna, ustedes son fuertes, capaces, ¡tienen toda una vida por delante! A Simón no lo derrotan tan fácilmente...esto es sólo un traspié. *(La retiene contra sí..)*

Luna Mariana...¿me podés sacar a tu marido de encima? No soporto ni la ironía sutil ni la imbecilidad optimista...salvo si viene acompañada de doscientos mil dólares.

Gregorio ¿Y de dónde querés que saque yo doscientos mil dólares?

Mariana *(Mirando con bronca a Gregorio)* Luna, no te preocupes. ¡Nosotros algo les podemos dar! ¡Algo para salir del paso les vamos a dar! Quiero que cuenten con Gregorio y conmigo.

Gregorio ¡Pará Mariana! Pará la mano...y consultame.

Mariana *(Fulminándolo con la mirada)* Gregorio.

Gregorio ¡Solamente te estoy pidiendo que me consultes!

Mariana *(A Luna)* En todos estos años en que Gregorio trabajó con papá hemos ido ahorrando para comprarnos una casa...pero...podemos darles una parte.

Gregorio *(Pálido)* ¿Una parte de qué?

Mariana *(Lo quiere matar.)* ¡No te hagas el imbécil en estas circunstancias, Gregorio!

Gregorio *(Gritando)* ¡Una parte de qué!

Mariana ¡Yo no voy a permitir que mi padre y Luna, que nos ayudaron siempre, pasen penurias!

Gregorio Yo creo que vos vivís en una nebulosa dorada.

Mariana ¡Y yo creo que vos sos un desagradecido!

Gregorio ¿Desagradecido? ¿Yo? ¿A que no te atrevés a decirlo delante de tu padre? ¿Dónde está Simón?

Luna En el inodoro. ¡El último inodoro Goldberg que nos queda! En estado de gracia…meditando. Y yo aquí…sola.

Mariana No estás sola, Luna.

Luna (*Abraza a Mariana. Luna está emocionada. Gregorio está furioso.*) Mariana, ¡yo sabía que vos no me ibas a fallar!

Mariana Te quiero…y siempre contamos con todo el apoyo de ustedes. Papá le dio trabajo a Gregorio y gracias a eso salimos adelante. Ahora nos toca a nosotros…(*Pausa. Le cuesta introducir el tema.*) pero también está mi…mi hermano Javier. De él se sabe que tiene una excelente posición económica.

Gregorio (*Sobresaltado*) ¿Javier?

Mariana Sí, mi hermano…mi único hermano. ¡Estamos al borde del abismo! ¡Basta de prejuicios! ¡Basta de rencores! Te lo digo de corazón. ¿Por qué no lo llamamos y le pedimos ayuda?

Gregorio Te escucho y no lo puedo creer…¡Ayuda a tu hermano Javier! ¡Es lo peor que le podés hacer a Simón, y vos lo sabés! Además me gustaría saber de dónde vas a sacar el coraje de…de enfrentarlo… después de…después de lo que pasó entre ustedes… (*Despechado*) ¡Yo creo que la desesperación genera grandes despropósitos! ¡En estado de desesperación surgen las miserias humanas! En estado de desesperación emerge en las almas un olor putrefacto…y las personas, incluida mi mujer,… dejan de parecer personas.

Mariana O quizás, empiezan por primera vez a darse cuenta de que realmente eran personas…quizás por desesperación se atraviesan los océanos que uno por cobardía no tuvo el coraje de atravesar en tiempos normales.

Gregorio Dejate de retórica. Vos le diste la espalda diez años igual que el resto de la familia.

Mariana Es una historia muy pesada…pero pasaron diez años…podemos pensar todo desde otro lugar…éramos muy jóvenes…podemos reconciliarnos.

Gregorio ¡Es una reconciliación bastante…interesada! Yo que tu hermano no creería en esta clase de reconciliación. Si se te hubiera ocurrido llamarlo el año pasado…¡pero hoy! ¡Mariana!

Mariana Hace mucho que quiero llamarlo…nunca me atreví…ahora estoy dispuesta.

Gregorio ¡Y él, sin duda, está dispuesto a mandarte a la mierda!

Mariana En esta situación tiene que estar aquí. (*Pausa*) Voy a pedirle ayuda.

(Esta última parte la escucha Simón que regresa).

Simón (*Retorciéndose*) ¡Ay! ¡Otra vez! ¡No puedo despegarme del inodoro! ¿A quién le quieren pedir ayuda?

Gregorio ¡Simón! (*Lo abraza.*) Simón, estás pálido...no te dejaron nada.

Simón ¿A quién le quieren pedir ayuda?

Gregorio No tiene importancia...son tonterías.

Luna ¡Claro que tiene importancia! ¡Tiene muchísima importancia que tu hijo sea rico y nos pueda salvar de la ruina!

Simón ¿Qué? ¿De qué hablan?

Luna Mariana, con mucha sensatez, le quiere pedir ayuda a tu hijo.

Simón ¿Ayuda a quién? Pero, ¿vos no sabés que "ése" ya no es más mi hijo? Mariana: ¿no me ves lo suficientemente humillado?

Gregorio (*Interviniendo a favor de Simón*) No se altere, Simón. ¡Yo no voy a permitir más humillaciones!

Simón ¡Y para colmo, usa mi nombre cada vez que abre un restaurant para maricones o una discoteca de hombres solos! ¡"Goldberg pito shop"! ¡"Goldberg culo beach!"! ¡"Preservativos de colores Goldberg"! ¡Usa mi apellido lleno de prestigio!

Luna (*Indignada*) ¿Prestigio?

Simón ¡Yo tuve un gran prestigio!

Luna (*Grita.*) ¡Te lo embargaron, Simón!

Simón (*Pausa. Está golpeado.*) ¡Lo eché a patadas de aquí cuando lo encontré en mi cama desnudo con el novio de Mariana! ¿O ya te olvidaste de eso, Mariana?

Luna ¿Eso hizo?

Gregorio (*A Mariana*) Nunca me contaste los detalles.

Mariana ¿Detalles? ¡Los detalles fueron preciosos! Yo estaba perdidamente enamorada de Nacho Bergman; tenía 28 años y el novio más hermoso de la tierra. Fijamos la fecha de boda, mandamos las invitaciones...todo era perfecto hasta que mi hermanito Javier se enamoró también de Nacho. Lo sedujo con su magnetismo irresistible...y ...quince días antes de la boda, papá y mamá los encontraron encamados.

Simón ¡En nuestra cama matrimonial!

Mariana Sí, yo había ido a visitar a una amiga...papá y mamá habían salido, pero volvieron temprano y...bueno...papá los echó a los dos.

Simón ¡Le dije que ésta ya no era su casa y que yo no era más su padre!

Mariana Y se fueron juntos de luna de miel a la India. Se raparon el pelo y me mandaban postales vestidos de naranja, al lado del Gurú Maharashi donde decían "Te amamos mientras hacemos el amor!" ¿Querés que te muestre las postales? Las tengo guardadas, ¡eran dos muchachos divinos! ¡Fue una experiencia inolvidable! Casi me suicido, ¡fue maravilloso! (*Todo este tema la angustia mucho. Pausa*) pero todo eso es parte del pasado...Papá, es tu hijo. Mi hermano. Es millonario...puede ayudar a su familia.

Simón ¿Ayudar? ¿ "Ése" ayudarme a mí? (*Pausa*) ¡Ustedes están todos en un complot! Pero para qué quieren heredar a un hombre fundido... me hubieran matado antes, algo no coincide con la realidad.

Luna ¿Qué realidad?

Simón Hay una realidad, un soplo que evoca que aquí vivió un tal Simón Goldberg, un hombre honrado que nunca estafó a nadie. Un hombre digno de llamarse hombre. ¿O ya ni siquiera hay una realidad?

Mariana La realidad indica que tenés un hijo que te puede ayudar.

Simón Quiero que sepan algo, los síntomas son contundentes.

(*Suspenso. Simón retorciéndose por el cólico da vueltas por el escenario y cae.*)

Luna Así no se infarta nadie, Simón. Así caminan los payasos en el circo...¡Ni infartarte sabés!

Simón (*Desde el suelo*) ¡Yo no tengo ningún hijo! ¿No es cierto Luna? (*Simón se levanta.*)

Luna Vos tenés un hijo. Yo no lo conozco. ¡Es una buena oportunidad!

Simón ¡Yo no tengo ningún hijo! Sólo tengo una gran atmósfera desasosegada e impía...(*Lo doblega un cólico.*) ¡Creo que me voy a desintegrar en el inodoro! Luna: con lo que quede de mí...¡no tenés más que tirar la cadena!

Mariana (*Encara a su padre con bronca.*) ¡Te advierto que voy a llamarlo!

Gregorio ¡No va a venir!

Mariana (*Decidida*) Yo voy a hacerlo venir. No puede negarnos su ayuda.

Gregorio Puede negarnos todo lo que se le ocurra.

Mariana Voy a traerlo.

Simón (*Desafiante*) Vos no vas a ridiculizarme más de lo que estoy...

Mariana Dejate de boludeces papá!

Simón ¡Me estás faltando el respeto! ¡Luna! ¡Decile algo!

Luna (*Irónica*) ¡Hijita!

Simón   (*Señalando a Luna*) Ella tampoco me respeta. Mi mujer me hubiera respetado en una circunstancia así.

Luna   Yo soy tu mujer y lamentablemente, en una circunstancia así.

Simón   Me refiero a la madre de mis hijos.

Mariana   ¿Ves como tenés un hijo?

Simón   No me confundan más. Todo esto me parece una pesadilla. ¿No será un sueño post-infarto?

Mariana   Vos no estas infartado papá. Estás en la calle.

Simón   (*Se apoya en Luna.*) Pediles, en nombre del respeto que alguna vez me tuvieron, pediles que no llamen a Javier.

Luna   Javier es TU hijo. Y yo lo quiero conocer.

Simón   ¿Conocer? Nunca tuviste esa inquietud.

Luna   Nunca viví con un filósofo del desasosiego. Nunca me faltó nada a tu lado y ahora me falta todo.

Simón   ¿Y eso qué tiene que ver con mi hijo?

Luna   Mariana dice que podemos pedirle que nos saque de esta atmósfera desasosegada e impía…y esa posibilidad me lo vuelve adorable. Sin conocerlo, lo quiero.

Simón   ¿Lo querés? ¿Ahora resulta que lo querés?

Luna   Tiene dinero. Yo no tengo prejuicios sexuales como vos.

Simón   Yo no tengo prejuicios sexuales… tengo vergüenza.

Luna   Estás viejo Simón. Viejo, pobre y con un falso orgullo de macho cabrío.

Simón   ¡Sí, macho! ¿O tenés alguna duda?

Luna   Últimamente…¡no sos lo que se dice el rey de la selva!

Simón   (*Cae de rodillas.*) ¡Piedad! ¡Un poco de piedad para Simón Goldberg, en sus últimos momentos!

Gregorio   ¡Basta! (*Se arrodilla al lado de él y le besa las manos.*) Yo te quiero…Simón…yo soy tu hijo…el otro es un fantoche.

Luna   ¡Un fantoche millonario!

Simón   ¡No me interesan sus millones!

Luna   ¡Te negás a pedirle ayuda al único miembro de la familia que nos la puede dar! (*Llora. Simón le da un pañuelo.*)

Simón   (*Llora.*) No soporto verte llorar.

Luna   Entonces llamá a tu hijo. (*Luna llora ostentosamente. Mariana la abraza y llora. Después llora Gregorio y finalmente los cuatro. Simón reparte pañuelos.*)

Simón   Todos ustedes me tiene…una especie de bronca que me hace pensar que mi único atractivo era el dinero.

(*Todos dejan de llorar.*)

Luna Era un atractivo fuerte Simón.

Simón (*Se agarra el corazón.*) ¡Siempre dijiste que el dinero era lo que menos te interesaba de mí!

Luna Eso creía.

Simón ¡Yo creo que si me decís con fuerza que te casaste conmigo por interés, puedo llegar a mi añorado infarto! ¿Empezamos?

Luna Me casé con vos, también por interés.

Simón ¿Así que todo mi erotismo era una fábrica de inodoros?

Luna Dije que el dinero era un fuerte atractivo en vos.

Simón Decí: "¡me casé con el viejo Simón Goldberg por su dinero!" ¡Vamos, que se viene el final! Decí: "¡era un asqueroso lascivo, pero tenía mucha guita!". ¡Vamos! ¡Vamos que lo logramos!

Mariana ¡Basta papá! Papá...estás desencajado...apoyate en mí.

Simón ¿En vos, que me querés ver de rodillas ante ese pervertido? Siento el intestino grueso en la oreja. ¿Eso es normal? Y el peritoneo me baila entre las dos cejas.   ¿Eso es siempre así? Entiérrenme en el cementerio judío, cerca de Dorita. Llamen al Rabino Steimberg, él sabe que soy un hombre de bien.

Luna (*Arrepentida*) ¿Qué sentís?

Simón Me siento...muy querido...soy un hombre amado. (*Cae redondo.*)

Luna ¡Así no son los infartos, Simón! (*Se exaspera.*)

Simón En la funeraria encarguen un cajón cómodo. Con aire acondicionado. No me gusta estar apretado bajo tierra ni pasar calor.

Mariana (*Al padre*) ¡Basta de chantajes! ¡Te anuncio que mi decisión es irrevocable!

Simón (*Se levanta.*) ¿Luna, me acompañás? No es muy sensual...pero...

Luna ¿Otra vez al baño?

Simón Es el único lugar donde me siento haciendo algo positivo. (*Salen.*)

Mariana (*A Gregorio*) Voy a proceder a llamarlo.

Gregorio (*Va hacia la puerta.*) Yo a esto no asisto.

Mariana Andá a dar una vuelta y traé algo para comer. En esta casa estamos todos muertos de hambre.

(*Gregorio sale. Mariana queda sola en escena. Busca su agenda en la cartera. Toma el teléfono inalámbrico y marca nerviosamente un número. Se arrepiente. Corta. Vuelve a marcar.*)

Mariana Buenas tardes...quisiera hablar con el señor Goldberg...sí sí...Goldberg (*Sorprendida*) ¿Dolly Goldberg? (*Incómoda*) No... disculpe...debo haber marcado mal. (*Controla.*) ¿Es el 0897? (*Escucha.*)

¿Sí?...¿pero Dolly Goldberg? (*Pausa*) Mire...quizás...quizás haya una Dolly Goldberg que no conozco...han pasado muchos años que no veo a mi hermano...Quizás se casó (*Le confirman.*) ¡Ah, se casó! ¿Hace mucho? (*Le responden.*) ¡Seis años! Bueno...¡qué sorpresa! ¡Me alegro por él! ¡Es un gran cambio! Mire...yo soy la hermana de Javier Goldberg y...hemos perdido contacto hace mucho tiempo...ni sabía que se había casado...bueno, yo también me casé y él tampoco lo sabe...(*Pausa*) Perdón, ¿con quién tengo el gusto de hablar? ¡Ah! ¡Usted es la secretaria de la señora Dolly! Bueno...yo le quiero dejar un mensaje a mi hermano...¿lo puede tomar? ¿Sí? ¡Muchas gracias! (*Mientras espera.*) ¡Se casó! ¡Se-ca-só! ¡Javier se casó! (*Vuelve la secretaria al teléfono.*) Ah, sí... (*Pausa. Se angustia.*) Dígale que le habló su hermana Mariana... (*Se larga a llorar.*) Disculpe...pero es para pedirle que venga urgentemente...que papá...que papá... (*Llora desesperadamente.*) Que papá está...dígale que... (*Se da manija y llora a los gritos con espasmos.*) ...venga ya...porque no nos queda tiempo...está en las últimas... (*Llora.*) Si es que no está muerto... (*Llora ostentosamente.*) ... Siento dar esta noticia por teléfono...pero sólo tiene dos hijos. Gracias ... muy amable. (*Cuelga. Cambio brusco.*) Le dejé un mensaje contundente.

Gregorio (*Entra Gregorio. Trae pizza.*) ¿Qué mensaje contundente? (*Abre la pizza y le sirve a su mujer.*)

Mariana Un mensaje definitivo. Tiene que venir sí o sí. Papá se muere ya.

Gregorio Te veo transformada. Ésa no es tu voz. ¡Vos estás planeando algo raro para traer ese maricón!

Mariana (*Lo encara.*) ¡No te voy a permitir que hables así de mi hermano! ¡Te informo que mi hermano se casó con una mujer llamada Dolly! ¡Es un señor casado! ¡Ha concluido su etapa gay!

Gregorio (*Pausa*) Te...te...¿te dijeron que se casó?

Mariana ¡Sí! ¡Hablé con la secretaria de su esposa! ¡La gente cambia!

Gregorio ¡Javier se casó! Bueno...¡qué noticia! ¡Rectificó el camino! ¡Todo un hombre! ¡Eso facilita las cosas con Simón! ¡Voy a decírselo!

Mariana Eso facilitará después...¡ahora hay que proceder!

Gregorio ¿Proceder?

Mariana Dije que papá...(*Mariana come pizza.*) agoniza...o quizás ya murió... (*Come ansiosamente.*) No fui clara, pero fui dura... (*Llora.*) Papá...te quiero... (*Llora.*)...pero tuve que matarte. ¡No había otra!

Gregorio Pero, ¿qué sentido tiene? En cuanto llegue se va a encontrar con su padre vivo.

Mariana (*Lógica*) Hay que matarlo.

Gregorio ¿Qué estás diciendo? *(Mariana y Gregorio comen pizza.)*

Mariana ¡Javier vendrá de un momento a otro, seguramente con su esposa Dolly, a llorar a su amado padre y aquí no tenemos amado padre muerto! *(Repite.)* Hay que matarlo.

Gregorio Los ojos se te ponen al revés...¡te sale bilis de las comisuras!

Mariana Una muerte leve...una muertecita transitoria.

Gregorio ¿Vos decís que hay que llevarlo a un estado de pre-infarto?

Mariana *(Furiosa con Gregorio)* ¿Yo dije eso? ¡Eso es tratarme de asesina...de mi propio padre!

Gregorio Marianita, ¡pará! ¡Marianita estás a tiempo de parar!

Mariana ¡Nada de "Marianita pará"! No querés solidarizarte con apoyo económico ni moral. ¡Pero nunca tuviste problemas en vivir a mi padre!

Gregorio Reconozco que yo era una rata cuando me casé con vos y que Simón me dio trabajo y nunca nos hizo faltar nada. Yo lo he querido como un hijo. Pero al fundirse él nosotros quedamos enganchados.

Mariana ¿Enganchados?

Gregorio Fundidos.

Mariana Pero...¿y nuestros ahorros? ¿Nuestra cuenta en Nueva York?

Gregorio Se lo di todo a tu padre...para tratar de salvarlo.

Mariana ¿Cómo no me dijiste nada? Ese dinero era de los dos.

Gregorio ¿Vos te hubieras opuesto a salvar a tu padre?

Mariana ¡No!

Gregorio Por eso ni te consulté.

Mariana ¿Nosotros también?

Gregorio Totalmente fundidos...*(Mariana y Gregorio se abrazan.)*

Mariana Entonces mi hermano tiene que salvar a toda la familia...

Gregorio ¿Qué razones puede tener para salvar a esta familia?

Mariana *(Baja la voz. Busca la complicidad de Gregorio.)* Bueno...papá grave...agonizando.

Gregorio Tu papá lo único que tiene es colitis. De eso no se muere nadie.

Mariana *(Sugiriendo)* ¿Cloroformo?

Gregorio Yo nunca fabriqué una muerte querida.

Mariana *(Lo acaricia para conquistarlo.)* Bueno, ¡algún día todas las personas hacemos lo que nunca hemos hecho! ¡Y hoy nuestro cielo indica que ha llegado ese día! ¡Cloroformo...cloroformo y coraje amor mío!

Gregorio No voy a ser tu cómplice en esto.

Mariana *(Lo besa.)* Yo sola no voy a poder...y Luna no va a querer.

Gregorio *(Hablan en voz muy baja.)* ¿Qué querés que haga?

Mariana Andá a la farmacia y volvé con algo que lo mate, sin matarlo...algo que lo...fulmine por un buen rato...

Gregorio ¿Un somnífero?

Mariana Un somnífero no sirve (*En secreto*) Algo contundente...

Gregorio Te brillan los ojos Mariana.

Mariana Es el brillo de la salvación.

Gregorio Es un brillo libidinoso, ¡me calienta! (*Se besan apasionadamente.*) Quizás haya algo que aniquile por contacto.

Mariana Vos, por ejemplo, a mí siempre me aniquilaste por contacto.

Gregorio (*Le acaricia los senos.*) ¿Y si se nos va la mano y lo matamos de verdad?

Mariana Vos movés muy bien las manos...(*Se besan.*) Andá...¡andá que hay que actuar antes de que lleguen Javier y su esposa Dolly!

Gregorio Esto es una locura...tengo miedo.

Mariana Yo también. Nunca maté a mi padre.

Gregorio ¡Y todo para impresionar a tu hermano!

Mariana Necesitamos que nos salve. Que no pueda negarse. Alto impacto. A mi hermano siempre le gustó sentirse un héroe. Démosle el gusto...¡ahora que es macho!

Gregorio Dame otro beso y me voy. (*Se besan apasionadamente.*)

Mariana ¡A vos también te brillan los ojos como carbones encendidos en la noche sin regreso! (*Pausa*) Debe haber productos nuevos.

Gregorio Te amo. (*Gregorio se desprende de ella y parte. Mariana queda sola. Entra luna a escena. Se sienta cerca de mariana. Está desencajada.*)

Mariana ¿Querés pizza?

Luna No tengo hambre, gracias. ¿Llamaste a tu hermano?

Mariana Sí, claro. ¡Tengo novedades! ¡Ya no es gay! ¡Se casó!

Luna ¿Pero sigue siendo millonario?

Mariana Multimillonario querida.

Luna No va a venir.

Mariana Yo creo que un hijo desea ver a su padre en un momento así.

Luna ¿Sí?

Mariana (*Le toma la mano.*) ¿Dónde está papá?

Luna En la cama de la mucama...es lo único que no nos embargaron...por dejarnos una cama.

Mariana Luna, no quiero ser brutal, pero papá está muy mal...pronóstico reservado...yo lo conozco...conozco muy bien a mi padre.

Luna Se quiere morir...no sabe cómo llegó a este desastre. Yo no sé como ayudarlo…creo que en este momento él quisiera tener a tu madre a su lado y no a mí… (*Pausa. Mariana la acaricia.*)   Yo fui feliz con Simón…pero él sin dinero es otra persona.

Mariana Luna…papá está realmente mal.

Luna Hecho polvo.

Mariana Algo más…no creo que sobreviva.

Luna ¿Qué estás diciendo?

Mariana   Comprendo que no hayas llamado al médico. (*Vuelve Gregorio. Tiene un pequeño paquete en la mano.*)

Gregorio ¿Y Simón?

Mariana (*Con complicidad de Gregorio*) Papá está descansando en el cuarto de la mucama…¿podés fijarte cómo está mientras nosotras terminamos una conversación privada?

Gregorio Sí, yo me ocupo…ustedes charlen tranquilas. (*Se mete en el interior del departamento.*)

Mariana (*Retomando*) Comprendo que no hayas llamado al médico… tal vez pensaste que si lo llamabas, papá se iba a asustar.

Luna Simón lo que necesita es descansar…y ahora encima va a reencontrarse con tu hermano después de diez años.

Mariana Tenemos la enorme ventaja de que, para hablar con el lenguaje de papá, Javier "volvió a la normalidad".

Luna La verdad es que va a ser la primera alegría del día para el pobre Simón. (*Vuelve Gregorio. Está pálido. Desencajado.*) Gregorio…a vos te pasa algo.

Gregorio (*Se larga a llorar en brazos de Luna.*) Para mí era más que un padre…y ahora…repentinamente.

Mariana Papá. (*Se abraza a Luna.*) Papá.

Luna   (*Pega un salto convencida de que se murió.*) ¿Qué le pasó a Simón?

Gregorio (*No deja de mover a Luna.*) Quedate tranquila Luna, ahora ya no hay apuro.

Luna ¿Cómo que no hay apuro?

Gregorio (*La sujeta con fuerza. Ella batalla por zafarse de Gregorio e ir a ver a su esposo.*)

Mariana (*Llora estruendosamente.*) Papá…papa.

Luna ¡Soltame, quiero verlo, tengo que verlo! (*Lo golpea.*) ¡Tengo que ver a mi marido! (*Pelean. Gregorio saca un algodón con cloroformo de su bolsillo y desmaya a Luna que cae redonda.*)

Mariana ¿A ella también?

Gregorio Se estaba poniendo pesada. (*Levanta a Luna en brazos. La* *sienta en una silla.*)

Voy a traer a tu papá acá, con cama y todo. Ayudame.

Mariana (*Como imaginando una "escena"*) A Luna la sentamos al lado de papá y le ponemos algo negro.

(*Van a buscar a Simón. Gregorio lo trae en brazos, desmayado, y Mariana trae la cama, que tiene ruedas. Arman el "cuadro": Simón en la cama, tapado. Luna, sentada a su lado, con el cuerpo sobre Simón. Mariana la envuelve en una mantilla negra.*)

Mariana Mirá lo que hiciste Gregorio.

Gregorio (*Orgulloso consigo mismo*) No está mal.

Mariana Y pensar que hasta hace una hora vos y yo éramos dos personas buenas.

Gregorio Vos seguís siendo buena, el ejecutor soy yo.

Mariana No sabés lo que te agradezco que hayas matado a mi papá.

Gregorio No lo maté. No lo digas así.

Mariana Para mí es como si lo hubieras matado...te felicito. (*Tomando distancia para observar la escena*) Un trabajo impecable. (*Le dan los últimos toque al "cuadro".*) Miralos: lívidos, inmóviles, rígidos. Una joya. ¿Te sentís poderoso?

Gregorio (*Los mira agrandado.*) Sí. Me siento bastante, bastante poderoso.

Mariana (*Orgullosa de su marido*) ¡Y el golpe maestro con Luna! Eso fue pura inspiración. Tenés arranques geniales.

Gregorio ¡Es la primera vez que siento que me admirás!

Mariana Es la primera vez que te admiro. (*Se besan largamente. Suena el timbre.*) ¡Puede ser mi hermano! (*Se pone algo negro y se coloca en pose de llorar. Se ubica al lado de la cama con la cabeza gacha como si estuviera tomada por el dolor. Estudia cuidadosamente su imagen.*

Gregorio va a abrir. Entra Dolly Goldberg. Dolly es una mujer espectacular. Tiene una figura impecable que sabe mover con extrema seducción, consciente todo el tiempo de lo que provoca. Lleva un vestido escotado y tacos altísimos. Un look muy moderno.)

Dolly (*Encantadora, frágil, conmovida*) Buenas noches...yo soy Dolly Gold-berg.

Gregorio (*Saludando a la supuesta mujer de Javier*) ¡Ah, sí...Dolly! Yo soy Gregorio Murray, el marido de Mariana. (*Está impactado por la belleza de Dolly.*)

Dolly Bueno, entonces somos...algo así como cuñados. (*Ambos dudan entre darse la mano y besarse. Gregorio define.*)

Gregorio ¡Sí! podemos darnos un beso. (*Se besan. Gregorio demora* *el beso.*)

Dolly   Y...los demás...(*Gregorio señala hacia el conjunto fúnebre formado por Simón y Luna sumidos en su sueño profundo y Mariana llorando. Dolly los mira y mira el espacio vacío.*) Pero...¿qué pasó? ¿Fue repentino...o?

Gregorio   Bueno, fue...consecuencia de un desastre económico...Simón quebró...está completamente arruinado...en bancarrota. Hoy le embargaron la casa y la fábrica...fue un impacto que lo llevó a este estado de colapso.

Dolly   ¡Ah...llegué a tiempo! ¡Yo sabía que lo encontraría con vida!

Gregorio   ¿Vino...viniste sola?

Dolly   Vine con mi marido...está estacionando el coche.

Gregorio   Mariana está impaciente por verlo.

Dolly   (*Sorprendida. No comprende.*) ¿A mi marido?

Gregorio   ¡Claro!

Dolly   ¿Y a mí?

Gregorio   A vos también...tiene curiosidad.

Dolly   ¿Curiosidad?

Gregorio   Bueno...es una curiosidad lógica. (*Suena el timbre. Gregorio abre. Es el marido de Dolly. Gregorio supone que es Javier. Es un hombre muy sexy. Viste un impecable traje blanco. Es alto, moreno, atlético, muy musculoso. Registra la casa vacía.*)

Paco   Disculpen no encontraba donde estacionar. (*A Gregorio*) Vos sos...

Dolly   (*Lo introduce.*) El marido de Mariana.

Gregorio   (*Emocionado, abraza a Paco.*) ¡No sabés qué importante es que estés aquí, hermano! (*Lo palmea efusivo.*) Gracias por el gesto de venir...a pesar de todo...

(*Paco vuelve a observar el espacio vacío. Mira a Dolly como interrogándola.*)

Dolly   Embargaron la casa y la fábrica...Simón no lo pudo soportar.

Gregorio   Gracias por tu capacidad de ser generoso.

Paco   (*Extrañado. No entiende bien.*) Yo vine por Dolly.

Gregorio   ¿Ella te ayudó a vencer los resquemores?

Paco   No...¡esta vez fui yo el que la ayudó a ella! ¿Verdad cielo? No le era fácil venir...(*Paco mira hacia donde están Simón, Mariana y Luna. Huele a cloroformo. Desconfía. Gregorio mira a Paco. Como para salir de la situación, se acerca a Mariana y la llama en voz baja. Mariana se acerca directamente a Paco, enjugándose las lágrimas. Ignora a Dolly.*)

Mariana   (*Perpleja.*) No...no...vos...no...pero ¿qué te hiciste Javier?

Vos eras más…menos…vos eras rubio…vos…¡vos no sos mi hermano!

Paco ¿Javier? Yo no soy Javier. Yo soy Paco Frías…el marido de Dolly.

Mariana *(Mira a Dolly de pies a cabeza.)* ¿Y mi hermano Javier no quiso venir?

Dolly Tu hermano Javier soy yo.

Gregorio y Mariana ¿Qué? *(Silencio petrificado)*

Mariana ¿Vos sos Javier Goldberg?

Dolly ¡Era Javier Goldberg, ahora, afortunadamente desde hace siete años soy Dolly Goldberg, estimada hermana mía!

Mariana ¿Te hiciste? ¿Te…te…convertiste en…mujer? *(No cabe en sí.)* ¿Te operaste?

Dolly Sí, claro, me operé en Londres con el mejor cirujano del mundo. Soy mujer de pies a cabeza. Saqué mis documentos en Chile. Donde dice sexo: femenino.

Mariana Quiero ver la cédula de identidad.

Gregorio ¿Para qué?

Mariana *(Está alteradísima.)* ¿Para qué? ¿Cómo para qué, Gregorio? *(Dolly saca del bolso su documento y se lo da.)* Cédula Nacional de Identidad N° 5.223.669. Fecha de nacimiento…12 de abril de 1964. Dolores Goldberg. Sexo femenino. *(Está atónita.)*

Dolly ¿No quedé divina?

Paco Divina!

Gregorio *(Se le escapa.)* ¡Divina! *(A Mariana que está anonadada.)* Bueno…¡espectacular! Nadie se daría cuenta. Yo, cuando entré vi un minón y ¡estaba convencido que era la esposa de Javier!

Mariana Pero te operaste…¿todo? Digo…¿las partes pudendas?

Paco Dolly tiene todo lo que hay que tener *(Le saca la cédula a Mariana y se la guarda.)* Todo. *(Paco se retira del grupo y comienza a observar el lugar.)*

Dolly Fue una decisión muy profunda y meditada. Me psicoanalicé mucho tiempo hasta que finalmente tuve claro mi deseo.

Mariana Psicoanalizada…y operada. ¿Con quién te psicoanalizaste, che?

Paco *(Desde la puerta que da al interior de la casa.)* Conmigo.

Gregorio ¿Vos sos psicoanalista?

Dolly ¡Por supuesto, no me voy a psicoanalizar con un veterinario! Me psicoanalicé con un post-lacaniano de primer nivel como Paco Frías. Cuando me dio el alta…¡me declaró su amor!

Mariana O sea que mientras era tu terapeuta no curtían.

Paco *(Está mirando el "cuadro" que armaron Gregorio y Mariana. Ha* *descubierto que todo es una escena armada*.) Tengo una ética profesional (*Comienza a acercarse a Mariana*.) No mezclemos todo. No mezclemos muerte con dinero.

Gregorio Se está poniendo intrigante.

Paco (*Sonríe a Dolly*.) ¡Dolly! ¡Tan inocente! (*La besa*.) ¡Tan valiente! (*Quedan entrelazados*.)

Dolly Fue el acto más valiente de mi vida…desde entonces…todo cambió…soy feliz. (*Mira a Paco enamorada*.)

Mariana ¿Feliz? ¡Para colmo es feliz! ¡Y lo dice tranquilamente! ¡No te creas que cualquiera puede decir soy feliz tan fácilmente! (*Pausa*) ¡Yo, por ejemplo, hace siglos que no soy feliz! (*Pausa. A Gregorio*) Qué te parece, ¡encima nos viene a refregar en la cara que es feliz!

Dolly ¡Soy muy feliz!

Mariana ¡Quedaste idéntica a mamá! ¡Idéntica a mamá!

Dolly (*Se desprende de Paco*.) Mariana, ¡dame un abrazo! Soy transexual pero no leprosa (*La quiere besar, ella pega un grito. Se asusta*.) Oíme, no contagia…¡dame un beso!

Mariana (*Furiosa*) ¿Un beso? ¡Ah, no Javier! Vos no podés seguir atacándome de este modo! ¡Me robaste a Nacho cuando me estaba por casar con él y ahora te convertiste en mujer cuando yo era la única hija de esta familia! ¡Para colmo en qué pedazo de mujer!

(*Paco ríe burlonamente por la reacción de Mariana y se acerca lentamente al cuadro armado por Simón y Luna. Los mira. Los toca*.)

Dolly ¿Por qué reaccionás así?

Mariana ¿Cómo reaccionarías vos si me vieras con bigotes, barba y un par de…entre las piernas?

Dolly Si eso te hiciera feliz…te diría ¡qué suerte que te atreviste!

Mariana ¡Lo que me parece increíble es que te hayas atrevido a venir!

(*Paco encuentra un algodón con cloroformo debajo de la cama. Lo huele. Lo guarda en el bolsillo*.)

Dolly ¡Recibí un llamado tuyo! ¡Papá agoniza!

Paco (*Desde su lugar. Provocando*) ¿Hay un diagnóstico? ¿Han llamado a un médico?

Gregorio (*Mira a Paco asustado*.)

Mariana No hubo tiempo…es decir…

(*Paco hace una seña a Dolly para que se acerque*.)

Dolly (*Decidida*) Quiero verlo.

Mariana (*Se interpone*.) Ni soñando.

Gregorio (*Quiere evitar un enfrentamiento. A Mariana*) Vino a ver a su padre… ¡Se llame Javier o Dolly, su padre está en el lecho de muerte!

Dolly ¡Hermana, yo no me transformé en mujer contra vos!

Mariana ¡A mí no me llames hermana!

Dolly (*A Dolly le duele esta respuesta.*) ¿Cómo querés que te llame? ¡Somos hermanas, Mariana!

Gregorio (*A Mariana. La separa de Dolly.*) ¡Superá, querida!

Mariana ¿Para qué te habré llamado? Me lo debí imaginar...siempre tengo que imaginarme que me vas a aplastar.

Gregorio (*Intercediendo. A Dolly*) Necesita tiempo...ella esperaba a Javier... ella llamó a Javier.

Dolly Ella tiene todo el tiempo del mundo. Yo me voy.

Paco (*Se acerca nuevamente al grupo. A Dolly, sugerente*) No Dolly...vos tenés que quedarte. Tenés que acercarte a tu padre.

Dolly ¡Mi padre! Mi querido padre... nunca tuvo el menor gesto de amor hacia mí.

Paco ¡Vos lo amás Dolly, vos mil veces me dijiste que lo amabas!

Dolly ¡Claro que lo amo! ¡Lástima que no sea recíproco! Por otra parte si mi hermana reaccionó con esta violencia, imaginate papá! Yo no puedo agregar más dolor a su dolor...¡vamos Paco! ¡Me equivoqué en venir! ¡Diganlé que su hijo Javier habló por teléfono para mandarle un gran abrazo final!

Paco Dolly, ¡no es bueno que vayas!

Dolly ¡Tomá conciencia Paco! ¡Si ni mi propia hermana se banca verme mujer! ¿Para qué lo voy a matar a mi padre con la novedad de que ahora tiene otra hija? ¡Que se muera de otra cosa! ¡Que se muera de su propia cobardía, de su fracaso vital, de su miedo a vivir!

Paco Vos sos la única que puede ayudarlo, mi amor...la solución no es que te vayas... Simón te necesita...aunque no sepa que te necesita...

Dolly Yo también lo necesitaba... Hace diez años que no veo a mi padre. (*Mariana está por hablar. Gregorio la fulmina con la mirada.*)

Paco No te vayas así. Por lo menos despedite. Está inconsciente. No te va a ver. ¡Yo te voy a acompañar hasta su cama! ¡Vení, acercate!

Mariana (*Se interpone.*) ¡No va a pasar ¡Yo tengo que defender a mi padre! Llamé a Javier y vino Dolly.

Dolly ¡Es mi padre, también!

Mariana ¿Y si abre los ojos? ¿Vos qué le vas a decir? ¿Que sos feliz?

Dolly ¿Por qué no?

Mariana ¡Yo a este lo mato! (*Se abalanza sobre Dolly. Dolly le da una piña contundente que la voltea. Paco levanta a Mariana.*)

Paco Ella tiene mucha fuerza física y espiritual. Vení...no vas a impedir que se acerque...y no es momento de armar todo este lío...vení. (*Paco* *aleja a Mariana. Ella se resiste con fuerza. Saca el algodón con cloroformo de su bolsillo y se lo encaja en la nariz a Mariana.*)

Gregorio (*Asustado. No sabe qué hacer. Confirma que Paco se ha dado cuenta de todo.*) ¡Sonamos!

(*Mariana se desmaya en brazos de Paco.*)

Paco (*Mientras acomoda teatralmente a Mariana en brazos de Gregorio.*) "Cuando la noche iguala al día, se alzan las tormentas del equinoccio. Cuando la luz artificial iguala a la violencia del sol, se desencadena la violencia del juego. Cuando dos mujeres se igualan en nuestra mente comienza el equinoccio del placer". ¿Has leído a Baudrillard?

Gregorio ¡Có...mo te...dis...te cuen...ta?

(*Dolly mira a Paco confundida. Trata de entender.*)

Paco Tu hermana sufrió un shock.

Dolly ¿Pero aquí todo el mundo sufre shocks?

Paco Sólo falta Gregorio...pero Gregorio va a portarse bien. ¿Verdad?

Gregorio (*Asustado y respetuoso de Paco*) ¡Muy bien! Creo que Dolly debería acercarse ya.

Paco Coincidimos. En algo coincidimos.

Dolly No creas que me resulta tan fácil acercarme... (*Dolly no se anima. Paco la lleva de la mano. La sostiene. Dolly se arrodilla en la cabecera del padre. Le toca la frente. La nariz. Le toma una mano y se la besa*). Papá...papá...papá (*Pone cara de asco. A Paco*) ¡Qué olor! (*Mira a Simón.*) Papá...papá... (*Se tapa la nariz.*) ¡Pero quién aguanta este olor!

(*Luna comienza a roncar.*)

Dolly ¿Y ella quién es?

Gregorio (*Sigue con Mariana en brazos, asustado y paralizado.*) Su esposa...se llama Luna...duerme profundamente...

Dolly ¡Ronca! ¡Está roncando! ¡Qué desagradable! Un olor sospechoso...gente roncando...esta "escena"...requiere silencio... requiere sensibilidad. (*Dolly le mueve la cabeza a Luna para que deje de roncar. Luna deja de roncar. Saca perfume con spray y los rocía.*) ¡Por lo menos que huelan a Kenzo! (*Dolly le tiende la mano a Paco que la ayuda a levantarse y a alejarse de ahí. Simón y Luna siguen dormidos. Cómplice a Paco*) Era muy importante verlo...sentirlo... (*A Gregorio*) o-ler-lo...después de todo este tiempo.

(*Gregorio asustado trata de despertar a Mariana.*)

Paco (*A Dolly*) Te diste cuenta .

Dolly Sí, me di cuenta al estar cerca...que todos ellos...succionando... (*Pausa*) Me di cuenta.

Paco Te diste cuenta de que te necesita de verdad.

(*Mariana abre los ojos en brazos de Gregorio. Lo mira y mira a Dolly.*)

Dolly (*A Mariana y Gregorio*) ¿Me quieren explicar qué es todo esto?

Mariana No sabía cómo hacerte venir.

Dolly Venir...y yo que venía a...

Gregorio (*Deja a Mariana y se para.*) Entonces...¿te vas?

Dolly Todo lo contrario. ¡Me quedo!

Paco (*Festejando*) ¡Se queda! ¡Se queda! ¡Se queda a pesar de ustedes! ¡Se queda con su papá! ¡Chicos algo les salió mal!

Mariana (*Se levanta del suelo ayudada por Gregorio.*) Cuando papá abra los ojos y te vea todo hecho una señora...los vuelve a cerrar para siempre.

Dolly Depende.

Mariana ¿Depende de qué?

Dolly Depende de mí.

Mariana Y de él.

Dolly Paco, necesito que te vayas.

Gregorio ¿Siempre sos así de rápida?

Paco Siempre. Ella "VE". Ella entiende más que nadie. De negocios, de la vida, de dinero, de padres...cambia de rumbo, cambia de sentido, improvisa, cambia de actitudes.

Mariana Cambia de sexo.

Paco Es una fuera de serie. Siempre gana...así hizo millones.

Dolly Andate Paco.

Paco ¿Estás seguro de lo que acabás de decidir?

Dolly Completamente. Quiero ayudarlo y quiero que me ame.

Mariana ¿Que te ame? ¿Que Simón Goldberg te ame?

Dolly ¡Va a adorar a Dolly!

Mariana Me rindo. Hacé lo que quieras.

Gregorio ¿Confiás en un milagro?

Dolly Confío en el amor.

Mariana (*Irónica*) "Te amamos mientras hacemos el amor" (*Se ríe.*) Te acordás de esa tarjeta que me enviaste de la India con Nacho. "Te amamos mientras hacemos el amor". Pobre viejo. ¡lo único que le faltaba!

Paco (*Decide irse.*) Me voy. (*Mira a Mariana y a Gregorio.*) ¡Ustedes esperaban un cheque al portador, pero llegó Dolly! ¡Dolly es mucho más que un cheque, Dolly es Dolly! (*Dolly acompaña a su marido a la puerta. Se despiden.*)

Paco (*Antes de irse*) Dolly sabe lo que hace... (*Paco se va.*)

Mariana (*Burlándose de Paco*) Dolly sabe lo que hace. (*Dolly se acerca, resuelta, a la cama. Gregorio y Mariana la siguen. Dolly sostiene una mano de su padre. Hablan en voz muy baja para no despertar a Simón ni a Luna. Irónica*) ¿Así que tenés tres hijas?

Dolly (*Asiente. Saca de su billetera una foto y la muestra.*)

Mariana (*Mirando la foto*) ¿Pero tuviste partos…normales?

Dolly (*Molestísima*) ¿A qué llamás…normales? Alquilamos un vientre.

Mariana (*Le pasa la foto a Gregorio.*) No quise molestarte Javier.

Dolly (*La corrige.*) Me llamo Dolly.

Gregorio (*Mirando la foto*) Parecen criaturas normales.

Mariana Sí... sí....parecen ... una familia feliz.

Dolly (*Frontal*) Hace mucho que espero que me llames.

Mariana ¿Y por qué no me llamaste vos, Javier?

Dolly (*Le saca la foto a Gregorio.*) Dolly.

Mariana Perdón. Es que no es fácil acostumbrarse. ¡Te pido que me tengas un poco de paciencia!

Dolly Yo también me tengo que acostumbrar… (*Mirando a Simón*) Cómo me gustaría que papá abriera los ojos.

(*Luna abre muy embotados los ojos. Debe advertirse que la droga que le dio Gregorio tiene efectos secundarios confusionales. No se ubica.*)

Luna ¿Se terminó la fiesta? ¿O vamos a seguir tomando champagne? (*A Simón*) Viejo, ¿vamos a casa? ¡No me gusta esta casa! Tiene una atmósfera desasosegada..

Gregorio (*Palmea a Luna.*) Luna…¡vamos…despertate!

Luna (*Por Dolly*) ¿Y esta mujer?

Dolly Hola... Soy la esposa de Javier Goldberg. (*Gregorio y Mariana se miran azorados.*) Soy Dolly Goldberg.

Luna (*La mira a Dolly de arriba abajo.*) Yo me imaginaba una esposa más…menos…bueno…no sé…no tan.

Dolly ¿Lo conocés a Javier?

Luna ¿Vino? ¡Me muero por conocerlo!

Dolly No. Me encargó a mí que viniera en su lugar.

Luna ¿Vos también sos millonaria?

Dolly Sí. ¿Eso te tranquiliza?

Luna Depende…porque si el hijo no quiso venir, la mujer no tiene porqué soltar un mango.

Gregorio (*Quiere matar a Luna.*) Luna…¿no tenés nada que hacer por ahí? Ventilarte…tirarte por la ventana.

Dolly (*Ríe divertida.*) Pero si es la única sincera.

Luna Soy la única sincera. ¿Viste Gregorio? Y te lo dice una millonaria.

Dolly Parece que te gustan los millones.

Luna Me enloquecen..son tan sexy. ¿No los encontrás afrodisíacos? Y pensar que me casé con un millonario que mirá...parece una bolsa de papas.

Dolly Sí, es una suerte que Javier no lo vea así.

Luna ¡Pero al contrario! Yo creo que si Javier venía en persona a decirle a Simón que se había convertido a la gran cofradía de los hombres...¡le perdonaba todo!

Dolly El que no le perdona todo a Simón es Javier.

Luna Entonces no va a soltar un mango.

Gregorio (*Se pone violentísimo.*) ¿Desde cuándo te interesa tanto el dinero de Javier Goldberg?

Luna ¿Por qué? ¿A vos qué te interesa? Sus manos, su voz, sus silencios? (*A Dolly*) ¡Se va a poner contento mi marido! (*Sacude a Simón.*) Simón, ¡sorpresa! Simón...¡tu hijo ya no es más gay...tiene una esposa divina!

Dolly (*Para con tranquilidad y firmeza los sacudones de* Luna) Volver es una decisión suya... (*Lo besa a Simón. Los mira a todos.*) ¡Ahora lo vamos a besar con concentración y amor!

Mariana (*Azorada*) ¿Qué vamos a hacer con Dolly Goldberg?

Luna (*A Mariana en voz baja*) Los millonarios son todos excéntricos, creen en la energía positiva y todas esas cosas. (*A Dolly*) ¡Voy a hacer todo lo que me digas!

Dolly ¡Besitos! ¡Vamos! ¡Todos juntos!

Mariana (*Contundente*) ¡Me opongo a esta ridiculez!

Gregorio (*Aparte. A Mariana*) Vos no te opongas a ninguna ridiculez.

Dolly Luna es sincera y tonta, pero Gregorio sabe negociar.

Luna No me gusta que me digas tonta.

Dolly Y a mí no me gusta que lo único que te interese a vos sean mis millones.

Luna También me gusta tu anillo. ¿Qué es? ¿Una esmeralda?

Gregorio (*Le tapa la boca a Luna.*) Te aseguro que ella está atontada...nunca la vi así.

Dolly También...¡con las drogas que vos repartís! (*Gregorio se pone pálido.*) ¡A besar a papi...vamos! ¡One...two...three! (*A una señal de Dolly todos, menos Mariana, lo llenan de besos.*)

Mariana (*Desesperada*) ¡Dolly Goldberg nos tiene en sus manos!

Dolly ¡Dolly Goldberg no quiere que Simón esté en manos de ustedes!

(*Simón mueve la cabeza y dormido murmura palabras confusas. Todos se quedan pendientes de él.*)

Luna Está reaccionando. (*Le levanta la cabeza.*) Simón.

Simón (*Mira a todos y se detiene en Dolly*) Dorita...qué joven estás. (*A los otros*) ¡Mi mujer! (*A Dolly*) ¡Al fin viniste, Dorita!

Dolly (*Le enfoca la cabeza hacia Luna. Contundentemente*) Ella es tu mujer.

Simón (*A Luna*) ¡Mi mujer es Dorita!

Dolly Gregorio, Luna quedó tonta, ¡pero Simón Goldberg quedó atrapado en la historia! ¡Arreglalo Gregorio, porque te meto en la cárcel!

Simón (*A Dolly*) ¿Te querés casar conmigo? Una gran boda.

Luna ¡Dorita se murió!

Dolly Yo...estoy casada con Javier, tu hijo.

Simón (*A todos*) Las cosas que dice... (*A Dolly*) Javier nos salió rarito...le gustan los señores...Dorita... ¡Sos tan linda! Te imagino vestida de novia...Dorita.

Dolly (*Categórica*) Gregorio Murray, ¡esta confusión es muy pesada para él y para mí!

Gregorio Simón, ¡cor-ta-la! ¡Estamos en el presente!

Mariana (*Le toma la cabeza la padre.*) Papá, no es mamá...es Dolly.

Simón (*Acariciando a Dolly que le quita las manos.*) ¡Do...Do... Dorita! ¡Cuánto tiempo te esperé...! ¡Sos mi gran amor!

Luna ¡Me hiere, me ofende, me mata que siga llamando a Dorita!

Dolly (*A Simón*) Ella es tu esposa actual. ¡Dorita murió! Vamos Luna, besa a Simón.

Luna ¡Que lo bese Dorita! (*Se va para adentro dando un portazo.*)

Dolly ¡Gregorio Murray! ¡Esto te va a salir muy caro!

Gregorio Simón, vamos viejo, saludá a tu nuera!

Simón Siempre quise a Dorita.

Dolly (*Harta*) ¡Soy Dolly, no Dorita!

Simón ¡Vení, metete en la cama conmigo! ¡Hagamos el amor y no la muerte! (*Simón trata de meter a Dolly en la cama. Forcejea para desnudarla. Dolly se defiende. Entra en pánico. Mariana interviene a favor de Dolly. Simón se la trata de sacar de encima para acostarse con Dolly. Desatado*) Vení mamita...no te ocupes tanto de los hijos...vení con papito. (*Logra montarse sobre ella.*)

Dolly (*A Gregorio*) ¡Hacé algo!

Gregorio ¡Basta! (*Gregorio saca a Simón de la cama y lo pone de pie. Mariana ayuda a Dolly a salir de la cama. Esta arregla inmediatamente su ropa. Vuelve Luna con un balde de agua en la mano.*)

Luna ¿Así que te querés acostar con tu nuera? ¡Desgraciado! ¡Te voy a matar! (*Roja de furia, le tira el balde de agua a Simán, quien cae al* *suelo.*) ¡Tu legítima esposa soy yo!

(*Dolly ayuda a levantar a Simón. Simón ve a Dolly.*)

Simón Gregorio, traé un balde de agua. *(Gregorio lo trae.)* Tirámelo sin miedo. *(Empapado, Gregorio no se atreve. Dolly se lo saca y le tira a Simón otro baldazo.)* ¡A mí no me mata nadie! ¡Nadie! ¿Entendido? Soñé que había vuelto Dorita, eso es todo. Luna, dame una toalla que tengo frío.

Luna Nos las embargaron, Simón.

Simón *(Dolly lo seca con las sábanas de la cama. Simón la mira extrañado.)* Gracias… *(Mira a Luna, Gregorio y Mariana.)* ¿Las lenguas también nos las embargaron?

Luna No querido.

Simón Entonces me pueden explicar ¿quién es este… esta… señora y qué hace en mi entierro?

Gregorio ¡Claro que sí! Ella es…

Mariana *(Cortando a su marido)* Llamamos a Javier.

Simón Me traicionaron. ¿Lo llamaste Mariana?

Mariana ¡Sí! ¡Lo llamé!

Simón Ya escuché. Llamaste…y…le pediste ayuda. ¡Te advierto que no voy a aceptar ni verlo ni que me ayude! ¡Soy pobre pero sigo siendo digno!

Mariana Con éste no se puede hablar.

Gregorio Simón… la gente cambia.

Luna Tu hijo no es más gay.

Simón ¿Qué?

Mariana Se casó. Javier se casó.

Simón ¡Sí, sí! ¡Mientras yo dormía! ¡Así que ahora me salen con el cuento de que se casó! ¡Yo necesito salir de este sueño absurdo, tengo que ir a trabajar, yo sin trabajo me vuelvo loco, yo soy un laburante, me hice de abajo, tengo que ir a la fábrica; las cosas que tengo que oír, por favor! Dame la corbata, poné el coche en marcha, vamos a trabajar Gregorio.

Gregorio No tenemos dónde ir a trabajar, Simón. Nos fundimos.

Simón Fundido yo deliro, ahora resulta que mi hijo se casó.

Mariana Te presento a Dolly Goldberg, la esposa de Javier.

Simón ¡Basta de tomarme el pelo! ¿Ahora me van a decir que mi hijo se casó con este pedazo de mujer?

Dolly Nos casamos hace siete años.

Simón ¡Que me lo diga el propio Javier en la cara!

Dolly Javier no quiere verlo.

Simón ¿Por qué?

Dolly ¿Cómo por qué?

Simón ¿Yo qué le hice?

Dolly ¡Lo echó a patadas de esta casa hace diez años y le dijo que no lo consideraba más su hijo!

Simón (*Pausa*) ¡Bueno...claro...pero...como verá, parece que...al muchacho le hicieron bien mis patadas!

Dolly (*Se le llenan los ojos de lágrimas.*) ¿Sus patadas? ¿Pero qué está diciendo, Simón Goldberg? ¡Sus patadas! ¡Le hicieron mucho mal!

Simón ¿Y usted cómo sabe?

Dolly (*Furiosa*) ¡Yo sé! ¡Yo sé que necesitó años para recuperarse de usted! ¡ Y también sé que no quiere volver a verlo!

Simón No quiero entrar en discusiones, pero a veces, de hombre a hombre.

Dolly (*Cortante*) No quiere verlo. (*Simón se queda mudo. Silencio general*)

Simón ¿Así que Javier...?

Dolly Tenemos tres nenas.

Simón ¿Soy abuelo?

Dolly Sí. Simón.

Simón Bueno...le agradezco...que al menos usted...

Dolly Sí, yo vine. Aquí me tiene.

Luna Bueno...ahora lo único que falta es que la otra parte.

Simón ¿Qué otra parte?

Luna Querido, la parte principal. Ella vino a traerte dinero.

Dolly ¿Dinero? ¿Quién dijo eso? Yo vine a traer amor.

Apagón

SEGUNDO ACTO

(*Varios meses después. Al encenderse las luces el espacio antes vacío, ahora está poblado de una moderna y audaz decoración. Todo tiene una suerte de alto vuelo, frescura, audacia y espíritu creativo. Gregorio se viste con un traje gris y una corbata muy tradicional como reacción frente a la modernización general del vestuario que advertiremos en todos. Entra cargado de rollos de papel higiénico de diversos colores muy brillantes: azul, rojo, violeta, verde, etc. Luna retoca su maquillaje.*)

Gregorio Luna…Luna, necesito hablar con vos.

Luna (*Le da un beso. Quiere ver los rollos.*) ¿Ya salieron?

Gregorio (*Indignado*) Estimada Luna, ¡te presento a nuestra nueva línea de papel higiénico Goldberg! Lanzado bajo el slogan: "Déle una alegría a sus rayas íntimas".

Luna (*Encantada, desenrolla y se envuelve en los papeles higiénicos como si fueran telas.*) ¡Son divinos!

Gregorio ¡Invendibles, Luna! ¡Hemos hecho una inversión enorme en este producto que no va a tener salida!

Luna· ¿Por qué ese pesimismo, Gregorio?

Gregorio Porque conozco a la gente. Estamos en una sociedad respetable. ¡El argentino siempre se ha limpiado con colores suaves! ¡El blanco es el predilecto! ¡Y los más arriesgados son amarillo patito, rosa bebé o celeste pálido! ¡Esa es la realidad de nuestras rayas íntimas!

Luna ¡El nuestro es un pueblo con humor! ¡Vas a ver como se impone esta nueva línea!

Gregorio ¡Pensá por ejemplo en un Ministro de Educación! ¡En un oficial del Ejército! ¡En el Gerente del Banco de Kioto! ¡Pensá en un obrero metalúrgico! ¡Pensá en todos ellos en el inexorable, cotidiano, inevitable momento de limpiarse la raya íntima!

Luna (*Cierra los ojos y los visualiza.*) Los tengo. Están con los pantalones caídos…a punto de cortar un pedazo de papel…

Gregorio Bien…¿a vos te parece que ese pedazo de papel puede ser verde lechuga o rojo violento o azul eléctrico?

Luna (*Vuelve a cerrar los ojos.*) Los veo..los estoy viendo ir y venir con el pedacito de papel…(*Festeja.*) ¡Les quedan muy simpáticos esos colores…en contraste con las nalgas!

Gregorio ¿Simpáticos?

Luna ¡Divertido! Total el culo se lo tiene que limpiar todo el mundo, así que resulta más alegre en technicolor.

Gregorio ¡Esto va a generar incomodidad en muchos sectores de nuestra sociedad! ¡Atenta contra los fundamentos de la vida familiar!

Luna Gregorio, ¡hasta ahora la innovación del diseño nos ha dado un gran resultado!

Gregorio ¡Hasta ahora! ¡Pero todo tiene un límite!

Luna ¿Y el límite son unos colores brillantes?

Gregorio ¡Es poco argentino limpiarse el trasero con colores brillantes!

Luna ¡No entiendo esta relación entre la argentinidad, el trasero y los colores brillantes!

Gregorio ¡Si no entendés eso, no entendés la esencia del hombre que habita nuestro país!

¡Se podría hacer un tratado sobre el tema! ¡La relación es más que directa!

(*Llega Mariana. Ve los papeles higiénicos.*)

Mariana ¿Ya salieron de la papelera? ¡Quedaron divinos!

Gregorio ¿Vos también?

Mariana ¿Vos no?

Gregorio Querida, ¡sabés que me opuse desde el primer momento!

Mariana Gregorio, ¡vos te opusiste a todo desde el primer momento!

Luna ¡Y todos los diseños nuevos se vendieron a raudales!

Gregorio Esta ERA la empresa de sanitarios más seria del país!

Mariana ¡Así nos fue, con tanta seriedad!

Gregorio Hay una sutil inculpación en lo que decís.

Luna ¿Sutil? Yo creo que Mariana te está diciendo directamente que a Simón le faltaba un socio con imaginación.

Mariana ¡Eso lo estás diciendo vos , Luna!

Luna Bueno…¡entonces decile vos lo que pensás!

Mariana Gregorio querido…

Luna Voy a dar instrucciones a la cocinera. Ya saben que Simón está a dieta.

Gregorio ¡Ya sabemos que Simón es un hombre nuevo! ¡Antes le gustaban los fideos con pesto y ahora adora la lechuga con limón a la Dolly! (*Quedan solos Mariana y Gregorio. Gregorio está muy ofuscado.*)

Mariana Creo que lo del papel higiénico ha desatado en vos...

Gregorio Oíme Mariana…en el baño de casa no se te ocurra ponerme papel "rojo fuego" porque…

Mariana Porque vos sos un hombre serio.

Gregorio Soy un hombre. Eso es todo.

Mariana Te veo exageradamente tomado por el tema: "Soy un hombre. Eso es todo".

Gregorio Por suerte en este grupo familiar hay alguien que no está tomado por el tema: "FUI un hombre. Eso es todo".

Mariana Gregorio…creo que estás enojado…injustamente.

Gregorio ¿Y quién hace justicia conmigo? ¡Yo estuve al lado de Simón en los momentos más duros…y ahora está empaquetado, envuelto con un moñito en una situación humillante..! ¡Esa psicópata, nos tiene bailando a todos! ¡Y sobre todo a él! Porque a mí no logra envolverme con sus mohines de…pervertida…ni con sus papelitos de colores. ¡Yo sé dónde está el bien y dónde está el mal! ¡Yo tengo todo mi aparato mohines!

Mariana ¿Y si fuera tu hermana o tu hermano, Gregorio?

Gregorio En MI familia somos todos normales. ¡Nor-ma-les! Los hombres somos hombres y nos gusta ser hombres y nos atraen las mujeres. ¡Pero en TU familia querida…está todo patas para arriba y un anormal se nos ha montado en la cabeza y nos dirige y nos demuestra que la vida es divertida! ¡Y propone negocios geniales que para colmo le salen bien! ¡Pero hay veces, como ahora, que yo veo con claridad que esta inversión en papeles higiénicos de colores no va a funcionar…y nadie me hace caso!

Mariana (*Tratando de calmar a su marido*) Gregorio, en poco tiempo, en menos de medio año, Dolly ha logrado imponer un tipo de sanitarios ultramodernos que evidentemente indican que ella sabe lo que el mercado de consumidores argentinos necesita… Es transexual…pero eso no le resta…talento comercial…ni capacidad de riesgo…su visión comercial.

Gregorio (*La corta.*) No voy a discutir su visión comercial…porque los números hablan por sí solos.

Mariana Mi amor , Dolly nos levantó los muertos, nos salvó las deudas, nos sacó del pozo. (*Le rodea el cuello con los brazos. Trata de calmarlo.*) ¡La única condición que puso para salvar a toda la familia fue apostar a un cambio en la empresa!

Gregorio ¡Estoy harto de tanto cambio!

Mariana ¿Harto de nuestro coche nuevo? ¿Harto de nuestra casa en Las Lomas*? (Lo besa seductora, le desanuda la corbata.)* ¡Te queda tan bien ganar dinero, Grek! Las corbatas de seda italiana te caen desde la nuez, en cascada hasta el sexo…tan provocativas. (*Le abre los botones de la camisa.*) ¡Hasta tu manera de besarme tiene un estilo…depurado…sin angustias económicas! Besar sin angustias económicas cambia la vida de una pareja. Los besos de las personas con agobio económico son tensos …desconcentrados. ¡En cambio estos besos ricos, opulentos! Compará nuestros besos con los de antes…vení, concentrate. (*Se besan. Él se aleja. Ella lo atrae hacia sí.*)

Gregorio En esta empresa soy un cero a la izquierda.

Mariana ¡Pero nuestra cuenta bancaria tiene cada vez más ceros a la derecha! (*Lo besa.*) ¿No nos propusimos eso cuando trajimos aquí a…? ¿No nos propusimos recuperar los ceros a la derecha? ¡No nos salió nada mál!

Gregorio ¿Cómo que no nos salió mal? ¡Se nos instaló! ¡Se adueñó de la empresa!

Mariana ¿Pero vos te creías que iba a soltar ceros a la derecha a cambio de nada? ¿Qué te pasa amor? ¿Todavía creés en los Reyes Magos? ¡Imponete!

Gregorio   Yo no me quedo nunca callado pero las votaciones son siempre iguales: dos a uno. ¡Simón nunca me apoya! ¿Qué carajo le hizo? ¡Está hipnotizado!

Mariana ¡Hipnotizalo vos! Gregorio...vos tenés con qué hipnotizar.

Gregorio (*La besa.*) Sí, claro, tenés razón. ¡Yo tengo con qué! (*Franelean. Caen sobre un sillón. Gregorio se exalta*). ¡No voy a dejarme aplastar! ¡Te lo juro!

(*Se enredan apasionadamente. Entra Dolly y los ve. Viene cargada de rollos de colores. No la perciben. Dolly los observa y después, casi chillando*)

Dolly ¿Interrumpo chicos? ¿Les corto algo importante? ¡Por mí no se inhiban! ¡Adoro el sexo incómodo, a quemarropa, en público!

Mariana (*Con bronca*) ¿Interrumpir? ¿Vos? ¡Siempre fuiste tan respetuosa con mi vida!

Gregorio Hablábamos precisamente de vos.

Dolly Me imaginaba...¿hay algo más calentante que yo?

Mariana ¡YO!

Gregorio (*Se levanta.*) Bueno chicas...¡no se peleen por mí! ¡Hay para todas!

Mariana (*Se levanta.*) ¿Qué? ¡Cómo que hay para todas!

Dolly ¡Yo sólo me peleo por los colores del papel higiénico! ¡Miren qué colores saqué de fábrica! ¡Dorado imperial! ¡Azul fluorescent, Amarillo Van Gogh! (*Buscando a Simón*) ¿Mi socio está?

Gregorio ¿Y yo qué soy? ¿Tu cadete?

Dolly Me refería a mi papá...es decir a mi suegro.

Gregorio Mariana...quiero hablar a solas con la mujer...quiero decir con tu hermano...¡quiero decir con la mujer de tu hermano!

Dolly (*Coqueteándole*) ¿A solas? ¿Conmigo?

Gregorio Sí tesorito. Sí angelito del cielo. Sí preciosura. A solas... contigo.

Mariana No jueguen con fuego que se van a quemar.

Dolly ¡Cuánta agitación! ¿Qué te pasa nena? ¿Vos creés que a mí tu marido me mueve algo?

Gregorio (*Herido*) Bueno, tan feo no soy. ¿O sí?

Dolly Qué querés mi vida, ¿que deschave que somos amantes?

Mariana ¡Yo me voy...porque si me quedo los mato! (*Mariana se retira dando un portazo*).

Gregorio (*Cambia el clima. Se pone serio.*) Dolly...yo...

Dolly Ya sé…te parecen horribles.

Gregorio Espantosos.

Dolly Ya están hechos.

Gregorio ¡Y a vos te encantan!

Dolly ¡Me parece una ruptura de la convención del acto pretendidamente solemne por excelencia! Si nos va bien.

Gregorio (*La corta*) Nos va a ir mal.

Dolly ¡Vos no apostás al juego como posibilidad de flexibilizar las mentes! (*Pausa*)

Gregorio Dolly…quizás lo tomes a mal pero…yo no me siento bien fabricando estos papeles. No los suscribo. Y por lo tanto…

Dolly ¿Sí?

Gregorio Sin intención de herir tu sensibilidad y reconociendo tu talento para innovar y pegarla…yo…yo…yo quisiera participar de algunos negocios…y de otros no… (*Pausa*) ¿Es eso posible en nuestra sociedad?

Dolly Por supuesto…pero no cometas esa tontería ahora.

Gregorio Yo quiero que me devuelvan mi parte en este negocio. Me retiro de este aspecto…digamos…de la empresa.

Dolly ¡No seas insensato! ¡Esto va a ser un éxito! ¡Hay que creer en la gente!

Gregorio Es porque creo en la gente y en mí que pido retirarme del rubro "Déle una alegría a sus rayas íntimas".

Dolly Bien, entonces retirás tu parte en esta inversión.

Gregorio Sí...solicito formalmente retirar mi parte.

Dolly ¿Querés esperar a Simón para comunicárselo o te extiendo un cheque por la cantidad que pusiste?

Gregorio Voy a esperarlo. Pero la decisión está tomada.

Dolly Te estás equivocando.

Gregorio La que se está equivocando sos vos.

Dolly Lo tuyo parece una cuestión de principios.

Gregorio Es una cuestión de principios.

Dolly ¿No deberías presentar una candidatura bajo el lema "Traseros aburridos, uníos"?

Gregorio Detesto tu ironía cuando está la moral en el medio.

Dolly Y yo detesto la moral cuando está la ironía en el medio.

Gregorio Dolly, que quede claro; yo no participo de este negocio.

Dolly ¡La dignidad no se negocia!

Gregorio ¡Exactamente!

(*Vuelven Mariana Y Luna.*)

Mariana Bueno, ¡mi marido está de buen humor!

Gregorio ¡Tu marido…se siente bien consigo mismo!

Dolly (*Irónica*) Tu marido…es un hombre…muy hombre.

Simón (*Llega radiante Simón. Su llegada debe contrastar enormemente con el Simón del primer acto. Se lo ve contento, dinámico, feliz. Lleva un traje moderno y una corbata de buen gusto y divertida.*) Dolly, Gregorio…familia…¡lo logramos!

Mariana ¿Qué logramos papá?

Simón ¡Traigo un notición!

Dolly ¿Qué pasó?

Simón ¡Pasó que cuatro cadenas de supermercados compraron la producción total de los papeles higiénicos de colores, pasó que hay que ponerse a producir el triple, pasó que la gente comenzó a comprarlo ni bien lo vio, pasó que esto es ya un suceso económico! ¡Eso pasó!

Dolly ¡Yo le dije, Simón!

Luna ¡Yo te dije, Simón!

Simón (*A Dolly*) ¡Todo lo que dijiste es poco! ¡Sos un genio del diseño! ¡Tenés un talento impresionante! ¡Sos una fuera de serie! (*Registra a Gregorio*) ¡Gregorio! ¡Te quedaste mudo! (*Pausa*) Gregorio (*Mira con silencio denso. Mariana mira implacable a su marido. Luna se ríe.*) Gregorio…¿no vas a darme un abrazo?

Gregorio ¿Un abrazo? Sí, por supuesto…

Mariana ¿Y?

Simón (*Atrae para sí a Gregorio y lo abraza.*) Vos y yo… tenemos que ser capaces de disfrutar este éxito y de valorarlo aún más…

Gregorio Sí.

Mariana Es que Gregorio no lo puede creer…

Gregorio No.

Simón Sentís una gran emoción, como yo…

Dolly (*Lo encara.*) ¿Es eso lo que verdaderamente sentís?

Luna Se siente feliz.

Dolly (*Lo increpa.*) ¿Te sentís feliz?

Gregorio Sí…estoy porque…veo. ¡Es maravilloso! ¡Me alegra tanto! (Gregorio *estalla. Agarra los papeles de colores y los tira por aire como serpentinas.*) ¡Me siento feliz de estar en este negocio! ¡Me siento feliz del éxito! ¡Me siento feliz de estar asociado a gente como Dolly Goldberg!

Mariana Gregorio…no hace falta que hagas tanto despliegue…

Luna Yo que vos me callaría la boca Gregorio…y me metería las ganancias en el bolsillo.

Gregorio   ¡Mariana! ¡Luna! Yo les dije que esto era lo que el país necesitaba para sentirse parte del primer mundo!

Dolly   (*Dura*) Gregorio, vos lo que dijiste es que te querías abrir de este negocio.

Gregorio   Bueno... ¡suelo ser impulsivo!

Dolly   Dijiste que ni bien llegara Simón ibas a pedir que te devolviéramos la inversión.

Gregorio   ¿Yo?

Mariana   Gregorio, ¿dijiste realmente eso?

Gregorio   ¡Lo que realmente importa no es lo que dije, sino que esto es un éxito!

Luna   Por supuesto. ¡Vamos a festejar! (*Luna sale.*)

Dolly   Gregorio...me imagino que vas a ser consecuente y te vas a retirar. ¿O acaso tu criterio en concepto de traseros nacionales desapareció por unos cuantos mangos?

Simón   Debés haber entendido mal, Dolly.

Dolly   (*Encara a Gregorio.*) ¡Hablo de que sos todo un hombre!

Gregorio   ¡Por supuesto!

Dolly   ¡Un hombre de palabra!

Gregorio   ¡De una sola palabra!

Dolly   Entonces sé coherente.

Mariana   Dolly...por favor.

Dolly   ¿Por favor qué?

Mariana   Vos dijiste que venías a esta casa a traer amor.

Dolly   Amor sí...pero a avalar mentiras, no.

Gregorio   (*Salta. Muy provocativo*) ¿No? No has venido a avalar ninguna mentira? Sos transparente y sincera todo el tiempo? ¿Estás segura? ¿Estás segura Dolly Goldberg de estar diciendo toda la verdad? (*Chantajeando*) ¿O querés que sea más explícito? Quiero decir...¿querés que yo la cante toda completa? ¿Querés que despleguemos toda la verdad Dolly querida? ¡Así que soy un hipócrita! ¿Querés que midamos nuestras respectivas capacidades de mentir?

Mariana   ¡Basta, Gregorio!

(*Dolly está muy tocada.*)

Gregorio   ¡La sincera, la impecable, la perfecta e inobjetable Dolly! (*Pausa*)

Dolly   ¿Me estás amenazando?

Gregorio   ¡Vos estás acusándome de mentiroso! ¡Es posible que yo ...a veces...no sea del todo consecuente...que a veces...bueno...no son cosas graves,   al menos no son las cuestiones de fondo! ¡No son cuestiones de fondo como las tuyas!

(*Entra Luna y mira a Simón interrogándolo.*)

Simón No entiendo nada, nos va bien, metimos un éxito sin precedentes y ellos se pelean.

Gregorio (*Atacando de nuevo*) ¿Vos estás segura de no ocultar nada?

Mariana ¡Gregorio! ¡No sigas!

Simón Dolly, ¿qué me ocultás?

Dolly (*Grave*) Gregorio sin duda se refiere a su hijo…Javier.

Gregorio ¡Exactamente! ¡Es el tema favorito de Simón!

Simón ¡Ay! ¿Por qué? ¿POR QUÉ, Luna?

Luna No me interesan los temas menores. ¡No me interesa la gente que no sabe gozar! ¡Hoy abro el champagne gigante! ¡Explotemos de felicidad! (*Besa a Simón.*) ¡Me prometiste la esmeralda, Simón y hoy ya no tenés excusas! (*Luna toca la campanilla.*)

Simón ¿Pero por qué?

Gregorio ¿Por qué, qué? ¿Por qué no viene a verlo ahora que es todo un hombrecito?

Mariana (*Intentando que su marido se calle*) Gregorio…

Simón ¡Gregorio tiene razón! Yo estoy dispuesto a arreglar las cosas. ¡Si soy capaz de ponerme este traje violeta, puedo reconciliarme con mi hijo! ¡Y hoy es el día indicado! ¡Este éxito también es suyo!

Luna ¿Hoy? ¿Justo hoy? ¡Hoy quiero disfrutar! ¿Por qué te empeñás en arruinarnos la felicidad de ser ricos? ¡Nunca fui tan rica! ¡Quién diría que unos cuantos papeles higiénicos eran la llave del paraíso!

(*Entran dos mucamos con champagne para todo.*)

Luna ¡Siempre quise tener mucamos hombres! ¡Champagne francés para todos!

(*Los mucamos abren las botellas gigantes de champagne. Producen una gran explosión.*)

Gregorio (*Irónico*) ¡Vivan los papeles higiénicos de colores!

(*Los mucamos sirven champagne en copas muy altas. Luna reparte copas.*)

Luna ¡Ahora sí que nos parecemos a nosotros! ¡Somos gente de mundo!

Dolly ¿De qué mundo, Luna?

Luna Del mundo de la gente bien.

Gregorio ¡Salud! (*Todos brindan.*)

Simón ¡Estamos todos reunidos! ¡Llamalo Dolly, decile que está perdonado!

Mariana (*Bebiendo*) ¡Pero si él no te pidió perdón!

Luna ¡Bebé, Simón y dejate de complicar las cosas! (*Luna sirve más* *champagne a todos.*)

Simón (*Bebe un trago.*) ¡No me pueden negar la alegría de ver a mi hijo!

Dolly (*Acercándose a Simón*) ¡Simón Goldberg! ¡No sé si usted es sordo, ciego o todo junto, pero ya le dije mil veces que Javier no quiere verlo!

Gregorio (*Provocando*) Pero usted puede mirarla a ella. ¿La ve, Simón?

Simón Sí, la veo.

Gregorio (*Bebe su champagne.*) ¿Y qué ve?

(*Simón cae redondo al piso.*)

Luna ¡Otra vez con los infartos!

(*Dolly y Mariana ayudan a Simón a levantarse.*)

Mariana (*A Gregorio*) Yo no seguiría molestando a una persona de la edad de papá.

Simón Por favor, un médico. (*Se sienta en un sillón. Cierra los ojos.*) Aire... Aire.

Luna (*Apantallando a su marido con una mano y con la otra bebiendo champagne.*) ¡Antes de infartarte definitivamente me vas a comprar el anillo de esmeraldas y un juego de gargantilla y pulsera de rubíes como los que usa la Reina de Inglaterra! ¿Me oíste amor?

Gregorio Abra los ojos y mire lo que ve ...¿qué ve, Simón?

Simón Veo que somos ricos...y me da colitis.

Luna ¿Todo te da colitis?

Simón Todo.

Dolly Bueno, papel higiénico sobra, Simón...así que puede permitirse una colitis.

Gregorio Pero antes me va a decir qué ve en vos.

Mariana (*Nerviosa*) Gregorio ¿qué te pasa?

Luna (*Intentando cambiar el clima*) necesita beber...trabajó demasiado para vernos felices. ¡Champagne para Gregorio! (*Luna sirve más champagne a Gregorio que bebe.*)

Gregorio ¿Por qué no la huele, Simón? ¿No siente un olor familiar?

(*Simón se para y huele a Dolly. Estornuda.*)

Simón ¿Cambiaste de perfume, Dolly? No soporto...me mareo...Luna ...agarrame.

Mariana (*Aparte. A Gregorio*) ¡Es un hombre mayor! ¡No soporta esta clase de pruebas!

(*Simón cae redondo al piso. Luna le tira champagne para reanimarlo.*)

Luna No lo mareen.

(*Simón se levanta solo. Se ríe.*)

Simón ¡Qué bien me siento de mal! No sé ni lo que veo...pero veo todo doble...Luna te prometo que si viene Javier te regalo la esmeralda y los rubíes.

Luna ¡Hay que traerlo, Dolly! ¡Es imprescindible!

Simón Si lo traen...¡muero de felicidad!

(*Luna abre otra botella de champagne y sirve a todos.*)

Luna ¡Ni se te ocurra morirte ahora! (*Todos brindan.*) ¡Salud, dinero y amor!

Dolly (*Con burlona ironía*) ¡Dinero, dinero y dinero!

Mariana (*Ídem*) ¡Amor, amor y amor!

Gregorio (*Ídem*) ¡Salud, salud y salud!

(*Chocan las copas con tal furia que derraman el champagne. Están todos bastante mareados. Suena el teléfono. Gregorio atiende.*)

Gregorio ¿Hola? Sí Leonor, soy yo...Gregorio. ¿De la Cámara de Diputados un pedido de 10.000 rollos de papel higiénico color Dorado Imperial? ¡Bravo! ¡Por supuesto...tómeles el pedido! ¡Voy para allá! (*Cuelga.*)

Mariana ¡Diez mil rollos!

Luna ¿Los diputados también tienen colitis?

Dolly Gregorio, en este negocio no cabemos los dos. O te vas vos o me voy yo.

Simón (*Imponiéndose*) ¡Se quedan los dos!

Dolly Pero...

Simón ¡Se quedan los dos porque lo digo yo!

Luna ¡Qué hombre de agallas! ¡Ese es el Simón que yo amo!

Simón ¡Yo también! ¡Este es el Simón Goldberg que yo amo! (*Simón está muy borracho.*) ¡El que tiene una vos potente y una autoridad indiscutible! (*Bebe champagne.*) ¡Y el que va a lograr que su hijo venga! ¡Porque para mí la familia es lo primero! ¡Quiero ver a mi familia unida! ¡Basta de peleas insípidas!

Dolly ¿Insípidas?

Simón (*Inapelable*) ¡Besá a Gregorio, Dolly!

Luna (*A Dolly*) ¡Es una orden!

Dolly ¿Yo? ¡Béselo usted!

Luna (*A Simón*) ¡Es una orden!

Simón ¡No tengo ningun inconveniente en besarlo! (*Simón se acerca a Gregorio y le da un beso muy teatral.*) ¡Yo no pierdo mi hombría de bien por estas nimiedades! ¿Soy menos macho por un besito insignificante? ¡Al contrario, mi masculinidad se asienta! (*Le da otro beso teatral a Gregorio.*)

Gregorio ¡Basta! ¡Otro beso más y vomito!

Simón ¡Esperaba una respuesta más romántica, Gregorio! ¡Besá a Dolly... No voy a permitir fisuras en el momento de mayor éxito!

Gregorio ¡Por qué me habré casado con esta familia! ¡Yo soy un tipo standard! ¡Un argentino normal! ¡Pero me estaré volviendo loco! ¡Loco! (*A Simón*) ¿Querés que bese a Dolly?

Simón ¡Claro que quiero que beses a Dolly!

Dolly y Mariana ¡No!

Luna ¡Sí!

(*Gregorio se acerca a Dolly y la besa en la boca. Dolly le da una cachetada. Mariana le da una cachetada a Dolly.*)

Gregorio ¡No aguanto más las pavadas familiares! ¡Me voy a la oficina! ¡Tengo que trabajar! ¡Alguien se tiene que ocupar de que el negocio funcione! (*Gregorio se va dando un portazo. Mariana y Dolly quedan enfrentadas. Simón llora.*)

Luna ¡Estás feliz! ¡Nunca te vi más feliz!

Simón (*Llorando*) Tengo ganas de ir al baño...Me gustaría estrenar ... papel higiénico Rosa Salvaje...

Luna (*Levanta varios rollos y se lleva a Simón para adentro.*) Permiso...yo también tengo colitis. ¡Voy a probar el amatista tropical! (*Salen. Mariana y Dolly quedan a solas.*)

Dolly ¿Qué te pasa?

Mariana Lograste que Gregorio esté loco por vos...todos estamos locos por vos...¿qué más querés?

Dolly ¡Irme!

Mariana ¡No, Dolly Goldberg! ¡Eso no te lo voy a permitir! ¡Ni eso ni que me robes a mi marido!

Dolly Oíme.

Mariana ¿Ya se acostaron? ¡Decime la verdad! ¿Fingen estar enfrentados para cubrir lo otro? (*Dolly se ríe y besa a Mariana. Mariana está tomada por los celos.*) ¡El beso que te dio no parecía el primero! ¡Siempre te gustaron mis hombres! ¡Siempre! Lo que me hiciste con Nacho nunca te lo perdoné..

Dolly Estoy enterada, darling. ¡Diez años sin hablarme!

Mariana ¡Yo estaba por casarme y vos!

Dolly Oíme..¿vas a seguir revolviendo viejas heridas?

Mariana No. ¡Ahora quiero revolver las nuevas!

Dolly ¿Y si no revolvieras nada?

Mariana (*No puede contenerse.*) ¿Hacen el amor en hoteles alojamiento?

Dolly Jamás en mi vida he pisado un hotel alojamiento. Y eso que soy dueña de cuatro. Uno para hombres gays. Otro para mujeres gays. Otro para militares que se acuestan con travestis...y otro para la tercera edad...

Mariana ¡Te estás yendo por la tangente! ¡Mirame a los ojos y decime la verdad! ¿Sos amante de mi marido?

Dolly ¿Yo? ¿Dolly Goldberg? ¿A vos te parece?

Mariana ¡Y pensar que fui yo la que te llamé! ¡Te entregué a mi esposo! ¡No me lo quites Dolly...yo lo amo! (*Reacciona.*) No pienso humillarme. Que Gregorio elija. (*Pausa*) Tuve que llamarte...¡papá agonizaba!

Dolly ¿Papá que? ¡Vos me llamaste para que los saque a todos de la ruina! ¡Para eso me llamaste! ¡Y yo vine...y satisfice tu pedido querida hermana! ¿O no? No queda ampliamente saldada mi deuda.

Mariana (*Interrumpe.*) ¿Cuánto hace que me meten los cuernos? Decime...no me mires con esa cara de víctima. Prefiero saber la verdad.

Dolly ¡La verdad! ¡La verdad es que me están usando como un forro! ¿Alguna otra acusación para hacerme? ¿Así que me acuesto con tu marido..? Si vos tenés problemas con tu marido.

Mariana ¿Problemas ¡Nunca tuvimos problemas...y vos no vas a ser mi problema!

Dolly ¡Yo, por el momento, soy tu solución! ¡Tu solución y la de tu marido y la de Luna y la de Simón Goldberg! ¡A mí me pidieron soluciones y traje soluciones! ¡Ahora...si encima querés tirar un balde de excrementos encima, tirámelo tranquila, total aquí colitis sobra...y papel higiénico, también! ¡Pero a mí, Gregorio no me gusta! ¡NO ME GUSTA! ¡Gregorio no me gusta!

(*Simón y Luna entran como para salir a la calle.*)

Simón ¡No es necesario que te guste, lo tenés que querer, querida!

Dolly ¡Yo tengo que querer a mi marido! ¡Tengo el mejor marido del mundo. Tengo un marido buenmozo...brillante...que me ama...y me aguanta todo!

Simón Javier. ¡Traémelo, Dolly!

Dolly No puede.

Luna Tiene que poder.

Simón ¡Yo quiero que venga!

Luna ¡Y yo, quiero las joyas!

Mariana ¡Y yo quiero que se vayan a pasear!

Simón En eso estábamos...me llevo papel para casos de apuro.

Luna ¿Y si llevaras la chequera para casos de apuro? ¡Harías más feliz a tu mujer! (*Luna arrastra a Simón hacia afuera. Se van. Dolly mira a*

Mariana con bronca.)
Dolly   ¡Me estabas acusando...no cortes...seguí querida hermana... quiero saber cuánta bronca acumulada tenés...seguí! ¿Qué más?
Mariana Dolly.
Dolly   ¡Fue un disparate quedarme! ¡Soy una desubicada!
Mariana Dolly...perdoname...estoy viendo fantasmas.
Dolly   (*Se encoge de hombros.*) Dejalo así.
Mariana Dolly ...quiero que sepas que yo...a pesar de que a veces no se me note...y otras veces yo me esfuerce para que no se me note...y otras veces, cuando se me nota, me esfuerce para que parezca lo contrario...quiero que sepas que te quiero.
Dolly   ¿Qué?
(*Mariana le da un beso.*)
Dolly   Basta de sentimentalismos absurdos, nena. Recién me acusabas de lo peor y ahora.
Mariana ¡Te pedí disculpas, che! ¿O no me escuchaste? (*Se miran. Ríen juntas.*)
Dolly   No te escuché. ¡Pedime más fuerte!
Mariana (*Grita con todo.*) ¡Andate a la mierda, Dolly Goldberg!
Dolly   (*Grita.*) Ahora sí que te escuché.
(*Se ríen. Todavía algo borrachas. Se abrazan.*)
Mariana ¿No tenés que ir a tu casa?
Dolly   Me peleé con Paco.
Mariana ¿Otra vez?
Dolly   Otra vez.
Mariana ¿Qué te pasa?
Dolly   Está celoso...¡se siente excluido del clan familiar!
Mariana ¡Tiene razón, ni siquiera le presentaste a papá!
Dolly   ¡Todos tienen razón! ¡No hay nadie que no tenga razón! ¡Gregorio tiene razón porque desde que yo aparecí pasó a segundo plano! ¡Paco tiene razón porque desde que entré en esta casa, no lo veo nunca! ¡Papá tiene razón porque está desesperado por ver a Javier que es su legítimo hijo y no a mí que soy su ilegítima nuera! Vos tenés razón porque .. porque...
Mariana (*Se ríe a carcajadas.*) ¿Por qué tengo razón, Dolly?
Dolly   Porque perdiste un hermano...y eras la única mujer...y...
Mariana ¿Y vos por qué tenés razón?
Dolly   ¡Yo perdí la razón! Entre tanta gente razonable, ¿qué fragmento de razón puede quedarme?
Mariana La razón de ser Dolly.

Dolly ¡Esa no es una razón, esa es una persona! ¡Y no me confundas Mariana!

Mariana ¡La confundida soy yo!

Dolly ¿Vos? Y a vos ¿qué te confunde?

Mariana Te veo y extraño a Javier.

Dolly A mí me pasa lo mismo: te veo y extraño a Javier.

Mariana ¡Ah, eso sí que no! ¡Vos eras Javier! ¡Y yo lo extraño! ¡A Javier la que lo extraña soy yo! Sobre todo…cuando te veo.

Dolly Mariana, ¡vos no vas a decretar la prohibición de que yo me extrañe a mí!

Mariana ¡Quizás extrañes ser Javier! ¡Pero yo extraño estar con Javier!

Dolly Yo extraño estar con vos…siendo Javier! ¡Qué bien la pasábamos!

Mariana (*Se enlazan físicamente.*) Sí, qué bien, qué bien…la pasábamos.

Dolly Me acuerdo de … cuando vivíamos en Flores…y nos escapábamos al parque Avellaneda a mangarle guita a la gente…disfrazados. ¡Fuimos todo un suceso barrial: THE GOLDBERG BROTHERS! ¡Nuestro primer trabajo! ¡Nuestro lanzamiento al mundo! Mariana, ¡qué épocas gloriosas!

Mariana (*Impactada*) ¿Vos realmente? (*Le parece increíble.*) Dolly, ¿vos extrañás en serio a Javier?

Dolly ¡Muchísimo…no solamente a Javier…nos extraño a nosotros de entonces…extraño a los Goldberg Brothers!

Mariana No sabés qué alegría me da que no hayas renegado…de…que no hayas renegado de nuestra adolescencia.

Dolly ¿Cómo se te ocurre? Yo recuerdo absolutamente todos los detalles …teníamos un camarín en el desván. Vos me maquillabas a mí y yo a vos. (*Pausa*) Fuimos tremendamente audaces.

Mariana Yo…(*Pausa, le confiesa algo muy secreto.*) Sabés cuántas veces en todos estos años en los que no nos vimos venía sola, sin que nadie lo supiera, al sótano de esta casa y sacaba nuestro equipo de … nuestra ropa.

Dolly No me digas que todavía queda algo de…Mariana, ¡es nuestra vida…es…no me digas que hay algo de aquella época!

Mariana Un día, buscando en el sótano un ventilador, descubrí una caja… la abrí y descubrí que mamá había guardado prolijamente con naftalina nuestros disfraces.

Dolly ¡Mamá! ¡Gracias! Sos un ángel.

Mariana ¿Querés verlos?

Dolly ¡Me muero por verlos! ¡Sí! The Goldberg Brothers … qué jóvenes, qué hermosos y qué insensatos.

Mariana Ayudame.

(Dolly y Mariana vuelven con una caja gigante y dos pares de zancos. Abren la caja y dentro hay disfraces de fracs, galeras y pantalones largos para cubrir los zancos. Hay juegos de malabarismo, bolos para tirar al aire, juegos de magia. Enloquecidas por descubrir esas cosas de la adolescencia se visten y se montan en los zancos. Mariana hace juegos malabares. Dolly da vueltas la manivela de un organillo donde suena la cumparsita y otros tangos remanidos con sonido a lata y calesita.)

Dolly ¡Señoras y señores del distinguido barrio de Flores, Floresta, Caballito, Primera Junta y todo aquél que por un motivo u otro vea en esta joven pareja de cómicos un futuro promisorio y próspero! Con ustedes, nosotros…¡The Goldberg Brothers!

Mariana ¡Nosotros hemos nacido para entretener a la gente, cosa que tiene su mérito porque…no hay nada más ofensivo que lograr que las personas se olviden por un momento…de sus reales vidas espantosamente…reales y vuelen como esta paloma que *(Se saca la galera y dentro hay una paloma embalsamada.)* que será embalsamada pero es legítima paloma del barrio de Flores, embalsamada especialmente por el artista Celedonio Marturano, para que cuando yo la muestre mi hermano comience su magnífico show!

Dolly ¿Qué show?

Mariana ¡Sacabas fuego por la boca Javier!

Dolly ¿Yo? ¿Fuego por la boca? ¿Y cómo hacía?

Mariana Te metías kerosene por delante de los dientes, encendías una antorcha, te la acercabas a la boca…y…¡flash! ¡Todo el público aplaudía …y nos tiraban monedas…muchas monedas. ¡Fue nuestro primer gran negocio!

Dolly ¡No me animo! ¡Es más fácil fabricar papel higiénico de colores! Mirá si me quemo la lengua, ¿con qué lo beso a Paco esta noche para reconciliarme?

Mariana Ves…¡ese es el Javier que yo extraño! ¡El que se incendiaba la boca!

Dolly ¡Pero teníamos más números…tan exitosos como lo del fuego ... teníamos una canción…y una coreografía!

Mariana Sí, después de tu fabuloso número del fuego, cantábamos y bailábamos…nuestro tema.

Dolly ¡Lo cantaba todo el barrio, podíamos haber sido famosos!

Mariana ¡Nuestro tema Javier!

(*Se preparan y recuerdan la canción de entonces. Bailan y cantan juntas.*)

> Querida mía, hoy que no llueve
> abrí el paraguas del sueño leve,
> azules días, dulces y breves,
> soplos de amores que nos suceden.
> Y NO TE DEJES BAJAR
> DE ESTE BELLO LUGAR
> Querida mía, hoy que no llueve,
> subí escaleras que al cielo lleguen
> absurdas tardes viajan en trenes
> locas pasiones que nos envuelven.
> Y NO TE DEJES BAJAR
> DE ESTE BELLO LUGAR
> Querida mía, hoy que no llueve
> ponte un vestido con luces verdes
> mágicos besos que la luz bebe
> somos ahora todos los siempres.
> Y NO TE DEJES BAJAR
> DE ESTE BELLO LUGAR
> Querida mía, hoy que no llueve
> vuela conmigo, juntos se puede
> el tiempo traza su gesto tenue
> vale la pena tocar su frente.
> Y NO TE DEJES BAJAR
> DE ESTE BELLO LUGAR

(*Se abrazan. Se tiran al suelo agotadas.*)

Mariana A veces siento que somos tres: Mariana, Javier y Dolly.

Dolly Es que somos tres…(*Se sacan los disfraces y los guardan en la caja.*)

Dolly y Mariana (*A la caja*) ¡Te queremos Javier! (*Al retrato de Dorita*) ¡Te queremos mamá! (*Ambas se abrazan. Están felices.*)

Dolly ¿Puedo poner "Casta Diva", en homenaje a mamá?

Mariana Por supuesto.

(*Dolly pone el compact con la callas cantando "Casta diva". Ambas se recuestan, agotadas, y escuchan el aria. Las luces van decreciendo hasta apagón. "La Callas" permanece a todo volumen. Al finalizar la música, se encienden las luces lentamente. Es otro día. En escena está Dolly, sola, trabajando con una computadora. Tiene anteojos puestos. Una montaña de papeles amontonados sobre su mesa de trabajo. Bebe un licuado de bananas. Tiene aspecto de ejecutiva de empresa norteamericana en febril actividad. Suena el teléfono, Dolly atiende.*)

Dolly   Sí ...¡ah Giménez! Estaba esperando su llamado ...¿Cómo? Nos convienen los importados...bueno, mitad nacionales y mitad importados, entonces...sí, compre...compre Giménez...estamos muy atrasados con las entregas. ¡Pero eso son detalles, Giménez!, ¡lo importante ahora es comprar! ¡Ud. compre! (*Suena el timbre.*) Lo tengo que dejar...pero manténgase en contacto! Chau...sí...muy bien...chau (*Cuelga.*)

(*Abre la puerta con una carpeta en la mano, sumergida en su trabajo y sin esperar en absoluto que quien llama es su marido. Cuando lo ve se le cae la carpeta. Se quita los anteojos. No puede creerlo.*)

Dolly   ¿Qué hacés vos acá?

Paco   ¿Puedo pasar?

Dolly   (*Duda. Finalmente lo deja pasar, consciente de que no hay nadie.*) Pasá. Pero...

Paco   Pero no tendría que haber venido. (*Paco recorre interesado el lugar.*) ¡Quedó muy divertida tu decoración! (*Paco se pasea por el ambiente. Dolly está muy nerviosa con su presencia. Lo mira pasearse.*) No parece ponerte contenta la sorpresa que te di...

Dolly   Paco...vos no viniste a ponerme contenta...

Paco   A un alma enamorada siempre le queda un resquicio de optimismo. Pensé: "Si Dolly me ve aparecer, aunque sea por piedad, va a divertirse con la idea".

Dolly   ¿Querés demostrarme algo?

Paco   Quiero advertirte...

Dolly   (*Lo corta.*) No me gusta el tomo.

Paco   A mí no me gusta el tono, la melodía, la letra de la canción, ni el lugar que me encajaste en todo esto.

Dolly   Lo siento mucho querido.

Paco   Lo siento mucho querido significa, "No pienso cambiar nada de todo este libreto querido."

Dolly   Yo...

Paco   (*La corta.*) ¡YO! ¡YO! ¡YO! Todo aquí pasa por vos ¿Y YO? Yo no me casé con la esposa de un tal Javier. Yo me casé con vos. Y dado que me casé con vos y que te amo...TE AMO, ¿entendés? Dado que te amo...

Dolly   Yo también te amo...pero estoy...muy metida en reparar mi propia...biografía, por llamar de algún modo a todo esto.

Paco   Dolly: esto no va más.

Dolly   Paco...necesito tu apoyo...

Paco Lo tuviste pero me cansé de estar solo. Te extraño.

Dolly   Yo también te extraño. Pero admito que tengo una terrible necesidad...una loca necesidad de...de... (*Le cuesta decirlo.*) de vengarme. Necesito que mi padre me necesite por un deseo terrible de vengarme...hacerlos girar a todos alrededor mío es...muy agradable ....muy...pero muy agradable.

Paco Ya está, Dolly. Misión cumplida. Lo sacaste de la ruina, le devolviste su prestigio empresarial, le renovaste las ideas, le hiciste sentir de nuevo ganas de vivir...creo que si querías tributo y reconocimiento lo tuviste...ahora te queremos en casa.

Dolly Paco...dame tiempo.

Paco No.

Dolly Necesito encontrar la manera de presentarte como mi marido...

Paco YO SOY tu marido. Tu padre es mi suegro. Juntanos, Dolly. O yo entro en esta casa por la puerta grande...o te retiro todo mi apoyo.

Dolly (*Furiosa*) ¡No podés hacerme esto!

Paco ¿Y vos sí podés borrarme del mapa con tanta facilidad? ¿Vos sí podés ningunearme? ¿Decidir que no existo? ¿Vos sí podés?

Dolly No seas cretino, Paco.

Paco ¿Cretino? ¡Me tiene cansado todo este circo que montaste por tu vanidad...la vanidad te sale por las orejas, la vanidad se enrosca en tu cintura y orbita alrededor de tu cabeza...tu vanidad me tiene HARTO! ¿Hasta cuándo creés que voy a ser cómplice de tu vanidad, darling? ¿Cuántos kilos de vanidad te quedan por satisfacer?

(*Dolly le da una cahetada. Paco no se la devuelve. Hay una tensa pausa.*)

Dolly Disculpame...nunca me hablaste de este modo.

Paco Nunca fui clandestino en tu vida. Nunca tuviste miedo, como ahora, de que llegara alguien y me sorprendiera. Nunca me hiciste sufrir así, para reparar no sé qué mierda irreparable, ¡i-rre-pa-ra-ble!

Dolly Me siento ridícula.

Paco Sos ridícula. Y estás arruinando nuestra pareja. Quiero que tomes, al menos, conciencia de eso: estás arruinando nuestra pareja.

Dolly Creí que contaba con todo tu respaldo.

Paco ¡No creíste nada! ¡Decidiste por mí! Decidiste que yo, lo menos que podía hacer, era desaparecer en silencio, - sin protestar - y cuidar NUESTRA casa y NUESTRA familia mientras vos te dabas el lujo de refregarle a toda TU familia qué mal hicieron en darte una patada en el culo hace diez años.

Dolly (*Dolly mira hacia la puerta d e entrada.*) Teneme un poco de paciencia.

Paco Se me acabó.

Dolly Me estás obligando.

Paco (*La corta.*) Vos me obligaste a mí. No des vuelta a todo. Yo no quiero más este lugar. Te lo devuelvo en un paquetito con moño. (*Harto*) ¿Por qué mirás tanto la puerta?

Dolly Puede llegar mi viejo en cualquier momento.

Paco ¿Y?

Dolly ¿En serio querés arruinarme todo lo que construí en este tiempo?

Paco Me muero de ganas.

Dolly Me querés aplastar.

Paco Quiero…recuperar a MI DOLLY…eso es lo que quiero.

Dolly ¿Recuperarla o aplastarla?

Paco Recuperarla o aplastarla (*Pausa*) Quiero ser parte de tu familia, quiero ser recibido como tu legítimo esposo, quiero que sepan que tuve el coraje de casarme con un hombre que se convirtió en mujer.

Dolly ¿Querés que mi padre te dé una medalla por casarte conmigo?

Paco ¡Debería dármela!

Dolly No sabía que vos eras el especial...creí que yo era la heroína de esta película.

Paco Yin y yang, lo crudo y lo cocido, lo posible y la invención ... nuestra pareja era un delicado equilibrio de disparate y técnica de intimidad cómplice. Ahora, que se te ha dado por volver a ser la hija por el hijo que no fuiste, nuestra pareja…se nos está yendo de las manos. Y cuando algo se te empieza a ir de las manos…hay que tener la claridad y el coraje de ponerle título al desastre.

Dolly No puedo decirle la verdad de golpe.

Paco (*Provocando*) ¿Y cómo se la vas a decir?

Dolly ¡Vos viniste a armar quilombo!

Paco Por supuesto, porque si no armo quilombo…un día volvés a casa y realmente no me encontrás más.

Dolly (*Llora.*) Encima venís a amenazarme con el estilo macho clásico, en casa de mi padre.

Paco Por ahora esta es la casa de tu suegro y tu esposo se llama Javier Goldberg y yo no existo.

Dolly No me contés mi vida resumida en comprimidos biodegradables.

Paco Quiero empezar a existir, Dolly…es decir, quiero volver a existir para vos.

Dolly Yo también quiero empezar a existir como hija de ese señor y no como nuera. Y también quiero existir como esposa de Paco Frías y no de mí mismo.

Paco (*Duro*) Vos inventaste todo esto…¡desinventalo, baby!

Dolly No puedo. (*Pausa*) Ayudame.

Paco A eso vine. Vine a ayudarte y a ayudarme…esto es una locura y una patraña. Y si seguís jugando este juego de la mentira, para que tu papito te deba la vida…jugalo solita, Dolly. Yo me abro..

(*Dolly se angustia. Llega Mariana cargada de paquetes. Espera encontrar a su hermana sola, se sorprende al ver a Paco.*)

Mariana ¿Eh? ¿Vos?

Paco Yo... sí…tu cuñadito…el fantasma. Pero no vayas a creer que estoy. Soy una visión. ¡Entre todos ustedes, para vivir a mi mujer, se han complotado para transformarme en un desaparecido!

Mariana ¿Qué? ¿Pero qué te pasa? ¡Yo fui informada, y no consultada, de lo que ustedes decidieron decirle al viejo!

Paco Mariana …¿vos creés que esto tiene arreglo?

Mariana Preguntale a tu marido, digo a mi hermano, es decir a tu mujer.

Paco (*Paco mira a las dos. Comienza su retirada.*) ¡Es tu ex-hermano y pronto va a ser mi ex-mujer! (*Paco se va furioso dado un portazo.*)

Dolly Supongo que pensás que soy una basura.

Mariana No, no exactamente una basura, pero creo que se nos acabó a todos la cuerda…pero…ojo cuñadita…un día las marionetas se van de escena.

Dolly (*Furiosa*) ¡No me llames cuñada!

Mariana Por ahora somos cuñadas. Ahora bien, si uno se atreve a preguntarse por qué mi cuñada es tan pero tan generosa, tan pero tan cariñosa…llegará a la conclusión que quiera.

Dolly Y vos ¿a qué conclusión llegaste?

Mariana (*Se encoge de hombros.*) ¡Yo estoy metida hasta las narices en todo esto, así que no puedo usarte y criticarte mi vida!

Dolly ¡Paco tiene razón! ¡Paco tiene razón! (*Dolly agarra su cartera.*) ¡Paco tiene razón! (*Se dirige hacia la puerta de salida.*) ¡Decile a papá que dentro un rato viene Javier! (*Dolly sale corriendo en busca de Paco.*)

Mariana (*Se dirige hacia los paquetes que trajo.*) ¡Por supuesto! ¡Paco tiene toda la razón! (*Comienza a recoger los paquetes del suelo. Los acomoda en un sillón. Mira las cosas que ha comprado. Llegan Luna y Simón.*)

Simón Buenos días hija…¿y Dolly?

Luna (*Dirigiéndose a lo que Mariana tiene en la mano.*) ¡Uy! ¡Qué lindo!

Mariana Papá, hoy viene Javier.

Simón ¿Qué?

Luna ¿Cómo?

Simón ¿Cuándo?

Mariana Dentro de un rato.

Simón ¿Estás segura de que no es una broma?

Mariana Dolly no hace esa clase de bromas. Luna, dejémoslos solos. Voy a llevar estas cosas al coche, en dos minutos subo a buscarte. (*Sale con sus paquetes.*)

Simón Entonces es en serio.

Luna ¿No es lo que querías?

Simón Sí.

Luna Venís hace meses queriendo ver a Javier.

Simón Sí ... sí...

Luna Bueno, ¡lo lograste Simón Goldberg!

Simón Pero ¿por qué tomó una decisión tan repentina...si se ha negado sistemáticamente?

Luna Simón...antes preguntabas por qué no, ahora preguntás por qué sí.

Simón No ... a mí me parece muy bien que después de tantos años, mi hijo y yo tengamos una conversación...frente a frente.

Mariana (*Abre la puerta con su llave. Viene a buscar a Luna.*) Vamos

Luna Debe estar por llegar.

Simón Esperen que llegue...no me dejen solo.

Luna Simón...fuiste vos el que provocó todo esto. Fuiste vos el que presionó a Dolly día tras día.

Mariana Es lo mejor que puede pasar. Todos necesitamos esto. Lo que no entiendo es por qué estoy tan nerviosa. (*Al padre*) Papá, espero que vos estés tranquilo.

(*Luna retoca su maquillaje como para salir.*)

Simón ¿Tranquilo? (*Tiembla.*) ¿Hace frío? ¿A dónde se van? Yo las necesito conmigo.

Mariana Coherencia, papá. Tus hijos demandamos conductas coherentes. Rompiste los tímpanos a todo el mundo diciendo que no podías vivir sin ver a mi hermano...ahora dejate de temblar...Javier ya salió para aquí. ¿Lo tenés claro?

Simón ¿Qué le digo?

Mariana ¡Pero si vos sos el que lo llamaste, viejo! ¿Así que ahora te tengo que decir YO, lo que tenés que decir VOS?

Simón Yo sé muy bien lo que decirle a mi hijo.

Mariana Él también habrá pensado un montón de cosas durante estos diez años... (*Pausa*) Papá...¿no era esto lo que querías?

Simón Sí, sí...pero parece que yo ya me había hecho a la idea de no verlo más...cuando, justo, él cambio de idea... (*Pausa*) Tengo miedo de meter la pata, de no saber qué decir.

Luna Decile lo que sientas, lo que te vaya saliendo...dale amor...es tu hijo.

Simón Sí, claro. (*Simón la mira serio.*)

Mariana Sonreí. (*Simón sonríe forzadamente.*) Si le ponés esa cara va a salir corriendo.

Simón (*Simón trata de relajarse. Sonríe.*) ¿Esta es una sonrisa más paternal?

Mariana ¿Más qué?

Simón Paternal.

Mariana ¿Y vos qué paternidad le querés vender a Javier?

(*Simón se pone serio.*)

Luna ¡Sonreí y basta!

(*Entra Gregorio.*)

Gregorio ¿Qué pasa que no bajan? Tengo el coche en marcha...y Dolly debe estar por llegar...digo Javier.

Simón ¿Viene con Dolly?

Gregorio (*Palmea a Simón.*) Histórico encuentro Simón ... ¿Está preparado?

Simón No.

Gregorio ¿Pero no me diga que le tiene miedo a ese salamín? Es pan comido...déle duro...no me afloje.

Mariana Gregorio...te estás convirtiendo en un tipo resentido...y la gente resentida se pone muy fea, la piel se le pone gris acerada, los ojos se le congelan sin remedio, la boca se le tuerce hacia el sudeste, las orejas se le pudren primero y después se le caen, el pelo se le enrula al revés y empieza a expander un tufo espantoso que hace que todos se tapen la nariz. (*Se tapa la nariz.*)

Gregorio ¿Estás enamorada de mí?

Mariana Muy enamorada.

(*Salen. Simón se queda solo esperando a Javier. Camina por la habitación. Se mira en el espejo. No le gusta la corbata que tiene. Se la cambia por otra. Se pone perfume. Se repasa el peinado. Está francamente impaciente. Suena el timbre. Abre. Es Javier. El actor que hace de Dolly llega vestido de hombre. Su vestuario es ultramoderno, de notable buen gusto y sobrio. Simón sonríe forzadamente. No saben si*

*saludarse con un beso o estrecharse las manos. Finalmente no hacen ni
una cosa ni la otra. Javier mira a su padre intensamente.*)
Simón Bueno…finalmente.
Javier Sí, finalmente.
Simón Pasá, ponete cómodo…estás en tu casa. (*Simón estudia a Javier.
Javier lo mira serio.*)
Javier Voy a intentar ponerme cómodo.
Simón Sí, yo también voy a intentar ponerme cómodo.
(*Hay tirantez y timidez. Mutua desconfianza.*)
Javier Tenés una casa muy divertida.
Simón La decoró Dolly.
Javier Ah...sí, sí, Dolly, claro…se nota la propuesta.
Simón A mí Dolly…me produjo una especie de revolución.   (*Simón
sonríe. Javier no sonríe.*)
Javier Hablemos de nosotros, Simón.
Simón Si, claro, para eso vine.
Javier Soy yo el que vine.
Simón Sí, claro…quise decir, que para eso viniste.
Javier Bueno…vos insististe mucho en verme.
Simón Sí, quería verte, bueno, quería volver a ver a Javier.
Javier Bueno, me estás viendo. ¿Qué ves?
Simón Te veo muy tenso. ¿Estás bien?
Javier Sí, gracias. (*Pausa*) ¿Me vas a tener parado?
Simón Sentate, por favor…sentate. (*Javier se sienta. Simón se queda
parado. Javier se pone de pie. Simón se sienta. Javier se sienta. Simón se
para.*) ¿Te sirvo un whisky?
Javier No bebo alcohol, Simón.
Simón ¿Vas a llamarme Simón?
Javier ¿Y no te llamas Simón?
Simón Soy tu papá.
Javier ¿Y querés que te llame papá?
Simón Me gustaría.
Javier Tengo que practicarlo.
Simón (*Angustiado*) Yo sí voy a tomar un whisky, Javier. Dolly me
regaló un escocés muy bueno.
Javier No quiero que me hables de Dolly. No nos vemos hace diez años.
Es lógico que intentemos hablar de nosotros dos.
(*Simón se sirve un whisky. Lo bebe.*)
Simón Es que ella es…es…única. Dolly es maravillosa, es dulce, es
buena persona, es creativa, ella es realmente inteligente, es una

personalidad fuera de serie, tiene todo lo que tiene que tener una mujer más algo más que la hace brillar por cuenta propia...ella ha cambiado realmente mi vida...para mí es alguien irremplazable, y ella lo sabe, ella lo sabe, ella sabe que se me instaló para siempre en el corazón, porque ella no es tonta, ella es muy lúcida, es muy talentosa, ella me ha devuelto mis ganas de vivir...ella...

Javier (*Lo corta.*) ¡Basta! Te ruego que no vuelvas a nombrar a Dolly. (*Simón calla.*) ¡Dolly, Dolly, Dolly! ¿Para eso me citaste con tanta insistencia? ¿Qué hago yo acá? Me siento ridículo hablando de Dolly ... Estás haciendo las cosas muy difíciles. Y ya de por sí son bastante difíciles... ¡O te creés que para mí es sencillo volver a la casita de los viejos! ¡Soy una persona ocupada, se supone que me citaste para algo! ¿Para qué querías verme? ¡Hablá!

Simón No es fácil entrar en materia. Y Dolly es un nexo entre vos y yo ... por eso la nombro...a modo de enlace.

Javier Bien, ahora que nombraste el enlace, podés zambullirte de lleno en lo que te hizo querer verme.

Simón (*Incómodo. No sabe qué decir.*) Sí, seguro.

Javier ¿Seguro? Y por qué te tiemblan las piernas.

Simón (*Simón controla su temblor.*) No creí que te afectara tanto Dolly.

Javier Conozco las virtudes de Dolly.

Simón Ella es realmente un tesoro.

Javier (*Javier lo quiere matar.*) ¿Otra vez?

Simón (*Incómodo*) ¿Cómo estás Javier? ¡Tanto tiempo! Pasaron muchos años desde que te fuiste.

Javier (*Interrumpe*) No me fui, me echaste.

Simón A patadas, te eché a patadas. Te encontré en...bueno (*Se interrumpe*) Para colmo era el novio de...¡A patadas! (*Pausa incómoda.*)

Javier Sí, a patadas.

Simón (*Se para.*) Esas patadas también me dolieron a mí, sos mi único hijo.

Javier (*Se para.*) Y vos sos mi único padre. Lamentablemente.

Simón No soy un monstruo.

Javier Yo tampoco.

Simón Te quiero decir que a pesar del espantoso concepto que tengas de mí, soy un tipo bueno.

Javier Yo también te quiero decir que a pesar del espantoso concepto que tengas de mí, soy un tipo bueno.

Simón ¿Vas a repetir todo lo que yo diga?

Javier Por ahora no dijiste nada papá.

Simón Me sonó bien ese papá...te salió bastante natural.

Javier Dolly me dijo que vos querías pedirme disculpas ... papito.

Simón Sentate, me pone nervioso verte de pie. (*Javier se sienta, cambia de posición las piernas y el cuerpo como si no encontrara comodidad. Pasea.*) Son los sillones de Dolly...divertidos pero a veces es difícil acomodarse.

Javier (*Se para.*) ¡Dolly me engañó! ¡Vos no tenés la menor intención de pedir disculpas!

Simón ' (*Lo sienta empujándolo contra el sillón.*) ¡Dolly es incapaz de engañar a nadie!

Javier ¿Dolly? ¿Incapaz de engañar a nadie? ¡No te creas!

Simón Si hay una persona sincera, un ser transparente hasta en los más mínimos gestos, si hay alguien verdaderamente veraz, esa es Dolly. Así que si ella te dijo que yo te quería pedir disculpas, ella te estaba diciendo la verdad. ¡La verdad! ¡Dolly es traslúcida como los vitrales de los templos góticos! No digo que no mienta, pero son mentiras tan piadosas ...son esa clase de mentiras que facilitan la verdad (*Javier se tapa los oídos. No quiere escuchar una sola palabra más de Dolly. Simón calla.*) ¡Javier! ¡Siempre tan teatral! (*Le destapa los oídos.*) Yo no estaba hablando de Dolly, sino de la verdad. Y la verdad es que mi deseo es (*Mecánicamente*) restablecer una relación cordial y afectuosa entre padre e hijo, basada en la tolerancia mutua y en el respeto extraordinario que siempre nos hemos tenido.

Javier (*Se pone de pie. Perplejo*) ¿Te aprendiste un discurso de memoria?

Simón ¿Cómo te diste cuenta?

Javier (*Sonríe.*) Oíme...¿te aprendiste un discurso de memoria para hablar conmigo?

Simón Es que tenía miedo de abatatarme.

Javier ¡Dame whisky, viejo!

Simón Pero si no bebés alcohol...

Javier Hasta hace un segundo. (*Simón le sirve.*) De aquí en más voy a pasar el resto de mi vida chupando whisky para olvidar esta pesadilla intitulada "EL REENCUENTRO CON EL VIEJO SIMÓN GOLDBERG, DESPUÉS DE DIEZ AÑOS DE NO VERLO"! ¡Salud!

Simón ¡Salud! (*Beben juntos.*)

Javier Repetime el discurso, no quiero que se me escape una sola palabra.

Simón "La verdad es que mi deseo es restablecer una relación cordial y afectuosa entre padre e hijo, basada en la tolerancia mutua y en el respeto extraordinario que siempre nos hemos tenido".

Javier ¡Es maravilloso! ¡Una verdadera pieza literaria! ¡Salud! ¡Por Dolly!

Simón Ahora fuiste vos el que la nombró. (*Pausa)* No fue fácil para mí aquella época tuya.

Javier ¿Para esto me llamaste, viejo?

Simón No, yo creí que lo tenía superado, pero no quiero mentirte, yo te puedo disculpar recién ahora.

Javier ¿Vos me podés qué?

Simón Disculpar...tu pasado.

Javier ¡Pero aquí el que tenía que pedir disculpas eras vos! Yo no te pido disculpas. No necesito disculpas. Me encanta mi pasado. Estoy feliz de ser quien soy. ¡Feliz!

Simón ¡Mirame a los ojos!

Javier (*Le clava la mirada. Simón se acerca a él.)* ¿Para qué carajo me llamaste, Simón Goldberg? ¡Me voy! Se te terminó el tiempo. Se nos terminó el tiempo. Hacé de cuenta que nunca viste a tu hijo, hacé de cuenta que yo nunca acepté venir, hacé de cuenta que estás soñando y que cuando te despiertes yo ya no voy a estar más en tu vida.

Simón Esperá. No seas tan tajante (*Javier lo agarra de la solapa y lo arrastra por la habitación.)* ¡Soltame!

Javier Mirame bien, por última vez.

Simón ¡Soltame! ¡Soltame maricón de mierda!

Javier (*Lo suelta. Se le llenan los ojos de lágrimas.)* ¡Ésa es tu verdad, eso es lo que me querías decir! (*Javier ríe. Pone música. Se hace el maricón. Agresivamente provocativo.)* ¿Bailamos mi amor? Qué lindos ojos tenés, lástima los dientes un poco torcidos.

Simón Disculpame, me hacés decir lo que no quiero ni pienso.

Javier (*Camina moviéndose provocativamente.)* ¿Te parece?

Simón Me salió todo al revés.

Javier (*Saca tacos altos y se los pone.)* ¿Te gusta este taco papi? ¿O preferís el taco chino?

Simón En serio Javier, no quise ofenderte.

Javier ¿No? ¿Cómo era la frase maravillosa? (*Pausa. Simón no contesta.)* No sabés nada de mí...nunca te importé...nunca te entendí... sigo sin entenderte.

Simón (*Interrumpe.)* Te quiero, Javier.

Javier "Te quiero si sos como yo quiero que seas". Pero resulta que los hijos no somos figuritas recortadas. No tenés el hijo que querías tener.

Simón Es cierto.

Javier ¡Ni yo tengo el padre que quería tener!

Simón Es cierto. Pero…a pesar de todo.

Javier A pesar de todo qué.

Simón Te quiero, hijo (*Lo quiere abrazar. Javier lo para en seco, ambos se miran.*)

Javier Pero con eso parece que no alcanza. (*Pausa*) ¿Te acordás cuando me llevabas a la cancha de Boca?

Simón ¿Seguís siendo de Boca?

Javier Por supuesto (*Juntos*) ¡Dale Boca, dale Boca, dale Boca dale Boca dale Boca! ¡Me querías sacar machito pero yo en vez de mirar el partido me distraía con las piernas de los jugadores…qué gambas, qué pectorales…qué bultos mama mía!

Simón (*Simón le da una cachetada. Con bronca. Provocando*) Con lo lindas que son las minas…yo me casé con una piba joven.

Javier (*Lo agarra de la cara.*) ¿Oíme viejo? Vos, en serio, ¿sos pelotudo o te hacés el pelotudo? (*Pausa. Es una pregunta clave.*)

Simón Me hago el pelotudo. (*Pausa. Javier está impactado.*)

Javier ¡Ah! ¿Entonces sabés?

Simón Pero si sos idéntico a tu madre.

(*Pausa prolongada. Ambos están muy impactados.*)

Javier Era…era eso lo que le querías decir a Javier.

Simón Sí.

Javier ¿Y desde cuándo sabés?

Simón Me fui dando cuenta de a poco.

Javier ¡Ah!

Simón Pero este es un secreto entre vos y yo. Yo…ante el mundo… no…no…yo no sé nada.

Javier Es un pacto entre hombres.

Simón Sí. (*Simón le extiende la mano. Javier se la estrecha. Ambos se miran.*)

Javier Bueno…creo que no tenemos nada más que decirnos, viejo…

Simón Quisiera encontrar las palabras para hablarle a mi hijo varón.

Javier (*Transición*) Ahora el que tiene colitis soy yo…¿puedo pasar al baño?

(*Simón toma un rollo de papel higiénico de color y se lo da.*)

Simón ¿Seremos una familia de cagones, che?

Javier (*Javier se ríe y le da un beso en la mejilla al padre.*) Vos sos un cagón… (*Se va para adentro. Simón queda solo en el escenario. Larga pausa.*)

Simón (*Le habla a su hijo.*) Javier…y si te volvieras a…digo…no hay modo de dar marcha atrás y… (*Pausa*) No tiene ningún rigor lo que estoy diciendo.   (*Pausa*) Javier…te agradezco el esfuerzo de haber venido…yo sé que te obligué…pero los dos lo necesitábamos… (*Pausa*) ¿Me oís o estoy hablando solo como un perejil?

Voz de Javier ¡El negro tulipán es aterciopelado!

Simón ¿El negro qué? (*Pausa*) Javier…se me ocurrió una cosa… podríamos inventarte un largo viaje. (*Pausa*) No me hagas caso, no sé ni lo que digo.

Voz de Javier (*Se ríe a carcajadas.*) A mí también se me ocurrió una cosa, papá.

Simón ¿Otra?

Voz de Javier (*En secreto como contando el argumento de un teleteatro.*) Javier y Dolly se separaron hace tiempo, hoy vos te enteraste …y ella trae a su verdadero marido a casa.

Simón ¡Hoy no Javier! Hoy te ruego que terminemos el día en paz.

Voz de Javier Precisamente.

Simón Seguro que ese tipo no me va a gustar.

Voz de Javier Lo importante es que le guste a Dolly.

Simón Yo no necesito conocer a nadie más…se va a meter entre ella y yo, va a opinar en todo.

Voz de Javier ¿Estas celoso?

Simón Terriblemente.

(***Dolly** sale espléndida del baño.*)

Dolly ¿Qué tal Simón?

Simón (*Está muy impactado.*) Dolly …

Dolly ¿Se siente mal, Simón?

(***Simón** cae redondo al piso. Dolly se acerca y lo mira. Sonríe.*)

Dolly ¿Te moriste papá?

Simón (*Se pone de un salto de pie.*) ¡A mí no me llames papá! ¡Llegaste demasiado lejos!

Dolly Quizás llegué demasiado cerca.

Simón Dolly…yo… (*Se interrumpe.*)

Dolly ¿Qué, Simón?

Simón ¡No me llames Simón!

Dolly Sí, papá.

Simón ¿Papá…? ¿Yo? De… (*Pausa*) ¡A mí decime Simón! ¡Y de usted!

Dolly Sí, Simón.

Simón La macana es que te quiero.

Dolly Y bueno, todo no se puede, Simón.

Simón ¡A las cosas hay que llamarlas por su nombre! ¡Llamame como corresponde!

Dolly Sí, papá.

Simón Dolly …yo no estoy en condiciones de ser yo ...

(*Simón cae redondo al suelo. Dolly lo mira. Pausa*)

Dolly Y bueno viejo…lo intentamos…al menos lo intentamos. (*Lo mira como esperando que se levante. Simón no se levanta. Dolly agarra su cartera, controla su maquillaje.*) Te aviso una cosa…si estás muerto de verdad yo no voy a sentirme culpable…y si no estás desmayado, ¡levantate!

(*Simón no se levanta. Dolly lo agarra en brazos y lo coloca en un sillón. Le toma el pulso. Con la otra mano agarra el teléfono inalámbrico y marca un número de teléfono.*)

Dolly ¿Hola? ¿Está la señora Mariana? Bueno, cuando llegue dígale que le habló la señora Dolly …es para pedirle que venga urgentemente…que su papá…que su papá. (*Llora.*) Que su papá está…dígale que... (*Se da manija y llora desesperadamente.*) venga ya…porque no nos queda tiempo…está en las últimas…si es que no está muerto. (*Llora ostentosamente.*) Siento dar esta noticia por teléfono. Gracias…muy amable. (*Cuelga. Cambio brusco*) Le dejé un mensaje contundente.

(*Dolly besa la mano de su padre que sigue desmayado. Se aleja.*)

Dolly Fue muy lindo conocerte…Papá.

(*Dolly ,lo mira. Mira el lugar y haciendo un chau con la mano se va. Simón queda solo en le escenario.*)

Simón (*Se incorpora repentinamente.*) ¡Señor Simón Goldberg!

Apagón